FREEDOM OF INFORMATION MANUAL

AUSTRALIA
Law Book Co.
Sydney

CANADA and USA
Carswell
Toronto

HONG KONG
Sweet & Maxwell Asia

NEW ZEALAND
Brookers
Wellington

SINGAPORE and MALAYSIA
Sweet & Maxwell Asia
Singapore and Kuala Lumpur

FREEDOM OF INFORMATION MANUAL

BY

MARCUS TURLE

LONDON
SWEET & MAXWELL
2005

First Edition 2005
Published in 2005 by Sweet & Maxwell Limited of
100 Avenue Road
London NW3 3PF
www.sweetandmaxwell.co.uk
Typeset by Interactive Sciences Ltd, Gloucester
Printed in England by
Athenaeum Press

No natural forests were destroyed to make this product; only farmed
timber was used and replanted

A CIP catalogue record for this book is available from the British Library

ISBN 0 421 922 400

Notes and Annotations to legislation reproduced by permission
of Reed Elsevier (UK) Limited trading as LexisNexis Butterworths.

Dedication

To the memory of my mother, and to my father, with love and gratitude.

Foreword

It is scarcely an exaggeration to say that freedom of information could be one of the most significant legal developments in the UK for a generation. The new regime is making a considerable impact on almost every corner of the public sector. The business community is beginning to understand how the new rules affect those supplying to government or regulated by it. Individuals, journalists, pressure groups and sophisticated companies are bringing a very wide range of traditionally closed information into the open.

The "right to know" became a reality on January 1, 2005. Its boundaries are still being tested. One year on, I am pleased to welcome a practical manual on the scope, application and use of the freedom of information rules. Marcus Turle's *Freedom of Information Manual* should be an invaluable resource for those affected by them, covering both the Freedom of Information Act and Environmental Information Regulations. It includes guidance on making and answering requests, and on the implications of the right to know for the private sector. Information officers at public authorities, practicing lawyers advising clients and users of the new rights should all find authoritative, in-depth guidance. I have a strong commitment to plain English and I especially welcome the effort in this manual to use clear and user-friendly language to make life easier for lawyers and non-lawyers alike.

Richard Thomas
Information Commissioner
September 2005

Preface[1]

It is a curious irony that in times of emergency, governments often react to perceived threats to our liberty by legislating in ways which seem to deprive us of it. Such has been the experience across Europe and the United States since 9/11. In 2001, one of the first acts of the newly appointed Home Secretary, David Blunkett, was to rush through Parliament the Anti-Terrorism Crime and Security Act (ATCS). The ATCS enabled the government to imprison foreign nationals without trial, thus reversing over 800 years of English legal history. Following a House of Lords' ruling that the ATCS broke human rights laws, we now have a system of "control orders", which in most respects is little different from the system it replaced (the principle differences being that internment is now imposed through house arrest, and can extend to cover British nationals as well as foreigners).[2]

Students of history will tell you that this is a familiar cycle. Go back through the statute book to 1911, for example, and you will find an Act of Parliament passed in a single day's sitting following the now long forgotten "Agadir Incident" in Morocco, after which the Congo passed from France to Germany, thereby putatively compromising Britain's imperial interests in Africa. That law is the Official Secrets Act—still with us today nearly a century on, having stubbornly resisted repeal ever since. The Official Secrets Act has a renowned history of abuse by governments trying to mask incompetence.[3]

The fact that there are historical parallels to our current predicament is scarce consolation of course. Individual freedom is fundamental to our

---

[1] Some of the ideas in this Preface are taken from an essay by A C Grayling which first appeared in the Guardian newspaper's Saturday Review, now collected in *The Reason of Things*, Weidenfeld & Nicolson, 2001

[2] One of the original 12 Belmarsh detainees who was released on bail because of deteriorating mental health has endured an extraordinary regime at his small flat in London since the middle of 2004. According to his bail conditions, he must "remain at all times" at home, telephoning a monitoring service everyday "at 7am, 11am, 3pm, 7pm and 11pm", and he must wear an electronic tag 24 hours a day. He is not allowed any visitors other than his wife, child, lawyer or "other such person approved by the Home Office by prior appointment", and he is forbidden the use of computers, mobile phones or "other electronic communication device". His flat may be searched at any time.

[3] In 1985, Clive Ponting was charged under the Official Secrets Act for leaking a Ministry of Defence document which caused Mrs Thatcher huge embarrassment by showing that the General Belgrano had been sailing *out* of the Falklands exclusion zone when it was attacked by a British submarine (thereby torpedoing the government line that the Belgrano was sunk because it posed a threat to British lives). Two years later, the Tories tried to gag Peter Wright who claimed in his book *Spycatcher* that MI5 had conspired to discredit Labour prime minister Harold Wilson. Quite recently, David Shayler was jailed for giving documents exposing malpractice in the security services to the Mail on Sunday.

democratic way of life, yet, as philosopher John Gray points out in his *Al Qaeda and What it Means to be Modern*, "The price of individualism is proving to be the loss of privacy".[4]

Take the government's national identity card scheme. Under current proposals, we will all be carrying a card by 2013. Without a card—which will contain biometric information such as fingerprints or iris scans stored on a microchip—access to state benefits, health care and the banking system will be blocked. The Home Secretary has said these cards will protect us from terrorists, organised crime, illegal immigration and benefit fraud. He may very well be right. But in the face of such compelling political imperatives, we should remember Kipling's words, written in 1899, but remarkably prescient still:

> He shall mark our goings, question whence we came,
> Set his guards about us, as in Freedom's name.
> He shall peep and mutter, and night shall bring
> Watchers 'neath our window, lest we mock the King.[5]

Kipling's point is that in times of upheaval and insecurity we must be at our most vigorous defending our freedoms, because that is when governments take steps to limit them, pleading necessity. In a very real sense, therefore, the Freedom of Information Act is a welcome counterweight to a trend which seems increasingly to be tipping the scales towards government interference and control.

It is instructive to reflect on the Official Secrets Act and the ATCS—both passed in great haste in times of "emergency"—and then to consider that the Freedom of Information Act is the culmination of something like 50 years of public debate on the rights of individuals to access information about the way they're governed. As we all know—yet still take for granted—freedoms have to be wrung out of our rulers, and usually only come after years of effort.

Inevitably, and with some justification, many in the public sector see freedom of information as complicated, unnecessary and vulnerable to misuse—in fact, all of the charges leveled at the Data Protection Act. These criticisms are not without substance, but we should always remember that freedom comes at a price, and part of that price is vigilance. The Freedom of Information Act gives us all the means to be vigilant and that, surely, is to be welcomed.

Part I of this book provides a detailed commentary on the Freedom of Information Act 2000 (FOIA) in Chapter 1, and the Environmental Information Regulations 2004 (EIRs) in Chapter 2, the latter often seen as

---

[4] John Gray, *Al Qaeda and What it Means to be Modern*, Faber and Faber, 2003
[5] The Old Issue, October 9 1899.

FOIA's lesser sibling, but in fact just as important, and in several significant respects wider reaching.

Part II offers commentary and guidance on several fundamental aspects of the freedom of information regime. Chapter 3 deals with the scope and application of the public interest, which is critical to the operation of all of the exceptions under the EIRs, and to the qualified exemptions under FOIA. Chapter 4 sets out practical guidance on how requests can be made, and how to enforce the legal rights of access which the new laws provide. Chapter 5 explores the procedures which public authorities need to consider when processing freedom of information requests, and Chapter 6 analyses the implications of freedom of information for the private sector.

The law is stated at September 2005.

Acknowledgements

A host of friends and colleagues deserve thanks for their support over the last 18 months. First, I would like to thank my research assistant, Emma Raleigh, for her efforts pulling together materials and ideas, and for her eye for detail and her honesty when reviewing my work. Several colleagues at Field Fisher Waterhouse deserve a mention, most notably Michael Chissick, without whose support this project may never have come to fruition, and to Colin Gibson and Charles Whiddington for input on, respectively, all things litigation related, and the procurement regulations.

Thanks of course go to the editorial team at Sweet & Maxwell, and particularly Julian Chase and Martine Henry and her team.

I am indebted to the work of others already published in this field, namely John McDonald QC and Clive Jones, John Wadham and Jonathan Griffiths, and Meredith Cook and the Constitution Unit at University College, London.

Finally, thanks must go to my partner, Louise, who has supported and encouraged me unfailingly, and whose enthusiasm has kept me going through the long hours at my desk at home.

Marcus Turle
Field Fisher Waterhouse
September 2005.

Contents

Contents

TABLE OF CASES

Table of Cases

TABLE OF TRIBUNAL DECISIONS

TABLE OF STATUTES

Table of Statutes

Australia

Canada

Ireland, Republic

New Zealand

TABLE OF STATUTORY INSTRUMENTS

TABLE OF TREATIES AND CONVENTIONS

TABLE OF SECONDARY LEGISLATION OF THE EUROPEAN COMMUNITIES

I

CHAPTER 1

FREEDOM OF INFORMATION ACT 2000

CHAPTER 36

PART II

EXEMPT INFORMATION

PART III

GENERAL FUNCTIONS OF SECRETARY OF STATE, LORD CHANCELLOR AND INFORMATION COMMISSIONER

PART IV

ENFORCEMENT

PART V

APPEALS

PART VI

HISTORICAL RECORDS AND RECORDS IN PUBLIC RECORD OFFICE OR PUBLIC RECORD OFFICE OF NORTHERN IRELAND

PART VII

AMENDMENTS OF DATA PROTECTION ACT 1998

Amendments relating to personal information held by public authorities

Other amendments

An Act to make provision for the disclosure of information held by public authorities or by persons providing services for them and to amend the Data Protection Act 1998 and the Public Records Act 1958; and for connected purposes

30th November 2000

BE IT ENACTED by the Queen's most Excellent Majesty, by and with the advice and consent of the Lords Spiritual and Temporal, and Commons, in this present Parliament assembled, and by the authority of the same, as follows:—

Part I

Access to Information Held by Public Authorities

Right to information

1 General right of access to information held by public authorities

(1) Any person making a request for information to a public authority is entitled—

    (a) to be informed in writing by the public authority whether it holds information of the description specified in the request, and

    (b) if that is the case, to have that information communicated to him.

(2) Subsection (1) has effect subject to the following provisions of this section and to the provisions of sections 2, 9, 12 and 14.

(3) Where a public authority—

    (a) reasonably requires further information in order to identify and locate the information requested, and

    (b) has informed the applicant of that requirement,

the authority is not obliged to comply with subsection (1) unless it is supplied with that further information.

(4) The information—

    (a) in respect of which the applicant is to be informed under subsection (1)(a), or

    (b) which is to be communicated under subsection (1)(b),

is the information in question held at the time when the request is received, except that account may be taken of any amendment or deletion made between that time and the time when the information is to be communicated under subsection (1)(b), being an amendment or deletion that would have been made regardless of the receipt of the request.

(5) A public authority is to be taken to have complied with subsection (1)(a) in relation to any information if it has communicated the information to the applicant in accordance with subsection (1)(b).

(6) **In this Act, the duty of a public authority to comply with subsection (1)(a) is referred to as "the duty to confirm or deny".**

NOTES

Initial Commencement

Specified date

Specified date: 30 November 2005 (unless the Secretary of State by order appoints this section before that date): see s 87(3) (as amended by SI 2001/3500, art 8, Sch 2, Pt I, para 8(1)(o) and SI 2003/1887, art 9, Sch 2, para 12(1)(c)). (See appointment note below.)

Appointment

Appointment: 1 January 2005: see SI 2004/3122, art 2.

GENERAL NOTE

As reflected in the heading to s.1, FOIA confers a "general right of access   1–003
to information held by public authorities". The right is retrospective, applies to all information regardless of format, provenance or degree of accessibility, and is exercisable by anyone (including companies and public authorities themselves) anywhere in the world, irrespective of nationality or place of residence. There are only very limited formalities necessary for making a request.[1]

Subsection (1)

Section 1(1) imposes two separate duties: 1–004

- the "duty to confirm or deny" (s.1(1)(a)); and

- the duty to communicate information (s.1(1)(b)).

Note that for the purpose of s.1(1), the right of access is engaged by mere possession of information—it does not depend on ownership or legal right of use. The single exception to this relates to information which an authority holds only on behalf of another person, which falls outside the rules by virtue of s.3(2)(a).

The duty to confirm or deny—Information Commissioner's Guidance[2]

The Commissioner's guidance indicates that the wording of a request is   1–005
likely to engage the duty to confirm or deny in different ways. As a rule, the

---

[1] See s.8.
[2] Information Commissioner's Awareness Guidance No.21: The Duty to Confirm or Deny.

more specific the request, the less likely the duty will arise. The guidance sets out an illustration of this using the example of requests to a hospital for medical records.

1. The first request is for information about general clinical outcomes and the incidence of particular medical conditions within its catchment area. The hospital will be likely to communicate this information because it is high level, and in the process confirm that it holds medical records relating to its patients.

2. The second request relates to the treatment by the hospital of a prominent individual who was involved in a road accident. Although the full details of the treatment might not be disclosed, it is likely the hospital would confirm that it held these, and disclose some limited information in response to the request.

3. The third request relates to this same prominent individual's heart condition. The hospital would almost certainly refuse to disclose any such information and it would probably also decline to confirm or deny holding it.

Transferring requests

1–006   If the authority believes that some or all of the information requested is held by another public authority, it should consider the most helpful way of assisting the applicant. In most cases this is likely to involve:

- contacting the applicant and telling her that the information requested may be held by another authority;

- suggesting that the applicant re-applies to that other authority; and

- providing her with contact details for that other authority.

If the authority believes it appropriate to transfer the request, then the authority should consult the other authority first to confirm whether it does in fact hold the information. Requests should not be transferred without this confirmation.

If the authority holds *some* of the information, then it is under a duty to comply with FOIA in relation to that information. However, where it is reasonable for the authority to transfer the request (for example, because another authority can answer it in full) then it will normally be permissible to pass the request on, provided the authority notifies the applicant (with reasons) accordingly.

The Government "Clearing House"

The government has now established a central "Clearing House" within the   **1–007**
DCA to which Whitehall departments may transfer FOIA requests in
certain circumstances. The Clearing House's role is threefold:

- to ensure a consistent government-wide position on round robin
  and potentially precedent-setting cases;

- to provide guidance on sensitive cases with a high public profile
  and to align the response to such cases with government policy
  and guidance; and

- to revise government guidance in the light of emerging case law
  and new policy imperatives.

The Clearing House's remit covers Whitehall departments (including non-
ministerial departments), and the Scottish Executive and the National
Assembly for Wales on issues which may have implications for the UK
administration.[3]

Information Officers should refer to the Access to Information Central
Clearing House Toolkit for further information.[4]

Exceptions to the general right of access—subsection (2)

Although the right of access is expressed to be "general", it is not unlimited.   **1–008**
An authority may be entitled to refuse a request, or impose conditions on
answering it. This is the case where:

- an exemption applies (see s.2 and Pt II);

- fees are payable (ss.9 and 13);

- the estimated costs of answering a request exceed certain limits
  (s.12); and/or

- the request is "repeated" or "vexatious" (s.14).

Note that apart from requests falling within s.14, FOIA is "purpose-blind"
meaning that the motive for an application is not relevant to the public
authority's obligations. Except in relation to s.14 therefore, public
authorities are not entitled to enquire into the reasons for a request.[5]

---

[3] Non-Departmental Public Bodies, Executive Agencies and other bodies sponsored by
government departments are expected to refer in the first instance to their sponsoring
Whitehall departments.
[4] Available at *www.foi.gov.uk/guidance/pdf/toolkit.pdf*.
[5] The Freedom of Information Bill did include such a right, but this did not make it into the
Act.

Subsection (4)

1–009   Public authorities must take care not to alter or destroy information which has been requested under FOIA. Section 77 makes it a criminal offence to alter, deface, block, erase, destroy or conceal any record with the intention of preventing FOIA disclosure.

Section 1(4) does permit the alteration or destruction of information which has been requested, but only where this would have happened anyway (*i.e.* where it occurs as a matter of routine rather than because of the request). This is necessary to ensure that authorities' work can continue while FOIA requests are processed, without the need to "freeze" files pending their completion.

2 Effect of the exemptions in Part II

1–010
(1) **Where any provision of Part II states that the duty to confirm or deny does not arise in relation to any information, the effect of the provision is that where either—**

   (a) **the provision confers absolute exemption, or**

   (b) **in all the circumstances of the case, the public interest in maintaining the exclusion of the duty to confirm or deny outweighs the public interest in disclosing whether the public authority holds the information,**

   section 1(1)(a) does not apply.

(2) **In respect of any information which is exempt information by virtue of any provision of Part II, section 1(1)(b) does not apply if or to the extent that—**

   (a) **the information is exempt information by virtue of a provision conferring absolute exemption, or**

   (b) **in all the circumstances of the case, the public interest in maintaining the exemption outweighs the public interest in disclosing the information.**

(3) **For the purposes of this section, the following provisions of Part II (and no others) are to be regarded as conferring absolute exemption—**

   (a) **section 21,**

   (b) **section 23,**

   (c) **section 32,**

   (d) **section 34,**

(e) **section 36 so far as relating to information held by the House of Commons or the House of Lords,**

(f) **in section 40—**

    (i) **subsection (1), and**

    (ii) **subsection (2) so far as relating to cases where the first condition referred to in that subsection is satisfied by virtue of subsection (3)(a)(i) or (b) of that section,**

(g) **section 41, and**

(h) **section 44.**

NOTES

Initial Commencement

Specified date

Specified date: 30 November 2005 (unless the Secretary of State by order appoints this section before that date): see s 87(3) (as amended by SI 2001/3500, art 8, Sch 2, Pt I, para 8(1)(o) and SI 2003/1887, art 9, Sch 2, para 12(1)(c)). (See appointment note below.)

Appointment

Appointment: 1 January 2005: see SI 2004/3122, art 2.

GENERAL NOTE

Although the entitlement to information under FOIA is very wide, the law   **1–011** recognises that certain areas of government need to retain some measure of secrecy and that freedom of access to information by the public should be balanced with legitimate commercial and confidential interests. A person making a request is therefore not entitled to have any information whatsoever. FOIA confers a general right-to-know, but with exemptions.

Section 2 identifies two types of exemption to the right of access. These are "absolute exemptions" and "qualified exemptions". An explanation of each is set out below and the table in Appendix 1 contains a full list. In essence, absolute exemptions protect whole categories of information, while qualified exemptions can apply only if disclosure would damage the particular interests which each is designed to protect and, even then, subject to the balance of the public interest.

Subsection 2(3)

Of the 23 exemptions in the Act, only eight are absolute. These are listed in   **1–012** s.2(3). They are:

(a) information accessible to the applicant by other means (s.21);

(b) security matters (s.23);

(c) court records (s.32);

(d) Parliamentary privilege (s.34);

(e) prejudice to the effective conduct of public affairs (so far as relating to information held by Parliament) (s.36);

(f) personal information (except to a limited extent, where the exemption is qualified) (s.40);

(g) confidential information (s.41); and

(h) other legal prohibitions on disclosure (s.44).

Absolute exemptions

1–013   The absolute exemptions apply to all information which falls within each of the categories set out in the sections listed above. In other words, the exemptions apply to whole *classes* of information. In assessing whether an absolute exemption applies, the only question is whether the information falls within one of the categories. If it does, then it is exempt. There is no test of public interest or prejudice.

If an absolute exemption applies, then the public authority does not have to disclose the information and may not even have to say whether it holds it. In every case, however, an authority must tell the applicant which exemption(s) it considers apply, and why (see s.17).

Qualified exemptions

1–014   The qualified exemptions operate on the basis that information can only be exempt if the public interest in maintaining the exemption outweighs the public interest in disclosing. This means that the default position for every request is to disclose (including where the arguments on both sides are equally balanced).

Public authorities are required to consider the balance of the public interest case-by-case. This therefore precludes reliance on rigid guidelines which may lead to specific categories of requests being rejected without allowing for the circumstances of each one.

The time limit for responding to a request to which a qualified exemption may apply is extended for "such time as is reasonable in the circumstances" to allow authorities to decide where the balance of the public interest lies. However, authorities are still required to tell applicants within 20 days that they are considering an exemption (s.17).

The test of prejudice

Many of the qualified exemptions are subject to a test of whether the   **1–015**
content of information or the consequences of its disclosure "would
prejudice" or "would be likely to prejudice" the particular interest which is
the subject of the exemption.[6] "Prejudice" is not defined but the
Information Commissioner's view is that it effectively means "harm" or
"damage".[7]

During Parliamentary consideration of the Freedom of Information Bill,
the government's view was that prejudice means prejudice that is actual,
real or of substance,[8] the intention being that authorities should not be
entitled to withhold information where prejudice would be trivial or
insignificant. In the event, the Act remains silent on the point, although it
is reasonable to assume that in the case of any qualified exemption, the less
significant the prejudice, the greater the chance of the public interest lying
in favour of disclosure.

The meaning of "would be likely" is also unclear, although we have judicial
guidance from Justice Munby in a data protection case[9] in which he states
that "likely" means a very significant and weighty chance of prejudice.
"The degree of risk," he says, "must be such that there 'may very well' be
prejudice . . . even if the risk falls short of being more probable than not."
This seems to mean that a risk of close to 50 per cent or greater is necessary
to engage the requirement that prejudice "would be likely".

3 Public authorities

    (1) **In this Act "public authority" means—**   **1–016**

        (a) **subject to section 4(4), any body which, any other
person who, or the holder of any office which—**

            (i) **is listed in Schedule 1, or**

            (ii) **is designated by order under section 5, or**

        (b) **a publicly-owned company as defined by section 6.**

    (2) **For the purposes of this Act, information is held by a
public authority if—**

---

[6] The prejudice-based exemptions are s.26 (defence), s.27 (international relations), s.28
(relations within the UK), s.29 (the economy), s.31 (law enforcement), s.33 (audit
functions), s.34 (Parliamentary privilege), s.36 (prejudice to the effective conduct of public
affairs), s.38 (health and safety), s.41 (information provided in confidence) and s.43
(commercial interests).

[7] Freedom of Information Act Awareness Guidance No.20: Prejudice & Adverse Affect.

[8] Hansard HL, April 20, 2000, Vol.612, Col.827.

[9] *R. (on the application of Alan Lord) v Secretary of State for the Home Department* [2003]
EWHC 2073 (Admin).

(a) **it is held by the authority, otherwise than on behalf of another person, or**

(b) **it is held by another person on behalf of the authority.**

NOTES

Initial Commencement

Royal Assent: **30 November 2000: see 87(1)(a).**

GENERAL NOTE

1–017   Schedule 1 to the Act contains a list of public authorities to which FOIA applies. The list starts with a series of generic categories. These cover all "government departments" (defined in s.84); Parliament and the devolved Assemblies in Wales and Northern Ireland; all parts of the armed forces; all local government; the NHS; schools and universities; and the police. There then follows a long list of organisations named individually.

Section 3(1)(b) brings publicly owned companies within the rules. "Publicly owned company" is defined in s.6.

There are currently reckoned to be around 120,000 FOIA-qualifying public authorities, but this will change continually as new bodies come into existence and existing ones disappear. Part of the remit of the Department for Constitutional Affairs (DCA) is to examine the evidence for bringing within the FOIA regime organisations which were either omitted when the original list was compiled, or which have since come to light as candidates for inclusion. Schedule 1 will be updated by a rolling process of amendment once or twice a year, and it is clear that many organizations not currently listed will be brought within the rules in future. There are two mechanisms by which this can happen.

Most amendments to Sch.1 will be made under FOIA s.4, which expressly contemplates the regular updating of the list. In addition, s.5 gives the Secretary of State power to designate public authorities individually.

Subsection (2)

1–018   As noted above in relation to s.1(1),[10] the right of access is engaged by mere possession of information. Ownership or legal right of use is not necessary. FOIA therefore applies to information held by a public authority which originated elsewhere. Furthermore, s.3(2)(b) extends FOIA to information held by another person on an authority's behalf. These two principles have very significant implications.

---

[10] At para.1–004.

Third party information

In general terms, information which originated from outside a public   **1–019**
authority will be FOIA accessible if held in an authority's files. All letters,
emails and other correspondence, as well as contracts, invoices, tenders,
technical data and other material authored by external organisations and
individuals will therefore be potentially accessible to the public (subject to
the rules about exemption, fees, costs and vexatious requests).

Such information which in the past may have been protected by law (*e.g.* on
grounds of confidentiality or commercial sensitivity) will not now be
protected unless FOIA permits. FOIA therefore applies, indirectly, to
information belonging to organisations which are not public authorities. In
particular, it applies to information from and about companies who supply
to the public sector, where the public authority customer is holding such
information.

The implications for third parties are even greater when one considers that
FOIA imposes no obligation on public authorities to notify or consult them
before disclosing. Nor does it provide any statutory mechanism for
preventing disclosure. Assessment of the exemptions and the decision
whether or not to apply them is entirely at the discretion of the public
authority (although there are good-practice guidelines to this effect in the
Lord Chancellor's Section 45 Code of Practice, on which see below). It is
open to a supplier to protect itself with contractual provisions requiring the
customer to notify and consult before disclosing, but in most cases this will
not be possible. The buck stops with the authority regardless of what any
contract says, so most authorities will be reluctant to accept contractual
terms which attempt to control their FOIA processes.

This leaves suppliers with limited options. Any pre-emptive challenge to an
authority's application of the Act will be contingent on the supplier
knowing a request has been made. The best advice to suppliers must
therefore be to try to ensure their customers tell them when a request comes
in. The key to risk management is a close working relationship between the
supplier's team and the authority's. Supplier liaison should be geared to
ensuring the authority's information handling process functions correctly,
but also allows the supplier to mitigate the risk of sensitive information
finding its way into the public domain.

If there is disagreement over information of material value, then the
supplier's only realistic legal remedy is an injunction preventing
disclosure—although for most companies, taking customers to court is not
a sensible way of doing business. It is possible that in some cases authorities
may actually invite a supplier to apply for an injunction (provided the
supplier meets the authority's costs) on the ground that an injunction will
provide solid legal justification for withholding information in a difficult
case.[11]

---

[11] An injunction would also bring the information with the FOIA exemption under s.44.

In the absence of some kind of early warning system, authorities will simply disclose information without the supplier knowing. In such a case, the supplier's options are limited. It can sue for damages under the common law—with all the difficulties this entails of quantifying loss—or it can seek judicial review. Both will be a long way short of satisfactory, however, involving uncertainty of outcome and further cost.

The Section 45 Code of Practice

1–020   Part VII of the Section 45 Code provides guidance on consultation with third parties where a request is made for information which an authority holds but which belongs to someone else. Its recommendations, in summary, are as follows:

> (a) Where disclosure of information cannot be made without the consent of a third party (*e.g.* because disclosure might be an actionable breach of confidence), the authority should consult with a view to obtaining consent unless this is not practicable (for example, because the third party cannot be located or the costs of consulting would be disproportionate).
>
> (b) Consultation should take place where the views of the third party may assist in determining whether an exemption applies or where the balance of the public interest lies.
>
> (c) Consultation will be unnecessary where:
>
>> (i) the authority does not intend to disclose, in reliance on some other legitimate ground under the Act;
>>
>> (ii) the views of the third party can have no effect on the authority's decision; or
>>
>> (iii) the information must be provided because no exemption applies.
>
> (d) Where the interests of a number of third parties may be affected by disclosure and those parties have a representative organisation which can express views on their behalf, the authority may consider it sufficient to consult the representative organisation. If there is no representative organisation, the authority may consider it sufficient to consult a representative sample of the third parties.
>
> (e) The fact that a third party has not responded to consultation does not relieve the authority of its duty to disclose under the Act, nor its duty to reply within the statutory time limit.
>
> (f) In all cases, it is for the public authority, not the third party or any representative, to determine whether or not information should be

disclosed under FOIA. A third party's refusal to consent does not in itself mean that information should be withheld.

Outsourcing of public authority functions and other transfers of information

Public authorities cannot escape FOIA by transferring information to third parties—the rules extend to information held on an authority's behalf. Importantly, where information *is* held by a third party, it remains the authority's responsibility to comply with requests. This means that public authorities which outsource services or otherwise transfer information to external organisations must ensure they can retrieve information in sufficient time. It is imperative that authorities have contractual arrangements to guarantee this. The contract should specify what assistance the supplier will provide, and at what cost.

1–021

4 Amendment of Schedule 1

(1) The [Secretary of State] may by order amend Schedule 1 by adding to that Schedule a reference to any body or the holder of any office which (in either case) is not for the time being listed in that Schedule but as respects which both the first and the second conditions below are satisfied.

1–022

(2) The first condition is that the body or office—

    (a) is established by virtue of Her Majesty's prerogative or by an enactment or by subordinate legislation, or

    (b) is established in any other way by a Minister of the Crown in his capacity as Minister, by a government department or by the National Assembly for Wales.

(3) The second condition is—

    (a) in the case of a body, that the body is wholly or partly constituted by appointment made by the Crown, by a Minister of the Crown, by a government department or by the National Assembly for Wales, or

    (b) in the case of an office, that appointments to the office are made by the Crown, by a Minister of the Crown, by a government department or by the National Assembly for Wales.

(4) If either the first or the second condition above ceases to be satisfied as respects any body or office which is listed in Part VI or VII of Schedule 1, that body or the holder of that office shall cease to be a public authority by virtue of the entry in question.

(5) The [Secretary of State] may by order amend Schedule 1 by removing from Part VI or VII of that Schedule an entry relating to any body or office—

    (a) which has ceased to exist, or

    (b) as respects which either the first or the second condition above has ceased to be satisfied.

(6) An order under subsection (1) may relate to a specified person or office or to persons or offices falling within a specified description.

(7) Before making an order under subsection (1), the [Secretary of State] shall—

    (a) if the order adds to Part II, III, IV or VI of Schedule 1 a reference to—

        (i) a body whose functions are exercisable only or mainly in or as regards Wales, or

        (ii) the holder of an office whose functions are exercisable only or mainly in or as regards Wales, consult the National Assembly for Wales, and

    (b) if the order relates to a body which, or the holder of any office who, if the order were made, would be a Northern Ireland public authority, consult the First Minister and deputy First Minister in Northern Ireland.

(8) This section has effect subject to section 80.

(9) In this section "Minister of the Crown" includes a Northern Ireland Minister.

NOTES

1–023   **Initial Commencement**

Royal Assent

Royal Assent: 30 November 2000: see s 87(1)(a).

Subordinate Legislation

Freedom of Information (Additional Public Authorities) Order 2002, SI 2002/2623 (made under sub-ss (1), (6)).
Freedom of Information (Additional Public Authorities) Order 2003, SI 2003/1882 (made under sub-ss (1), (6)).
Freedom of Information (Removal of References to Public Authorities) Order 2003, SI 2003/1883 (made under sub-s (5)).

Freedom of Information (Additional Public Authorities) Order 2004, SI 2004/938 (made under sub-ss (1), (6), (7)).
Freedom of Information (Removal of References to Public Authorities) Order 2004, SI 2004/1641 (made under sub-s (5)).
Freedom of Information (Additional Public Authorities) (Amendment) Order 2004, SI 2004/1870 (made under sub-ss (1), (6)).

GENERAL NOTE

Inevitably, some bodies which should be listed in Schedule 1 are not. Under s.4, Schedule 1 will be updated by a rolling process of amendment once or twice a year. The process of rolling amendments will be administered by the DCA, which is responsible for assessing evidence of qualification and liaising with the relevant Minister or department before making a decision. For the most part, new public authorities will be added where the DCA judges an organisation to qualify under the s.4 criteria. For this, there are two tests. The first applies to an organisation's establishment, the second, to the appointment of its officers. **1–024**

Under the first test, a body can only qualify if it is established by Royal Prerogative, by statute or subordinate legislation, or if it was set up by a Minister or a government department. Where this is the case, the second requirement must also then be met, namely: that at least one of the organisation's appointees or officers must be made or appointed by the Crown, a Minister or a government department. It is clear that very many organisations not currently covered by FOIA which will meet these criteria and will therefore be brought within the rules in due course.

Where DCA decides that an organisation should be added, this will be done by negative resolution, whereby an order is signed and put before Parliament giving MPs 40 days to object. Once an organisation is brought within Schedule 1 it will have a specified period within which to meet FOIA's publication scheme requirements, and to ensure that it is in a position to comply with information requests as and when received. Grace periods are likely to be either three, six or nine months, depending on the DCA's assessment.

Section 4(5) gives a corresponding power to remove bodies from Schedule 1 where they cease to qualify.

5 Further power to designate public authorities

    (1) **The [Secretary of State] may by order designate as a public authority for the purposes of this Act any person who is neither listed in Schedule 1 nor capable of being added to that Schedule by an order under section 4(1), but who—** **1–025**

        (a) **appears to the [Secretary of State] to exercise functions of a public nature, or**

    (b) **is providing under a contract made with a public authority any service whose provision is a function of that authority.**

(2) **An order under this section may designate a specified person or office or persons or offices falling within a specified description.**

(3) **Before making an order under this section, the [Secretary of State] shall consult every person to whom the order relates, or persons appearing to him to represent such persons.**

(4) **This section has effect subject to section 80.**

NOTES

Initial Commencement

Royal Assent

Royal Assent: 30 November 2000: see s 87(1)(a).

GENERAL NOTE

1–026 Section 5 confers on the Secretary of State the power to designate as a public authority any body which:

    (a) "appears to the Secretary of State" to be exercising functions of a public nature; or

    (b) provides a public service under contract with a public authority.

These categories are intended to sweep up organisations which fall outside the s.4 criteria but which ought to be included in Schedule 1 nevertheless.

There are very many organisations which perform functions which, intuitively, seem FOIA qualifying but which are not currently listed in Schedule 1. Examples include the Press Complaints Commission, The Law Society and the British Board of Film Classification.[12]

---

[12] The government has so far resisted calls for the Press Complaints Commission to be brought within FOIA. Just prior to the General Election in 2005 Estelle Morris, the Minister for Culture, Media and Sport, replied to a question from Clive Soley MP by saying "The government strongly believes that a press free from state intervention is fundamental to democracy. Designating the PCC a public authority would not be compatible with the government's support for an independent body overseeing press regulation." This is odd. The PCC's remit is to regulate the press to ensure compliance with proper standards. It is therefore clearly exercising a function of a public nature. There is no obvious reason why the PCC should be FOIA-proof when numerous other regulators (the Parliamentary Ombudsman, the Police Complaints Commission and the Information Commissioner, to name but three) are not.

Part (1)(b) is likely to affect a large number of companies supplying to the public sector. Public service delivery is increasingly being outsourced, particularly for IT-heavy functions and for specialised services relating to security, prisons, health care and waste management. Companies which supply in these sectors are prime candidates for s.5 designation, particularly as designation need not apply to the whole of an organisation but can be restricted to particular functions.

6 Publicly-owned companies

(1) A company is a "publicly-owned company" for the purposes of section 3(1)(b) if— 1–027

    (a) it is wholly owned by the Crown, or

    (b) it is wholly owned by any public authority listed in Schedule 1 other than—

        (i) a government department, or

        (ii) any authority which is listed only in relation to particular information.

(2) For the purposes of this section—

    (a) a company is wholly owned by the Crown if it has no members except—

        (i) Ministers of the Crown, government departments or companies wholly owned by the Crown, or

        (ii) persons acting on behalf of Ministers of the Crown, government departments or companies wholly owned by the Crown, and

    (b) a company is wholly owned by a public authority other than a government department if it has no members except—

        (i) that public authority or companies wholly owned by that public authority, or

        (ii) persons acting on behalf of that public authority or of companies wholly owned by that public authority.

(3) In this section—

    "company" includes any body corporate;

    "Minister of the Crown" includes a Northern Ireland Minister.

NOTES

Initial Commencement

Royal Assent

Royal Assent: 30 November 2000: see s 87(1)(a).

7 Public authorities to which Act has limited application

1–028

(1) Where a public authority is listed in Schedule 1 only in relation to information of a specified description, nothing in Parts I to V of this Act applies to any other information held by the authority.

(2) An order under section 4(1) may, in adding an entry to Schedule 1, list the public authority only in relation to information of a specified description.

(3) The [Secretary of State] may by order amend Schedule 1—

(a) by limiting to information of a specified description the entry relating to any public authority, or

(b) by removing or amending any limitation to information of a specified description which is for the time being contained in any entry.

(4) Before making an order under subsection (3), the [Secretary of State] shall—

(a) if the order relates to the National Assembly for Wales or a Welsh public authority, consult the National Assembly for Wales,

(b) if the order relates to the Northern Ireland Assembly, consult the Presiding Officer of that Assembly, and

(c) if the order relates to a Northern Ireland department or a Northern Ireland public authority, consult the First Minister and deputy First Minister in Northern Ireland.

(5) An order under section 5(1)(a) must specify the functions of the public authority designated by the order with respect to which the designation is to have effect; and nothing in Parts I to V of this Act applies to information which is held by the authority but does not relate to the exercise of those functions.

(6) An order under section 5(1)(b) must specify the services provided under contract with respect to which the

designation is to have effect; and nothing in Parts I to V of this Act applies to information which is held by the public authority designated by the order but does not relate to the provision of those services.

(7) Nothing in Parts I to V of this Act applies in relation to any information held by a publicly-owned company which is excluded information in relation to that company.

(8) In subsection (7) "excluded information", in relation to a publicly-owned company, means information which is of a description specified in relation to that company in an order made by the [Secretary of State] for the purposes of this subsection.

(9) In this section "publicly-owned company" has the meaning given by section 6.

NOTES

Initial Commencement   1–029

Royal Assent

Royal Assent: 30 November 2000: see s 87(1)(a).

Subordinate Legislation

Freedom of Information (Additional Public Authorities) Order 2002, SI 2002/2623 (made under sub-s (2)).
Freedom of Information (Additional Public Authorities) Order 2003, SI 2003/1882 (made under sub-s (2)).

GENERAL NOTE

Section 7 allows for specific derogations from the right of access as it applies   1–030
to certain individual public authorities, and for such derogations to be set out in Schedule 1. So, for example, FOIA only applies to the BBC and Channel 4 in relation to information held for purposes *other than* journalism, art or literature. It only applies to the Bank of England in relation to information held for purposes *other than* its monetary policy functions, its operations which provide financial stability to financial institutions, and its private banking services.

8 Request for information

(1) In this Act any reference to a "request for information" is   1–031
a reference to such a request which—

(a) is in writing,

    (b) **states the name of the applicant and an address for correspondence, and**

    (c) **describes the information requested.**

  (2) **For the purposes of subsection (1)(a), a request is to be treated as made in writing where the text of the request—**

    (a) **is transmitted by electronic means,**

    (b) **is received in legible form, and**

    (c) **is capable of being used for subsequent reference.**

NOTES

Initial Commencement

Royal Assent

Royal Assent: 30 November 2000: see s 87(1)(a).

GENERAL NOTE

1–032 There are very few formalities necessary for a request to be valid and therefore enforceable under FOIA. A request need not be in a particular format, nor be addressed to a particular person, nor mention that it is a request under the Act, nor otherwise refer to the Act (although for applicants this will always be prudent). Public authorities must understand that any written communication could contain a FOIA request, even if it is buried in the text of a document which is otherwise unrelated to open government.

Note that the duty to advise and assist under s.16 applies whether or not the request meets the s.8 requirements. This means, for example, that requests made orally should be answered with a recommendation to submit the request again in writing, rather than outright rejection.

Subsection (2)

1–033 Requests submitted by electronic means must be legible and capable of being used for subsequent reference. It is unclear whether an email address alone is sufficient for this purpose (arguably not, if, for example, the information requested is held only in hard copy and therefore cannot be sent by email unless scanned to soft copy first). However, the duty to advise and assist would probably mean that in cases where an email address is not sufficient on its own, the authority should advise the applicant of this fact together with the reason why, and request a postal or other address instead, rather than simply rejecting the request outright.

9 Fees

(1) A public authority to whom a request for information is made may, within the period for complying with section 1(1), give the applicant a notice in writing (in this Act referred to as a "fees notice") stating that a fee of an amount specified in the notice is to be charged by the authority for complying with section 1(1).

1–034

(2) Where a fees notice has been given to the applicant, the public authority is not obliged to comply with section 1(1) unless the fee is paid within the period of three months beginning with the day on which the fees notice is given to the applicant.

(3) Subject to subsection (5), any fee under this section must be determined by the public authority in accordance with regulations made by the [Secretary of State].

(4) Regulations under subsection (3) may, in particular, provide—

    (a) that no fee is to be payable in prescribed cases,

    (b) that any fee is not to exceed such maximum as may be specified in, or determined in accordance with, the regulations, and

    (c) that any fee is to be calculated in such manner as may be prescribed by the regulations.

(5) Subsection (3) does not apply where provision is made by or under any enactment as to the fee that may be charged by the public authority for the disclosure of the information.

NOTES

Initial Commencement

1–035

Royal Assent

Royal Assent (in so far as this section confers powers to make any order, regulations or code of practice): 30 November 2000: see s 87(1)(m).

Specified date

Specified date (for remaining purposes): 30 November 2005 (unless the Secretary of State by order appoints this section before that date): see s 87(3) (as amended by SI 2001/3500, art 8, Sch 2, Pt I, para 8(1)(o) and SI 2003/1887, art 9, Sch 2, para 12(1)(c)). (See appointment note below.)

Appointment

Appointment (for remaining purposes): 1 January 2005: see SI 2004/3122, art 2.

Subordinate Legislation

Freedom of Information and Data Protection (Appropriate Limit and Fees) Regulations 2004, SI 2004/3244 (made under sub-ss (3), (4))

GENERAL NOTE

1-036　The law recognises that freedom of access to information imposes a financial and administrative burden on public authorities which should not be solely the responsibility of the taxpayer. Sections 9 and 13 therefore give authorities discretion, within parameters set by the Secretary of State, to charge a fee. Section 9 deals with notices about fees. Fees themselves are covered under s.13.

10 Time for compliance with request

1-037

(1) Subject to subsections (2) and (3), a public authority must comply with section 1(1) promptly and in any event not later than the twentieth working day following the date of receipt.

(2) Where the authority has given a fees notice to the applicant and the fee is paid in accordance with section 9(2), the working days in the period beginning with the day on which the fees notice is given to the applicant and ending with the day on which the fee is received by the authority are to be disregarded in calculating for the purposes of subsection (1) the twentieth working day following the date of receipt.

(3) If, and to the extent that—

(a) section 1(1)(a) would not apply if the condition in section 2(1)(b) were satisfied, or

(b) section 1(1)(b) would not apply if the condition in section 2(2)(b) were satisfied,

the public authority need not comply with section 1(1)(a) or (b) until such time as is reasonable in the circumstances; but this subsection does not affect the time by which any notice under section 17(1) must be given.

(4) The [Secretary of State] may by regulations provide that subsections (1) and (2) are to have effect as if any

reference to the twentieth working day following the date of receipt were a reference to such other day, not later than the sixtieth working day following the date of receipt, as may be specified in, or determined in accordance with, the regulations.

(5) Regulations under subsection (4) may—

    (a) prescribe different days in relation to different cases, and

    (b) confer a discretion on the Commissioner.

(6) In this section—

"the date of receipt" means—

    (a) the day on which the public authority receives the request for information, or

    (b) if later, the day on which it receives the information referred to in section 1(3);

"working day" means any day other than a Saturday, a Sunday, Christmas Day, Good Friday or a day which is a bank holiday under the Banking and Financial Dealings Act 1971 in any part of the United Kingdom.

NOTES

Initial Commencement   1–038

Royal Assent

Royal Assent (in so far as this section confers powers to make any order, regulations or code of practice): 30 November 2000: see s 87(1)(m).

Specified date

Specified date (for remaining purposes): 30 November 2005 (unless the Secretary of State by order appoints this section before that date): see s 87(3) (as amended by SI 2001/3500, art 8, Sch 2, Pt I, para 8(1)(o) and SI 2003/1887, art 9, Sch 2, para 12(1)(c)). (See appointment note below.)

Appointment

Appointment (for remaining purposes): 1 January 2005: see SI 2004/3122, art 2.

Subordinate Legislation

Freedom of Information (Time for Compliance with Request) Regulations 2004, SI 2004/3364 (made under sub-ss (4), (5)).

GENERAL NOTE

1–039   The overriding requirement for compliance with s.1 is promptitude, with a long stop period of 20 working days in any event (s.10(1)). "Prompt" is presumably intended to mean "without delay" although the Act gives no further guidance.

On a strict reading of s.10(1) it is arguable that authorities are not entitled to take the full 20 working days unless absolutely necessary. Taken in the abstract, however, it is difficult to imagine circumstances in which a 20 working day response would be judged too long. There is nothing to suggest, for example, that authorities must try to act more quickly where necessary to meet newspaper copy deadlines. On the contrary, there have been numerous complaints to the Commissioner under s.50 where authorities have taken longer than 20 days to respond and in every case, while identifying the breach of the statutory time limit, the Decision Notice has not required any action to be taken.[13]

When does the 20-day clock start to run?

1–040   The 20 working day clock starts the day *after* the authority receives the request or, if it reasonably requires further information to identify and locate the information, the day it receives such further information.

A request is received when it is delivered to the authority (regardless of who the addressee is) or when it is delivered to an individual's inbox. The date of receipt is *not* the date the request reaches the right person within the organisation. That said, where a request is made by email and an out-of-office message gives instructions for re-directing it, the email will be treated as received when delivered to the inbox of the alternative contact.

Where an authority transfers a request to another authority (because the transferring authority does not hold the information), then the 20 working day clock starts when the second authority receives the request. Authorities are of course required to act promptly when redirecting requests.

Circumstances in which the time for compliance may be extended

1–041   There are four circumstances in which the time for compliance may be extended:

- If the authority requires further information to identify and locate the information (s.1(3)), then time will not start to run unless and until that further information is provided.

- If the authority issues a fees notice (s.9), then the clock stops on the day the notice is given and re-starts on the day the fee is

---

[13] See for example Decision Notices FS50067858 (June 20, 2005), FS50079178 (June 13, 2005) and FS50061644 (May 16, 2005).

received (which, in the case of a cheque, means the day the cheque is cleared).[14] If the fee is not received within three months of the fees notice, then the request lapses and the authority is not required to respond.

- If the authority notifies the applicant that the information is subject to a qualified exemption (s.17(1)), then the authority is entitled to take "such time as is reasonable in the circumstances" to assess the balance of the public interest. Note however that notification under s.17(1) must be served promptly, and in any event within 20 working days. Section 17(2) requires the authority to give an estimate of the date by which it expects to reach a decision on the public interest, and under the Section 45 Code of Practice any estimate must be realistic and reasonable (taking account, for example, of the need to consult third parties). The authority is expected to comply with its estimate unless there are good reasons for exceeding it, in which case it should explain the reason for the delay.

- Where special dispensation is made under s.10(4). Section 10(4) provides for an extension of the time limit up to a maximum of 60 working days. To date, four cases have been identified for such treatment:

  - to deal with school holidays, since schools will not be staffed at that time;

  - when frontline units of the armed forces are impossible to reach for operational reasons;

  - if a public authority needs to consult posts, governments or companies abroad to obtain information; and

  - when the National Archives need to determine whether requested information in a transferred public record that has not been designated as open information is exempt, or whether the duty to confirm or deny is excluded under Pt II.[15]

It will be apparent that the time limits for compliance take no account of resource limitations. The Act gives no grace for understaffing, nor for inefficient, obsolete or non-existent record management systems. In cases where 20 days look likely to be insufficient, the best advice is to seek the applicant's agreement to an extension of time or, failing that, to provide a partial response to the request within the time allowed, with the balance of information to follow. The latter is still a breach of s.10, but may serve to

[14] Authorities are of course required to ensure that cheques are banked promptly.
[15] See s.66 in relation to transferred records, together with the commentary under s.67.

mitigate an adverse assessment by the Information Commissioner in the event of a complaint.

Information Commissioner's Guidance[16]

1–042   It is in public authorities' interests to ensure that mail is distributed and acted upon promptly. Authorities also need to give thought to their procedures for dealing with communications where an addressee is unexpectedly absent. The following good practice guidelines are recommended:

- It may be helpful to provide and publicise a separate email address for FOI requests (although the duty to deal with requests applies regardless of where they are received within the organisation).

- Staff should use the out-of-office facility for email to cover absences and provide alternative contact details.

- Where an alternative contact is provided in an out-of-office message, that contact should advise the original recipient of action taken.

- Acknowledge receipt of requests and refer to the 20 working day time limit so that applicants know their request is being dealt with. If possible, tell applicants when they might expect a full response.

11 Means by which communication to be made

1–043   **(1) Where, on making his request for information, the applicant expresses a preference for communication by any one or more of the following means, namely—**

(a) the provision to the applicant of a copy of the information in permanent form or in another form acceptable to the applicant,

(b) the provision to the applicant of a reasonable opportunity to inspect a record containing the information, and

(c) the provision to the applicant of a digest or summary of the information in permanent form or in another form acceptable to the applicant,

the public authority shall so far as reasonably practicable give effect to that preference.

---

[16] Freedom of Information Awareness Guidance No.11: Time for Compliance.

(2) **In determining for the purposes of this section whether it is reasonably practicable to communicate information by particular means, the public authority may have regard to all the circumstances, including the cost of doing so.**

(3) **Where the public authority determines that it is not reasonably practicable to comply with any preference expressed by the applicant in making his request, the authority shall notify the applicant of the reasons for its determination.**

(4) **Subject to subsection (1), a public authority may comply with a request by communicating information by any means which are reasonable in the circumstances.**

NOTES

Initial Commencement

Specified date

Specified date: 30 November 2005 (unless the Secretary of State by order appoints this section before that date): see s 87(3) (as amended by SI 2001/3500, art 8, Sch 2, Pt I, para 8(1)(o) and SI 2003/1887, art 9, Sch 2, para 12(1)(c)). (See appointment note below.)

Appointment

Appointment: 1 January 2005: see SI 2004/3122, art 2.

GENERAL NOTE

Authorities may communicate information by any means which are reasonable in the circumstances, unless the applicant expresses a preference in accordance with s.11(1). If so, the authority must oblige "so far as reasonably practicable", having regard to all the circumstances, including the cost. **1–044**

Circumstances in which authorities need not meet an applicant's preference

There may be cases where providing a digest or summary of information will be difficult or impossible: **1–045**

- Information which is quantitative (*e.g.* statistics, accounts and other numeric data) may not easily be distilled.

- A transcript of a video might convey the text of a speech but not the inflection or facial expressions of the speaker and may therefore not accurately convey all the information in the original.

- Summarising information may constitute an infringement of copyright or database right.

In circumstances where it is not reasonably practicable to meet the applicant's preference the authority is entitled to decline to do so.

12 Exemption where cost of compliance exceeds appropriate limit

1–046

(1) Section 1(1) does not oblige a public authority to comply with a request for information if the authority estimates that the cost of complying with the request would exceed the appropriate limit.

(2) Subsection (1) does not exempt the public authority from its obligation to comply with paragraph (a) of section 1(1) unless the estimated cost of complying with that paragraph alone would exceed the appropriate limit.

(3) In subsections (1) and (2) "the appropriate limit" means such amount as may be prescribed, and different amounts may be prescribed in relation to different cases.

(4) The [Secretary of State] may by regulations provide that, in such circumstances as may be prescribed, where two or more requests for information are made to a public authority—

(a) by one person, or

(b) by different persons who appear to the public authority to be acting in concert or in pursuance of a campaign,

the estimated cost of complying with any of the requests is to be taken to be the estimated total cost of complying with all of them.

(5) The [Secretary of State] may by regulations make provision for the purposes of this section as to the costs to be estimated and as to the manner in which they are to be estimated.

NOTES

Initial Commencement

Royal Assent

1–047

Royal Assent (in so far as this section confers powers to make any order, regulations or code of practice): 30 November 2000: see s 87(1)(m).

Specified date

Specified date (for remaining purposes): 30 November 2005 (unless the Secretary of State by order appoints this section before that date): see s 87(3) (as amended by SI 2001/3500, art 8, Sch 2, Pt I, para 8(1)(o) and SI 2003/1887, art 9, Sch 2, para 12(1)(c)). (See appointment note below.)

Appointment

Appointment (for remaining purposes): 1 January 2005: see SI 2004/3122, art 2.

Subordinate Legislation

Freedom of Information and Data Protection (Appropriate Limit and Fees) Regulations 2004, SI 2004/3244 (made under sub-ss (3)–(5)).

GENERAL NOTE

Section 12 permits authorities to decline requests altogether where the cost of complying would exceed "the appropriate limit". **1–048**

The Fees Regulations (SI 2004/3244)

Under the Fees Regulations "the appropriate limit" is £600 for central **1–049**
government (*i.e.* the public authorities listed in Pt 1 of Schedule 1) and £450 for everyone else. In calculating the cost, authorities can take into account the total cost of identifying, locating, retrieving and extracting information. Time spent on these activities by authority staff or by anyone on the authority's behalf must be assessed at a rate of £25 per hour. This applies regardless of any published or agreed hourly rates which may be charged by external service providers. In effect, therefore, the £600 limit equates to 24 hours, or around three and a half days' work; the £450 limit equates to 18 hours, or two and a half days' work.

One anomaly in the Fees Regulations is that they take no account of the authority's level of sophistication. You are likely to get a lot more for your money if you petition an authority which operates an up-to-date electronic document management system as opposed to one whose files are all held in unstructured paper records in the basement.

The Fees Regulations do not apply:

- to material made available under a publication scheme under s.19;

- to information which is reasonably accessible by other means (within the meaning of s.21); or

- where provision is made by or under any enactment for the fee that may be charged.

In relation to the last of these, authorities should ensure that charges made in accordance with other legislation are within the terms of any relevant guidance issued or approved by HM Treasury or the Northern Ireland Department of Finance and Personnel (applicable to devolved bodies in Northern Ireland).

Multiple requests and "campaigns"

1–050   Section 5 of the Fees Regulations permits authorities to treat multiple requests from the same person as a single request, provided they relate to the same or similar information and are received within any period of 60 consecutive working days. In effect, it should not be possible to come in below the appropriate limit by dividing one request into several smaller requests. The same applies to multiple requests from different applicants who appear to be acting in concert or as part of an organised campaign.

13 Fees for disclosure where cost of compliance exceeds appropriate limit

1–051
(1) A public authority may charge for the communication of any information whose communication—

   (a) is not required by section 1(1) because the cost of complying with the request for information exceeds the amount which is the appropriate limit for the purposes of section 12(1) and (2), and

   (b) is not otherwise required by law,

   such fee as may be determined by the public authority in accordance with regulations made by the [Secretary of State].

(2) Regulations under this section may, in particular, provide—

   (a) that any fee is not to exceed such maximum as may be specified in, or determined in accordance with, the regulations, and

   (b) that any fee is to be calculated in such manner as may be prescribed by the regulations.

(3) Subsection (1) does not apply where provision is made by or under any enactment as to the fee that may be charged by the public authority for the disclosure of the information.

NOTES

Initial Commencement

Royal Assent

Royal Assent (in so far as this section confers powers to make any order, regulations or code of practice): 30 November 2000: see s 87(1)(m).

Specified date

Specified date (for remaining purposes): 30 November 2005 (unless the Secretary of State by order appoints this section before that date): see s 87(3) (as amended by SI 2001/3500, art 8, Sch 2, Pt I, para 8(1)(o) and SI 2003/1887, art 9, Sch 2, para 12(1)(c)). (See appointment note below.)

Appointment

Appointment (for remaining purposes): 1 January 2005: see SI 2004/3122, art 2.

Subordinate Legislation

Freedom of Information and Data Protection (Appropriate Limit and Fees) Regulations 2004, SI 2004/3244 (made under sub-ss (1), (2)).

GENERAL NOTE

Section 12 permits authorities to decline requests if they exceed a specified **1–052**
cost, but s.13 gives them the option to offer a response anyway, in return for
a fee. The manner in which fees notices should be issued is dealt with in
s.9.

Fees Regulations (SI 2004/3244)

The fees which an authority can charge must not exceed the total costs **1–053**
which it reasonably expects to incur in complying with s.1. In assessing
costs, the regulations expressly permit accounting for:

- compliance with s.11, where an applicant expresses a preferred means of communication;

- reproduction of any document; and

- postage and other forms of transmitting information.

Authorities are not permitted to include costs attributable to time spent by
others on the authority's behalf. This therefore excludes costs incurred by

third parties who hold information on behalf of an authority. It also presumably excludes the cost of any external professional advice relating to the request.

14 Vexatious or repeated requests

1–054
(1) Section 1(1) does not oblige a public authority to comply with a request for information if the request is vexatious.

(2) Where a public authority has previously complied with a request for information which was made by any person, it is not obliged to comply with a subsequent identical or substantially similar request from that person unless a reasonable interval has elapsed between compliance with the previous request and the making of the current request.

NOTES

Initial Commencement

Specified date

Specified date: 30 November 2005 (unless the Secretary of State by order appoints this section before that date): see s 87(3) (as amended by SI 2001/3500, art 8, Sch 2, Pt I, para 8(1)(o) and SI 2003/1887, art 9, Sch 2, para 12(1)(c)). (See appointment note below.)

Appointment

Appointment: 1 January 2005: see SI 2004/3122, art 2.

GENERAL NOTE

1–055   Section 14 permits an authority to refuse any request which is vexatious, or which is identical or substantially similar to a previous request by the same person unless a reasonable period has elapsed.[17] Authorities must notify applicants of any reliance on s.14.[18]

Subsection (1)

1–056   In legal terms, "vexatious" normally refers to something done without sufficient grounds or for the purpose of causing inconvenience, harassment

---

[17] Interestingly, under s.50(2) the Commissioner is not obliged to investigate a complaint if it appears to him to be "*frivolous or* vexatious" (author's emphasis). The inclusion of "frivolous" in s.50(2) suggests that the grounds for the Commissioner refusing to investigate a complaint are slightly wider than the s.14 grounds on which an authority may refuse a request in the first place.
[18] See s.17 in relation to notices.

and expense out of all proportion to any likely gain. However, FOIA confers access to information *as of right* which means that the merits of a request and the motives or grounds for making it will usually be irrelevant. In effect, FOIA is "purpose-blind" or "applicant-blind"—requesters do not have to establish any interest or need-to-know before they become entitled to information.

On this basis, "vexatious" can only refer to the nature and effect of the request itself, *e.g.* where the request requires the unreasonable diversion of resources (although the fees regulations will prevent this in many cases), or to supplementary requests from the same applicant for further and further clarification where no further information can reasonably be provided.

It is arguable that requests made simply to waste an authority's time rather than because the applicant genuinely wants the information fall within s.12(1), but then it is difficult to see how an authority could determine this without straying into the supposedly forbidden territory of scrutinising the applicant's motives. The reality is that an applicant's conduct and motives *will* sometimes be relevant. This is borne out by freedom of information cases in Australia, New Zealand and Canada (on which, see below).

Subsection (2)

There are two questions to consider in relation to s.14(2), namely: what **1–057** constitutes a "substantially similar request" and how long is a "reasonable interval"? There is very little to go on in either case but, given FOIA's overriding purpose, the words "substantially similar" should not be interpreted too broadly. The length of a reasonable interval will depend on the circumstances. For information which changes rapidly, the period could be relatively short. So, for example, two requests received from the same applicant a month apart requesting an authority's most recent monthly performance statistics would not normally be considered a repeated request even if the content of the two requests is identical. Indeed, even if there were no new monthly statistics, the request would still merit a response by informing the applicant of this fact (unless of course he had been told as much in the response to the first request).

It is also likely that authorities will receive requests which simply ask whether information has changed since it was last requested. Whether the information has changed or not, the request must be answered (unless the applicant knows that the information is the same, and is asking the question simply to create a nuisance).

Circumstances in which repeated requests may nevertheless require an answer

There will be some cases where a repeated request should be answered on **1–058** grounds of good practice, even though technically it is invalid. For example:

- where the applicant has lost or disposed of the information but subsequently discovered that he still requires it;

- where the applicant reasonably requires another copy, *e.g.* because he has supplied the original to another body;

- where a request includes some information which is new but also some information previously supplied.

Department for Constitutional Affairs Guidance

1–059   DCA Guidance states that "vexatiousness needs to be assessed in all the circumstances of an individual case, but if a request is not a genuine endeavour to access information for its own sake, but is aimed at disrupting the work of an authority, or harassing individuals in it, then it may well be vexatious."[19]

Information Commissioner's Guidance[20]

1–060   The Commissioner's general approach is to be sympathetic to authorities where a request would impose a significant burden and display any of the following characteristics:

- it carries no serious purpose or value;

- it is designed to cause disruption or annoyance (*e.g.* because the applicant makes this clear or the authority has independent knowledge of his intentions from previous dealings);

- it has the effect of harassing the authority (*e.g.* because the request is for information which the applicant clearly understands is exempt);

- it can otherwise be characterised as obsessive or manifestly unreasonable.

Further, if a reasonable person would conclude that the main effect of the request would be "disproportionate inconvenience or expense", then the Commissioner considers it appropriate to treat it as vexatious.

Lessons from other countries

1–061   Freedom of information guidance from New Zealand, Australia and Canada suggests that the standard necessary for demonstrating

---

[19] Department for Constitutional Affairs, Procedural Guidance, Ch.03: The limits of your duty to answer requests.

[20] Freedom of Information Act Awareness Guidance No.22: Vexatious and Repeated Requests.

vexatiousness will normally be high, and also that the conduct and motives of applicants may well be relevant.

In New Zealand, the Ombudsman has commented that:

- to be vexatious the request must be such that no reasonable person could properly treat it as bona fide; and

- for a request to be refused on grounds of vexatiousness a requestor must be believed to be patently abusing the rights granted by the legislation.

Past experience can indicate that a new request is simply an abuse of the right of access rather than a request made in good faith. The Ombudsman has stated that "it seems plainly wrong that an unbalanced, mischievous or malicious individual should be able to inundate a department with time wasting requests."[21] Clearly, the requestor's conduct and the purpose of the request may be relevant to these issues.

In Australia, under the Northern Territory's Information Act 2002 the **1–062** Information Commissioner can make a declaration that a person is a vexatious applicant so long as the Commissioner is satisfied that:

- over a period of time the person has repeatedly applied to the same organisation for access or for review; and

- the repeated applications are unnecessary, an improper use of the right of access or review, or made for the purpose of harassing or obstructing or otherwise interfering with the operation of the organisation.

In Canada, Regulation 823 (passed to supplement Canada's freedom of information statutes) indicates that a request may well be vexatious if it is part of a pattern of conduct that amounts to an abuse of the right of access or would interfere with the operations of the institution, or it is made in bad faith of for a purpose other than to obtain access.[22]

The Ontario Information and Privacy Commissioner (OIPC) has made a number of decisions based on this guidance. These indicate that:

- a "pattern of conduct" requires recurring incidents of related or similar requests on the part of the requestor;

- "an abuse of the right of access" can be understood as an excessive volume of requests and appeals combined with the following factors:

[21] *Towards Open Government*, Supplementary Report, 1981, para.4.38(2), p.31, Danks Committee.
[22] RRO 1990 Reg.823, s.5.1.

- the varied nature and broad scope of the requests;

- the appearance they were submitted for 'nuisance' value;

- increased requests following the initiation of court proceedings;

- the requestor's working in concert with another requestor who has stated that he aims to harass government.

- "bad faith" follows a dictionary definition, namely "the conscious doing of a wrong because of a dishonest purpose or moral obliquity".[23]

Note, however, that the OIPC has also stated that public authorities who can only provide speculative reasons for a requestor's bad faith or attribute questionable motives to him do not satisfy the test for vexatiousness.[24]

1–063 The British Columbia Information and Privacy Commissioner (BCIPC) has also issued guidance on vexatious requests under British Columbia's Freedom of Information and Protection of Privacy Act 1996. He states that before agreeing to disregard a request on grounds of vexatiousness, the Commissioner would expect an authority to provide:

- evidence that it has exercised considerable restraint and made every effort to assist the requestor; and

- an explanation of the repetitious or systematic nature of the requests in question.[25]

The BCIPC has also said that:

- "a pleading is vexatious of it is without *bona fides,* is 'hopelessly oppressive' or causes the other party anxiety, trouble or expense"; and

- the dictionary definition of vexatious is "an annoying or distressing thing . . . without reasonable or probable cause or excuse."[26] (In this case, the Commissioner decided that the request was vexatious because the authority faced multiple requests from an individual who should have known that it had already disclosed to him all the information he had requested.)

---

[23] Order M-850, Appeal M-9600149, Town of Midland, 24 October 1996; Order MO-1841, Appeal MA-030249-1, Regional Municipality of Peel, 30 September 2004.

[24] Order PO-2348, Appeal PA-030172-2, Ministry of Natural Resources, 26 November 2004.

[25] See *www.oipcbc.org.*

[26] Auth (s.43) 02-02 Insurance Corporation of British Columbia, 8 November 2002, David Loukidelis, Information and Privacy Commissioner.

15 Special provisions relating to public records transferred to Public Record Office, etc

(1) Where—   1–064

    (a) the appropriate records authority receives a request for information which relates to information which is, or if it existed would be, contained in a transferred public record, and

    (b) either of the conditions in subsection (2) is satisfied in relation to any of that information,

that authority shall, within the period for complying with section 1(1), send a copy of the request to the responsible authority.

(2) The conditions referred to in subsection (1)(b) are—

    (a) that the duty to confirm or deny is expressed to be excluded only by a provision of Part II not specified in subsection (3) of section 2, and

    (b) that the information is exempt information only by virtue of a provision of Part II not specified in that subsection.

(3) On receiving the copy, the responsible authority shall, within such time as is reasonable in all the circumstances, inform the appropriate records authority of the determination required by virtue of subsection (3) or (4) of section 66.

(4) In this Act "transferred public record" means a public record which has been transferred—

    (a) to the Public Record Office,

    (b) to another place of deposit appointed by the Lord Chancellor under the Public Records Act 1958, or

    (c) to the Public Record Office of Northern Ireland.

(5) In this Act—

    "appropriate records authority", in relation to a transferred public record, means—

        (a) in a case falling within subsection (4)(a), the Public Record Office,

        (b) in a case falling within subsection (4)(b), the Lord Chancellor, and

        (c) in a case falling within subsection (4)(c), the Public Record Office of Northern Ireland;

"responsible authority", in relation to a transferred public record, means—

(a) in the case of a record transferred as mentioned in subsection (4)(a) or (b) from a government department in the charge of a Minister of the Crown, the Minister of the Crown who appears to the Lord Chancellor to be primarily concerned,

(b) in the case of a record transferred as mentioned in subsection (4)(a) or (b) from any other person, the person who appears to the Lord Chancellor to be primarily concerned,

(c) in the case of a record transferred to the Public Record Office of Northern Ireland from a government department in the charge of a Minister of the Crown, the Minister of the Crown who appears to the appropriate Northern Ireland Minister to be primarily concerned,

(d) in the case of a record transferred to the Public Record Office of Northern Ireland from a Northern Ireland department, the Northern Ireland Minister who appears to the appropriate Northern Ireland Minister to be primarily concerned, or

(e) in the case of a record transferred to the Public Record Office of Northern Ireland from any other person, the person who appears to the appropriate Northern Ireland Minister to be primarily concerned.

NOTES

Initial Commencement

Specified date

Specified date: 30 November 2005 (unless the Secretary of State by order appoints this section before that date): see s 87(3) (as amended by SI 2001/3500, art 8, Sch 2, Pt I, para 8(1)(o) and SI 2003/1887, art 9, Sch 2, para 12(1)(c)). (See appointment notes below.)

Appointment

Sub-ss (4), (5): Appointment: 1 January 2005: see SI 2004/1909, art 2(1), (2)(a), (3).

Sub-ss (1)–(3): Appointment: 1 January 2005: see SI 2004/3122, art 2.

GENERAL NOTE

This section should be read in conjunction with s.66.   **1–065**

Sections 15 and 66 contain provisions relating to information held by the Public Records Office (PRO). These provisions are necessary because although the PRO is itself a public authority and therefore subject to FOIA, its function has never been to respond to individual requests, but instead to provide the general public with physical access to records for the purposes of inspection and copying.

Sections 15 and 66 set out an elaborate procedure for the PRO to handle FOIA requests for information contained in records in its custody. In essence, where the PRO receives a FOIA request for information which has been transferred to it under the Public Records Act 1958, it must consult the body from which that information was passed (known as the "transferring authority") before deciding whether the information is exempt. In effect, it is the transferring authority which makes this decision rather than the PRO.

The obligation to consult does not apply to information which the transferring authority has designated as open information. "Open information" is not defined but effectively means information which the transferring authority decided at the time of transfer to the PRO was not eligible for exemption.

16 Duty to provide advice and assistance

(1) It shall be the duty of a public authority to provide advice   **1–066**
and assistance, so far as it would be reasonable to expect the authority to do so, to persons who propose to make, or have made, requests for information to it.

(2) Any public authority which, in relation to the provision of advice or assistance in any case, conforms with the code of practice under section 45 is to be taken to comply with the duty imposed by subsection (1) in relation to that case.

NOTES

Initial Commencement

Specified date

Specified date: 30 November 2005 (unless the Secretary of State by order appoints this section before that date): see s 87(3) (as amended by SI 2001/3500, art 8, Sch 2, Pt I, para 8(1)(o) and SI

2003/1887, art 9, Sch 2, para 12(1)(c)). (See appointment note below.)

Appointment

Appointment: 1 January 2005: see SI 2004/3122, art 2.

GENERAL NOTE

1–067　Public authorities can only answer requests once they know what the applicant is requesting. To put it another way, the right of access necessarily depends on the ability of applicants to describe what they want—and that is an inherent weakness in the rules. It means that FOIA's effectiveness depends in part on the attitude of civil servants. An authority could attempt to thwart requests by taking a wilfully narrow and obstructive approach. Section 16 exists to prevent this by imposing a wide ranging duty to advise and assist both prospective and actual applicants, and to do so at all stages of the process.

Note that the 20 working day clock for compliance with a request does not stop whilst an authority is providing advice and assistance.

Information Commissioner's Guidance[27]

1–068　The Commissioner's guidance emphasises that authorities should be flexible when assessing what reasonable advice and assistance might be. Examples include:

- keeping an applicant advised of the progress of his request;

- advising a potential applicant of his rights;

- helping an applicant focus his request, perhaps by describing the types of information available within the requested category[28];

- advising an applicant if information is available elsewhere and explaining how to access this (*e.g.* via the authority's publication scheme).

---

[27] Freedom of Information Awareness Guidance No.23: Advice and Assistance.

[28] In a complaint involving Ferryhill Town Council, an applicant who requested information about Council allotments was told that the Council would only supply the information on receipt of the Council's full costs (which were set out in a Fees Notice) because the cost of complying with the request would exceed the appropriate limit set out in the Fees Regulations. The Commissioner upheld the Council's estimation of its costs but also directed the Council to offer advice and assistance, either by giving the complainant the opportunity to refine his request, or by offering to supply whatever information could be provided within the parameters of the appropriate limit. Decision Notice FS50075378, July 14, 2005.

In all cases, the Commissioner recommends that early contact be made with the applicant and that all advice and assistance should be clear and intelligible.

Authorities should also be mindful of other legislative requirements which may affect how advice and assistance is provided. *e.g.* the Disability Discrimination Act 1995, the Welsh Language Act 1976 and the amended Race Relations Act 1976.

The Section 45 Code of Practice

The Section 45 Code specifically addresses the question of advice and assistance. It requires all public authorities to publish their procedures for dealing with requests. It also requires them to ensure that appropriate assistance is given to applicants who are unable to frame their requests in writing. This might mean advising the applicant to contact a Citizens Advice Bureau or other body for help, or offering to take a note of the application over the telephone and then sending the note to the applicant for confirmation.

1–069

The Code states that the aim of providing assistance is to clarify the nature of the information sought, not to determine the aims or motives of the applicant.

According to the Code, appropriate assistance might include:

- providing an outline of the different kinds of information which meet the terms of the request;

- providing access to detailed catalogues and indexes to help the applicant ascertain the nature and extent of the information held by the authority;

- providing a general response to the request setting out options for further information which could be provided on request.

Authorities must bear in mind that applicants cannot be expected to have identifiers such as file reference numbers or a description of a particular record, unless made available by the authority.

Authorities are not expected to seek further clarification if, having provided assistance in accordance with the Code, the applicant is still unable to identify the information they want.

Refusal of request

17 Refusal of request

(1) **A public authority which, in relation to any request for information, is to any extent relying on a claim that any**

1–070

provision of Part II relating to the duty to confirm or deny is relevant to the request or on a claim that information is exempt information must, within the time for complying with section 1(1), give the applicant a notice which—

(a) states that fact,

(b) specifies the exemption in question, and

(c) states (if that would not otherwise be apparent) why the exemption applies.

(2) Where—

(a) in relation to any request for information, a public authority is, as respects any information, relying on a claim—

(i) that any provision of Part II which relates to the duty to confirm or deny and is not specified in section 2(3) is relevant to the request, or

(ii) that the information is exempt information only by virtue of a provision not specified in section 2(3), and

(b) at the time when the notice under subsection (1) is given to the applicant, the public authority (or, in a case falling within section 66(3) or (4), the responsible authority) has not yet reached a decision as to the application of subsection (1)(b) or (2)(b) of section 2,

the notice under subsection (1) must indicate that no decision as to the application of that provision has yet been reached and must contain an estimate of the date by which the authority expects that such a decision will have been reached.

(3) A public authority which, in relation to any request for information, is to any extent relying on a claim that subsection (1)(b) or (2)(b) of section 2 applies must, either in the notice under subsection (1) or in a separate notice given within such time as is reasonable in the circumstances, state the reasons for claiming—

(a) that, in all the circumstances of the case, the public interest in maintaining the exclusion of the duty to confirm or deny outweighs the public interest in disclosing whether the authority holds the information, or

(b) that, in all the circumstances of the case, the public interest in maintaining the exemption outweighs the public interest in disclosing the information.

(4) **A public authority is not obliged to make a statement under subsection (1)(c) or (3) if, or to the extent that, the statement would involve the disclosure of information which would itself be exempt information.**

(5) **A public authority which, in relation to any request for information, is relying on a claim that section 12 or 14 applies must, within the time for complying with section 1(1), give the applicant a notice stating that fact.**

(6) **Subsection (5) does not apply where—**

    (a) **the public authority is relying on a claim that section 14 applies,**

    (b) **the authority has given the applicant a notice, in relation to a previous request for information, stating that it is relying on such a claim, and**

    (c) **it would in all the circumstances be unreasonable to expect the authority to serve a further notice under subsection (5) in relation to the current request.**

(7) **A notice under subsection (1), (3) or (5) must—**

    (a) **contain particulars of any procedure provided by the public authority for dealing with complaints about the handling of requests for information or state that the authority does not provide such a procedure, and**

    (b) **contain particulars of the right conferred by section 50.**

NOTES

Initial Commencement

Specified date

Specified date: 30 November 2005 (unless the Secretary of State by order appoints this section before that date): see s 87(3) (as amended by SI 2001/3500, art 8, Sch 2, Pt I, para 8(1)(o) and SI 2003/1887, art 9, Sch 2, para 12(1)(c)). (See appointment note below.)

Appointment

Appointment: 1 January 2005: see SI 2004/3122, art 2.

GENERAL NOTE

Section 17 requires authorities to give written notice whenever they refuse   **1–071**
to disclose information. All notices must describe the authority's

complaints procedure or state that no procedure exists if that is the case.[29] Notices must also explain to the applicant their rights of appeal under s.50. Failure to include these particulars will invalidate the notice. This would mean an applicant's right to complain and/or appeal continues without time limit.

In addition to these general requirements, s.17 contemplates four different types of notice.

(a) Where the authority is relying on an exemption, it must specify which one and explain why it applies, unless this would itself involve disclosure of exempt information.

(b) Where the authority is relying on a qualified exemption but has not yet completed its assessment of the balance of the public interest, it must notify the information referred to in (a) above, and also state that a decision is pending and provide an estimated date for a decision. Note that where the information requested is a public record transferred to the Public Records Office (or another records authority) under the Public Records Act 1958, the assessment of the public interest lies with the "responsible authority", *i.e.* usually the authority which transferred the record (rather than the records authority which is now holding it).

(c) A statement of the reasons for claiming that the public interest in withholding information outweighs the public interest in disclosing it. This form of notice would normally be issued following a notice in the form of (b) above. Such a statement need not be made if doing so would itself involve disclosure of exempt information.

(d) A statement that the authority is refusing a request for reasons of excessive cost (s.12) or because the request is vexatious or repeated (s.14). This form of notice must be given within the time limits set out in s.1(1). Note that a notice need not be given if already provided in relation to a previous request.

The Information Commissioner and the Information Tribunal

18 The Information Commissioner and the Information Tribunal

1–072

(1) The Data Protection Commissioner shall be known instead as the Information Commissioner.

---

[29] Where no formal complaints process exists it is submitted that the authority should still offer to applicants a review of the handling of their request. Reviews should be conducted by someone who was not involved in processing the request in the first place.

(2) The Data Protection Tribunal shall be known instead as the Information Tribunal.

(3) In this Act—

(a) the Information Commissioner is referred to as "the Commissioner", and

(b) the Information Tribunal is referred to as "the Tribunal".

(4) Schedule 2 (which makes provision consequential on subsections (1) and (2) and amendments of the Data Protection Act 1998 relating to the extension by this Act of the functions of the Commissioner and the Tribunal) has effect.

(5) If the person who held office as Data Protection Commissioner immediately before the day on which this Act is passed remains in office as Information Commissioner at the end of the period of two years beginning with that day, he shall vacate his office at the end of that period.

(6) Subsection (5) does not prevent the re-appointment of a person whose appointment is terminated by that subsection.

(7) In the application of paragraph 2(4)(b) and (5) of Schedule 5 to the Data Protection Act 1998 (Commissioner not to serve for more than fifteen years and not to be appointed, except in special circumstances, for a third or subsequent term) to anything done after the passing of this Act, there shall be left out of account any term of office served by virtue of an appointment made before the passing of this Act.

NOTES

Initial Commencement

Royal Assent

Sub-s (4): Royal Assent (for certain purposes): 30 November 2000: see s 87(1)(i).   1–073

Specified date

Sub-s (1): Specified date: 30 January 2001: see s 87(2)(a).
Sub-ss (2), (3), (5)–(7): Specified date: 30 November 2005 (unless the Secretary of State by order appoints these subsections before that date): see s 87(3) (as amended by SI 2001/3500, art 8, Sch 2, Pt

I, para 8(1)(o) and SI 2003/1887, art 9, Sch 2, para 12(1)(c)). (See appointment note below.)

Sub-s (4): Specified date (for certain purposes): 30 January 2001: see s 87(2)(c).

Sub-s (4): Specified date (for remaining purposes): Specified date: 30 November 2005 (unless the Secretary of State by order appoints this subsection before that date): see s 87(3) (as amended by SI 2001/3500, art 8, Sch 2, Pt I, para 8(1)(o) and SI 2003/1887, art 9, Sch 2, para 12(1)(c)). (See appointment notes below.)

Appointment

Sub-ss (2), (3), (5)–(7): Appointment: 14 May 2001: see SI 2001/1637, art 2(a).

Sub-s (4): Appointment (for certain purposes): 14 May 2001: see SI 2001/1637, art 2(b).

Sub-s (4): Appointment (for remaining purposes): 30 November 2002: see SI 2002/2812, art 2(h).

GENERAL NOTE

1–074   The Information Commissioner and the Information Tribunal are responsible for policing freedom of information. Their records are public records for the purposes of the Public Records Act 1958. The Commissioner's functions are set out in s.47. Enforcement procedures are set out in Pt IV (ss.50–56), appeals procedures in Pt V (ss.57–61).

The Information Commissioner as a public authority

1–075   The Information Commissioner is himself listed in Schedule 1 as a public authority which means that any information he holds is subject to the right of access. This could oblige him to disclose information which he obtained only by virtue of his duty to investigate FOIA complaints, even though the public authority under investigation had withheld it under an exemption. There are some limited procedures designed to address this anomaly, set out in a Memorandum of Understanding (MoU) between the Commissioner and the Department for Constitutional Affairs.[30]

Paragraph 9 of the MoU states that the Commissioner will not disclose to a complainant or to any third party any information provided to him by a government department either under the terms of the MoU or as a result of serving a notice under s.50 or 51 of FOIA, unless the department consents to the disclosure, or all appeal proceedings have been exhausted. The Commissioner has also undertaken to inform departments where such requests are made and to resist them by all reasonable means. Thirdly, he has agreed not to hold information for longer than necessary, and to return or dispose of it as appropriate.

---

[30] The MoU is available from the Department for Constitutional Affairs website at *www.dca.gov.uk.*

For particularly sensitive information, the Commissioner has agreed to inspect documents *in situ* so that such information is not "held" by him and therefore not subject to the right of access.

There is a further restriction on the disclosure of information acquired under or for the purposes of FOIA, where that information "relates to an individual or identifiable individual or business" and is not otherwise available to the public.[31] In these circumstances, the Data Protection Act prohibits disclosure unless it is made "with lawful authority". This sounds encouraging. Unfortunately, since disclosure by the Commissioner pursuant to a FOIA request would effectively be with lawful authority, it is unclear how much use this restriction will be in practice.

The MoU only applies to information provided by government departments, so other public authorities will presumably have to hope that the law enforcement exemption under s.31 protects their information in the Commissioner's hands, and that he is prepared to apply it.

Publication schemes

19 Publication schemes

    (1) It shall be the duty of every public authority—   1–076

        (a) to adopt and maintain a scheme which relates to the publication of information by the authority and is approved by the Commissioner (in this Act referred to as a "publication scheme"),

        (b) to publish information in accordance with its publication scheme, and

        (c) from time to time to review its publication scheme.

    (2) A publication scheme must—

        (a) specify classes of information which the public authority publishes or intends to publish,

        (b) specify the manner in which information of each class is, or is intended to be, published, and

        (c) specify whether the material is, or is intended to be, available to the public free of charge or on payment.

    (3) In adopting or reviewing a publication scheme, a public authority shall have regard to the public interest—

---

[31] Para.19 of Schedule 2 of FOIA extends s.59 of the Data Protection Act 1998 in this regard to include information obtained under FOIA.

(a) in allowing public access to information held by the authority, and

(b) in the publication of reasons for decisions made by the authority.

(4) A public authority shall publish its publication scheme in such manner as it thinks fit.

(5) The Commissioner may, when approving a scheme, provide that his approval is to expire at the end of a specified period.

(6) Where the Commissioner has approved the publication scheme of any public authority, he may at any time give notice to the public authority revoking his approval of the scheme as from the end of the period of six months beginning with the day on which the notice is given.

(7) Where the Commissioner—

(a) refuses to approve a proposed publication scheme, or

(b) revokes his approval of a publication scheme,

he must give the public authority a statement of his reasons for doing so.

NOTES

1–077   **Initial Commencement**

Royal Assent

Royal Assent (so far as relating to the approval of publication schemes): 30 November 2000: see s 87(1)(b).

Specified date

Specified date (for remaining purposes): 30 November 2005 (unless the Secretary of State by order appoints this section before that date): see s 87(3) (as amended by SI 2001/3500, art 8, Sch 2, Pt I, para 8(1)(o) and SI 2003/1887, art 9, Sch 2, para 12(1)(c)). (See appointment notes below.)

Appointment

Sub-ss (1)–(4): Appointment (in relation to certain specified public authorities): 30 November 2002: see SI 2002/2812, art 3, Sch 1, and Sch 1, paras 1–3, 5 hereto.
Sub-ss (1)–(4): Appointment (in relation to certain specified public authorities): 31 October 2003: see SI 2003/2603, art 2, and Sch 1, Pts III, VII hereto.

Sub-ss (1)–(4): Appointment (in relation to certain specified public authorities): 29 February 2004: see SI 2003/2603, art 3, Sch 1, and s 6, Sch 1, Pt IV hereto.

Sub-ss (1)–(4): Appointment (in relation to certain specified public authorities): 28 February 2003: see SI 2002/2812, art 4, Sch 2, and Sch 1, paras 7, 8, 10–16, 18–36 hereto.

Sub-ss (1)–(4): Appointment (in relation to certain specified public authorities): 30 June 2003: see SI 2002/2812, art 5, Sch 3, and Sch 1, paras 6, 57–64 hereto.

Sub-ss (1)–(4): Appointment (in relation to certain specified public authorities): 30 June 2004: see SI 2003/2603, art 4, the Northern Ireland Act 1998, s 56(4), and Sch 1, para 17 hereto.

Sub-ss (5)–(7): Appointment (for remaining purposes): 30 November 2002: see SI 2002/2812, art 2(a).

GENERAL NOTE

Every public authority must have a publication scheme drawn up in compliance with s.19 and approved by the Information Commissioner. Each authority is free to publish its scheme as it thinks fit, but all schemes must at least specify: **1–078**

(a) the classes of information which the authority publishes or intends to publish;

(b) the manner in which information of each class is, or is intended to be, published; and

(c) whether the material is, or is intended to be, available to the public free of charge or on payment.

Authorities must publish information in accordance with their schemes and review them from time to time.

Publication schemes are a means by which authorities can release information voluntarily, which FOIA very clearly encourages—under s.21, information accessible under a publication scheme is exempt from FOIA's s.1 requirements, which makes the inclusion of information within a scheme extremely advantageous.

20 Model publication schemes

(1) **The Commissioner may from time to time approve, in relation to public authorities falling within particular classes, model publication schemes prepared by him or by other persons.** **1–079**

(2) **Where a public authority falling within the class to which an approved model scheme relates adopts such a scheme without modification, no further approval of the Commissioner is required so long as the model scheme**

remains approved; and where such an authority adopts such a scheme with modifications, the approval of the Commissioner is required only in relation to the modifications.

(3) The Commissioner may, when approving a model publication scheme, provide that his approval is to expire at the end of a specified period.

(4) Where the Commissioner has approved a model publication scheme, he may at any time publish, in such manner as he thinks fit, a notice revoking his approval of the scheme as from the end of the period of six months beginning with the day on which the notice is published.

(5) Where the Commissioner refuses to approve a proposed model publication scheme on the application of any person, he must give the person who applied for approval of the scheme a statement of the reasons for his refusal.

(6) Where the Commissioner refuses to approve any modifications under subsection (2), he must give the public authority a statement of the reasons for his refusal.

(7) Where the Commissioner revokes his approval of a model publication scheme, he must include in the notice under subsection (4) a statement of his reasons for doing so.

NOTES

Initial Commencement

Royal Assent

Royal Assent (so far as relating to the approval and preparation by the Commissioner of model publication schemes): 30 November 2000: see s 87(1)(c).

Specified date

Specified date (for remaining purposes)pecified date: 30 November 2005 (unless the Secretary of State by order appoints this section before that date): see s 87(3) (as amended by SI 2001/3500, art 8, Sch 2, Pt I, para 8(1)(o) and SI 2003/1887, art 9, Sch 2, para 12(1)(c)). (See appointment note below.)

Appointment

Appointment (for remaining purposes): 30 November 2002: see SI 2002/2812, art 2(a).

Part II

Exempt Information

21 Information accessible to applicant by other means

(1) Information which is reasonably accessible to the applicant otherwise than under section 1 is exempt information.

1–080

(2) For the purposes of subsection (1)—

    (a) information may be reasonably accessible to the applicant even though it is accessible only on payment, and

    (b) information is to be taken to be reasonably accessible to the applicant if it is information which the public authority or any other person is obliged by or under any enactment to communicate (otherwise than by making the information available for inspection) to members of the public on request, whether free of charge or on payment.

(3) For the purposes of subsection (1), information which is held by a public authority and does not fall within subsection (2)(b) is not to be regarded as reasonably accessible to the applicant merely because the information is available from the public authority itself on request, unless the information is made available in accordance with the authority's publication scheme and any payment required is specified in, or determined in accordance with, the scheme.

NOTES

Initial Commencement

Specified date

Specified date: 30 November 2005 (unless the Secretary of State by order appoints this section before that date): see s 87(3) (as amended by SI 2001/3500, art 8, Sch 2, Pt I, para 8(1)(o) and SI 2003/1887, art 9, Sch 2, para 12(1)(c)). (See appointment note below.)

Appointment

Appointment: 1 January 2005: see SI 2004/3122, art 2.

GENERAL NOTE[32]

1-081   The purpose of s.21 is to ensure that public authorities do not become the natural first choice for information which is already available elsewhere. FOIA may supplement existing means of accessing information—whether through library and archive services or through the commercial electronic and print media—but it does not duplicate or cut across them. Nor does it replace existing legal regimes for access.[33]

Uniquely among the FOIA exemptions, s.21 does not apply to the duty to confirm or deny, so even if s.21 permits an authority to refuse to communicate information, it will still have to say whether or not it holds it.

Where an authority does rely on this exemption, it should try as a matter of good practice to point the applicant to existing alternative sources of the information.

Meaning of "reasonably accessible"

1-082   Information is "reasonably accessible" if it is made available in accordance with the authority's publication scheme or if it is available by virtue of other legislation (*e.g.* information accessible under the subject access rules in the Data Protection Act 1998 or information about the environment which is available under the Environmental Information Regulations 2004).[34]

Information will not be exempt by virtue of its availability under other legislation if the relevant statutory obligation is only to make the information available for inspection.[35] This is because FOIA requires

---

[32] Section 21 is an absolute exemption, but note that it applies only to the duty to communicate information. It does *not* apply to the duty to confirm or deny.

[33] See, for example, Freedom of Information Act 2000, ss.32, 39 and 40, which expressly preserve existing legal regimes for access.

[34] On which, see ss.40 and 39 respectively.

[35] For example, s.1 of the Commons Registration Act 1965 requires the keeping of registers of commons and town or village greens. Section 3 provides that "any register maintained under this Act shall be open to inspection by the public at all reasonable times". Although this does not preclude the provision of copies on request, the obligation does not go beyond allowing inspection and would therefore not engage the FOIA s.21 exemption. By contrast, s.67(1) of the Trade Marks Act 1994 states that "after publication of an application for registration of a trade mark, the registrar shall on request provide a person with such information and permit him to inspect such documents relating to the application, or to any registered trade mark resulting from it, as may be specified in the request . . . any request must be made in the prescribed manner and be accompanied by the appropriate fee (if any)". This meets all the requirements of FOIA s.21(2)(b). The fact that payment of a fee may be required is irrelevant. Similarly, s.33(1) of the Births and Deaths Registration Act 1953 provides that "any person shall, on payment of a fee . . . and on furnishing the prescribed particulars, be entitled to obtain from the Registrar General, a superintendent registrar, or a registrar a short certificate of the birth of any person." This would qualify for FOIA s.21 exemption.

authorities actively to "communicate" information[36] (unless an applicant expresses a preference to inspect).[37]

Information may still be "reasonably accessible" even if it is only available on payment of a fee (the Land Registry, for example, charges fees for copies of entries in the Land Register, but such information would still be FOIA exempt under s.21). Only where the cost of obtaining information by other means would be excessive will a requirement to pay preclude use of the exemption.

Department for Constitutional Affairs Guidance[38]

Some factors to consider when assessing whether information is readily accessible:

1–083

- Is it is available to purchase through commercial outlets, or is it out of print?

- Is it mass produced in a large print-run, or distributed only through scarce or specialist outlets?

- Is it available over the internet or through a public library?

- How easily can it be identified? Has it been catalogued or indexed?

- Is it ephemeral or has it been archived?

- Is it subject to onerous conditions of access or subsequent use?

Note that there is a subjective element to the exemption, in the sense that the information must be reasonably accessible "to the applicant". Consider the following:

- Are any legal access rights available to the particular applicant (for example, s.3 of the Access to Health Records Act 1990 which provides that the holder of a health record shall allow access to the health record of a deceased person on application by that person's personal representative, by supplying them with a copy or an extract)?

- Does the applicant have access to otherwise closed or private sources of information, by virtue of some particular quality, entitlement or qualification?

---

[36] Freedom of Information Act 2000, s.1(1)(b).
[37] Freedom of Information Act 2000, s.11.
[38] See *www.foi.gov.uk/guidance/exguide/sec21/index.htm*.

- Does the applicant possess enhanced skills or resources which may bring otherwise inaccessible information within their reach (*e.g.* research, technical or linguistic skills)?

- Is the applicant disadvantaged in some way (*e.g.* because of disability or educational or economic circumstances) which might render information inaccessible which would otherwise be readily accessible to the general public?

Public Archives and Public Records

1–084 Information held in public archive or by the Public Records Office may be FOIA exempt under s.21 if the information requested is catalogued and included in the relevant authority's publication scheme (or its parent authority's publication scheme).

The Public Services Quality Group of the National Council on Archives has produced a Standard for Access to Archives providing guidance on what constitutes an acceptable level of service for archive repositories, including availability to the public. Where a personal visit to an archive is not practicable, some alternative should be made available, such as a paid research service or reference to a list of professional researchers.

22 Information intended for future publication

1–085   (1) **Information is exempt information if—**

        (a) **the information is held by the public authority with a view to its publication, by the authority or any other person, at some future date (whether determined or not),**

        (b) **the information was already held with a view to such publication at the time when the request for information was made, and**

        (c) **it is reasonable in all the circumstances that the information should be withheld from disclosure until the date referred to in paragraph (a).**

    (2) **The duty to confirm or deny does not arise if, or to the extent that, compliance with section 1(1)(a) would involve the disclosure of any information (whether or not already recorded) which falls within subsection (1).**

NOTES

Initial Commencement

Specified date

Specified date: 30 November 2005 (unless the Secretary of State by order appoints this section before that date): see s 87(3) (as

amended by SI 2001/3500, art 8, Sch 2, Pt I, para 8(1)(o) and SI 2003/1887, art 9, Sch 2, para 12(1)(c)). (See appointment note below.)

Appointment

Appointment: 1 January 2005: see SI 2004/3122, art 2.

GENERAL NOTE[39]

Most public authorities now release information proactively, irrespective of **1–086** their FOIA obligations. Section 22 is intended to ensure that individual FOIA requests do not interfere with this, on the sensible ground that authorities themselves are best placed to determine the manner and timing of their own arrangements for publication.

To qualify for this exemption, information must meet three conditions:

(a) it must be held by the authority with a view to its publication (by the authority or by someone else) at some future date, although the precise date need not have been determined;

(b) the intention to publish must exist at the time the FOIA request is made; and

(c) it must be reasonable in all the circumstances for the authority to withhold the information until the future date of planned release.

A typical example would be where an authority has commissioned a report for which a date has been set for publication. Section 22 would normally permit withholding the content of the report until the official publication date, to allow advanced disclosure to those most directly affected by it, or to enable the authority to prepare administrative resources to ensure that it can respond effectively to queries about published information.

Meaning of "publication"

"Publication" means any information which is addressed to the public or **1–087** any section of the public. For most public authorities this will include the scheduled publication of announcements, press releases, speeches, interviews and articles, email bulletins, information available online and information retrievable electronically, including books, journals, periodicals and newspapers. For central government it will also include consultation papers, white papers and green papers, reports, and responses to select committee reports. Publication of research and statistics may also be covered.

---

[39] Section 22 is a qualified exemption. It applies to the duty to communicate information and the duty to confirm or deny.

Meaning of "with a view to publication"?

1–088 Section 22 can apply whether or not the actual date of publication has been determined, and whether or not publication will be by the authority itself or by someone else. The requirement that information must *already* have been held with a view to publication at the time the request is made means only that an authority cannot avoid disclosing something by deciding *when it receives a request* that the information will be published at some future date.

Information which an authority intends to pass on to another organisation for publication by them would normally also engage the exemption, even where the authority has no intention of its own to publish. Naturally, the exemption cannot apply where a decision whether or not to publish is pending.

Any "view to publication" must be current and continuing. In this sense, it will cover information which appears in the current draft of a document, but once a draft has been superseded, information which is absent from the current draft will not normally be s.22 exempt unless there remains a justifiable ground on which that information can still be said to be held with a view to publication (although, of course, other exemptions may still apply).

Department for Constitutional Affairs Guidance[40]

1–089 It will be apparent that where disclosure of information is already planned, the public interest will turn not on *whether* to disclose but on *when*. In other words, is it reasonable to withhold disclosure under s.22 until the planned future date?

The public interest in allowing authorities to release information in a manner and form and at a time of their own choosing is important. In the general run of public affairs, publication is planned and managed according to prevailing circumstances, and authorities should rightfully be able to make their own arrangements. Considerations relevant to assessing the public interest might therefore include:

- the nature of the proposed publication timetable itself (the more distant, contingent or indeterminate the prospective publication date, the less heavily it will weigh in favour of exemption and the less reasonable delay might be);

- possible detrimental affects of early/delayed publication—for example, if disclosure might damage a third party's private interests or give rise unnecessarily to public concern, then this might favour withholding;

[40] See *www.foi.gov.uk/guidance/exguide/sec22/index.htm.*

- where simultaneous disclosure is a consideration in itself—*e.g.* because advanced disclosure to an FOI applicant might be unfair to others;

- pre-publication procedures—where immediate disclosure might undermine consultation with, or pre-publication disclosure to, a particular person (it is normally good practice, for example, to disclose information about a complaint to the complainant or the subject of the complaint before publication);

- publication procedures—*e.g.* the reports of public enquiries are often published under the protection of the Parliamentary Papers Act to avoid defamation or other civil action;

- previous undertakings—*e.g.* if ministers have promised to inform Parliament first about certain information, or where family members should be informed first about matters relating to a relative.

Delay in publication may be unreasonable where information in circulation is inaccurate or where there is some other urgent need for release.

23 Information supplied by, or relating to, bodies dealing with security matters

   (1) **Information held by a public authority is exempt**   **1–090**
information if it was directly or indirectly supplied to the
public authority by, or relates to, any of the bodies
specified in subsection (3).

   (2) **A certificate signed by a Minister of the Crown certifying**
that the information to which it applies was directly or
indirectly supplied by, or relates to, any of the bodies
specified in subsection (3) shall, subject to section 60, be
conclusive evidence of that fact.

   (3) **The bodies referred to in subsections (1) and (2) are—**

     (a) **the Security Service,**

     (b) **the Secret Intelligence Service,**

     (c) **the Government Communications Headquarters,**

     (d) **the special forces,**

     (e) **the Tribunal established under section 65 of the**
Regulation of Investigatory Powers Act 2000,

     (f) **the Tribunal established under section 7 of the**
Interception of Communications Act 1985,

     (g) **the Tribunal established under section 5 of the**
Security Service Act 1989,

(h) the Tribunal established under section 9 of the Intelligence Services Act 1994,

(i) the Security Vetting Appeals Panel,

(j) the Security Commission,

(k) the National Criminal Intelligence Service,

(l) the Service Authority for the National Criminal Intelligence Service, and

(m) the Serious Organised Crime Agency.

(4) In subsection (3)(c) "the Government Communications Headquarters" includes any unit or part of a unit of the armed forces of the Crown which is for the time being required by the Secretary of State to assist the Government Communications Headquarters in carrying out its functions.

(5) The duty to confirm or deny does not arise if, or to the extent that, compliance with section 1(1)(a) would involve the disclosure of any information (whether or not already recorded) which was directly or indirectly supplied to the public authority by, or relates to, any of the bodies specified in subsection (3).

NOTES

Initial Commencement

Specified date

1-091   Specified date: 30 November 2005 (unless the Secretary of State by order appoints this section before that date): see s 87(3) (as amended by SI 2001/3500, art 8, Sch 2, Pt I, para 8(1)(o) and SI 2003/1887, art 9, Sch 2, para 12(1)(c)). (See appointment note below.)

Appointment

Appointment: 1 January 2005: see SI 2004/3122, art 2.

Amendment

Sub-s (3): para (m) inserted by the Serious Organised Crime and Police Act 2005, s 59, Sch 4, paras 158, 159.
     Date in force: to be appointed: see the Serious Organised Crime and Police Act 2005, s 178(8).

GENERAL NOTE[41]

The s.23 exemption operates by reference to the list of security bodies in   **1–092**
s.23(3). None of these are themselves public authorities for FOIA
purposes, but they operate under the auspices of bodies which are, such as
the Home Office, and of course other public authorities may come into
possession of information from or relating to them. This necessitates
specific FOIA protection.

The first part of s.23 refers to information "directly or indirectly supplied"
by any of the security bodies. Whether or not this applies will therefore turn
on the source rather than the content of the information—the content is
irrelevant.

Insofar as the application of the exemption turns on the second part of
s.23—*i.e.* whether information "relates" to any of the security bodies—then
the exemption will be capable of covering a range of subject matter, whether
of a policy, operational or administrative nature.

In relation to any particular item of information, it will be a question of fact
whether it falls within s.23. Where the origin of information is unclear, the
exemption should be applied with care, and if possible after consultation
with the author.

FOIA does not specify how remote from the original source information
needs to be before it ceases to be "indirectly" supplied by or related to one
of the security bodies. As such, if it is possible to trace a discrete piece of
information back through each transmission to its original source, then this
would seem to be sufficient, however many hands it has passed through,
and even if the wording has changed, along the way.

The s.23 exemption applies to all records, regardless of their age, including
historical records, except that for historical records held by the National
Archives or the Public Record Office of Northern Ireland, s.23 ceases to be
an absolute exemption after 30 years.

Ministerial Certificates

Ministerial certificates require the signature of either a cabinet minister, the   **1–093**
Attorney General or the Advocate General. It is not necessary to have a
certificate in order to rely on s.23 but a certificate will normally reinforce a
department's position in any legal proceedings, and determine the forum
for hearing an appeal (the Information Tribunal rather than the
Information Commissioner).[42] As such, certificates are primarily relevant

---

[41] Section 23 is an absolute exemption, except in relation to information contained in any
"historical record" (see s.64 and the commentary under s.66 below) for which it is
qualified. In either case, it applies to the duty to communicate information and the duty to
confirm or deny.
[42] Freedom of Information Act 2000, s.60.

to enforcement proceedings and need not be served until then. Serving a certificate when answering a request will normally be premature and might involve unnecessary work, although departments should consider the need for a certificate at a reasonably early stage to take account of the time needed to prepare one. Note also that the Information Commissioner advises against the use of a s.23 certificate unless there are good reasons for preventing him considering complaints under s.50 in the normal way.

Although s.23(2) provides that it is "conclusive evidence" that information falls within this exemption where it is certified as such by a minister, this can still be challenged under s.60.[43] Further, s.23 only permits ministers to certify specific information—which precludes the preparation of certificates in expectation of future requests (but note that certificates issued under s.24 (national security) *can* be general and prospective).

Interaction with other exemptions

1–094   The security matters exemption may overlap with a number of other exemptions, namely: national security (s.24), defence (s.26), international relations (s.27) and the economy (s.29). There is nothing to prevent a department claiming exemption under several or indeed all these heads if appropriate.

It is worth remembering however that, except for national security, the other exemptions do not provide for ministerial certificates. Further, all of them are qualified exemptions and will therefore be subject to the public interest. This could give rise to procedural difficulties if an applicant challenges their efficacy. For example, if a department claimed exemption under both the s.23 (security matters) and s.26 (defence) exemptions, then the route for appeal would be:

- an appeal to the Information Tribunal under s.60 against the s.23 certificate, by either the applicant or the Commissioner;

- a challenge by the applicant to the Commissioner on the balance of the public interest (although this may be adjourned pending the outcome of any s.60 appeal);

- a challenge by the applicant to the Commissioner on the s.26 exemption, although again, it may be appropriate for the Commissioner to adjourn this, pending hearing of the s.60 appeal.

24 National security

1–095   **(1) Information which does not fall within section 23(1) is exempt information if exemption from section 1(1)(b) is**

---

[43] See the commentary on s.60 at para.1–296.

required for the purpose of safeguarding national security.

(2) The duty to confirm or deny does not arise if, or to the extent that, exemption from section 1(1)(a) is required for the purpose of safeguarding national security.

(3) A certificate signed by a Minister of the Crown certifying that exemption from section 1(1)(b), or from section 1(1)(a) and (b), is, or at any time was, required for the purpose of safeguarding national security shall, subject to section 60, be conclusive evidence of that fact.

(4) A certificate under subsection (3) may identify the information to which it applies by means of a general description and may be expressed to have prospective effect.

NOTES

Initial Commencement

Specified date

Specified date: 30 November 2005 (unless the Secretary of State by order appoints this section before that date): see s 87(3) (as amended by SI 2001/3500, art 8, Sch 2, Pt I, para 8(1)(o) and SI 2003/1887, art 9, Sch 2, para 12(1)(c)). (See appointment note below.)

Appointment

Appointment: 1 January 2005: see SI 2004/3122, art 2.

GENERAL NOTE[44]

Information which is not covered by the security matters absolute exemption under s.23 will still be exempt if exemption is "required" to safeguard national security. This exemption applies also to the duty to confirm or deny.   **1–096**

Interaction with other exemptions

The national security exemption may overlap with a number of other exemptions, namely: security matters (s.23), defence (s.26), international relations (s.27) and the economy (s.29). There is nothing to prevent a department claiming exemption under several or indeed all these heads if appropriate.   **1–097**

---

[44] Section 24 is a qualified exemption. It applies to the duty to communicate information and the duty to confirm or deny.

Meaning of "national security"

1–098 The term "national security" has never been defined in UK legislation and both domestic and European courts have considered that the assessment of threats is essentially a matter for government.[45] The courts here have accepted that it is proper to take a precautionary approach.[46] This means considering two things, namely: circumstances where actual harm has occurred or will occur, and measures to prevent harm occurring or avoid the risk of harm occurring. It goes without saying that the courts will not accept government claims that information should be suppressed, without sufficient justification.[47]

Despite the absence of a definition, it is possible to infer certain statements about the meaning of national security from case law and statute[48]:

- the security of the nation includes its well being and the protection of its defence and foreign policy interests, as well as its survival;

- the nation does not refer only to the territory of the UK, but includes its citizens, wherever they may be, or its assets wherever they may be, as well as the UK's system of government; and

- there are a number of matters which UK law expressly recognises as constituting potential threats to, or otherwise being relevant to, the safety or well-being of the nation, the pursuit of the Government's defence and foreign policies, and the economic well-being of the UK, including terrorism, espionage and subversion. However, these matters are not exhaustive. The Government would regard a wide range of other matters as being capable of constituting a threat to the safety or well being of the nation. Examples include the proliferation of weapons of mass destruction and the protection of the Critical National Infrastructure, such as the water supply or national grid, from actions intended to cause catastrophic damage.

As common sense would suggest, national security is not the same as the interests of the government of the day. Official information that would be embarrassing or inconvenient to the government if made public is not of itself a matter of national security.

As a qualified exemption, s.24 is contingent on two things. First, the test for reliance on the exemption is that non-disclosure should be "required" for

---

[45] See, for example, *Chandler v DPP* [1964] AC 673.

[46] See the House of Lord's Judgement in the appeal of Shafiq Ur Rehman against deportation, Secretary of State for the Home Department (October 11, 2001) [2001] UKHL 47.

[47] See, for example, *Lord Advocate v The Scotsman Publications Ltd* [1990] 1 AC 809.

[48] *E.g.* the Security Service Act 1989, Intelligence Services Act 1994, Radioactive Substances Act 1993, Water Industry Act 1991, Control of Pollution Act 1974, Offshore Safety Act 1992, Town and Country Planning Act 1990.

the purpose of safeguarding national security. An authority must be prepared to demonstrate the need to withhold the information requested, and if steps could be taken to allow information to be disclosed while safeguarding national security in some other way, those steps will need to be considered. Second, even if exemption is "required" for this purpose, the application of the exemption is still subject to the public interest.

Department for Constitutional Affairs Guidance[49]

The public interest requires consideration of: **1–099**

(a) whether, in all the circumstances of the case, the public interest in disclosing the information outweighs the public interest in withholding it; and

(b) if it is decided to withhold the information, whether the exemption from the duty to confirm whether or not the information is held is required for the purpose of safeguarding national security, and whether there is any overriding public interest in communicating the fact that a department holds the information, while not actually disclosing it.

In reality, the public interest and the maintenance of national security are very closely allied and it is difficult in the abstract to envisage circumstances where the former would override the latter. The circumstances would seem to have to be fairly extraordinary, and presumably such that national security and the public interest were somehow in conflict, although this seems like a contradiction in terms.

Ministerial Certificates

Ministerial certificates require the signature of either a cabinet minister, the   **1–100** Attorney General or the Advocate General. It is not necessary to have a certificate in order to rely on s.24 but a certificate will normally reinforce a department's position in any legal proceedings, and determine the forum for hearing an appeal (the Information Tribunal rather than the Information Commissioner).[50] Further, a certificate under s.24 can be general and prospective, which means that it can be prepared in expectation of future requests. This is distinct from s.23 certificates which must realate to specific information.

Although s.24(3) provides that it is "conclusive evidence" that information falls within this exemption where it is certified as such by a minister, this can still be challenged under s.60.[51]

---

[49] See *www.foi.gov.uk/guidance/exguide/sec24/index.htm*.
[50] Freedom of Information Act 2000, s.60.
[51] See the commentary on s.60 at para.1–296.

25 Certificates under ss 23 and 24: supplementary provisions

1–101

(1) A document purporting to be a certificate under section 23(2) or 24(3) shall be received in evidence and deemed to be such a certificate unless the contrary is proved.

(2) A document which purports to be certified by or on behalf of a Minister of the Crown as a true copy of a certificate issued by that Minister under section 23(2) or 24(3) shall in any legal proceedings be evidence (or, in Scotland, sufficient evidence) of that certificate.

(3) The power conferred by section 23(2) or 24(3) on a Minister of the Crown shall not be exercisable except by a Minister who is a member of the Cabinet or by the Attorney General, the Advocate General for Scotland or the Attorney General for Northern Ireland.

NOTES

Initial Commencement

Specified date

Specified date: 30 November 2005 (unless the Secretary of State by order appoints this section before that date): see s 87(3) (as amended by SI 2001/3500, art 8, Sch 2, Pt I, para 8(1)(o) and SI 2003/1887, art 9, Sch 2, para 12(1)(c)). (See appointment note below.)

Appointment

Appointment: 1 January 2005: see SI 2004/3122, art 2.

26 Defence

1–102

(1) Information is exempt information if its disclosure under this Act would, or would be likely to, prejudice—

(a) the defence of the British Islands or of any colony, or

(b) the capability, effectiveness or security of any relevant forces.

(2) In subsection (1)(b) "relevant forces" means—

(a) the armed forces of the Crown, and

(b) any forces co-operating with those forces,

or any part of any of those forces.

(3) **The duty to confirm or deny does not arise if, or to the extent that, compliance with section 1(1)(a) would, or would be likely to, prejudice any of the matters mentioned in subsection (1).**

NOTES

Initial Commencement

Specified date

Specified date: 30 November 2005 (unless the Secretary of State by order appoints this section before that date): see s 87(3) (as amended by SI 2001/3500, art 8, Sch 2, Pt I, para 8(1)(o) and SI 2003/1887, art 9, Sch 2, para 12(1)(c)). (See appointment note below.)

Appointment

Appointment: 1 January 2005: see SI 2004/3122, art 2.

GENERAL NOTE[52]

Section 26 is a qualified exemption which turns entirely on the effects of 1–103 disclosure. In every case, s.26 requires an assessment of the risk of prejudice that disclosure may cause to the matters in subss.(1)(a) and (b), regardless of the content of the information, the kind of document in which the information is contained, or its source.

Section 26 should generally be considered alongside s.23 (security matters), s.24 (national security), s.27 (international relations) and s.29 (the economy). Note in particular that information from or relating to UK special forces, or units assisting GCHQ, will normally be exempt under s.23.

Relevant examples falling within this exemption might be:

- defence policy and strategy, military planning and defence intelligence;

- the size, shape, organisation, logistics, order of battle, state of readiness and training of the armed forces;

- the actual or prospective deployment of those forces in the UK or overseas, including their operational orders, tactics and rules of engagement;

---

[52] Section 26 is a qualified exemption. It applies to the duty to communicate information and the duty to confirm or deny.

- the weapons, stores, transport or other equipment of those forces and the invention, development, production, technical specification and performance of such equipment and research relating to it;

- plans and measures for the maintenance of essential supplies and services that are or would be needed in time of conflict;

- plans for future military capabilities;

- plans or options for the defence or reinforcement of a colony or another country;

- analysis of the capability, state of readiness, performance of individual or combined units, their equipment or support structures; and

- arrangements for co-operation, collaboration, consultation or integration with the armed forces of other countries, whether on a bilateral basis or as part of a defence alliance or other international force.

Department for Constitutional Affairs Guidance[53]

1–104　The public interest in avoiding prejudice to defence matters will be strong in most cases and so is likely to prevail unless the harm or prejudice likely to result from disclosure would be trivial or minor.

There is at the same time widespread public interest in defence policy and the activities of the armed forces, so it is appropriate that the public should be able to understand how and why key decisions are taken. Where disclosure will inform debate, the public interest in disclosure will be weightier. Examples might include disclosure of information relating to:

- the safety of military personnel or loss of life;

- risks to the safety of civilians;

- the use of land or the environmental impact of military activity (for which s.39 may also be relevant);

- the factual and analytical bases used to develop defence policies; and

- the use of public funds.

---

[53] See *www.foi.gov.uk/guidance/exguide/sec26/index.htm*.

Clearly the public interest will weigh against disclosure where it might undermine the conduct of a specific military operation or have an adverse impact on security or safety. Further, the disclosure of information in the face of an objection from an allied country, or in breach of a clear undertaking to preserve confidentiality, may well prejudice the UK's defence relations by restricting exchanges of information or by jeopardising military co-operation.[54]

Information Commissioner's Guidance[55]

Where there is a choice between relying on the s.23 (national security) and **1–105** s.26 exemptions, the Commissioner strongly encourages use of the latter. This is because s.26 will generally be less emotive.

The Commissioner gives the following guidance on the application of s.26:

- Information will be exempt under s.26 if its disclosure would or would be likely to assist an enemy or potential enemy.

- The timing of disclosure will often be critical in the context of s.26. For example, the likelihood of prejudice may depend on whether any related military operation is still underway or has concluded, or on whether information about tactics or weaponry may prejudice the chances of a similar operation being successful in the future.

- Consideration should be given to what information is already in the public domain. Where information is available from other (reliable) sources, it may be difficult to argue that repeated disclosure would cause prejudice.

Applying the Public Interest Test

The Commissioner's Guidance sets out the following examples of public **1–106** interest considerations:

- Government decisions whether to deploy troops are self-evidently very difficult and sensitive but this must be weighed against the public interest in facilitating an informed public debate on the merits of such decisions.

- Information about the behaviour of British troops is also of legitimate public interest.

- The public have a clear interest in understanding how the very large sums involved in defence have been spent.

---

[54] See also the exemption under s.27 (International Relations) in this regard.
[55] Freedom of Information Act Awareness Guidance No.10: The Defence Exemption.

- Where military operations lead to loss of life, the safety of equipment and the direction of those operations will be of legitimate public interest.

Related issues

1–107   Authorities which deal routinely with defence information will usually have their own specific clearance procedures for dealing with requests. Officials should always comply with such procedures because they will have been written to reflect the legal restrictions which apply to the organisation. FOIA preserves all existing statutory prohibitions on disclosure, the breach of some of which is a criminal offence.

In many cases, it will also be appropriate for an authority to consult the Ministry of Defence before disclosing potentially exempt defence information.

27 International relations

1–108

(1) **Information is exempt information if its disclosure under this Act would, or would be likely to, prejudice—**

(a) **relations between the United Kingdom and any other State,**

(b) **relations between the United Kingdom and any international organisation or international court,**

(c) **the interests of the United Kingdom abroad, or**

(d) **the promotion or protection by the United Kingdom of its interests abroad.**

(2) **Information is also exempt information if it is confidential information obtained from a State other than the United Kingdom or from an international organisation or international court.**

(3) **For the purposes of this section, any information obtained from a State, organisation or court is confidential at any time while the terms on which it was obtained require it to be held in confidence or while the circumstances in which it was obtained make it reasonable for the State, organisation or court to expect that it will be so held.**

(4) **The duty to confirm or deny does not arise if, or to the extent that, compliance with section 1(1)(a)—**

(a) **would, or would be likely to, prejudice any of the matters mentioned in subsection (1), or**

(b) **would involve the disclosure of any information (whether or not already recorded) which is** confidential information obtained from a State other than the United Kingdom or from an international organisation or international court.

(5) In this section—

"international court" means any international court which is not an international organisation and which is established—

(a) by a resolution of an international organisation of which the United Kingdom is a member, or

(b) by an international agreement to which the United Kingdom is a party;

"international organisation" means any international organisation whose members include any two or more States, or any organ of such an organisation;

"State" includes the government of any State and any organ of its government, and references to a State other than the United Kingdom include references to any territory outside the United Kingdom.

NOTES

Initial Commencement

Specified date

Specified date: 30 November 2005 (unless the Secretary of State by order appoints this section before that date): see s 87(3) (as amended by SI 2001/3500, art 8, Sch 2, Pt I, para 8(1)(o) and SI 2003/1887, art 9, Sch 2, para 12(1)(c)). (See appointment note below.)

Appointment

Appointment: 1 January 2005: see SI 2004/3122, art 2.

GENERAL NOTE[56]

Section 27 is in two parts. Section 27(1) is a prejudice-based exemption **1–109** which turns on the effect of disclosure on the UK's relations abroad. Section 27(2) protects confidential information obtained from a foreign state, an international organisation, or an international court. Confidential

---

[56] Section 27 is a qualified exemption. It applies to the duty to communicate information and the duty to confirm or deny.

information from these bodies is exempt irrespective of any question of prejudice (but still subject to the public interest test).

The exemption exists to protect national interests generally, not the interests of specific groups or bodies (such as the authority holding the information) within the state.

Section 27 should generally be considered alongside s.23 (security matters), s.24 (national security), s.26 (defence) and s.29 (the economy).

Subsection (1)

1–110   Information which may engage this exemption could include:

- reports on, or exchanges with, foreign governments or international organisations such as the EU, NATO, the UN, Commonwealth, World Bank or International Monetary Fund;

- information about the UK's activities relating to UK citizens or companies abroad, particularly their consular and commercial interests;

- information about other states' views or intentions provided in the course of diplomatic and political exchanges of views;

- information about international trade partnerships and international funding matters;

- details about international events (*e.g.* the Olympics);

- details of inward and outward state visits and visits by Ministers and officials;

- information supplied by other states through diplomatic or other channels;

- discussion within the UK government on approaches to particular states or issues;

- information relevant to actual or potential cases before an international court; and

- details of the UK's position in multilateral or bilateral negotiations.

It is worth bearing in mind that differences in culture, religion, legislation and infrastructure may affect the question of whether disclosure would be prejudicial in any given case.[57]

---

[57] See Freedom of Information Act Awareness Guidance No.14: International Relations.

Meaning of "international organisation"

An "international organisation" is one whose members include two or more   **1–111**
states. A "state" for this purpose includes the government of any state and
any organ of government, such as a state's legislature and executive. UK
territories outside the UK are also states, which will include Crown
Dependencies like Jersey and Guernsey and British Overseas Territories
like Gibraltar. Territorial entities not recognised as states in international
law but which may be the subject of international law or international
agreements (*e.g.* Antarctica) also qualify as states for FOIA purposes.

The UK itself need not be a member of an international organisation for the
organisation to qualify as such under FOIA (but see below in relation to
"international courts"). As well as the United Nations and European
Union, OPEC is covered, as is the World Trade Organisation and the
Organisation of American states. The definition also extends to any organ
of such an organisation, which would include, for example, the European
Commission and European Parliament.

Meaning of "international court"

An "international court" is one established by a resolution of an   **1–112**
international organisation of which the UK is a member, or by an
international agreement to which the UK is a party. The International
Court of Justice, European Court of Justice, International Criminal Court
and European Court of Human Rights all qualify as international courts for
FOIA purposes.

Subsections (2) and (3)

"Confidential information" is defined in s.27(3) as "information   **1–113**
obtained . . . at any time while the terms on which it was obtained require
it to be held in confidence or while the circumstances in which it was
obtained make it reasonable for the state, organisation or court to expect
that it will be so held". This allows for the possibility that a duty of
confidence may arise by reasonable expectation or by express agreement. It
is therefore wider than the s.41 exemption for confidential information,
which reflects the common law position rather than the conventionally
wider restrictions which parties agree by written contract. Also in contrast
with s.41, s.27 is not conditional on a breach being "actionable".

Department for Constitutional Affairs Guidance[58]

The fundamental question when applying the public interest under s.27 is   **1–114**
whether the public interest in disclosure outweighs the damage or likely
damage that disclosure would cause to the UK's international relations, its
interests abroad or its ability to protect and promote those interests.

---

[58] See *www.foi.gov.uk/guidance/exguide/sec27/index.htm.*

For prejudice which is likely to be trivial—for example where disclosure about the content of a discussion with a foreign official would be unlikely to provoke any significant negative reaction or have any significant detrimental effect on other states' willingness to have similar discussions with the UK in the future—the public interest in disclosing is likely to prevail.

Correspondingly, for prejudice likely to be more serious—such as disclosure about the UK's attitude to an international issue of concern to a particular state which would provoke a strong negative reaction and could (say) make it less likely British companies would be awarded government contracts in future with that state—the public interest in disclosing would have to be more specific and compelling to justify disclosure. The same would be true of a disclosure which would be likely to weaken significantly the UK's bargaining position in international negotiations, inhibit other governments' willingness to share sensitive information, or inhibit frankness and candour in diplomatic reporting.

Some examples of factors to consider when assessing the public interest as it relates to confidential information falling within s.27:

- would disclosure be contrary to international law (*e.g.* a breach of a treaty obligation)?

- would disclosure undermine the UK's reputation for honouring its international commitments and obligations?

- would disclosure be likely to undermine the willingness of the state, international organisation or court that supplied the information to supply other confidential information in future (or would it be likely to have such an affect on the willingness of states, international organisations or courts in general)?

- would disclosure be likely to provoke a negative reaction from the state, international organisation or court that supplied the information which would damage the UK's relations with them and/or its ability to protect and promote UK interests?

- would disclosure be likely to result in another state, international organisation or court disclosing—contrary to the UK's interests—confidential information supplied by the UK?

- has the state, international organisation or court that supplied the confidential information objected to its disclosure, and would good relations with them be likely to suffer if the objection were ignored?

Authorities should also consider consulting the Foreign and Commonwealth Office when considering disclosing information which may affect the UK's international relations.

28 Relations within the United Kingdom

(1) Information is exempt information if its disclosure under this Act would, or would be likely to, prejudice relations between any administration in the United Kingdom and any other such administration.

    1–115

(2) In subsection (1) "administration in the United Kingdom" means—

  (a) the government of the United Kingdom,

  (b) the Scottish Administration,

  (c) the Executive Committee of the Northern Ireland Assembly, or

  (d) the National Assembly for Wales.

(3) The duty to confirm or deny does not arise if, or to the extent that, compliance with section 1(1)(a) would, or would be likely to, prejudice any of the matters mentioned in subsection (1).

NOTES

Initial Commencement

Specified date

Specified date: 30 November 2005 (unless the Secretary of State by order appoints this section before that date): see s 87(3) (as amended by SI 2001/3500, art 8, Sch 2, Pt I, para 8(1)(o) and SI 2003/1887, art 9, Sch 2, para 12(1)(c)). (See appointment note below.)

Appointment

Appointment: 1 January 2005: see SI 2004/3122, art 2.

GENERAL NOTE[59]

Section 28 applies, regardless of the nature or content of the information in question, where disclosure would, or would be likely to, prejudice relations between the UK government and any of the devolved administrations in Scotland, Northern Ireland and Wales, and also between any of the devolved administrations themselves. The exemption recognises that it is legitimate for different administrations to take a different view of a wide range of different matters and that from time to time these differences may

    1–116

---

[59] Section 28 is a qualified exemption. It applies to the duty to communicate information and the duty to confirm or deny.

give rise to disagreements which will be the subject of negotiations, particularly between the UK administration and the devolved administrations.

Administrations in the UK

1–117   There are three devolved administrations within the UK and the UK government represents UK interests only in matters which are not devolved.[60]

There are two distinct circumstances in which s.28 might apply, namely: where information requested under FOIA has been obtained from or shared between administrations; and where information held by one administration could prejudice relations because that administration does not want other administrations to see it, or because other administrations would not want the information to be disclosed.

Information obtained from, or shared between, administrations

1–118   By the terms of the Memorandum of Understanding between the UK administrations ("MoU"), all four are committed to the principle of good communication with one another, especially where one administration's work may have some bearing on the responsibilities of another. To enable each to operate effectively, they provide each other with policy information, including scientific and technical statistics, research and, where appropriate, representations from third parties. Where necessary, they will in confidence:

- alert each other to relevant developments within their areas of responsibility, wherever possible prior to publication (although there are certain areas, notably national security and budget proposals, where prior notification is much less likely);

- give consideration to the views of the other administrations; and

- where appropriate, establish arrangements that allow for policies to be developed jointly between administrations.

The MoU also includes safeguards to ensure that information shared with other administrations is appropriately protected. In certain circumstances, this means that confidentiality is expected. In particular, the MoU provides that administrations will:

- state what restrictions there should be on information they share;

---

[60] Details of the relationships between the administrations, and their respective responsibilities, are set out in CM 5240, an inter-administration Memorandum of Understanding, a summary of the terms of which is available at *www.foi.gov.uk/guidance/exguide/sec28/annex_a.htm*.

- treat information received in accordance with the restrictions they have agreed to respect;

- comply with FOIA but in difficult cases refer back to the originator of the information;

- accept that some information is subject to statutory or other restrictions and that there will be a common approach to the classification and handling of sensitive material.

An expectation of confidentiality will not be conclusive demonstration of prejudice likely to result from disclosure, but it will be a relevant consideration.

Other information

There will be all kinds of circumstances in which information shared between administrations might be prejudicial to relations if disclosed. Some examples might be: **1–119**

- sensitive information about devolved matters which pre-date devolution, held by UK government departments but concerning devolved administrations;

- information held by devolved administrations relating to reserved or excepted matters;

- briefings or comments on another administration's plans or policies;

- an options analysis in an area of reserved policy which also includes an assessment of the operation of policy in a devolved area;

- information about another administration which has come direct from a third party.

Note that, as with the other qualified exemptions, embarrassment is not enough to justify use of s.28.

Department for Constitutional Affairs Guidance[61]

The demands of open government have to be balanced with the political imperatives underlying the devolution settlement, namely: trust, co-operation, information sharing and respect. The prospect of harming the effective functioning of the devolved relationships will be a significant factor in assessing whether to disclose information.   **1–120**

---

[61] See *www.foi.gov.uk/guidance/exguide/sec28/index.htm.*

In weighing the public interest it is important to consider the following:

- the wider public interest in freedom of information and any particular commitments given by administrations;

- the commitment to sharing information between the four administrations;

- the commitment to respecting confidential information shared between bodies;

- the nature and extent of prejudice to the relationships between administrations that might be caused by the disclosure of a particular piece of information;

- the importance of ensuring appropriate frankness and candour of discussion between administrations; and

- the extent to which other exemptions may be relevant.

The following are some examples where the public interest might favour withholding information:

- confidential briefings for UK ministers, provided for ministerial meetings;

- policy plans received from devolved administrations on a confidential basis which have not yet been announced;

- details of meetings between the four administrations the disclosure of which could impact the effectiveness of such meetings;

- details of a sensitive UK negotiating position in the EU which, though reserved, impacts on devolved matters;

- UK government assessments of politics and policies in the devolved administrations.

And examples where the public interest might favour disclosure:

- information which helps public understanding of the devolution settlement;

- information which would explain how decisions were taken (after an announcement has been made);

- details of negotiations which are no longer sensitive because of the passage of time; and

- cases where the administration which provided the information would have disclosed the information (even if a case can be made for non-disclosure).

Information Commissioner's Guidance[62]

The Commissioner's guidance states that there are two principle grounds   **1–121** for relying on s.28, namely: where the disclosure of information may compromise negotiating positions or the formulation of policy towards other administrations, or where it would breach the MoU. In relation to the MoU, the Commissioner will generally expect authorities to provide applicants with a reasonably detailed explanation and reference to the relevant documents.

Information originating from an authority which is not a central government department or a devolved administration is unlikely to be exempt under s.28.

29 The economy

> (1) **Information is exempt information if its disclosure under   1–122 this Act would, or would be likely to, prejudice—**
>
>> (a) **the economic interests of the United Kingdom or of any part of the United Kingdom, or**
>>
>> (b) **the financial interests of any administration in the United Kingdom, as defined by section 28(2).**
>
> (2) **The duty to confirm or deny does not arise if, or to the extent that, compliance with section 1(1)(a) would, or would be likely to, prejudice any of the matters mentioned in subsection (1).**

NOTES

Initial Commencement

Specified date

Specified date: 30 November 2005 (unless the Secretary of State by order appoints this section before that date): see s 87(3) (as amended by SI 2001/3500, art 8, Sch 2, Pt I, para 8(1)(o) and SI 2003/1887, art 9, Sch 2, para 12(1)(c)). (See appointment note below.)

Appointment

Appointment: 1 January 2005: see SI 2004/3122, art 2.

GENERAL NOTE[63]

The s.29 exemption recognises that the disclosure of certain information   **1–123** could cause instability and damage to the UK economy, either as a whole

---

[62] Freedom of Information Awareness Guidance No.13: Relations within the UK.
[63] Section 29 is a qualified exemption. It applies to the duty to communicate information and the duty to confirm or deny.

or where disclosure could damage a regional or local economy, *e.g.* because it would deter investment within a particular area.

Authorities should always consider consulting HM Treasury and/or other relevant government departments before releasing information which might fall within s.29.

Section 29 should generally be considered alongside s.23 (security matters), s.24 (national security), s.26 (defence) and s.27 (international relations).

Section 29(a)—meaning of "economic interests"

1–124   These will include the government's economic and financial management in support of a stable macroeconomic environment, the maintenance of sound public finances and the promotion of UK economic prospects and productivity. Associated with these are the oversight of a competitive financial services market and efficient tax and benefits systems.

Section 29(a)—the economic interests of the UK

1–125   The exemption does not cover the economic interests of states other than the UK unless those interests impact on the UK economy also.

The UK's economic interests cover a considerable range of subject matter. It is likely that prejudice could result from disclosure of some of the following, where the information in question is sensitive:

- Tax, National Insurance and benefits policy;

- IMF loan programmes;

- financial stability discussions and support operations;

- company specific financial regulatory information;

- discussions with overseas financial authorities;

- analyses of macro-economic policy;

- marketing trends, including interest rates and the framework of monetary policy and forecasts of government borrowing;

- analyses of the effects of increases in public spending on wage and inflation pressures.

In most of these areas the potential for prejudice is likely to turn on the timing of disclosure, particularly in cases where premature release could cause market instability.

Meaning of "financial interests"

These include the financial aspects of government administration, to **1–126** minimise the cost of government to the taxpayer. Public accountability requires sufficient information to assess the probity and cost effective nature of such dealings. This must be balanced against the damage to an administration's financial interests which might result if too much information is disclosed, or too soon after the event. This component of the exemption recognises the long-term cost to the taxpayer which could result from disclosure (premature or otherwise) of certain information.

The expression "an administration in the UK" has the same meaning as in s.28.

The financial interests of an administration in the UK

The financial interests of an administration in the UK are clearly much **1–127** narrower than the interests of the economy as a whole. The administrations in question are the UK government, the Scottish Administration, the Executive Committee of the Northern Ireland Assembly and the National Assembly for Wales.

The scope of the exemption covers a broad spectrum of subject matter. Examples of likely prejudicial disclosures include:

- allocation of gilts and Treasury bills at auctions/tenders to particular investors or market-makers;

- government cash dealing and banking arrangements;

- UK reserves and foreign currency liabilities' management and foreign exchange dealings;

- timing of large cash and stock transactions in the future;

- intended investment strategies;

- contract details of PFI and PPP deals;

- auction bidding details (*e.g.* gilts, spectrum licenses); and

- finances of public corporations.

Some examples of potentially prejudicial disclosures

These examples are drawn from the DCA guidance on s.29. The list is only **1–128** illustrative.

- Information contained in Standing Committee and financial stability papers (of, for example, HM Treasury, the Bank of England, the Financial Services Authority).

- Vulnerability assessments—for example of emerging market economies.

- Gilt auctions—the size of offering at a gilt auction has a short term but nevertheless significant sensitivity which could influence price and therefore the cost of borrowing for the government.

- Budget information—release of budget information ahead of formal announcement, particularly in relation to tax and national insurance, might lead to pre-emptive action by companies and individuals, leading to a reduction in tax payable to the government.

- Government cash flows and borrowing requirements—premature disclosure is likely to be market sensitive.

- Terrorism reinsurance—disclosure of information about claims could potentially prejudice the economic interests of a part of the UK.

Department for Constitutional Affairs Guidance[64]

1–129 There is a legitimate public interest in the UK's economic policy, taxation and financial management, and release of some information will promote public understanding and informed debate (and, indeed, it has been government policy for some time to release information such as Monetary Policy Committee minutes and the annual borrowing plans and gilt auctions calendar).

Some specific factors will weigh in favour of disclosure:

- the need to hold public authorities to account for their stewardship of public resources (*e.g.* when investing large sums in schemes for economic regeneration); and

- the objective of building public trust and establishing transparency in the operation of the economy so as to increase the credibility of economic policy decision-makers and enhance the UK's reputation as a fair and honest business environment (*e.g.* in relation to financial assistance provided to private sector companies).

Factors weighing in favour of withholding information might include:

- where disclosure could result in financial instability within institutions or countries, either in the UK or abroad;

---

[64] See *www.foi.gov.uk/guidance/exguide/sec29/index.htm*.

- where disclosure could pre-empt announcements on taxation, National Insurance or benefits;

- where selective disclosure of the information could affect financial markets—financial regulation and government policy requires the transparent release of market sensitive data simultaneously to the whole market because this reinforces confidence in market integrity, thereby reducing the cost of capital in financial markets; selective or premature release of information undermines confidence in dealing in UK markets;

- where information has been obtained from confidential sources (*e.g.* overseas governments or regulators) and these would be damaged by disclosure and reduce the likelihood of information being made available in the future;

- where the information consists of assessments of an institution's or economy's viability; and

- where information could jeopardise relationships with private sector organisations and thereby inhibit future private sector investment.

Information Commissioner's Guidance[65]

The Commissioner provides some examples of how information held by a public authority might affect the local or national economy even though the authority itself may not be responsible for economic management: **1–130**

- information relating to the setting or influencing of interest rates, taxation, currency rates or controls on public spending;

- information about the promotion of regional economic interests or overseas trade;

- information about trade embargoes and European integration;

- information about social, health or environmental policy (such as relating to drinking, smoking or the use of public transport versus the private car);

- information about planning (whether at the local or national level and including policy information on things like transport and airports).

All public authorities are also of course major customers, employers and investors in their local area.

---

[65] Freedom of Information Act Guidance No.15: The Economy.

30 Investigations and proceedings conducted by public authorities

(1) Information held by a public authority is exempt information if it has at any time been held by the authority for the purposes of—

    (a) any investigation which the public authority has a duty to conduct with a view to it being ascertained—

        (i) whether a person should be charged with an offence, or

        (ii) whether a person charged with an offence is guilty of it,

    (b) any investigation which is conducted by the authority and in the circumstances may lead to a decision by the authority to institute criminal proceedings which the authority has power to conduct, or

    (c) any criminal proceedings which the authority has power to conduct.

(2) Information held by a public authority is exempt information if—

    (a) it was obtained or recorded by the authority for the purposes of its functions relating to—

        (i) investigations falling within subsection (1)(a) or (b),

        (ii) criminal proceedings which the authority has power to conduct,

        (iii) investigations (other than investigations falling within subsection (1)(a) or (b)) which are conducted by the authority for any of the purposes specified in section 31(2) and either by virtue of Her Majesty's prerogative or by virtue of powers conferred by or under any enactment, or

        (iv) civil proceedings which are brought by or on behalf of the authority and arise out of such investigations, and

    (b) it relates to the obtaining of information from confidential sources.

(3) The duty to confirm or deny does not arise in relation to information which is (or if it were held by the public

authority would be) exempt information by virtue of subsection (1) or (2).

(4) In relation to the institution or conduct of criminal proceedings or the power to conduct them, references in subsection (1)(b) or (c) and subsection (2)(a) to the public authority include references—

   (a) to any officer of the authority,

   (b) in the case of a government department other than a Northern Ireland department, to the Minister of the Crown in charge of the department, and

   (c) in the case of a Northern Ireland department, to the Northern Ireland Minister in charge of the department.

(5) In this section—

   "criminal proceedings" includes—

      (a) proceedings before a court-martial constituted under the Army Act 1955, the Air Force Act 1955 or the Naval Discipline Act 1957 . . . ,

      (b) proceedings on dealing summarily with a charge under the Army Act 1955 or the Air Force Act 1955 or on summary trial under the Naval Discipline Act 1957,

      (c) proceedings before a court established by section 83ZA of the Army Act 1955, section 83ZA of the Air Force Act 1955 or section 52FF of the Naval Discipline Act 1957 (summary appeal courts),

      (d) proceedings before the Courts-Martial Appeal Court, and

      (e) proceedings before a Standing Civilian Court;

   "offence" includes any offence under the Army Act 1955, the Air Force Act 1955 or the Naval Discipline Act 1957.

(6) In the application of this section to Scotland—

   (a) in subsection (1)(b), for the words from "a decision" to the end there is substituted "a decision by the authority to make a report to the procurator fiscal for the purpose of enabling him to determine whether criminal proceedings should be instituted",

    (b) **in subsections (1)(c) and (2)(a)(ii) for "which the authority has power to conduct" there is substituted "which have been instituted in consequence of a report made by the authority to the procurator fiscal", and**

    (c) **for any reference to a person being charged with an offence there is substituted a reference to the person being prosecuted for the offence.**

NOTES

Initial Commencement

Specified date

1–132   **Specified date: 30 November 2005 (unless the Secretary of State by order appoints this section before that date): see s 87(3) (as amended by SI 2001/3500, art 8, Sch 2, Pt I, para 8(1)(o) and SI 2003/1887, art 9, Sch 2, para 12(1)(c)). (See appointment note below.)**

Appointment

Appointment: 1 January 2005: see SI 2004/3122, art 2.

Amendment

Sub-s (5): in definition "criminal proceedings" in para (a) words omitted repealed by the Armed Forces Act 2001, s 38, Sch 7, Pt 1.
    Date in force: 28 February 2002: see SI 2002/345, art 2.

GENERAL NOTE[66]

1–133   There are two distinct exemptions within s.30.

Section 30(1) is intended to protect the law enforcement and prosecution functions of the police and other bodies with powers to investigate and prosecute criminal offences. It applies to information which has been held "at any time" for criminal investigations or proceedings. Subject to the public interest, the exemption therefore protects information even after the related investigations or proceedings have closed. Sections (a), (b) and (c) within s.30(1) presumably apply to distinct groups of public authorities. Unfortunately the scope of each subsection, and therefore the lines of demarcation, are not at all clear.

---

[66] Section 30 is a qualified exemption. It applies to the duty to communicate information and the duty to confirm or deny.

Section 30(2) turns on the reasons for the acquisition of information and is intended to protect informers and witnesses. It applies to information "obtained or recorded" from "confidential sources" for a range of investigations or proceedings. These include, but also go beyond, criminal investigations and proceedings.

Subsection (1)

The s.30(1) exemption has three separate parts.   **1–134**

Section 30(1)(a) covers information held for the purpose of any investigation into a specific offence, including information and evidence which leads to the bringing of charges or which leads to a conviction.

Section 30(1)(b) is presumably intended to be wider. It relates to investigations which may lead to "criminal proceedings". This seems more general than investigations into specific offences, to which s.30(1)(a) applies, but the reason for the difference is not clear (it is odd having two separate sections when the wider section seems to cover both).

Section 30(1)(c) further complicates matters because it too refers to information held for "criminal proceedings", thus repeating that expression from s.30(1)(b). The difference is that s.30(1)(c) does not mention "investigations".

The fact that s.30(1) contains three subsections must mean that each is intended to be distinct. Clearly, the exemption protects the law enforcement and prosecution functions of the police and other public authorities with powers or duties to conduct criminal investigations or proceedings (such as the National Crime Squad and the Serious Fraud Office) but beyond this it is difficult to venture far with any confidence. Other bodies whose activities would presumably fall within s.30(1) include the Crown Prosecution Service, HM Revenue & Customs, the Department for Trade and Industry, the Department for the Environment, Food and Rural Affairs, the Food Standards Agency, the Environment Agency, the Health and Safety Executive, the Financial Services Authority and the Office of Fair Trading. How the activities of these bodies might divide between ss.30(1)(a), (b) and (c) is something of a mystery however. Presumably it will depend on the derivation of each body's ability to conduct criminal investigations and proceedings, and the nature of the powers or duties involved. The Information Commissioner's guidance states that he will expect public authorities relying on s.30(1) to be able to explain the legal basis of any investigations or proceedings which they conduct,[67] so in cases where public authorities believe that s.30(1) applies, they should take care to assess thoroughly which element of the section is relevant, and why.

---

[67] Freedom of Information Awareness Guidance No.16: Investigations.

There has been considerable debate about the application of s.30(1) generally. Critics argue that there is no justification for exempting whole classes of information simply because it underlies particular criminal investigations or proceedings (recent examples being the foot-and-mouth crisis and the Paddington rail crash).[68] Section 30(1) nevertheless remains a class-based exemption. The balance lies with the requirement to assess the public interest. As a general principle (and see below for a more detailed examination of public interest factors), the public interest in disclosure will tend to increase once investigations and proceeding are complete. Conversely, while investigations and proceedings are current the right to a fair trial under the Human Rights Act 1998 (and Article 6 of the European Convention) may tip the scales in favour of exemption. Clearly, the Information Commissioner has a deal of responsibility for ensuring that the public interest is applied correctly in the context of s.30(1).[69]

Subsection (2)

1–135   Section 30(2) is limited by two quite specific requirements. First, it can only apply if the information in question was "obtained or recorded" for the purposes of the authority's "functions" in relation to one of four categories listed in s.30(2)(a)(i)–(iv). Second, the information must have come from "confidential sources", which will usually mean witnesses or informants.

This sounds straightforward. It is anything but. In fact, the categories in s.30(2)(a)(i)–(iv) are excessively convoluted, referring to:

   (i) investigations of the type referred to in s.30(1)(a) (see above); or

---

[68] This was also the conclusion of the Macpherson report (Cm. 4262-I) in 1999, commissioned to identify lessons for the investigation and prosecution of racially motivated crimes following the death of Stephen Lawrence. Macpherson puts forward five arguments in support of his conclusion:
   (a) Information which merely describes the circumstances of a crime or which reveals how thoroughly and competently it has been investigated will often be capable of release without harmful consequences.
   (b) In certain circumstances, information will be incapable of prejudicing a trial, for example:
      (i) where an investigation has been closed without a suspect being identified;
      (ii) where the trial is complete but where relevant evidence was not presented because the defendant pleaded guilty;
      (iii) where the prosecution was unsuccessful and the defendant cannot therefore face charges for the same offence in future; or
      (iv) where the defendant has died before the trial.
   (c) Information of positive value to victims of crime may be withheld needlessly.
   (d) Crucial evidence of police incompetence may be concealed by a blanket exemption.
   (e) Restrictions on information held by the police may have implications for information held by other law enforcement bodies.
[69] Note also that the s.30(1) exemption falls away once records are 30 years old and become historical records (s.63). See the commentary under s.67 for an analysis of the treatment of historical records.

(ii) criminal proceedings which the authority has power to conduct; or

(iii) investigations conducted under the authority's statutory or prerogative powers for any of the "specified purposes" (see below); or

(iv) civil proceedings brought by an authority, or on its behalf.

As with s.30(1), it is far from clear how categories (i) and (ii) differ. An explanation of categories (iii) and (iv) is set out below.

Statutory or prerogative powers

There are very many investigations carried out under either statutory or prerogative powers, too numerous to cover here. Two examples are: inquiries under s.14 of the Health and Safety at Work etc. Act 1974 and investigations under s.169 of the Financial Services and Markets Act 2000. **1–136**

As a rule, most investigations carried out by statutory bodies will be statutory investigations, and investigations carried out by central government departments will be either statutory investigations or carried out under prerogative powers.

Meaning of "civil proceedings"

"Civil proceedings" is not defined but will certainly include legal proceedings which are not criminal proceedings before a court or tribunal. It is possible that in some cases the phrase might have a wider meaning, perhaps including certain forms of statutory regulatory enforcement action. **1–137**

Meaning of "the specified purposes"

The specified purposes are: **1–138**

(a) for ascertaining whether any person has failed to comply with the law;

(b) for ascertaining whether any person is responsible for any conduct which is improper;

(c) for ascertaining whether circumstances exist or may arise which would justify regulatory action in pursuance of any enactment;

(d) for ascertaining a person's fitness or competence in relation to the management of bodies corporate or in relation to any profession or other activity which he is, or seeks to become, authorised to carry on;

(e) for ascertaining the cause of an accident;

(f) for protecting charities against misconduct or mismanagement (whether by trustees or other persons) in their administration;

(g) for protecting the property of charities from loss or misapplication;

(h) for recovering the property of charities;

(i) for securing the health, safety and welfare of persons at work; and

(j) for protecting persons other than persons at work against risk to health or safety arising out of or in connection with the actions of persons at work.

One effect of the wording of s.30(2) appears to be that if an authority sets up an inquiry which may reveal illegality, but which the authority does not have express statutory or prerogative power to conduct, then the information obtained or recorded for that inquiry will not be exempt, even if obtained from confidential sources.

Confidential sources

1–139   "Confidential sources" will usually be informants or whistle-blowers whose identity an authority wants to protect. It will not normally extend to personnel working covertly to gather information, nor to information gathered using covert technology.

To engage s.30(2), the information itself need not be confidential, it is the relationship with the source which must be confidential. In practice, the personal information and confidential information exemptions may also apply to information obtained from confidential sources. Sections 40 and 41 should therefore be considered before looking at s.30(2). Examples of information which is likely to fall outside ss.40 and 41 but within s.30(2) are:

• a diary with recorded appointments to meet an unnamed informer;

• details of surveillance and investigative techniques associated with the management of external confidential sources;

• an indication that certain information has been obtained from an unnamed confidential source.

Department for Constitutional Affairs Guidance[70]

At the heart of s.30 lies the importance to law enforcement of public **1–140** confidence in the investigations and proceedings to which the exemption refers. Public confidence can obviously be fostered by transparency, but it also requires the processes themselves to deliver justice effectively. As the White Paper on Open Government stated:

> "*There should be no commitment to disclose information which would help potential lawbreakers and criminals, put life, safety or the environment in danger . . . Investigation of suspected crime must normally be kept secret from the suspect and others. Witness statements, names and addresses of witnesses and reports from the police and others to prosecutors could, if disclosed other than as required by the courts, jeopardise law enforcement or the prevention or prosecution of crime, or be extremely unfair to a temporary suspect against whom (in the event) no real evidence existed. It is in the interests of both the individuals concerned and the integrity of the prosecution process that material relating to both live and completed prosecutions and to prosecutions which do not go ahead can be kept confidential.*"

In balancing public interest considerations, public authorities will need to consider the potential effects of a disclosure and the nature and seriousness of the matter being pursued.

The ability of the police, HM Revenue & Customs and other public authorities to obtain information in pursuance of their investigative processes is critical to the prevention and detection of crime and to the integrity and effectiveness of the criminal justice system. Certain disclosures, particularly in relation to confidential sources, could have extremely serious consequences, lead to serious risk of injury or loss of life and be damaging to the willingness of other individuals to supply information.

When considering the balance of the public interest, a weighty consideration will be the extent to which disclosing or withholding information would:

- promote or diminish the chances of a successful prosecution, bringing future charges or making arrests;

- promote or diminish the chances of a fair trial;

- be fair to those who have not been prosecuted, in cases where a decision has been taken not to proceed;

- assist or hamper the gathering of intelligence information from confidential sources such as informants, whistle-blowers or calls to Crimestoppers;

---

[70] See *www.foi.gov.uk/guidance/exguide/sec30/index.htm.*

- further the interests of justice through the participation of victims, witnesses, informants, suspects or offenders in investigations and proceedings—and either protect or endanger them as they do so;

- assist or impede other ongoing or future proceedings;

- prevent or facilitate the commission of crime.

31 Law enforcement

1–141

(1) **Information which is not exempt information by virtue of section 30 is exempt information if its disclosure under this Act would, or would be likely to, prejudice—**

    (a) **the prevention or detection of crime,**

    (b) **the apprehension or prosecution of offenders,**

    (c) **the administration of justice,**

    (d) **the assessment or collection of any tax or duty or of any imposition of a similar nature,**

    (e) **the operation of the immigration controls,**

    (f) **the maintenance of security and good order in prisons or in other institutions where persons are lawfully detained,**

    (g) **the exercise by any public authority of its functions for any of the purposes specified in subsection (2),**

    (h) **any civil proceedings which are brought by or on behalf of a public authority and arise out of an investigation conducted, for any of the purposes specified in subsection (2), by or on behalf of the authority by virtue of Her Majesty's prerogative or by virtue of powers conferred by or under an enactment,**

    (i) **or any inquiry held under the Fatal Accidents and Sudden Deaths Inquiries (Scotland) Act 1976 to the extent that the inquiry arises out of an investigation conducted, for any of the purposes specified in subsection (2), by or on behalf of the authority by virtue of Her Majesty's prerogative or by virtue of powers conferred by or under an enactment.**

(2) **The purposes referred to in subsection (1)(g) to (i) are—**

    (a) **the purpose of ascertaining whether any person has failed to comply with the law,**

    (b) **the purpose of ascertaining whether any person is responsible for any conduct which is improper,**

(c) the purpose of ascertaining whether circumstances which would justify regulatory action in pursuance of any enactment exist or may arise,

(d) the purpose of ascertaining a person's fitness or competence in relation to the management of bodies corporate or in relation to any profession or other activity which he is, or seeks to become, authorised to carry on,

(e) the purpose of ascertaining the cause of an accident,

(f) the purpose of protecting charities against misconduct or mismanagement (whether by trustees or other persons) in their administration,

(g) the purpose of protecting the property of charities from loss or misapplication,

(h) the purpose of recovering the property of charities,

(i) the purpose of securing the health, safety and welfare of persons at work, and

(j) the purpose of protecting persons other than persons at work against risk to health or safety arising out of or in connection with the actions of persons at work.

(3) The duty to confirm or deny does not arise if, or to the extent that, compliance with section 1(1)(a) would, or would be likely to, prejudice any of the matters mentioned in subsection (1).

NOTES

Initial Commencement

Specified date

Specified date: 30 November 2005 (unless the Secretary of State by order appoints this section before that date): see s 87(3) (as amended by SI 2001/3500, art 8, Sch 2, Pt I, para 8(1)(o) and SI 2003/1887, art 9, Sch 2, para 12(1)(c)). (See appointment note below.)

Appointment

Appointment: 1 January 2005: see SI 2004/3122, art 2.

GENERAL NOTE[71]

1–142   Section 31 operates by reference to a list of law enforcement functions which might be prejudiced by disclosure of information. Some are very wide, others very specific.

Section 31 turns on the likely effects of disclosure rather than the source of the information or the purpose for which it is held. Sources and purposes are covered under s.30 and so s.31 will only be relevant in cases where s.30 is not. This excludes from s.31 most substantive information relating to an authority's own law enforcement functions. However, s.31 is considerably broader than s.30 because it can apply to information which authorities hold for the law enforcement purposes of other bodies.

Subsection (1)

1–143   As will be clear, sections (a)–(f) stand by themselves and refer to a series of law enforcement "interests" which could be prejudiced by disclosure. Sections (g)–(i) can only apply in relation to the purposes set out in subs.(2).

There follows an analysis of each section, together with examples of public interest considerations for each.

Sections 31(1)(a) and (b)—meaning of "the prevention or detection of crime" and "the apprehension of prosecution of offenders"

1–144   These terms appear throughout English law and have no special meaning within FOIA. They may apply specifically or in general. Examples of circumstances which might engage the exemption are:

- intelligence about anticipated criminal activities (disclosure here has a high potential to prejudice the prevention or detection of the crime in question, and the apprehension of the alleged offenders);

- information relating to planned police operations, including specific planned operations, and policies and procedures relating to operational activity;

- information relating to the identity and role of police informers (to which a number of other exemptions are also likely to be relevant, including those under ss.30, 38, 40 and 41);

- information relating to police strategies and tactics in seeking to prevent crime (the disclosure of such information has a high

---

[71] Section 31 is a qualified exemption. It applies to the duty to communicate information and the duty to confirm or deny.

potential to undermine legitimate police objectives carried out in the public interest);

- information the disclosure of which would facilitate the commission of any offence[72]; and

- information the disclosure of which would prejudice the fair trial of any person against whom proceedings have been or may be instituted (to which, again, a number of other exemptions may also be relevant, particularly, with reference to s.44, in relation to disclosures which would breach Article 6 of the European Convention on Human Rights).

Department for Constitutional Affairs Guidance[73]

Maintaining confidence in law enforcement and the criminal justice system is obviously crucial to the public interest, but it is a consideration which can weigh both for and against disclosure. Much is done through police and community consultation and the media to keep citizens informed about the ways in which the police carry out their responsibilities. But on occasions, there will be some tension between this emphasis on openness and the need to maintain the confidentiality of specific operations or policies. Similar considerations will apply to other law enforcement bodies. **1–145**

It is also important to be aware that prejudice may arise incrementally as well as from a single disclosure. Clearly, disclosure of information on a single specific police operation designed to apprehend alleged offenders could be prejudicial but so could disclosures of more general information relating to police strategies and tactics. The latter might undermine legitimate police objectives and hamper future operational activity by limiting the value of those strategies and tactics once disclosed (or providing valuable intelligence to perpetrators of crime).

Examples of specific considerations which might be relevant to this section include:

---

[72] The Commissioner upheld a refusal by Essex Police to disclose the identity of the 20 fixed camera locations in Essex which catch the most drivers speeding, how many drivers per month or year are caught at each location, and how much money was raised from each location per month or year. The refusal was based partly on s.31. In his Decision Notice the Commissioner states that while recognising "the value of improving public awareness and the opportunity disclosure would bring to further the debate on the effectiveness and purpose of speed cameras, he was not persuaded that the public interest in furthering this debate would outweigh the public interest in ... avoiding ... an increase in non compliance with road traffic laws." He was also persuaded that "if the perception of the risk of being caught by speed cameras was reduced this may force Essex Constabulary to consider more widespread installation of speed cameras incurring additional public expenditure." Decision Notice FS50068601, August 3, 2005. See also Decision Notices FS50067279 and FS50068017, both of August 2, 2005, on the same issues in relation to Hampshire Police.

[73] See *www.foi.gov.uk/guidance/exguide/sec31/index.htm*.

- the effects of crime on individuals—for example, it would not be in the public interest to disclose details of a surveillance operation and thus potentially compromise that operation, where the target was a person suspected of a series of violent assaults;

- the effects of crime on society—for example, it may not serve the public interest to disclose in advance the arrangements for an operation to combat graffiti and other criminal damage in a specific area; and

- the effects of crime on the economy—for example, it may be against the public interest to disclose specific police strategies for action against those failing to pay fines or other penalties.

Section 31(1)(c)—meaning of "the administration of justice"

1–146   There is no definition of the administration of justice, but it should be interpreted broadly. In particular:

- the exemption is not just about the courts—justice is administered through courts and tribunals, through arbitrators, and through alternatives to litigation;

- all categories of justice are included: criminal, civil, family, or administrative, as are matters which may not fit that classification or which are general in nature;

- justice may be administered by professional judges and adjudicators, or by lay magistrates or panel members, or by jurors;

- administration of justice need not imply an adversarial context—it includes non-contentious or uncontested business, and inquisitorial processes (such as inquiries and coroners' courts);

- ensuring people's access to justice is part of the administration of justice;

- the administration of justice may be prejudiced in an individual case, or by something happening to the general process by which justice is delivered.

In the normal course, the administration of justice could be prejudiced by disclosures relating to:

- the operation of the judicial appointments system;

- the ability of a judge to deliver justice effectively, fairly and fearlessly in a particular case;

- the ability of a judge, or of the judiciary, to perform this function more generally;

- the business of the running of the courts and tribunals (though other exemptions might also be relevant);

- the enforcement of sentences and the execution of judgments;

- the ability of litigants to bring their cases, or a particular case, to court;

- the prospects of a fair trial taking place;

- the effectiveness of relationships between different agencies involved in the administration of justice (for example, premature disclosure of plans to redistribute functions between different agencies could lead to a breakdown of co-operation);

- a range of other matters and systems that support the administration of justice (*e.g.* the operation of the legal aid system, or IT systems—disclosure of the security measures on computer systems would facilitate unauthorised access and thereby make them vulnerable to interference);

- the maintenance of an independent and effective legal profession.

Department for Constitutional Affairs Guidance[74]

Self evidently, the public interest in the administration of justice is very high. However, in addition to this, there is a public interest in the separation of powers between courts and the executive. This effectively means that there is a public interest in the government acknowledging the administration of justice as the courts' particular domain, and in recognising that the courts are themselves ultimately the constitutional arbiters within the law.   **1–147**

As such, although the nature, degree and likelihood of prejudice to the administration of justice will be an essential part of weighing the balance of public interest, government recognition of the courts' position means that authorities should take particular care whenever concluding that the public interest in avoiding such prejudice is outweighed. One example of where the balance might come down in favour of disclosure might be circumstances where prejudice in a particular case is outweighed by the prevention of prejudice more generally. There may be other circumstances, particularly at the administrative margins (as opposed to the judicial centre)

---

[74] *Ibid.*

of the administration of justice, where the operational impact of a prejudicial disclosure is more diffuse, and considerations of administrative transparency weigh more strongly. Precisely because prejudice to the administration of justice encompasses such a wide range of circumstances, the specific factors relevant to individual cases may be particularly important to the operation of this exemption.

Section 31(1)(d)—meaning of "tax or duty or any imposition of a similar nature"

1–148   "Taxes, duties and impositions of a similar nature" includes:

- income tax;

- corporation tax;

- VAT;

- insurance premium tax;

- petroleum revenue tax;

- national insurance contributions;

- climate change levy;

- excise duties (for example, on tobacco, oil, beer, spirits and wine);

- motor vehicle duties;

- air passenger duty; and

- stamp duty.

Disclosures likely to be prejudicial to the assessment or collection of these include:

- details of plans to close tax loopholes;

- information held in relation to the tax affairs of companies or individuals;

- information which informs plans for future investigations;

- third party information which aids the collection of tax or duties; and

- details of strategies, investigative practices or even negotiating tactics used to assist in the collection of taxes or duties.

Department for Constitutional Affairs Guidance[75]

There is a strong public interest in having stable and secure public finances. **1–149** These are crucial to the stability and sustainable growth of the UK economy and to deliver the resources to fund public services. An efficient and well administered tax system also improves the competitiveness of business and supports the government's social and welfare objectives. A central requirement of a modern and fair tax system is that everyone pays the proper amount of tax and receives the benefits they are entitled to. Tax avoidance and evasion distort the incentives that the tax system aims to deliver and unfairly shifts a greater tax burden onto honest and compliant taxpayers. They also reduce the revenue available for delivering public services.

Of course, disclosure of information promotes public awareness of how taxes work, which helps make it simpler for people and business to pay taxes. Authorities should take into account the public interest in the proper administration of taxation both in general and in particular cases, and in avoiding disruption and distortion of markets or of the successful delivery of tax policy objectives.

Section 31(1)(e)—meaning of "operation of immigration controls"

"Immigration controls" is not defined in FOIA but it will obviously cover **1–150** the physical immigration controls at points of entry into the UK, as well as the arrangements made (whether in or under legislation, or as a matter of policy or procedure) in connection with entry into and stay in the UK, including the investigation of offences relating to immigration. Clearly, the disclosure of information would be prejudicial under this head if its release into the public domain would help people to evade immigration controls (although, as long as that is likely to be the consequence of release, the information itself need not be "about" immigration controls).

Examples of circumstances where disclosure might prejudice the operation of immigration controls include disclosure of:

- Information about the counterfeiting of travel documents of a particular country, on the basis of which travel documents issued by that country should be subjected to particular scrutiny. In this case, the disclosure of the information or the identity of the targeted country might be prejudial because it could alert counterfeiters and persons making use of their services.

- Information which would reveal an incidence of suspected illegal working which is to be investigated by the immigration service. In this case, the disclosure of the information about the proposed investigation might be prejudial because it could alert those

---

[75] *Ibid.*

employing illegal workers and allow them to escape investigation.

- Information on proposed changes to visa regimes. The imposition or amendment of visa regimes usually takes place with little or no notice being given to the public. This is because visa regimes are generally introduced to prevent evasion or abuse of immigration controls by nationalities who, over time, have been shown to pose a higher risk of evasion or abuse when seeking to enter the UK. Therefore, the disclosure of information relating to visa regimes could, in some cases, prejudice the operation of immigration controls because it would encourage persons from the countries which are due to be affected to seek to enter the UK before the changes are introduced, thus avoiding the more stringent regime which has necessarily been developed.

Department for Constitutional Affairs Guidance[76]

1–151   There is a clear public interest in the existence and efficient operation of immigration controls to regulate entry to and settlement in the UK.

In the immigration context there are a number of public interest considerations which may, in relation to a particular request, favour disclosure. There is a public interest in fostering public confidence in the operation of our immigration controls, and one way of ensuring this is to keep the public informed of policies, developments and proposals for the future, together with explanations of them. Linked with this is the public interest in ensuring that the public have access to correct information. Immigration is an emotive issue and inaccurate information circulating in the public domain should be corrected.

It will be in the public interest to provide information which confirms the performance of immigration control—for example, by providing statistics on the number of passengers and applications that are handled by the Immigration and Nationality Directorate. There is also a public interest in establishing that the implementation of immigration control is carried out in accordance with published statements and policies by providing, wherever possible, details of its implementation.

Equally there are a number of public interest considerations which may, in the context of a particular request, favour non-disclosure. For example, there is a public interest in ensuring that:

- people are not able to evade or abuse our immigration controls in order to enter the UK illegally;

---

[76] *Ibid.*

- the efficiency and integrity of our immigration controls are not undermined; and

- investigations into suspected immigration offences can be conducted effectively.

Section 31(1)(f)—meaning of "maintenance of security and good order in prisons"

"Security" and "good order" are not defined in FOIA but common sense   1–152
suggests that "security" will include everything related to the secure
custody of detainees, the safety of the prison population, and the detection
and prevention of activity (criminal or otherwise) prohibited under prison
rules. "Good order" presumably means things intended to counter
individuals' disobedience or concerted indiscipline, and which promotes a
safe and orderly prison regime. Note, however, that the exemption is
intended to preserve not only security and good order in prisons but also in
"other institutions where persons are lawfully detained". This will include
Young Offenders Institutions, Secure Hospitals, Secure Training Centres,
Local Authority Secure Accommodation and Immigration Detention and
Removal Centres.

Since the exemption focuses on the effects of disclosure, information would
presumably cause harm if its release would compromise security, lead to the
breakdown of good order or impaire an institution's ability to restore
either.

A key aspect of all this is the need to ensure that changes to prison routine
are introduced in a carefully managed way, with the prisoner reaction
assessed and expectations managed so that when the change is introduced,
there is not an immediate adverse reaction that might put staff and
prisoners at risk. Premature release of information about a potentially
unpopular policy change might therefore be prejudicial. Hypothetical
examples of information relevant to "good order" might be information
about proposed changes in the Home Detention Curfew (or "tagging")
policy or Incentives and Earned Privileges scheme, or information about
changes in meal times or visiting arrangements.

Examples of security related information might be information detailing the
times and routes of prisoner escorts. Information relating to good order
would be things like the strategy for dealing with concerted prisoner
indiscipline or the contingency plans for responding to other types of
incident.

Conversely, information on physical security at a prison which was assessed
as having little or no impact on the risk of prisoner escape if disclosed might
not be considered to prejudice security and should therefore be
disclosed.

Department for Constitutional Affairs Guidance[77]

1-153　There is a public interest in fostering public confidence in the operation of the prison system, and one way of ensuring this is to keep the public informed of policies, developments, proposals for the future and the like. The public interest is clealy not served, however, by releasing information which may abett escape, unrest or put anybody within an institution at risk.

Sections 31(1)(g), (h) and (i)

1-154　As noted above, these exemptions operate only where:

- disclosure would prejudice one of the authority's functions, *and*

- the function in question is for one of the purposes listed in s.31(2), *and*

- the public interest allows.

Section 31(1)(g)—meaning of an authority's "functions"

1-155　"Functions" refers to an authority's powers and duties. These derive either from statute or from royal prerogative, and the connected purposes in s.31(2) indicate that we are really concerned with those systems operated by authorities for ensuring proper standards of conduct and safety. That said, s.31 does not limit the application of the exemption to particular "central" functions, since in reality very many authorities and departments will exercise functions for the purpose of ascertaining whether any person has complied with the law (s.31(2)(a)), ascertaining whether any person is responsible for any conduct which is improper (s.31(2)(b)), ascertaining the cause of an accident (s.31(2)(e)), or securing the health, safety and welfare of persons at work (s.31(2)(i)).

Section 31(1)(h)—civil proceedings arising out of statutory or prerogative investigations

1-156　"Civil proceedings" certainly comprises non-criminal legal action before a court or tribunal, but it could stretch to include other proceedings such as for example some forms of regulatory enforcement proceedings. Much will depend on the circumstances and on the terms of any regulatory regime involved.

The "prejudice" in question must be to the civil proceedings themselves, but there is no need to give that an artificially narrow interpretation. It is capable, for example, of applying to prejudice to the authority's position in such proceedings.

[77] *Ibid.*

The proceedings must arise, directly or indirectly, out of an investigation. The investigation, in turn, must have been conducted for one of the specified purposes in s.31(2), though the proceedings themselves need not have been (even if, in practice, this will be likely). For example, having ascertained that someone has improperly disclosed sensitive information to journalists, a public authority may attempt to prevent publication of that material by a breach of confidence action.

The investigation must have been conducted either:

- by virtue of the Royal Prerogative (many investigations undertaken by government departments are undertaken under prerogative powers because the residual source of their legal powers—where not expressly conferred by statute, for example—resides in the Crown; this is particularly the case for investigations into the internal management of government departments), or

- by or under an enactment—that is to say, by virtue of provisions in an Act of Parliament or in an instrument made under powers contained in an Act (that will include, in particular, statutory regulations).

Both the civil proceedings and the investigation may be undertaken either by the authority itself, or by another body on the authority's behalf.

This provision has potential to overlap with s.31(1)(c) (the administration of justice) and with ss.32 (court records) and 42 (legal professional privilege). The general public interest considerations likely to be engaged are therefore those relating to the administration of justice and the proper conduct of legal proceedings

Section 31(1)(i)—inquiries under the Fatal Accidents and Sudden Deaths Inquiry (Scotland) Act 1976

The 1976 Act provides for public inquiries to be held in respect of fatal **1–157** accidents, deaths of persons in legal custody, sudden, suspicious, or unexplained deaths, or deaths which occur in circumstances giving rise to serious public concern. As the Lord Advocate's powers to investigate deaths in Scotland under this legislation are wide-ranging, this provision will have relevance to UK government departments operating in Scotland in a wide variety of circumstances where a death occurs, even where the death does not occur in "legal custody". For Whitehall departments, these will of course be in areas of 'reserved' policy/operations, such as, for example, defence (deaths of MoD service personnel based in Scotland) or immigration (deaths of asylum seekers in Home Office detention in Scotland).

Like s.31(1)(h), this provision is limited by the following factors:

- the prejudice must be to the inquiry;

- the exemption applies only to the extent that the inquiry arises out of an investigation;

- the investigation must have been conducted for one of the purposes specified in s.31(2);

- the investigation must have been conducted under statutory or prerogative powers (although not necessarily under the 1976 Act itself).

Some statutes, which have their own provisions about inquiries into deaths, expressly allow for the disapplication of the 1976 Act, to prevent a death triggering two parallel statutory inquiries. Examples include section 14(7) of the Health and Safety at Work etc Act 1974, and section 271(6) of the Merchant Shipping Act. Such provisions will limit the application of this provision.

The section 31(2) purposes most likely to be relevant to the investigations referred to in connection with the 1976 Act are:

- ascertaining whether any person has failed to comply with the law;

- ascertaining whether any person is responsible for any conduct which is improper;

- ascertaining whether circumstances which would justify statutory regulatory action exist;

- ascertaining the cause of an accident.

32 Court records, etc

1–158

(1) **Information held by a public authority is exempt information if it is held only by virtue of being contained in—**

    (a) **any document filed with, or otherwise placed in the custody of, a court for the purposes of proceedings in a particular cause or matter,**

    (b) **any document served upon, or by, a public authority for the purposes of proceedings in a particular cause or matter, or**

    (c) **any document created by—**

        (i) **a court, or**

        (ii) **a member of the administrative staff of a court,**

for the purposes of proceedings in a particular cause
or matter.

(2) Information held by a public authority is exempt
information if it is held only by virtue of being contained
in—

    (a) any document placed in the custody of a person
conducting an inquiry or arbitration, for the
purposes of the inquiry or arbitration, or

    (b) any document created by a person conducting an
inquiry or arbitration, for the purposes of the inquiry
or arbitration.

(3) The duty to confirm or deny does not arise in relation to
information which is (or if it were held by the public
authority would be) exempt information by virtue of this
section.

(4) In this section—

    (a) "court" includes any tribunal or body exercising the
judicial power of the State,

    (b) "proceedings in a particular cause or matter"
includes any inquest or post-mortem examination,

    (c) "inquiry" means any inquiry or hearing held under
any provision contained in, or made under, an
enactment, and

    (d) except in relation to Scotland, "arbitration" means
any arbitration to which Part I of the Arbitration Act
1996 applies.

NOTES

Initial Commencement

Specified date

Specified date: 30 November 2005 (unless the Secretary of State by
order appoints this section before that date): see s 87(3) (as
amended by SI 2001/3500, art 8, Sch 2, Pt I, para 8(1)(o) and SI
2003/1887, art 9, Sch 2, para 12(1)(c)). (See appointment note
below.)

1–159

Appointment

Appointment: 1 January 2005: see SI 2004/3122, art 2.

See Further

See further, the disapplication of sub-s (2) above in relation to
information contained in documents that, in pursuance of rules

under the Inquiries Act 2005, s 41(1)(b), have been passed to and are held by a public authority: the Inquiries Act 2005, s 18(3).

GENERAL NOTE[78]

1-160 Information contained in court records and other similar documents is absolutely exempt from FOIA disclosure. In essence, the exemption covers:

(a) any document served on or by a public authority; and

(b) documents held or created by a court, or a person conducting an inquiry or arbitration, in each case where this is for the purposes of proceedings. "Proceedings" means court proceedings and also any inquest or post-mortem.

Note that the exemption can only apply where proceedings have actually started. Information relating to proceedings which are merely contemplated will not be exempt under s.32 (although s.42 (legal privilege) may apply).[79]

The point about s.32 is that there are separate and specific regimes applying to courts and tribunals which give those bodies control over the information they hold. FOIA does not duplicate or cut across these. Section 32 simply preserves the courts' own procedures for disclosure.

By way of example, the Civil Procedure Rules or "CPR" set out a comprehensive code governing the disclosure of court records and documents served in the course of proceedings. Rule 5.4 of the CPR deals with access to court documents in civil proceedings in county courts, the High Court and the Court of Appeal. It allows anyone, on payment of a fee, to inspect and take a copy of a claim form which has been served, a judgment or order given or made in public and, if the court gives permission, any other document. Where a person has the right to inspect a document without permission, a request can be made to the court staff; where permission is required, application must be made to a judge.

For certain types of proceedings (such as in the family court, where children need to be protected), only limited classes of persons may access court documents.

The "administrative staff of a court"—subsection (1)(c)(ii)

1-161 Documents produced by the courts' administrative staff (such as court listings) will not be accessible under FOIA. So, for example, a copy of a

---

[78] Section 32 is an absolute exemption. It applies to the duty to communicate information and the duty to confirm or deny.

[79] Information Commissioner's guidance: Freedom of Information Act Awareness Guidance No.9: Information contained in court records.

court case transcript obtained from the Court and paid for by Bridgnorth District Council was exempt under s.32(1)(c) on the grounds that the information was taken from court tapes, which were created by the administrative staff of the court. If an authority only holds information because it was obtained from a source to which s.32 applies, then the exemption stands irrespective of the format into which the authority may later convert the information.[80]

There is a distinction between the courts themselves—which are not public authorities under FOIA—and the government departments responsible for organising the court and tribunal systems (*i.e.* the Court Service and the Northern Ireland Court Service)—which are public authorities. Information held by the latter is accessible under FOIA in the normal way, as is information held by the police, the Legal Services Commission and the Legal Services Ombudsman.

Documents served on or by a public authority

This covers documents created by the parties to litigation and will include   **1–162** information contained in:

- claim forms and statements of defence;

- committal documents in criminal proceedings;

- witness statements, medical and other experts' reports and exhibits;

- skeleton arguments;

- standard disclosure lists;

- public interest immunity applications and certificates;

- allocation questionnaires or pre-trial checklists (listing questionnaires);

- notices of a Part 36 payment into court (a payment of money into court which is made pursuant to Part 36 of the Civil Procedure Rules);

- application notices;

- applications under ss.76 and 78 of the Police and Criminal Evidence Act 1984;

- trial bundles;

[80] Decision Notice FAC0065282, May 17, 2005.

- response to a Request for Further and Better Particulars (Civil Procedure Rules Part 18); and

- any other documents which are placed before a court for the purpose of a decision or ruling.

Where an authority is party to litigation, documents provided to it by the other parties as part of the disclosure process will normally be exempt. However, the exemption will not apply to information which is also held by the public authority in non-exempt form. So, for example, if an authority is litigating over a contract, the contract will not be exempt (assuming the authority holds a copy in its files) just because that contract is included in the authority's statement of case. This is because the opening line in s.32 reads "Information held by a public authority is exempt information if it is held *only* by virtue of being held in [court documents etc.]" (author's italics).

In practical terms, this means that information will usually only be susceptible to the s.32 exemption where it is known to the public authority solely because it is contained in documents served on the authority by another party in litigation, or where it is held by the authority solely because it was recorded in connection with litigation.

Documents held or created by a court

1–163 For the purposes of s.32, a "court" includes a tribunal or other body exercising the judicial power of the State (s.32(4)(a)). As well as the civil and criminal courts (comprising magistrates' courts, county courts, the Crown Court, the High Court and the Court of Appeal), this includes the Judicial Committees of the House of Lords and the Privy Council, and the judicial functions of coroners.[81] It probably excludes the European Court of Justice and the European Court of Human Rights which are not UK domestic courts.[82]

This part of the exemption would cover information contained in things like:

- judgments and orders of the court which have not been published;

---

[81] The definition reproduces the definition in s.19 of the Contempt of Court Act 1981. Bodies such as Mental Health Review Tribunals and Employment Tribunals are regarded as exercising the judicial power of the state, but bodies exercising purely administrative functions, such as a local rating court, are not (*Attorney-General v BBC* [1981] AC 303).

[82] Although because s.32 is phrased to "*include* any tribunal or body exercising the judicial power of the State" (author's italics) it is arguable that this covers courts or tribunals which exercise judicial powers outside the UK.

- notebooks of judges, tribunal members, coroners and other judicial officers;

- notices of hearings;

- summaries prepared by judicial assistants; and

- court or tribunal internal memoranda and correspondence which relate to particular proceedings.

Documents held or created by a person conducting an inquiry

Inquiries will be subject to FOIA unless they are legally independent of the sponsoring department. A public authority may therefore hold information which falls within s.32 either because it conducted an inquiry itself or because it was the inquiry's sponsoring department. However, there is a very important limitation on the application of the exemption to inquiries. The exemption can only apply where an inquiry has statutory constitution or is set up under Royal Prerogative (even if a judge heads the proceedings). This might include: **1–164**

- inquiries which are required to be held by specific statutory provision;

- a discretionary inquiry or hearing designated by an order under s.16(2) of the Tribunals and Inquiries Act 1992 (the relevant order is the Tribunals and Inquiries (Discretionary Inquiries) Order 1975, as amended);

- an inquiry set up by the exercise of a statutory power (*e.g.* under s.250 of the Local Government Act 1972 or s.81 of the Children Act 1989);

- any inquiry to which the provisions of the Tribunals of Inquiry (Evidence) Act 1921 apply.

There are numerous examples of specific inquiries set up under an enactment. The Bloody Sunday Inquiry was set up under the Tribunals of Inquiry (Evidence) Act 1921, the Marchioness Inquiry under the Merchant Shipping Act 1995, and the Victoria Climbie Inquiry under the Children Act 1989, the NHS Act 1971 and the Policy Act 1996. Examples of inquiries which would normally fall outside the scope of s.32 are:

- departmental leak inquiries;

- Lord Butler's reivew of the intelligence published prior to the invasion of Iraq on weapons of mass destruction;

- Sir Michael Bichard's inquiry arising from Ian Huntley's murder of Soham schoolgirls Holly Wells and Jessica Chapman;

- Lord Penrose's inquiry into Equitable Life; and

- Lord Philip's inquiry into BSE.

Documents held or created by a person conducting arbitration

1–165 Arbitration is defined by reference to Pt 1 of the Arbitration Act 1996, which applies only where there is a written arbitration agreement. Arbitration involves an impartial, independent third party hearing both sides (usually in private) and issuing a final and legally binding decision to resolve the dispute.

The exemption would normally apply to information contained in, for example:

- notes taken by an arbitrator;

- written decisions or reports of the arbitration;

- a written arbitration agreement that is created by a person conducting an arbitration;

- internal correspondence between persons involved in the conduct of an arbitration; and

- a letter from a person conducting an arbitration requesting further evidence.

33 Audit functions

1–166

(1) **This section applies to any public authority which has functions in relation to—**

    (a) **the audit of the accounts of other public authorities, or**

    (b) **the examination of the economy, efficiency and effectiveness with which other public authorities use their resources in discharging their functions.**

(2) **Information held by a public authority to which this section applies is exempt information if its disclosure would, or would be likely to, prejudice the exercise of any of the authority's functions in relation to any of the matters referred to in subsection (1).**

(3) **The duty to confirm or deny does not arise in relation to a public authority to which this section applies if, or to the extent that, compliance with section 1(1)(a) would, or would be likely to, prejudice the exercise of any of the authority's functions in relation to any of the matters referred to in subsection (1).**

NOTES

Initial Commencement

Specified date

Specified date: 30 November 2005 (unless the Secretary of State by order appoints this section before that date): see s 87(3) (as amended by SI 2001/3500, art 8, Sch 2, Pt I, para 8(1)(o) and SI 2003/1887, art 9, Sch 2, para 12(1)(c)). (See appointment note below.)

Appointment

Appointment: 1 January 2005: see SI 2004/3122, art 2

GENERAL NOTE[83]

This exemption is intended to protect the effectiveness of the audit   **1–167** functions of certain public authorities.[84] It applies to authorities which exercise audit functions but not to other authorities which are subject to audit, even though the latter may hold information which relates to public audits. In addition, bodies which are appointed by the Audit Commission and exercise functions under the Audit Commission Act 1998 will not be covered by s.33 unless they are public authorities.

While much of the information an auditor holds may be disclosable (and indeed much of it is prepared with a view to publication), there may be cases where disclosure might prejudice the audit function:

- Relations with audited bodies and audit third parties—there may be information that originates from an audited body which, if disclosed, could harm relations between the auditors and that body, and so affect the ability of the auditors to carry out their functions effectively.

- Audit methods—in the interests of an audit's effectiveness, it may be important that details of the audit method, including, for example, the specific files that the auditor intends to examine, are kept from the audited body before the audit takes place. Disclosure of audit methods after an audit may also prejudice subsequent audits where, for example, an auditor intends to use the same method. Releasing information about how the auditing

---

[83] Section 33 is a qualified exemption. It applies to the duty to communicate information and the duty to confirm or deny.

[84] Authorities which exercise the functions set out in subs.(1) include the National Audit Office, the Audit Commission, the Northern Ireland Audit Office, the Commission for Healthcare Audit and Inspection, HM Magistrates' Court Services Inspectorate, HM Inspectorate of Constabulary, HM Inspectorate of Prisons, Ofsted and the Commission for Social Care Inspection.

body derives its conclusions could also prejudice the audit function.

- Public reporting and scrutiny—before publication, many public sector auditors discuss their emerging findings and draft report with the audited body itself and other affected parties to ensure accuracy and completeness of the evidence on which they base their conclusions and recommendations. In the case of the National Audit Office, they may also be under a duty to inform Parliament first of the findings of their reports. If information on an audit were disclosed before official publication, this might pre-empt the proper reporting process, were preliminary findings which had not been fully tested given the same currency as fully tested conclusions. This might undermine the fairness of the audit process and create a misleading impression of both the auditor and the body being audited, causing unwarranted damage to either reputation. In these circumstances the audit function would be prejudiced.

Department for Constitutional Affairs Guidance[85]

1–168 There is a strong public interest in ensuring that auditors can effectively carry out audits of public authorities. Much of the information that auditors produce is made available for the same general public interest reasons that support the principles of FOIA. These include:

- making the reasons for a public body's decisions evident;

- enhancing the scrutiny and improving the accountability of public bodies;

- contributing to public debate; and

- increasing public participation in decision making.

The audit process facilitates the accountability and transparency of public authorities for decisions taken by them, which in turn facilitates accountability and transparency in the spending of public money. Most value-for-money audits lead to a public report with these express aims. There is therefore a clear public interest in protecting the effectiveness of the audit process. But there is also a counter-balancing public interest in making available information which would lead to greater public confidence in the integrity of the audit process by allowing scrutiny, not only of the audited body, but also the auditor's performance. In many cases the balance of the public interest will change over time, with the key issue likely to be whether the final report has been published.

---

[85] See *www.foi.gov.uk/guidance/exguide/sec33/index.htm.*

Auditing departments and agencies will need to be aware of the confidentiality requirements of legislation that governs the particular bodies they audit. For example, the National Audit Office, the external auditor of the Inland Revenue, is bound by the Finance Act 1989, which makes it a criminal offence to disclose taxpayers' information.

34 Parliamentary privilege

(1) Information is exempt information if exemption from   1–169
   section 1(1)(b) is required for the purpose of avoiding an infringement of the privileges of either House of Parliament.

(2) The duty to confirm or deny does not apply if, or to the extent that, exemption from section 1(1)(a) is required for the purpose of avoiding an infringement of the privileges of either House of Parliament.

(3) A certificate signed by the appropriate authority certifying that exemption from section 1(1)(b), or from section 1(1)(a) and (b), is, or at any time was, required for the purpose of avoiding an infringement of the privileges of either House of Parliament shall be conclusive evidence of that fact.

(4) In subsection (3) "the appropriate authority" means—

   (a) in relation to the House of Commons, the Speaker of that House, and

   (b) in relation to the House of Lords, the Clerk of the Parliaments.

NOTES

Initial Commencement

Specified date

Specified date: 30 November 2005 (unless the Secretary of State by order appoints this section before that date): see s 87(3) (as amended by SI 2001/3500, art 8, Sch 2, Pt I, para 8(1)(o) and SI 2003/1887, art 9, Sch 2, para 12(1)(c)). (See appointment note below.)

Appointment

Appointment: 1 January 2005: see SI 2004/3122, art 2.

GENERAL NOTE[86]

1–170 Parliamentary privilege is not intrinsically a reason for secrecy. Nevertheless, it is deemed a form of immunity necessary for the House of Commons and House of Lords to function independently and without external interference.

The most significant privilege is the right of freedom of speech and proceedings in Parliament, which effectively means that MPs and peers cannot be sued or prosecuted for anything they say in debates or proceedings.[87] Privilege also gives each House the freedom to control its own affairs (known as "exclusive cognisance") and freedom to control publication of its proceedings. As it applies to FOIA, this means that no external authority can interfere with Parliament's right to withhold information where that right is exercised on grounds of parliamentary privilege.[88]

Both the House of Commons and the House of Lords are public authorities for the purposes of FOIA (individual MPs and peers are not) and both have publication schemes. Information included in these publication schemes will be exempt under s.21. For the most part, the s.34 exemption will apply to information generated and held by the Commons or Lords which is unpublished, such as:

- committee reports and report drafts;

- memoranda submitted to committees, and draft memoranda;

- internal papers prepared by the Officers of either House directly related to the proceedings of the House or committees (including advice of all kinds to the Speaker or Lord Chancellor or other occupants of the Chair in either House, briefs for the chairmen and other members of committees, and informal notes of deliberative meetings of committees);

- papers prepared by the Libraries of either House, or by other House agencies such as the Parliamentary Office of Science and Technology, either for general dissemination to Members or to assist individual Members, which relate to, or anticipate, debates and other proceedings of the relevant House or its committees, and are intended to assist Members in preparation for such proceedings;

---

[86] Section 34 is an absolute exemption. It applies to the duty to communicate information and the duty to confirm or deny.

[87] Article 9 of the Bill of Rights 1689. This applies both to civil liability (*e.g.* for defamation) and criminal liability (*e.g.* for breach of the Official Secrets Act).

[88] Further information on Parliamentary privilege is available at *www.direct.gov.uk*. See also *Erskine May's Parliamentary Practice.*

- correspondence between Members, Officers, Ministers and Government officials directly related to House proceedings;

- papers relating to investigations by the Parliamentary Commissioner for Standards;

- papers relating to the Registers of Members' Interests;

- bills, amendments and motions, including those in draft, where they originate from Parliament or a Member rather than from Parliamentary counsel or another government department.

The Conclusive Certificate—section (3)

Section 34(3) gives the Speaker of the House of Commons and the Clerk   **1–171** of the Parliaments at the House of Lords the power to certify that exemption is necessary to avoid an infringement of privilege. Certification is conclusive evidence of exemption. There is no statutory appeal against a certificate, which is consistent with the principle that it is for Parliament to decide whether its privilege has been infringed.[89] There are no formalities required for a s.34(3) certificate but it would be good practice to specify which privilege would be infringed by disclosure and why.

The Information Commissioner's guidance states that evidence will not be required to establish that the appropriate official has issued a certificate, nor that certification was based on reasonable grounds or sound judgment. However, the Commissioner *will* be entitled to verify the existence and authenticity of the certificate. He will also be entitled to investigate complaints which arise under other parts of FOIA in relation to the request—such as fees, time limits and the provision of advice and assistance.[90]

As well as information generated and held by the Commons or Lords themselves, s.34 could extend to information held elsewhere (for example, by central government departments) if related to Parliamentary proceedings. If so, then the department concerned will need to consult with the appropriate House authorities before disclosing. Importantly, although it is open to a department to refuse disclosure on s.34 grounds, only the House authorities can conclusively certify the exemption (as permitted by s.34(3)). Since any person breaching privilege may be punished by Parliament, failure to apply the exemption where it is available may result in serious sanctions. Departments should normally therefore seek advice

---

[89] *Pepper v Hart* [1993] AC 593, 645, HL, where the House of Lords stated that "it is for the courts to decide whether a privilege exists and for Parliament to decide whether such a privilege has been infringed." This effectively means that while a .34(3) certificate may be conclusive evidence that a particular disclosure would infringe privilege, it would be open to the Commissioner to refuse to accept a certificate which purported to rely on a "new" privilege not previously recognised by the courts.

[90] Freedom of Information Awareness Guidance No.28: Parliamentary Privilege.

from the relevant officials to ensure that privilege is asserted (and duly certified) where it is proper to do so (for the House of Commons, the relevant official is the Speaker of the House, for the House of Lords, it is the Clerk of the Parliaments—each House asserts privilege over its own material). The Information Commissioner's guidance on s.34 recommends that authorities should contact the Freedom of Information Officer at the appropriate House to discuss the details of any request before relying on s.34.

1–172 Particular care should be taken with requests for information contained in:

- any of the unpublished working papers of a select committee of either House, including factual briefs or briefs of suggested questions prepared by the committee staff for the use of committee chairmen and/or other members, and draft reports (most likely to be held by a department where a Minister is or has been a member of such a committee);

- any legal advice submitted in confidence by the Law Officers or by the legal branch of any other department, to the Speaker, a committee chairman or a committee, or any official of either House;

- drafts of motions, bills or amendments which have not otherwise been published or laid on the Table of either House;

- any unpublished correspondence between Ministers or department officials on the one hand, and any member or official of either House on the other, relating specifically to proceedings on any Question, draft bill, motion or amendment, either in the relevant House or in a committee;

- any correspondence with or relating to the proceedings of the Parliamantary Commissioner for Standards or the Registrar of Members' Interests in the House of Commons;

- papers (including drafts) prepared by external special advisers and academics appointed for their specific expertise in a given area;

- papers prepared by the Libraries of either House at the request of an MP relating to constituency matters and expected to be the subject of a forthcoming debate or parliamentary committee.

Much information which is privileged is now routinely published by Parliament anyway, and this goes well beyond the record of proceedings. It includes internal administrative documents and even individual members' expenditure against parliamentary allowances. Information published in this way does not cease to be privileged (it remains Parliament's decision whether or not to continue publication) but disclosure of published information cannot be taken as "infringing" Parliamentary privilege in a way which would engage the s.34 exemption (although the information may be eligible for exemption under s.21, being reasonably accessible to the applicant other than under FOIA).

Note that s.34 is not intended to enable the withholding of information which would be disclosable but for its being contained in Parliamentary papers. So, while the draft of a memorandum responding to a select committee report may itself be privileged, factual information included in it may not be. Unless the factual information cannot be extracted without revealing what else is in the draft report, then the factual information would normally have to be disclosed.

There will also be a range of information which is not published by Parliament but which is also not related to Parliamentary proceedings. This will therefore not be protected by Parliamentary privilege. The best examples of this are:

1–173

- papers prepared by the Libraries of either House or other House agencies, intended to provide general or specific background information on matters not currently under examination or expected or planned to be considered in formal proceedings of either House or their committees;

- Members' correspondence and other communications not specifically related to proceedings of either House or of one of its formally constituted committees (correspondence between a Member and a Minister about a constituency issue that is not the subject of proceedings is not privileged, but correspondence about a draft motion, amendment or Question is privileged);

- the deliberations of parliamentary bodies established by statute (although if they are discussing matters relating to the preparation of formal proceedings in Parliament, those deliberations may well be privileged);

- meetings of political parties and other committees.

35 Formulation of government policy, etc

(1) **Information held by a government department or by the National Assembly for Wales is exempt information if it relates to—**

1–174

    (a) **the formulation or development of government policy,**

    (b) **Ministerial communications,**

    (c) **the provision of advice by any of the Law Officers or any request for the provision of such advice, or**

(d) the operation of any Ministerial private office.

(2) Once a decision as to government policy has been taken, any statistical information used to provide an informed background to the taking of the decision is not to be regarded—

    (a) for the purposes of subsection (1)(a), as relating to the formulation or development of government policy, or

    (b) for the purposes of subsection (1)(b), as relating to Ministerial communications.

(3) The duty to confirm or deny does not arise in relation to information which is (or if it were held by the public authority would be) exempt information by virtue of subsection (1).

(4) In making any determination required by section 2(1)(b) or (2)(b) in relation to information which is exempt information by virtue of subsection (1)(a), regard shall be had to the particular public interest in the disclosure of factual information which has been used, or is intended to be used, to provide an informed background to decision-taking.

(5) In this section—

        "government policy" includes the policy of the Executive Committee of the Northern Ireland Assembly and the policy of the National Assembly for Wales;

        "the Law Officers" means the Attorney General, the Solicitor General, the Advocate General for Scotland, the Lord Advocate, the Solicitor General for Scotland and the Attorney General for Northern Ireland;

        "Ministerial communications" means any communications—

        (a) between Ministers of the Crown,

        (b) between Northern Ireland Ministers, including Northern Ireland junior Ministers, or

        (c) between Assembly Secretaries, including the Assembly First Secretary,

        and includes, in particular, proceedings of the Cabinet or of any committee of the Cabinet, proceedings of the Executive Committee of the Northern Ireland Assembly, and proceedings of the executive committee of the National Assembly for Wales;

"Ministerial private office" means any part of a government department which provides personal administrative support to a Minister of the Crown, to a Northern Ireland Minister or a Northern Ireland junior Minister or any part of the administration of the National Assembly for Wales providing personal administrative support to the Assembly First Secretary or an Assembly Secretary;

"Northern Ireland junior Minister" means a member of the Northern Ireland Assembly appointed as a junior Minister under section 19 of the Northern Ireland Act 1998.

NOTES

Initial Commencement

Specified date

Specified date: 30 November 2005 (unless the Secretary of State by order appoints this section before that date): see s 87(3) (as amended by SI 2001/3500, art 8, Sch 2, Pt I, para 8(1)(o) and SI 2003/1887, art 9, Sch 2, para 12(1)(c)). (See appointment note below.)   1–175

Appointment

Appointment: 1 January 2005: see SI 2004/3122, art 2.

GENERAL NOTE[91]

The purpose of s.35 is to protect the internal deliberative process as it   1–176
relates to policy-making; in other words, to allow the government "private thinking space" where the threat of publication might otherwise compromise candid and robust discussions about policy. The exemption is intended to ensure that FOIA does not deter policy makers from full and proper deliberation where, for example, the prospect of disclosure might discourage the exploration of extreme options, the keeping of detailed records and the taking of hard choices, or where disclosure might prejudice good working relationships, the neutrality of civil servants and ultimately the quality of government.

---

[91] Section 35 is a qualified exemption. It applies to the duty to communicate information and the duty to confirm or deny.

The application of s.35 turns on whether the information in question "relates to" the categories listed under subs.(1). This means that it is broad enough to capture not only information which actually describes government policy or which is contained in documents which are actual ministerial communications, but also any information which simply refers to these. So, for example, information contained in papers discussing whether or not to seek the Law Officers' advice may be related to the provision of the advice itself, and a note of a meeting or a reference in correspondence to a conversation may include the record of the communication itself and therefore fall within the exemption.

Whether or not particular information is covered will be a question of fact, and certain information may fall into more than one category. Interestingly, whereas the title of s.35 is "Formulation of government policy etc.", only the first of the four categories of exempted information in s.35(1) actually refers to policy. The absence of this qualification in subss.(b), (c) and (d) means that they are considerably wider and will apply regardless of whether or not the information in each case relates to policy at all. That said, the content of information should not be overlooked because the content will invariably affect the balance of the public interest.

The commentary which follows considers each category in turn, with an analysis of the public interest considerations relating to each.

Formulation or development of government policy

1–177   Section 35(1)(a) has always been controversial. This is partly because it is expressed so widely but also because it applies even after a policy has finally been adopted. Section 35(2) alleviates matters slightly. In effect, "statistical information" used to provide an informed background to a policy decision emerges from the exemption once the decision has been taken. There is no definition of statistical information in FOIA itself, but there is a definition in Annex A to the Department for Constitutional Affairs Guidance on s.35. In any event, s.35(4) attempts to address potential difficulties separating statistics from facts by stating that authorities must consider disclosing factual information as well where the public interest allows.[92]

Meaning of government "policy"

1–178   "Policy" is not defined. According to the Information Commissioner, it will usually cover the development of options and priorities for Ministers who determine which options should be translated into political action, and when.[93]

---

[92] The government's intention is that factual information must be disclosed unless there is good reason not to do so: see Hansard HL, November 14, 2004, col. 156–7.
[93] Freedom of Information Awareness Guidance No.24: Policy Formulation, Ministerial Communications, Law Officers' Advice, and The Operation of Ministerial Private Office.

The Modernising Government White Paper[94] refers to policy as the process by which governments translate their political vision into programmes and actions, to deliver outcomes or desired changes in the real world.

Policy can be sourced and generated in various ways. For example, it may come from ministers' ideas and suggestions, manifesto commitments, significant incidents (such as a major outbreak of foot-and-mouth disease), EU policies or public concern expressed through letters, petitions and the like. Proposals and evidence for policies may come from external legal advisers, stakeholder consultation, or external researchers, as well as civil servants.

Importantly, policy is unlikely to include purely operational or administrative matters, or decisions about individuals. For instance, decisions about applications for licenses or grants are not likely to involve the formulation of policy, but rather its application. Similarly, in most cases, information about an individual's FOI application will not fall into the category of information relating to the formulation or development of policy.

"Government policy" is seen as distinct from departmental or other types of policy. This implies policy which has had Cabinet input or represents the collective view of ministers or which applies across government. It also implies some political process. Departmental policy will frequently be derived from and be identical to government policy, but where departmental policy applies only to the internal workings of the department it would not be caught (for example, departmental policy about working hours or estate management).

An example of government policy might be a policy to promote equality of opportunity by imposing a positive duty across the public sector. By contrast, policies developed in support of that policy by a department's personnel unit would not be 'government' policy but merely departmental policy.

Meaning of "formulation" and "development" of policy

These terms do not have precise meanings.   1–179

"Formulation" suggests the output from the early stages of the policy process, where options are generated and sorted, risks are identified, consultation occurs and recommendations and submissions are put to a minister.

"Development" is sometimes used interchangeably with "formulation", but also goes beyond it. It may refer to the processes involved in improving on or altering existing policy, for example through piloting, monitoring,

[94] Cm 4310, March 1999.

reviewing, analysing or recording the effects of existing policy. At the very least, "formulation and development" suggests something dynamic—in the sense that something must be happening to the policy. The exemption cannot apply to a finished product, or a policy which has been agreed, is in operation or has already been implemented.

The Information Commissioner's view is that the exemption can only apply where there is clear, specific and credible evidence that the formulation or development of government policy would be materially undermined by the threat of disclosure under FOIA.[95]

This sort of information will be found in a wide range of documents from officials' emails to Cabinet Committee papers. These will include such documents as submissions to Ministers, correspondence with other departments and public bodies in connection with policy development, minutes and proceedings of both Ministerial and officials' committees and internal departmental correspondence. Drafts of such documents are also likely to be covered, as well as ancillary documents such as e-mails discussing points arising on drafts. Of course, it is not the nature of the document which is determinative but the substance of the information contained within it.

Public interest considerations—Department for Constitutional Affairs Guidance[96]

1–180   The following questions may be relevant when assessing the application of the exemption:

- Would release of the information in this particular case make civil servants less likely to provide full and frank advice or opinions on policy proposals? (Would it, for example, prejudice working relationships by exposing dissenting views?)

- Would the prospect of future release inhibit consideration and debate of the full range of policy options (for example, if on reflection some of them seem extreme)?

- Would the prospect of release lead to civil servants defending everything that is or has been raised during deliberation (in anticipation, for example, of certain things later being discounted)?

- Would the possibility of future release deter the giving of advice which is ill-considered, vague, poorly prepared or written in unnecessarily brusque or defamatory language? Would the

---

[95] See Freedom of Information Awareness Guidance No.24: Policy Formulation, Ministerial Communications, Law Officers' Advice, and The Operation of Ministerial Private Office.

[96] See *www.foi.gov.uk/guidance/exguide/sec35/index.htm.*

prospect of release in fact enhance the quality of future advice? (If so, then this would weigh in favour of release.)

- Is the main reason for applying the exemption to spare a civil servant or minister embarrassment? (If so, then the exemption is not appropriate.)

Arguments in favour of applying the exemption might include:

- Maintaining the quality of government policy making by facilitating free and frank exchanges between civil servants and the thorough consideration of all policy options, however extreme, without inducing the need to defend them.

- Maintaining the quality of records, working relationships and a neutral civil service.

- The particular circumstances of the case indicate that public participation in the policy is inappropriate.

Arguments in favour of disclosure might include:

- public participation in the policy is appropriate (in the sense of permitting people to contribute to policy prior to a final decision). Note:

  - participation cannot be meaningful without access to relevant recorded information about how policy decisions are reached, what options are being considered and why some are excluded and others preferred;

  - without public participation in key policy decisions, certain individuals or groups will enjoy undue influence in the policy making process;

  - a key driver for freedom of information is to provide access to information which will facilitate informed participation in the development of government proposals or decisions which are of concern to them;

  - information disclosed prior to a decision being taken will facilitate more informed public debate.

- accountability for government decisions (*i.e.*, the need for government to explain why something has happened, or to demonstrate sufficient rigour in taking account of all relevant considerations, including addressing legitimate objections, or that it is keeping its word and delivering what it has promised). Note:

– disclosure of information is desirable where it may expose wrongdoing, the fact that wrongdoing has been dealt with or dispels suspicions of wrongdoing;

– access to information under FOIA may facilitate objective assessment, particularly where information obtained direct from the civil service (as opposed to government press offices) has not been spun;

– there will usually be a strong public interest in favour of disclosure where a policy decision is going to lead to large scale public expenditure;

– similarly, there will usually be a strong public interest in favour of disclosure where a policy decision involves departure from routine procedures or standard practice.

Subsection (4)—meaning of "factual information"

1–181   Subsection (4) applies to factual information relating to the formulation or development of government policy (but not the other categories in s.35(1)).

In contrast with the provision in subs.(2) relating to statistical information, subs.(4) refers to information "which is intended to be used" in providing an informed background to a decision, so there is no requirement that a decision must actually have been taken.

There is no definition of "factual information" within FOIA. Advice from officials to Ministers is not "factual", although that advice could and normally should be supported by evidence which may well be. Thus, a report submitted by an external body, or research commissioned by a government department may be factual information.

Poor quality or inaccurate factual information should be treated in the same way as any other factual information.

Any assessment that the public interest favours withholding information which could be classified as factual background information requires particularly clear evidence in support. If it is not in the public interest to release such information this is likely to be for one of two reasons:

• because the information is covered by another exemption as well as s.35(1)(a); or

• because the factual information is so closely associated with the advice that it forms part of the argument rather than simply the informed background to the decision. This may particularly be the case for information which pre-dates FOIA, when the distinction was less relevant. In the future, advice to Ministers should be constructed so that it is possible to identify clearly relevant background factual information.

Ministerial communications

There are a number of important points related to the definition in subs.(5): **1–182**

- It refers to "any communication". This means the exemption is not confined to formal correspondence (it will include records of telephone conversations, meetings and ministerial discussions), nor is it limited by the definition of information in s.84 (*i.e.* recorded information)—theoretically at least, it could cover communications which have never been recorded, and communications the records of which have been lost or destroyed.

- The term "between" indicates the exemption can only apply to communications between one Minister and another.

- Communications must be between Ministers of the Crown or between ministers of the same administration. Information relating to communications between a Minister of the Crown and ministers of devolved administrations are not exempt (though they may still qualify for exemption under s.28 (relations within the UK).

Because the exemption applies to information which "relates to" Ministerial communications, it applies not just to the content of communications but may also apply to information *about* the content. So, correspondence setting up a ministerial meeting or going over the matters to be discussed by Ministers may be exempt. Similarly, internal correspondence such as a submission to a Minister proposing that he writes in certain terms to a ministerial colleague would be covered, as would papers prepared for discussion at Cabinet.

As noted above, the exemption does not require that the communication relates to the formulation or development of policy. All communications are exempt, irrespective of their subject matter. However, communications between Ministers can only be exempt insofar as they are communications made in their ministerial capacity. The exemption will not cover private discussions of party matters or personal correspondence unconnected to ministerial duties.

Proceedings of the Cabinet or of any committee of the Cabinet

The reference to committees of Cabinet includes both standing committees and ad hoc committees. **1–183**

Proceedings of Cabinet and other meetings covered by s.35(1)(b) are not confined to the formal minutes of meetings, but include information relating to timing, agendas, memoranda and other tabled papers. Where a committee does much of its business by correspondence the correspondence of the committee is covered by s.35(1)(b) and may also be covered by s.35(1)(a).

Applying the public interest—Department for Constitutional Affairs Guidance[97] and Information Commissioner's Guidance[98]

1–184 Although the content of Ministerial communications does not affect its eligibility for exemption it may well have a significant bearing on the public interest for and against disclosure. The Commissioner's view is that authorities must apply the public interest robustly. Not all ministerial communications will cause harm if disclosed and information should not be withheld unless there is good reason to believe that harm would result. Passage of time may be critical, embarrassment will not be.

Considerations which may weigh in favour of a decision to disclose:

- ministers' decisions have a significant impact on the general public and there is therefore a public interest in their deliberations being transparent;

- it is no secret that there can be differences between ministers —disclosure would merely confirm that decisions are made after healthy debate.

Considerations which may weigh against a decision to disclose information:

- The maintenance of collective ministerial responsibility—ministers should be able to express their views frankly in the expectation that they can argue freely in private while maintaining a united front once decisions have been made. If the risk of subsequent disclosure acted to inhibit ministers' frankness and candidor in debate, then the quality of the debate underlying collective decisions would be diminished.

- Ultimate responsibility for government decisions lies with the Cabinet—collective responsibility seeks to ensure that decisions do not become personalised.

Meaning of "statistical information"—subsection (2)

1–185 In relation to ss.35(1)(a) and (b) (but not to subss.(c) and (d)), statistical information ceases to be exempt once a policy decision has been taken.

---

[97] *Ibid.*
[98] Freedom of Information Act Awareness Guidance No.24: Policy Formulation, Ministerial Communications, Law Officers' Advice, and The Operation of Ministerial Private Office.

There is no definition of statistical information in the Act but Annex A to the Department for Constitutional Affairs Guidance on s.35 defines statistical information as follows:

> *"Statistical information used to provide an informed background to government policy and decision making or in Ministerial communications will usually be founded upon the outcomes of mathematical operations performed on a sample of observations or some other factual information. The scientific study of facts and other observations allows descriptive approximations, estimates, summaries, projections, descriptions of relationships between observations, or outcomes of mathematical models, etc. to be derived.*
>
> *A distinguishing feature of statistical information is that it is founded to at least some degree on accepted scientific or mathematical principles. Statistical information is therefore distinguished by being i) derived from some recorded or repeatable methodology, and ii) qualified by some explicit or implied measures of quality, integrity, and relevance.*
>
> *This should not imply that the term 'statistical information' only applies where standards of methodology and relevant measures are particularly high. What distinguishes statistical information is that the limitations of the methodology, and the relevant measures of quality, etc., allow for a rational assessment of the validity of the information used as an informed background to the formulation and development of government policy.*
>
> *Departmental policy papers and Ministerial communications may contain headline statistical information, but are less likely to contain all the available methodology and qualifications that support the statistics, nor the underlying observations or facts from which the statistics are derived. Therefore it is good practice when producing such papers and communications to include a footnote or annex containing an outline of the statistical methodology, any available qualifications of quality, relevance and integrity, and the source of the underlying observations or facts. When the headline statistical information is disclosed to an applicant, the footnote or annex should be disclosed simultaneously."*

Even with the benefit of this guidance it is not entirely clear when such **1–186** information will emerge from the exemption because FOIA does not say when a "decision as to government policy" is taken. Clearly, a decision can be inferred once a public announcement of policy has been made, but there are other less clear-cut cases such as interim decisions, conditional or contingent decisions and decisions which are a small part of a wider policy issue, and unannounced or unrecorded decisions.

If a decision is an interim decision necessary to proceed to the next stage of the formulation of policy, then s.35 is likely to apply. A decision not to proceed with a policy which has been under consideration is equally a decision as to government policy.

The DCA guidance on this areas emphasises that applying the test of when a decision has been taken will require careful judgement. The general idea is that when the policy-making process has reached a point at which the statistical information essentially becomes a part of the historical explanation rather than a continuing and integral part of the policy-making itself, then the considerations which protect the policy-making process are separable from, and need no longer apply to, that statistical information. Section 35(2) focuses on statistical information used to provide an informed background to the taking of the decision, so once information can properly be assigned that background characteristic, then it ceases to be exempt under this part of s.35, but if it has a continuing integral rather than background role, then the exemption may continue to apply.

In these circumstances, it will be important for departments to be as clear as possible about their decision-making processes. If the nature of those decisions is properly identified and recorded at the time, decisions about the application of the provisions on background statistical information are likely to be much easier to take

The Law Officers' advice

1–187 While government departments have access to lawyers at the Government Legal Service, legal advice functions are also carried out by appointees who must either be an MP or a peer qualified as a solicitor or a barrister. These are the Law Officers defined in s.35(5).

Section 35(1)(c) covers "advice" and "any request for" advice relating to any aspect of government policy and operations. It is not limited to information which attracts legal professional privilege (on which see s.42), but information relating to the *functions* of the Law Officers (which is distinct from information relating to the provision of *advice*) is not covered (although it may fall under one of the other parts of s.35, or another exemption).

Functions of the Law Officers

1–188 The policy and operational functions of the Law Officers include:

- chief legal adviser to government (the Attorney General, Solicitor General and Advocate General for Scotland);

- chief legal adviser to the Scottish Executive (the Lord Advocate and the Solicitor General for Scotland);

- chief legal adviser to the UK Parliament (the Attorney General and Solicitor General);

- representing the public interest in litigation, in such matters as the administration of charities, family law cases, and contempt of court cases (the Attorney General, Solicitor General, Lord Advocate);

- consenting to prosecutions in certain types of cases, such as unduly lenient sentences, nolle prosequi cases, HM Revenue &

Customs cases (the Attorney General, Solicitor General, Lord Advocate and the Solicitor General for Scotland);

- each of the Law Officers exercises policy responsibilities, in particular in relation to the criminal justice system; and

- departmental responsibilities:

  - the Attorney General and Solicitor General are responsible for the Crown Prosecution Service, the Serious Fraud Office, the Treasury Solicitor, the Legal Secretariat to the Law Officers, the Crown Prosecution Services Inspectorate, and prosecutions by HM Revenue & Customs;

  - the Lord Advocate and the Solicitor General for Scotland are responsible for the Crown Office and Procurator Fiscal Service; and

  - each of them exercise devolution functions, such as questions on the competence of devolved legislation.

Meaning of "advice"

"Advice" could relate to any of the Law Officers' functions but is most likely to be given in their roles as legal advisers. In general:

- The exemption applies to both legal and non-legal advice given by the Law Officers to others, or requested from them.

- It will not normally apply to decisions taken by the Law Officers exercising their own functions, or the reasons for such decisions. Examples of these are decisions about whether to consent to a prosecution, commence contempt proceedings or refer a question on the competence of devolved legislation (see the list above). Each case should be examined carefully to determine whether advice formed part of the decision.

Applying the public interest—Department for Constitutional Affairs Guidance[99]

The following factors should be considered:

1–189

- Where the advice of the Law Officers is legal advice, the public interest considerations will normally be the same as for s.42[1] (although as noted above, s.35(1)(c) covers more than just information which is legally privileged).

---

[99] See *www.foi.gov.uk/guidance/exguide/sec35/index.htm.*
[1] See para.1–239 for commentary on the public interest considerations relevant to s.42.

- There is a long-standing convention, based on the principle that the government is entitled to frank and confidential legal advice (and now included in the Ministerial Code),[2] that the government does not disclose either the content of the Law Officers' advice nor even whether advice has been requested, without their authority. The argument for this is that if advice (or information relating to it) is revealed, future governments may feel inhibited about asking for advice on other matters and that may threaten properly informed policy making. Irrepsective of the merits of this argument, departments should normally consult the Law Officers before disclosing whether they have advised, or the advice itself.[3]

- It would be impossible for the Law Officers to advise on every aspect of government policy having legal implications, bearing in mind the enormous range of legal advice that government requires.

- At present, it is a matter for Ministers, Departments and the devolved administrations to decide whether to ask the Law Officers for advice. However, if the government routinely disclosed the occasions on which the Law Officers had given advice, then that could lead to questions about why they have not advised in other cases, and create political pressure for them to advise in cases where their involvement is not justified. This could in turn undermine their constitutional position as principal legal advisers who advise only on matters that ministers, Departments and the devolved administrations consider to be of particular significance. It could also undermine the position of Departmental legal advisers. This would not be conducive to the effective conduct of public affairs and given the impracticality of the law officers advising on everything, lead to poorer decision making.

Ministerial private offices

1–190 All government ministers have their own private office comprising a small team of civil servants who form the bridge between the minister and their department. The private office exists to provide administrative support so

---

[2] The Code is available at *www.cabinetoffice.gov.uk/propriety_and_ethics/ministers/ministerial_code/*.

[3] The Ministerial Code states that Ministers should consult the Law Officers in any case where the legal consequences of government action might have foreign or domestic repurcussions, where there is doubt concerning the legality of legislation, subordinate legislation or administrative action, where two or more departments are in disagreement on legal questions, or on any other matter raising particularly difficult legal issues. The last time advice was disclosed was in 1993 during the Maastricht controversy. The Attorney-General's advice to the Prime Minister on the legality of invading Iraq was the subject of numerous FOIA applications when the Act first came into force in January 2005. The government refused to disclose, but in the event the advice was leaked.

that the minister can concentrate on meetings, reading documents, weighing facts and advice, and making policy decisions.

Section 35(1)(d) only covers information relating to the "operation" of ministerial private offices. The Information Commissioner's view is that this should be interpreted quite narrowly to include only such practical matters as routine emails, and the *procedures* for handling ministerial papers, travel expenses, staffing, organisation and the like. So, for example, the process of the management of the minister's diary may be covered, but the entries themselves will not be. Information will not be exempt simply because it has passed through a ministerial office.

Information relating to a Minister's private affairs is not exempt under 35(1)(d) but may be exempt under s.40 (personal information).

It will be aparent that many aspects of the operation of ministerial offices has nothing to do with policy formulation, and in this sense it is strange that s.35(1)(d) exists at all. Some commentators have suggested that it reflects the fact that Ministers themselves are best placed to assess the affect of any disclosure. The Information Commissioner's guidance says that the exemption is concerned with circulation lists and whether the Minister has seen a document, initialled it and signed it off. The guidance states: "In this regard, the exemption reflects the convention that whilst advisers advise on policy matters, only a minister may decide and implement that policy. The purpose of the exemption is therefore to protect the anonymity of civil servants who may have drafted speaches or letters."

Applying the public interest—Department for Constitutional Affairs Guidance[4]

Considerations which may weigh in favour of a decision to disclose: **1–191**

- information caught by this exemption may demonstrate that ministers are complying with their duties under the Ministerial Code;

- the public interest in ensuring that private offices operate efficiently;

- the public interest in ensuring private offices are used appropriately.

Considerations which may weigh against a decision to disclose information include:

[4] See *www.foi.gov.uk/guidance/exguide/see 35/index.htm.*

- the fact that the private office is an important aspect of the space around ministers which needs to be protected so that good decision making is not threatened;

- ministers expect to receive advice from their private office about a range of matters that other officials are not able to give and such advice should not be inhibited by fear of publication.

Other related issues—Consultation, and the papers of previous administrations

Consultation

1–192 Given the wide range of s.35 there are potentially a large number of bodies that should be consulted. DCA guidance sets out the following general points:

- Requests for information relating to the formulation and development of policy should be referred to the department with lead responsibility for the policy.

- Requests for information which relates to communications between ministers should be referred to all the departments whose ministers were party to the communications.

- If the request relates to sensitive or significant information, or its release might create a precedent for Government, the DCA should be consulted.

- If the request relates to Cabinet or Cabinet committee proceedings, DCA will consult the Cabinet Office so that there can be a consistent approach to such requests across government.

- In the case of requests relating to the proceedings of the Executive Committee of the Northern Ireland Assembly, DCA will consult the Office of First Minister and Deputy First Minister (and, likewise, DCA will consult the National Assembly of Wales in relation to proceedings of its executive committee).

- Requests relating to the provision of advice by the Law Officers should be referred to the office of the relevant law officer.

- Where disclosure of the information would affect the interests of a third party, and it is possible to do so, the views of the third party should be sought to ensure that adequate consideration is given to those interests, and where relevant to avoid the effect disclosure may have on their future co-operation.

Duration of the Exemption; Papers of Previous Administrations

The public interest in withholding information under s.35 is likely to **1–193** diminish with the passage of time. In any event, the exemption falls away once a document or file is over 30 years old.[5]

There is a long-standing convention that governments are not permitted to see the papers of Ministers of previous administrations of a different political persuasion. The purpose of this is to give Ministers and their officials a secure space in which to develop and document their thinking on policy options. The convention guards against the risk of Ministers being subject to improper political attacks by their opponents in the future. Requests for papers of a previous administration (within the 30-year period) should therefore be considered on the same public interest principles as papers of the current administration. To ensure consistency, DCA recommends that such requests be referred to it for processing. Those cases requiring Ministerial intervention will be handled by the Attorney-General. The relevant former Minister should be consulted before a decision is made. As a general principle, the harm to the public interest from disclosure of such documents will need to be weighed with special care.[6]

36 Prejudice to effective conduct of public affairs

(1) This section applies to—   **1–194**

    (a) **information which is held by a government department or by the National Assembly for Wales and is not exempt information by virtue of section 35, and**

    (b) **information which is held by any other public authority.**

(2) **Information to which this section applies is exempt information if, in the reasonable opinion of a qualified person, disclosure of the information under this Act—**

    (a) **would, or would be likely to, prejudice—**

        (i) **the maintenance of the convention of the collective responsibility of Ministers of the Crown, or**

---

[5] See ss.62 and 63 in relation to historical records. It is of course possible that information contained in the classes of records covered by s.35 will be exempt for longer than 30 years under a different exemption. Accordingly, information in a Cabinet minute more than 30 years old cannot be exempt under s.35, but may for instance be exempt under s.27 if its disclosure would damage relations between the UK and another state.

[6] This convention was the subject of much debate after the Treasury released papers in February 2005 (only two months before a General Election) relating to the UK's exit from the Exchange Rate Mechanism under the Conservatives in 1992.

(ii) the work of the Executive Committee of the Northern Ireland Assembly, or

(iii) the work of the executive committee of the National Assembly for Wales,

(b) would, or would be likely to, inhibit—

(i) the free and frank provision of advice, or

(ii) the free and frank exchange of views for the purposes of deliberation, or

(c) would otherwise prejudice, or would be likely otherwise to prejudice, the effective conduct of public affairs.

(3) The duty to confirm or deny does not arise in relation to information to which this section applies (or would apply if held by the public authority) if, or to the extent that, in the reasonable opinion of a qualified person, compliance with section 1(1)(a) would, or would be likely to, have any of the effects mentioned in subsection (2).

(4) In relation to statistical information, subsections (2) and (3) shall have effect with the omission of the words "in the reasonable opinion of a qualified person".

(5) In subsections (2) and (3) "qualified person"—

(a) in relation to information held by a government department in the charge of a Minister of the Crown, means any Minister of the Crown,

(b) in relation to information held by a Northern Ireland department, means the Northern Ireland Minister in charge of the department,

(c) in relation to information held by any other government department, means the commissioners or other person in charge of that department,

(d) in relation to information held by the House of Commons, means the Speaker of that House,

(e) in relation to information held by the House of Lords, means the Clerk of the Parliaments,

(f) in relation to information held by the Northern Ireland Assembly, means the Presiding Officer,

(g) in relation to information held by the National Assembly for Wales, means the Assembly First Secretary,

(h) in relation to information held by any Welsh public authority other than the Auditor General for Wales, means—

    (i) the public authority, or

    (ii) any officer or employee of the authority authorised by the Assembly First Secretary,

(i) in relation to information held by the National Audit Office, means the Comptroller and Auditor General,

(j) in relation to information held by the Northern Ireland Audit Office, means the Comptroller and Auditor General for Northern Ireland,

(k) in relation to information held by the Auditor General for Wales, means the Auditor General for Wales,

(l) in relation to information held by any Northern Ireland public authority other than the Northern Ireland Audit Office, means—

    (i) the public authority, or

    (ii) any officer or employee of the authority authorised by the First Minister and deputy First Minister in Northern Ireland acting jointly,

(m) in relation to information held by the Greater London Authority, means the Mayor of London,

(n) in relation to information held by a functional body within the meaning of the Greater London Authority Act 1999, means the chairman of that functional body, and

(o) in relation to information held by any public authority not falling within any of paragraphs (a) to (n), means—

    (i) a Minister of the Crown,

    (ii) the public authority, if authorised for the purposes of this section by a Minister of the Crown, or

    (iii) any officer or employee of the public authority who is authorised for the purposes of this section by a Minister of the Crown.

(6) Any authorisation for the purposes of this section—

(a) may relate to a specified person or to persons falling within a specified class,

(b) may be general or limited to particular classes of case, and

(c) may be granted subject to conditions.

(7) A certificate signed by the qualified person referred to in subsection (5)(d) or (e) above certifying that in his reasonable opinion—

(a) disclosure of information held by either House of Parliament, or

(b) compliance with section 1(1)(a) by either House,

would, or would be likely to, have any of the effects mentioned in subsection (2) shall be conclusive evidence of that fact.

NOTES

Initial Commencement

Specified date

Specified date: 30 November 2005 (unless the Secretary of State by order appoints this section before that date): see s 87(3) (as amended by SI 2001/3500, art 8, Sch 2, Pt I, para 8(1)(o) and SI 2003/1887, art 9, Sch 2, para 12(1)(c)). (See appointment note below.)

Appointment

Appointment: 1 January 2005: see SI 2004/3122, art 2.

GENERAL NOTE[7]

1–195　Section 36 recognizes the critical role in effective government of free and frank discussion. However, s.36 can only apply in cases where the information in question is not exempt under s.35 (although the two may be claimed in the alternative). It is therefore likely that s.36 will tend to apply to areas which do not relate to policy—areas such as management, delivery and operations. As such, s.36 is broader than s.35 and is capable of applying to advice and discussion taking place below ministerial level.

---

[7] Section 36 is an absolute exemption insofar as it relates to information held by the House of Commons or the House of Lords. In all other respects it is a qualified exemption. In either case, it applies to the duty to communicate information and the duty to confirm or deny.

The fundamental difference between ss.35 and 36 is that the latter turns on the effects of disclosure rather than the nature of the information itself. In other words, s.36 can apply irrespective of what the information is, if disclosure "would, or would be likely to . . . *inhibit* the free and frank provision of advice . . . or the free and frank exchange of views for the purposes of deliberation . . . or would otherwise *prejudice*, or would be likely to prejudice, the effective conduct of public affairs" (author's italics).

Importantly, s.36 is contingent on "the reasonable opinion of a qualified person" which means that it can only apply with the authority of one of the officials listed in s.36(5). Section 36 must therefore be used with great deliberation.

Meaning of "reasonable opinion"

The Information Commissioner considers a reasonable opinion to be one   **1–196** which "lies within the bounds of reasonableness or range of reasonable opinions and can be verified by evidence. Any opinion which is not outrageous, or manifestly absurd or made with no evidence, or made on the basis of irrelevant factors or without consideration of all relevant factors, will satisfy such a test."[8]

Meaning of "collective responsibility of Ministers"

The collective responsibility of ministers is a long-standing constitutional   **1–197** convention now formalized in the Ministerial Code.[9] Collective responsibility means that ministers may express their views freely and frankly in ministerial meetings in the expectation that these will remain private, and thereafter maintain a united front when decisions have been reached.[10]

Meaning of "advice" and "exchange of views"

There is very little guidance on these points. "Advice" can be internal (*e.g.*   **1–198** by officials to ministers) or external (*e.g.* from third parties). It includes advice whether made by or to an authority. Any exchange of views is limited only by having to be "for the purposes of deliberation". This will include processes of decision making, opinion forming or evaluation, but is likely to exclude casual or trivial exchanges.

The term "inhibit" does not feature elsewhere in FOIA. It suggests a suppressive effect, *i.e.* where communications would be less likely to be

---

[8] Freedom of Information Act Awareness Guidance No.25: Effective Conduct of Public Affairs.
[9] The Code is available at *www.cabinetoffice.gov.uk/propriety_and_ethics/ministers/ministerial_code/*.
[10] Collective responsibility used to imply an obligation of confidentiality but this has been undermined in recent years by disclosures in former ministers' memoirs about Cabinet disagreements.

made, or would be made in a more reticent or circumscribed fashion, or would be less inclusive.

In considering what effect disclosure might have, it may be relevant to consider the following:

- Would it make it more likely that the person offering advice will be unwilling to do so in future?

- Would it inhibit that person from offering unwelcome advice?

- Would it make it more likely that the person being advised will not ask for advice in future?

- Would it have a similar inhibiting effect on other people in future?

- Would it make it more likely that advice will be given that is materially different because of the possibility of disclosure?

- Will it make people less likely to engage in discussion (whether oral or written) as part of the deliberative process?

- Would it distort or restrain that discussion?

- Would it result in pressure being brought to bear on officials to provide particular advice?

Meaning of "effective conduct of public affairs"

1–199 This provision deals with situations which fall outside the other specific circumstances covered by s.36. We have next to no guidance on it but, during debates on the Bill, Lord Falconer explained that it is intended to cover residual cases which cannot be foreseen, but where it is necessary to withhold information in the interests of good government. Because it is a broadly expressed residual exemption, a clear justification would have to be provided when seeking to rely on it (and it is also subject to Ministerial authorization). The Information Commissioner's view is that s.36(2)(c) will only be available in cases where disclosure would prejudice the authority's ability to offer an effective public service, or to meet its wider objectives or purpose (rather than simply to function) due to the disruption caused by the disclosure and the diversion of resources in managing the impact of the disclosure.

Statistical information

1–200 The authorisation of a qualified person is not necessary if the information requested is statistical.

In relation to *statistical* information, it will be exempt (without authorisation) if disclosure would prejudice:

(a) the free and frank provision of advice; or

(b) the free and frank exchange of views for the purposes of deliberation; or

(c) would otherwise prejudice the effective conduct of public affairs.

Statistical information incorporates analyses, projections and meta-data, as well as the statistics themselves—numerical data which may take the form of a table or graph or simply a sum total. Statistics must be derived from a recorded or repeatable methodology, and commentary on this is also statistical information.[11]

Note that in relation to information held by the House of Commons or House of Lords, s.36 is an absolute exemption (presumably for reasons of Parliamentary privilege).

37 Communications with Her Majesty, etc and honours

(1) Information is exempt information if it relates to—   1–201

    (a) communications with Her Majesty, with other members of the Royal Family or with the Royal Household, or

    (b) the conferring by the Crown of any honour or dignity.

(2) The duty to confirm or deny does not arise in relation to information which is (or if it were held by the public authority would be) exempt information by virtue of subsection (1).

NOTES

Initial Commencement

Specified date

Specified date: 30 November 2005 (unless the Secretary of State by order appoints this section before that date): see s 87(3) (as amended by SI 2001/3500, art 8, Sch 2, Pt I, para 8(1)(o) and SI 2003/1887, art 9, Sch 2, para 12(1)(c)). (See appointment note below.)

Appointment

Appointment: 1 January 2005: see SI 2004/3122, art 2.

---

[11] See Annex A to the Department for Constitutional Affairs Guidance on s.35 (*www.foi.gov.uk/guidance/exguide/sec35/index.htm*) for a comprehensive definition of statistical information.

GENERAL NOTE[12]

1-202   The Royal Household is not defined in FOIA but can be taken to mean those individuals who are authorised to act on behalf of a member of the Royal Family (such as their employees, agents and servants, and including members of the Private Offices of each of the Royal Family) in the carrying out of public, official and constitutional affairs.[13] Contractors who supply to the Royal Household (*e.g.* holders of Royal Warrants) do not form part of it. Certain members of the government Whips' offices in both Houses of Parliament are formally members of the Royal Household (senior government Whips in the Commons are designated the Treasurer and Comptroller of the Household; the Vice Chamberlain also serves as a Senior government Whip; Junior government Whips in the Lords are Lords and Baronesses in Waiting). The activities of these individuals as government Whips are not covered by s.37.

Because the exemption applies to information which "relates to" the matters in subss.(a) and (b) it will cover notes of meetings between public authority officials and a member of the Royal Household as well as letters and other documents.

Information Commissioner's Guidance[14]

1-203   A number of factors may influence the assessment of the public interest in the context of s.37(1)(a):

- the Queen's constitutional position, and the fact she holds office for life, may mean that views expressed by her relating to government policy or individuals may remain sensitive even after the policy has been implemented or the individual has moved on;

- the timing of a request may be significant, for example where a request relates to royal visits which have not yet taken place.

However, any assessment of the public interest should not take account of the status of the member of the Royal Family concerned.

Note that the exemption can also apply to information even after the death of a member of the Royal Family.

In certain cases it may be important to consider the distinction between the public and private roles and functions of the Royal Family. Requests for

---

[12] Section 37 is a qualified exemption. It applies to the duty to communicate information and the duty to confirm or deny.

[13] See *www.royal.gov.uk* for further information about the Royal Family and the Royal Household.

[14] Freedom of Information Guidance No.26: Communications with Her Majesty and the Awarding of Honours.

information relating to private matters may be subject to the exemption for personal information under s.40. Article 8 of the Human Rights Act 1998 (respect for family and private life) may also be relevant.

Honours and dignities

Section 37(1)(b) only relates to honours conferred by the Crown so it cannot exempt honours bestowed by any other institution.   **1–204**

Some examples of the kind of honours and dignities which may be subject to the exemption are:

- honours comprising the various Orders of Knighthood;

- Appointment of Knights Bachelor;

- Military medals and decorations;

- Gallantry awards;

- Foreign or international awards where the Queen's permission is required or sought to accept and wear them;

- Creation of life peers;

- Creation of hereditary titles;

- Appointment as Lords and Vice Lords Lieutenant;

- Appointment of Governor-Generals, Governors and Lieutenant-Governors;

- Appointments to the Privy Council.

38 Health and safety

(1) **Information is exempt information if its disclosure under**   **1–205**
this Act would, or would be likely to—

(a) **endanger the physical or mental health of any individual, or**

(b) **endanger the safety of any individual.**

(2) **The duty to confirm or deny does not arise if, or to the extent that, compliance with section 1(1)(a) would, or would be likely to, have either of the effects mentioned in subsection (1).**

NOTES

Initial Commencement

Specified date

Specified date: 30 November 2005 (unless the Secretary of State by order appoints this section before that date): see s 87(3) (as amended by SI 2001/3500, art 8, Sch 2, Pt I, para 8(1)(o) and SI 2003/1887, art 9, Sch 2, para 12(1)(c)). (See appointment note below.)

Appointment

Appointment: 1 January 2005: see SI 2004/3122, art 2.

GENERAL NOTE[15]

1–206   The purpose of s.38 will be self-evident. Note that it refers to "any" individual, so it is not limited to the applicant or the supplier of the information.

"Endanger" in subs.(1) connotes risk of harm rather than harm itself. The Information Commissioner has said that he does not consider the use of "endanger" rather than "prejudice" to be a departure from the test of prejudice applying to other exemptions.

The following are examples of disclosures with the potential for the kind of risk to which this exemption applies:

- those which would allow individuals, groups or firms to be identified or located and consequently targeted and attacked for their beliefs or practices, including work in controversial scientific areas;

- disclosure of plans and policies relating to the accommodation of individuals, or groups of individuals, where disclosure could lead to their being threatened or harassed (*e.g.* asylum seekers);

- disclosing information about negotiations with kidnappers, where disclosure could endanger the safety of hostages;

- the disclosure of sensitive or graphic information about deceased individuals which could cause serious distress to particular individuals such as family members if disclosed, particularly if they were not previously aware of it.

Information relating to health and safety may very often be environmental information within the meaning of the Environmental Information Regulations. If such information is environmental information, then s.39

---

[15] Section 38 is a qualified exemption. It applies to the duty to communicate information and the duty to confirm or deny.

will be the appropriate exemption and the request should be considered under the Environmental Information Regulations.

In a series of Decision Notices relating to the location of speed cameras, the Commissioner refused to enforce disclosure on the basis that "the value of improving public awareness and the opportunity disclosure would bring to further the debate on the effectiveness and purpose of speed cameras [did not] outweigh the public interest in . . . avoiding . . . the likely increased risk to the health and safety of the public."[16]

Department for Constitutional Affairs Guidance[17]

It is never in the public interest to endanger the health and safety of any individual. However, more generally, details to be considered will include: **1–207**

- the size of the risk involved, the likelihood of the outcome in question, and the extent to which steps might be taken to reduce or manage that risk;

- the nature and seriousness of the resulting outcome if the risk was to come about;

- the possibility that disclosure would help to protect the health or safety of other individuals;

- the possibility that the anticipated danger could be prevented or managed by other reasonable precautions.

There is a public interest in disclosing information in order to reduce the potential danger to people and to increase their personal freedom by making them aware of various risks and enabling them to take appropriate action. If the recommendations and information supplied by departments with specific responsibilities to inform the public of health and safety issues are to be trusted and acted upon, this may be enhanced by a high level of disclosure.

Other statutes and policies

There may be legal prohibitions on disclosing information which would endanger an individual's health or safety. The most relevant examples include the Rehabilitation of Offenders Act 1974 and s.28 of the Health and Safety at Work Act 1974. It is important to be alert to the possibility of such information being environmental information within the meaning of   **1–208**

---

[16] See Decision Notices FS50068601 (August 3, 2005) and FS50067279 and FS50068017 (both August 2, 2005).
[17] See *www.foi.gov.uk/guidance/exguide/sec38/index.htm.*

the Environmental Information Regulations, in which case, exemption from FOIA under s.39 is the necessary route.

39 Environmental information

1–209

(1) Information is exempt information if the public authority holding it—

    (a) is obliged by [environmental information regulations] to make the information available to the public in accordance with the regulations, or

    (b) would be so obliged but for any exemption contained in the regulations.

[(1A) In subsection (1) "environmental information regulations" means—

    (a) regulations made under section 74, or

    (b) regulations made under section 2(2) of the European Communities Act 1972 for the purpose of implementing any Community obligation relating to public access to, and the dissemination of, information on the environment.]

(2) The duty to confirm or deny does not arise in relation to information which is (or if it were held by the public authority would be) exempt information by virtue of subsection (1).

(3) Subsection (1)(a) does not limit the generality of section 21(1).

NOTES

1–210   **Initial Commencement**

Specified date

Specified date: 30 November 2005 (unless the Secretary of State by order appoints this section before that date): see s 87(3) (as amended by SI 2001/3500, art 8, Sch 2, Pt I, para 8(1)(o) and SI 2003/1887, art 9, Sch 2, para 12(1)(c)). (See appointment note below.)

Appointment

Appointment: 1 January 2005: see SI 2004/3122, art 2.

Amendment

Sub-s (1A): inserted by SI 2004/3391, reg 20(1), (3).
    Date in force: 1 January 2005: see SI 2004/3391, reg 1.

GENERAL NOTE[18]

Section 39 exempts information which an authority is obliged to make 1–211
available in accordance with the Environmental Information Regulations
2004 ("**EIRs**"), or would be obliged to make available but for an
exemption in those Regulations.

The duty to confirm or deny does not apply to information which is exempt
under s.39.

In essence, information which falls within the EIRs must be processed in
accordance with those Regulations. The public interest test is applied by
the Regulations in the same was as it applies under FOIA.

The EIRs are dealt with in full in Ch.2.

40 Personal information

(1) Any information to which a request for information 1–212
relates is exempt information if it constitutes personal
data of which the applicant is the data subject.

(2) Any information to which a request for information
relates is also exempt information if—

(a) it constitutes personal data which do not fall within
subsection (1), and

(b) either the first or the second condition below is
satisfied.

(3) The first condition is—

(a) in a case where the information falls within any of
paragraphs (a) to (d) of the definition of "data" in
section 1(1) of the Data Protection Act 1998, that the
disclosure of the information to a member of the
public otherwise than under this Act would
contravene—

(i) any of the data protection principles, or

(ii) section 10 of that Act (right to prevent
processing likely to cause damage or distress),
and

(b) in any other case, that the disclosure of the
information to a member of the public otherwise than
under this Act would contravene any of the data

---

[18] Section 39 is a qualified exemption. It applies to the duty to communicate information and
the duty to confirm or deny.

protection principles if the exemptions in section 33A(1) of the Data Protection Act 1998 (which relate to manual data held by public authorities) were disregarded.

(4) The second condition is that by virtue of any provision of Part IV of the Data Protection Act 1998 the information is exempt from section 7(1)(c) of that Act (data subject's right of access to personal data).

(5) The duty to confirm or deny—

(a) does not arise in relation to information which is (or if it were held by the public authority would be) exempt information by virtue of subsection (1), and

(b) does not arise in relation to other information if or to the extent that either—

(i) the giving to a member of the public of the confirmation or denial that would have to be given to comply with section 1(1)(a) would (apart from this Act) contravene any of the data protection principles or section 10 of the Data Protection Act 1998 or would do so if the exemptions in section 33A(1) of that Act were disregarded, or

(ii) by virtue of any provision of Part IV of the Data Protection Act 1998 the information is exempt from section 7(1)(a) of that Act (data subject's right to be informed whether personal data being processed).

(6) In determining for the purposes of this section whether anything done before 24th October 2007 would contravene any of the data protection principles, the exemptions in Part III of Schedule 8 to the Data Protection Act 1998 shall be disregarded.

(7) In this section—

"the data protection principles" means the principles set out in Part I of Schedule 1 to the Data Protection Act 1998, as read subject to Part II of that Schedule and section 27(1) of that Act;

"data subject" has the same meaning as in section 1(1) of that Act;

"personal data" has the same meaning as in section 1(1) of that Act.

NOTES

Initial Commencement

Specified date

Specified date: 30 November 2005 (unless the Secretary of State by order appoints this section before that date): see s 87(3) (as amended by SI 2001/3500, art 8, Sch 2, Pt I, para 8(1)(o) and SI 2003/1887, art 9, Sch 2, para 12(1)(c)). (See appointment note below.)

Appointment

Appointment: 1 January 2005: see SI 2004/3122, art 2.

GENERAL NOTE[19]

An understanding of s.40 is impossible without a basic understanding of the Data Protection Act 1998 ("**DPA**"). A detailed explanation of the DPA is outside the scope of this book but, in summary, it regulates the processing of information which identifies living individuals (such information being known as "personal data"). All processing of personal data must comply with eight data protection "principles" which are designed to ensure that data is collected, stored and used fairly and in a manner consistent with the DPA rules. Individuals who are the subject of personal data are known as "data subjects".

In so far as it applies to public authorities, FOIA now extends the meaning of personal data to include unstructured manual files. This category of data is known as "category (e)" data, because it appears in the DPA under a new s.1(1)(e). Previously, the DPA only covered electronic records, and manual records held in filing systems which were structured in a way which enabled a user to find the personal data held therein without flicking through the pages.[20] The DPA still applies in this way to manual records held by organisations in the private sector.

In relation to FOIA, the rules for dealing with requests for personal data depend on who is making the request—*i.e.* whether the requestor is the data subject him or herself, or a third party. There are also special rules in FOIA dealing with costs, designed to reduce the administrative burden which requests for information are likely to place on public authorities. See ss.9, 12 and 13 in relation to costs.

---

[19] Section 40 is an absolute exemption, except where s.40(2) applies because disclosure would contravene a notice given under s.10 of the Data Protection Act 1998 (*i.e.* disclosure would, or would be likely to, cause damage or distress). In such a case the exemption is qualified. In either case, it applies to the duty to communicate information and the duty to confirm or deny.

[20] Note that s.70 of FOIA introduces a new s.33A into the DPA which exempts category (e) data from much of the DPA.

Subject Access Requests—*i.e.* requests made by the data subject him or herself

1–215   Subject access requests are absolutely exempt from FOIA because they are covered by the regime in s.7 of the DPA. Section 40 exists to ensure that the FOIA regime does not duplicate or cut across the access regime under the DPA. Any request for personal data made by the data subject him or herself should therefore be treated as a subject access request under s.7 of the DPA (although note that public authorities' obligations under s.7 of the DPA will now also apply to unstructured manual files). The duty to confirm or deny also does not apply to such information.

Requests for personal data by third parties

1–216   These requests *do* fall within the FOIA regime, but the obligations vary. In a nutshell, information which is protected from disclosure under the DPA cannot be obtained using FOIA.

Section 40(2) provides that personal data requested under FOIA by someone other than the data subject him or herself is exempt where either of two conditions apply, set out in ss.40(3) and 40(4). The duty to confirm or deny is also excluded if either of these conditions apply.

Section 40(3)—the First Condition

1–217   Personal data is exempt where disclosure would contravene:

- any of the data protection principles; or

- in the case of all data except category (e) data, the right under s.10 of the DPA to prevent processing likely to cause damage or distress.

The First Condition effectively requires authorities to ask whether the release of someone's personal data to a third party would be fair, bearing in mind the purposes for which the data was originally obtained and the authority's relationship with the data subject (for example, information relating to an individual's public life may be less likely to be exempt than information relating to their private life).

When dealing with requests for personal data, authorities should always bear in mind the confidential information exemption under s.41. This may apply to data subjects' salary or disciplinary records. Authorities should also bear in mind that where personal data can be redacted this will usually mean that other information contained in the document must be disclosed.

Section 40(4)—the Second Condition

1–218   Personal data is exempt from FOIA disclosure if any of the DPA exemptions to subject access apply (DPA, ss.27–39).

The Information Commissioner's Guidance[21]

The Commissioner's guidance sets out some factors to consider when   **1–219**
assessing whether to disclose under s.40:

- Would disclosure cause unnecessary or unjustified distress or damage to the person who the information is about?

- Would the individual expect that his or her information might be disclosed to others?

- Has the person been led to believe that his information will be kept secret?

- Has the individual expressly refused consent to disclosure?

In thinking about whether it is fair and lawful to disclose, one factor may be whether the information relates to the private or public life of the individual. Information about a person's home or family life or their personal finances will deserve much greater protection than information about someone in their official capacity. On this basis, information about officials' names, grades, job functions and decisions should normally be disclosed, as should expenses incurred on official business and, in the case of senior staff, salary details.[22]

Status of the section 40 exemption

Section 40 is an absolute exemption except where s.40(2) applies because   **1–220**
disclosure would contravene a notice given under s.10 of the DPA (*i.e.*
disclosure would be likely to cause damage or distress). In such a case, exemption is subject to the public interest.

41 Information provided in confidence

    (1) Information is exempt information if—   **1–221**

        (a) it was obtained by the public authority from any other person (including another public authority), and

---

[21] Freedom of Information Awareness Guidance No 1: Personal Information. See also Freedom of Information: access to information about public authorities' employees.

[22] There has been one complaint brought before the Commissioner on this point. It concerned a request for details of the full qualifications, experience and duties of each member of the Northern Ireland Department of Finance and Personnel's Web Design Team by grade. The Department withheld information about the full qualifications and experience of each individual, citing s.40(2) on the basis that it was personal information and its disclosure would breach the provisions of the Data Protection Act 1998. The Commissioner agreed: "in that [the information withheld] could be linked to identifiable individuals". Decision Notice FS50063659, July 12, 2005.

(b) the disclosure of the information to the public (otherwise than under this Act) by the public authority holding it would constitute a breach of confidence actionable by that or any other person.

(2) The duty to confirm or deny does not arise if, or to the extent that, the confirmation or denial that would have to be given to comply with section 1(1)(a) would (apart from this Act) constitute an actionable breach of confidence.

NOTES

Initial Commencement

Specified date

Specified date: 30 November 2005 (unless the Secretary of State by order appoints this section before that date): see s 87(3) (as amended by SI 2001/3500, art 8, Sch 2, Pt I, para 8(1)(o) and SI 2003/1887, art 9, Sch 2, para 12(1)(c)). (See appointment note below.)

Appointment

Appointment: 1 January 2005: see SI 2004/3122, art 2.

GENERAL NOTE[23]

1–222 Information which a public authority obtained from outside the organisation (including from another public authority) is exempt from disclosure if disclosure would be an "actionable" breach of confidence. Public authorities are also not obliged to confirm or deny possession of confidential information to the extent that this would in itself be an actionable breach of confidence.

Importantly, the exemption cannot apply to an authority's own confidential information (although it can still apply to information which is confidential to an authority's officers and staff) because s.41 refers to information "obtained by the public authority *from another person*" (author's italics). Further, although government departments are treated as separate entities for FOIA purposes,[24] a government department is unlikely to be able to claim s.41 exemption on the grounds that disclosure of information would be actionable by another government department—for the sensible reason that the government cannot sue itself. The same applies between Northern Ireland departments, although not between a Northern Ireland department and a UK department.

---

[23] Section 41 is an absolute exemption. It applies to the duty to communicate information and the duty to confirm or deny.
[24] Freedom of Information Act 2000, s.81.

Meaning of "breach of confidence"

The legal rules which define confidentiality have developed considerably in   **1–223**
recent years. In essence, information can only be confidential if:

(a) it has the necessary "quality of confidence" about it (*i.e.* the information is worthy of protection and is not trivial); *and*

(b) it was imparted in circumstances importing an obligation of confidence, or the receiving/acquiring party ought reasonably to know that it is confidential (information which is generally accessible or in the public domain will not be confidential); *and*

(c) disclosure of it would be detrimental to the party wishing to keep it confidential.[25]

Even if these conditions are met, an action for breach of confidence will fail (and therefore the exemption will not apply) if disclosure is in the public interest. This is known as the "public interest defence" to an action for breach of confidence and derives from common law, not FOIA.[26] So, although the FOIA exemption for information provided in confidence is absolute (*i.e.* not subject to a public interest test), if a public authority judges that a breach of confidence will not be actionable because the authority has a public interest defence to a claim in the courts, then the authority would normally have to disclose that information notwithstanding its confidentiality.[27] Further, whereas in the past the public interest has tended only to protect necessary disclosures to an appropriate recipient (such as the police or a regulatory authority) rather than the public at large,[28] decisions on the public interest under FOIA must be made on the assumption that the public now have a general right of access to information.[29]

---

[25] *Coco v AN Clark (Engineers) Ltd* [1969] RPC 41; *Attorney-General v Guardian Newspapers (No. 2)* [1990] 1 AC 109; *Hellewell v Chief Constable of Derbyshire* [1995] 1 WLR 804; *Campbell v MGN Ltd* [2004] 2 WLR 1232, HL.

[26] So, for example, a person seeking to enforce an obligation of confidence will not be able to do so where the information reveals some form of iniquity (see *Garside v Outram* [1856] 26 LJ Ch 113) or where there is some other just cause or excuse for disclosing the information (see *Lion Laboratories v Evans* [1984] 2 All ER 417).

[27] This effectively mirror's the court's own task in matters of confidentiality, namely: to balance the public interest in maintaining an obligation of confidence with the public interest in disclosing: *X v Y* [1988] 2 All ER 417.

[28] *Attorney-General v Guardian Newspapers (No.2)* [1990] 1 AC 109, per Lord Griffiths.

[29] Recent jurisprudence on media intrusion into the private lives of celebrities indicates that the courts decide issues of confidentiality very much on their particular facts. In *Campbell v MGN Ltd* [2004] 2 WLR 1232, HL and *Von Hannover v Germany* [2005] 40 E.H.R.R. 1 the courts narrowed the circumstances in which confidential information could be published, basing their decision on a test of whether the information contributed to a debate of general interest.

Meaning of "actionable"

1-224 FOIA does not say what might qualify as an "actionable" breach for the purposes of s.41. It is likely that "actionable" requires a claimant to have a fairly good case which will not fall apart on initial examination.

Confidential information in practice

1-225 Information with commercial value which is not easily available from other sources may be confidential, as may information which an individual would consider confidential (*e.g.* a staff appraisal or salary details).

Three important factors must be assessed whenever a public authority is applying s.41:

- whether or not information is protected by confidentiality will depend largely on the circumstances in which it was obtained and whether, at the time, the authority expressly agreed to keep it confidential (there are guidelines in the Section 45 Code of Practice (see below) on when an authority should agree to confidentiality restrictions);

- special considerations apply if the information in question is personal data (see s.40); and

- if information is disclosed in breach of a duty of confidence, then the authority may be liable to a claim for damages; if, on the other hand, information is withheld when it should be disclosed, sanctions under FOIA may apply. The application of s.41 must therefore be approached with care, and legal advice sought where appropriate.

Even if information *is* confidential, it can be lawfully disclosed with the consent of the person to whom the confidence is owed.

Document designations and protective markings

1-226 Government departments routinely make use of a standardised system of protective markings: Restricted, Confidential, Secret and Top Secret.[30] FOIA does not affect this system and authorities are free to continue classifying documents according to current rules and procedures (although it is highly recommended that all protective markings are accompanied by a date, a period of time for which the marking is anticipated to be relevant and any other information which might assist a FOIA assessment in the future. Authorities would also be well advised to review key documents to ensure that designations are correct).

---

[30] For an explanation of the different designations, see the Cabinet Office Manual of Protective Security.

At the same time, designations on documents will not in themselves mean that information is protected from FOIA disclosure. A document may have been marked confidential because it was sensitive at the time of creation, but this does not mean that such sensitivity still exists. There is also a tendency to put designations on anything which might conceivably be sensitive, or to use blanket designations without distinguishing between those sections of a document which merit protection and those which do not.

As a rule, protective markings mean that one or more FOIA exemptions should be considered, subject to checking that the classification is still current. Note, however, that FOIA may override a designation and authorities should therefore not follow them slavishly.

The Section 45 Code of Practice

The overriding purpose of freedom of information is to ensure openness   1–227
and transparency in the public sector. Sweeping confidentiality restrictions on information held by public authorities are incompatible with this principle. The Section 45 Code of Practice sets out guidance on when public authorities should accept information in confidence, and also on when to consult third parties where an authority plans to disclose their confidential information.

In relation to information provided to a public authority by a third party:

- the public authority should only accept information "in confidence" where possession of the information is necessary in connection with the authority's functions and where it would not otherwise be provided;

- the public authority should not agree to hold information "in confidence" unless the information is genuinely confidential; and

- the public authority should only agree to written confidentiality restrictions where these are capable of justification to the Information Commissioner.

The Section 45 Code does not have the legal force of FOIA itself. Nevertheless, the Information Commissioner has a duty to promote its observance and a legitimate expectation that authorities will comply with it. The courts will also normally refer to the Code when determining any question of compliance.

Here are some useful pointers when considering whether to agree to hold information in confidence:

- consider the nature of the interest to be protected and whether it is really necessary to hold information in confidence to protect that interest;

- consider whether it is possible to agree a limited duty of confidentiality, for example by clearly stating the circumstances in which the authority would disclose information;

- if the information will only be provided on condition that it is kept confidential, how important is the information in relation to the authority's functions?

- consider the nature of the person from whom the information is to be obtained and whether that person is also a public authority to whom FOIA and the Section 45 Code applies (departments must be particularly cautious about agreeing to keep information confidential where the supplier of the information is also a public authority).

1–228   The Section 45 Code also deals with consultation with third parties where an authority cannot disclose third party material without risking a breach of confidence. The Code says that:

- where disclosure cannot be made without consent (*e.g.* because this would in itself be a breach of confidence) the authority should consult the third party with a view to getting their consent to disclose, unless this is not practicable (for example because the third party cannot be located or because the costs of consulting would be disproportionate);

- if the authority believes the cost of consulting to be disproportionate, then it should consider what is the reasonable course of action in light of the requirements of FOIA and the circumstances of the request.

In essence, if an authority has consent to disclose, then it will not be able to rely on s.41. If the authority notifies a third party of its intention to disclose and they object, the authority may still disclose if it chooses, and the third party can only prevent disclosure by injunction (there is no statutory mechanism within FOIA for the third party to prevent disclosure). If the authority discloses without consulting at all, then the third party will have no redress under FOIA. The only remedy would be a claim against the authority for damages (with all the difficulties that entails of quantifying loss), perhaps with an injunction to prevent further disclosure.

The public interest defence to breach of confidence

1–229   When considering the application of s.41, an authority must assess whether a public interest defence to a claim exists. If so, then the exemption cannot apply. The following principles should be applied when assessing the likelihood and force of a public interest defence:

- where a duty of confidence exists, there is a general public interest in favour of keeping that confidence;

- there is no general public interest in the disclosure of confidential information in breach of a duty of confidence—in other words, for a public interest defence to arise, there must be a specific factor in favour of disclosure;

- there is a public interest in ensuring public scrutiny of the activities of public authorities, so, if disclosure would enhance this scrutiny, this will weigh in favour of disclosure; examples might be:

  - information revealing misconduct or mismanagement of public funds;

  - information demonstrating that a public contract is not providing value for money;

  - information which would correct untrue statements or misleading acts by an authority;

- on the other hand, where the interests of a private person (whether an individual or an organisation) are protected by a duty of confidence, the public interest in scrutiny of public authority information is unlikely to override that duty (although this will be less compelling where a substantial period of time has passed since the information was obtained, as a result of which the harm which may be caused by disclosure has diminished);

- FOIA itself has no influence on the nature of any public interest which attaches to the disclosure of information—so the fact that FOIA might require disclosure were it not for s.41 is irrelevant;

- public authorities must have regard to the interests of the person to whom the duty of confidence is owed, but the authority's own interests are not relevant;

- the identity of the person requesting the information and the reason for the request are both irrelevant—the question is not whether disclosure to the applicant would be a breach of confidence, but whether disclosure "to the public" would be a breach (a request from a journalist or pressure group must be treated in the same way as a request from a person who is conducting historical research).

There is unlikely to be a public interest defence in cases where:

- the duty of confidence arises from a professional relationship;

- disclosure would affect the continued supply of important information (*e.g.* information from whistleblowers); or

157

- disclosure would involve some risk to public administration or public or personal safety.

42 Legal professional privilege

1–230

(1) **Information in respect of which a claim to legal professional privilege or, in Scotland, to confidentiality of communications could be maintained in legal proceedings is exempt information.**

(2) **The duty to confirm or deny does not arise if, or to the extent that, compliance with section 1(1)(a) would involve the disclosure of any information (whether or not already recorded) in respect of which such a claim could be maintained in legal proceedings.**

NOTES

Initial Commencement

Specified date

Specified date: 30 November 2005 (unless the Secretary of State by order appoints this section before that date): see s 87(3) (as amended by SI 2001/3500, art 8, Sch 2, Pt I, para 8(1)(o) and SI 2003/1887, art 9, Sch 2, para 12(1)(c)). (See appointment note below.)

Appointment

Appointment: 1 January 2005: see SI 2004/3122, art 2.

GENERAL NOTE[31]

1–231 Legal professional privilege ("**LPP**") protects material from disclosure on the ground that a client must be sure that what he and his lawyer discuss in confidence will not be disclosed to third parties without his consent. LPP is a creature of common law rather than statute and so s.42 is necessary to ensure that FOIA does not cut across the common law rules.

In any situation where an individual in their personal capacity instructs a solicitor for the purpose of legal advice, the existence of LPP will be a relatively straightforward matter. In other contexts, however, the application of LPP has been significantly undermined following a Court of Appeal decision in *Three Rivers DC v The Governor and Company of the Bank of England*[32] ("**Three Rivers**"). Widely criticised as artificial and impractical, it is fair to say the ramifications of the ruling have yet to be fully

---

[31] Section 42 is a qualified exemption. It applies to the duty to communicate information and (subject to the wording of s.42(2)) the duty to confirm or deny.

[32] CA [2003] EWCA Civ 474.

worked out. We are therefore in a state of considerable uncertainty. This is exacerbated by FOIA's imposition of a public interest test in relation to LPP. Pre-January 1, 2005, LPP applied to information in perpetuity. Under FOIA, the duration of the LPP exemption will be subject to the public interest, which as a rule will tend to favour disclosure as time goes on.[33] This is another significant shift in the application of a previously settled legal principle.

As a result of these changes, there are likely to be documents to which authorities would expect LPP to apply, but which are not in fact protected. Further, there may be documents to which LPP did apply at the time the document was produced, but to which privilege has now ceased to apply. In both cases, information which an authority would wish and expect to be FOIA exempt will not be exempt under s.42.

It is absolutely essential to understand how LPP works before attempting to apply the s.42 FOIA exemption on the basis of it. The recent developments in the scope of LPP necessitate a more detailed examination of the general legal principles than would otherwise be appropriate. If in doubt, authorities should always seek professional legal assistance.

LPP is divided into two categories: legal advice privilege and litigation privilege.

Legal Advice Privilege

A communication is protected by legal advice privilege if it is made: **1–232**

 (a) confidentially; and

 (b) between a client and his/her lawyer; and

 (c) for the dominant purpose of seeking or giving legal advice or assistance.

Litigation Privilege

A communication is protected by litigation privilege if it is made: **1–233**

 (a) confidentially; and

 (b) for the dominant purpose of conducting or giving advice in relation to litigation, either pending or contemplated.

---

[33] And note that s.42 will fall away altogether after 30 years when records become historical records (s.63). See the commentary under s.67 for an analysis of the treatment of historical records.

"Litigation" for this purpose covers adversarial proceedings. Adversarial proceedings include Court proceedings and arbitration. Non-adversarial proceedings such as inquiries or investigations are excluded.

Unlike litigation privilege, legal advice privilege can only apply to communications passing directly between a lawyer and his client. Legal advice privilege cannot apply to correspondence between a lawyer and a third party, or between a client and a third party, even if the communication is for the purpose of obtaining information to be submitted to the client's lawyer. This means that the question of who acts or qualifies as the "client" is critical in any assessment of whether legal advice privilege applies.

The Three Rivers case

1–234   The change to privilege introduced by the Three Rivers decision is that the Court of Appeal confined within narrow limits the persons who qualify as the "client" for the purpose of determining whether legal advice privilege applies. The Three Rivers case arose out of the collapse of BCCI following fraud on a vast scale by its senior staff. The creditors and the liquidators of BCCI sued the Bank of England for misfeasance in public office in respect of its supervision of BCCI. The Bingham Inquiry was set up to consider whether the action taken by the Bank had been appropriate and timely. Shortly after the Inquiry was established, three Bank of England officials were appointed by the Governor to deal with all communications between the Bank and the Inquiry, and with the Bank's solicitors in relation to the Inquiry. They became known as the Bank's Inquiry Unit (BIU).

The Bank received legal advice from its lawyers on every aspect of the presentation of its evidence and submissions to the Inquiry. Preparatory work was carried out by the BIU, including discussions with present and former Bank staff involved in the licensing or supervising of BCCI. The flow of factual information from the Bank to its lawyers was usually channelled through the BIU. Specific requests for factual matters to be investigated and reported to its lawyers were often made by its lawyers to the BIU who then delegated those fact finding tasks to others within the Bank.

The Court of Appeal held that only the members of the BIU should be regarded as the client for the purpose of legal advice privilege.

1–235   The Bank argued that communications from any employee should be treated as from "the client" because a company can only act through its employees. The Court of Appeal accepted that a company can only act through its employees but did not regard that as sufficient for determining whether privilege should apply. It said that *"information from an employee stands in the same position as information from an independent agent"* and was thus not protected by legal advice privilege. This is of fundamental significance in matters relating to legal advice privilege, because it means that not every employee of the client will be regarded as the client for the purpose of determining whether a document is protected.

The Court held that confidential internal documents prepared for the purpose of instructing lawyers were not protected by legal advice privilege because such documents were not in themselves a communication between lawyer and client, or a document evidencing such communication. The Court decided that legal advice privilege did not extend to documents prepared by the Bank's employees who were not part of the BIU:

- with the intention that they should be sent to and were in fact sent to the Bank's lawyers;

- which were said to have been prepared with the dominant purpose of the Bank obtaining legal advice but which were not in fact sent to the Bank's lawyers, whether or not prepared for submission to or at the direction of the Bank's lawyers, even if their effect was incorporated into documents which were sent to the lawyers;

- otherwise than for the dominant purpose of obtaining legal advice but which were in fact sent to the lawyers.

In short, Three Rivers has made absolutely critical the question of who stands in the capacity of "client" for the purpose of determining whether a document is protected by legal advice privilege. At the same time however, the Court of Appeal gave no guidance about how to determine who the client is. The client would seem to include in-house lawyers, senior officers whose duties include instructing the client's lawyers and those appointed to communicate with the client's lawyers on specific matters.

Communications between an employer and his in-house lawyer where the lawyer is providing legal advice in his capacity as legal adviser will qualify for LPP, but where the lawyer acts in an administrative or executive capacity the communications will not be privileged.

This issue is of the utmost importance because, increasingly, public authorities are turning to personnel seconded from external consultants and other professional organisations to help staff large projects. As a result of Three Rivers, it is doubtful that communications made or received by seconded personnel on behalf of a public authority will qualify for LPP.

Can Privilege be Lost?

Privilege can be lost where the underlying confidentiality in a document is **1–236** lost or where the client waives the right to LPP in a document.[34] Waiver of LPP for one document in a series of documents may, depending on the facts, also waive privilege in other related documents. The Court will ensure fairness, and prevent a party from cherry picking and waiving privilege only in those documents which assist it. Waiver of privilege in

[34] See *Calcraft v Guest* [1898] 1 QB 759 in relation to waiver of privilege by the client.

respect of part of a document will extend to the entire document unless the subject matter of the remaining part is completely different.

Partial waiver should be distinguished from redaction of a document whereby privileged material is edited out: disclosure of the unprivileged part of the document will not waive privilege in the privileged part.

Privilege will not apply in any case where non-disclosure would conceal fraud, crime or innocence.[35]

Meaning of "legal advice" for the purposes of LPP

1–237   Most, but not all, communications between a lawyer and his client will qualify as "advice" for the purpose of LPP. Legal advice is not confined to telling the client the law, provided that the advice is directly related to the performance by the solicitor of his professional duty as legal adviser of his client.

In the *United States of America v (1) Philip Morris Inc & Ors and British American Tobacco (Investments) Ltd (Intervener)*,[36] the Court of Appeal said that the leading modern authority on the practical application of the principles governing privilege is still *Balabel v Air India*.[37] In that case Taylor LJ said (at pp.330–331):

> "*The test is whether the communication or other document was made confidentially for the purposes of legal advice. Those purposes have to be construed broadly. Privilege obviously attaches to a document conveying legal advice from a solicitor to client and to a specific request from the client for such advice. But it does not follow that all other communications between them lack privilege. In most solicitor and client relationships, especially where a transaction involves protracted dealings, advice may be required or appropriate on matters great or small at various stages. There will be a continuum of communication and meetings between the solicitor and client. Where information is passed by the solicitor or client to the other as part of the continuum aimed at keeping both informed so that advice may be sought and given as required, privilege will attach. A letter from the client containing information may end with such words as 'please advise me what I should do'. But, even if it does not, there will usually be implied in the relationship an overall expectation that the solicitor will at each stage, whether asked specifically or not, tender appropriate advice. Moreover legal advice is not confined to telling the client the law; it must include advice as to what should prudently and sensible be done in the relevant legal context.*"

A little later (at pp.331–2) Taylor LJ said that the scope of the privilege had to be kept within justifiable bounds. He stated in relation to documents recording information or transactions or recording meetings that:

[35] *R v Cox and Railton* [1884] 14 QBD 153.
[36] [2004] EWCA CIV 330.
[37] [1988] Ch 317.

"Whether such documents are privileged or not must depend on whether they are part of that necessary exchange of information of which the object is the giving of legal advice as and when appropriate."

There will always be borderline cases in which it is difficult to decide whether or not the advice is given in a legal context. Much will depend upon whether it is reasonable for the client to consult the special professional knowledge and skills of a lawyer. However, there will normally be a relevant legal context when a client seeks advice from a lawyer.

Application of litigation privilege

The test for determining whether litigation privilege can be invoked in relation to any communication where litigation has not commenced is whether there was a real likelihood that litigation was reasonably in prospect at the time when the communication was made. There must be a real prospect of litigation as distinct from a mere possibility, but the prospect does not have to be more likely than not. The requirement that litigation be reasonably in prospect is satisfied if the party seeking to claim privilege can show that he was aware of circumstances which rendered litigation between himself and a particular person a real likelihood.   **1–238**

Department for Constitutional Affairs Guidance[38]

The public interest in maintaining the legal privilege exemption will normally be substantial because legal privilege itself derives from the public interest in maintaining confidentiality between lawyer and client. The DCA guidance on s.42 underlines this. It notes that where legal privilege applies, the balance of the public interest will usually only weigh in favour of disclosure in exceptional circumstances.   **1–239**

There are a number of factors which, as a matter of principle, will weigh in favour of maintaining LPP in the face of a FOIA request for privileged information:

- decisions by public authorities must be taken in a fully informed legal context;

- authorities require legal advice for the effective performance of their operations and that advice must be given by lawyers who are fully apprised of the factual background;

- legal advisers must be able to present the full picture, which will include arguments in support of their final conclusions and arguments that may be made against these (it is in the nature of legal advice that it will set out the arguments both for and against

---

[38] See *www.foi.gov.uk/guidance/exguide/sec42/index.htm.*

a particular view, weighing up their relative merits, and highlighting perceived weaknesses in any position);

- without such comprehensive advice, authority decision making may be compromised because it would not be fully informed;

- disclosure of legal advice could materially prejudice an authority's ability to protect and defend its legal interests;

- disclosure might unfairly expose a legal position to challenge and diminish the reliance which may be placed on the advice;

- even where litigation is not in prospect, disclosure of legal advice may carry a risk of prejudicing an authority in future litigation, and legal advice connected with one department could have wider implications for other departments.

Public interest factors weighing in favour of disclosing privileged information might include:

- the circumstances are such that the government would waive privilege if litigation were afoot;

- departments should be accountable for the quality of their decision making and this may require transparency in the decision making process and access to the information on which decisions were made;

- in some cases there may be a public interest in knowing whether or not legal advice was followed.

43 Commercial interests

1–240

(1) Information is exempt information if it constitutes a trade secret.

(2) Information is exempt information if its disclosure under this Act would, or would be likely to, prejudice the commercial interests of any person (including the public authority holding it).

(3) The duty to confirm or deny does not arise if, or to the extent that, compliance with section 1(1)(a) would, or would be likely to, prejudice the interests mentioned in subsection (2).

NOTES

Initial Commencement

Specified date

Specified date: 30 November 2005 (unless the Secretary of State by order appoints this section before that date): see s 87(3) (as amended by SI 2001/3500, art 8, Sch 2, Pt I, para 8(1)(o) and SI 2003/1887, art 9, Sch 2, para 12(1)(c)). (See appointment note below.)

Appointment

Appointment: 1 January 2005: see SI 2004/3122, art 2.

GENERAL NOTE[39]

Section 43 recognises that the operation of open government should take account of legitimate commercial interests.   **1–241**

There are two separate qualified exemptions under s.43 which serve to protect the legitimate commercial interests of both public authorities and others.

Section 43(1) applies to trade secrets. There is no requirement in s.43(1) to assess the prejudice which disclosure might cause, because trade secrets arise precisely *because* disclosure would be damaging. If information is a trade secret then it will be exempt, subject to the public interest.

Section 43(2) provides a more general category of exemption for commercially sensitive information if disclosure would, or would be likely to, prejudice someone's commercial interests (whether the authority's own or anyone else's).

Subsection (1)—trade secrets

There is no definition of a trade secret, either in FOIA or in English law generally. Typically, trade secrets comprise secret formulae or processes   **1–242**

---

[39] Section 43 is a qualified exemption. It applies to the duty to communicate information and the duty to confirm or deny, except that there is no exemption to the duty to confirm or deny where the information requested is a trade secret. FOIA assumes that while disclosure of a trade secret may be harmful, mere confirmation that it is in an authority's possession is not.

associated with particular products or services. The essence of a trade secret is generally taken to comprise three elements[40]:

- it must be specific information used in a trade or business;

- it must not generally be known—which usually means that the owner must have limited, or at least not permitted, its widespread publication; and

- it must be information which, if disclosed to a competitor, would be liable to cause real or significant harm to the owner.

In 1997, the Law Commission, seeking views on the criminalisation of trade secrets as part of a Consultation Paper, identified four categories:

- formulae for highly specific products;

- technological secrets;

- strategic business information; and

- collations of publicly available information, such as databases.

These have not been formerly drafted into protected categories, however.

Subsection (2)—commercial interests generally

1–243 "Commercial interests" are wider than trade secrets and apply—theoretically, at least—to any activity related to the business, trade or profession of any person or organisation. An organisation's commercial interests might, for example, be prejudiced where a disclosure would be likely to:

- damage its business reputation or the confidence that customers, suppliers or investors may have in it;

- have a detrimental impact on its commercial revenue or threaten its ability to obtain supplies or secure finance; or

- weaken its position in a competitive environment by revealing market-sensitive information or information of potential usefulness to its competitors.

Examples of information the disclosure of which may have particular potential to damage commercial interests include:

---

[40] Cited in *Lansing Linde Ltd v Kerr* [1991] 1 WLR 251.

- information relating to payments for services, where disclosure could prejudice active and contemporaneous negotiations for other similar services[41];

- research and plans relating to a potential new product;

- product manufacturing cost information;

- product sales forecast information;

- strategic business plans, including, for example, plans to enter, develop or withdraw from a product or geographical market sector;

- marketing plans, to promote a new or existing product;

- information relating to the preparation of a competitive bid;

- information about the financial and business viability of a company; and

- information provided to a public authority in respect of an application for a licence or as a requirement of a licence condition or under a regulatory regime.

Importantly, s.43(2) can apply to an authority's own commercially sensitive information as well as to such information held by the authority relating to outside organisations.

Prejudice to a third party's commercial interests

Public authorities will hold lots of information which falls within s.43(2) **1–244** because disclosure would cause commercial damage to third parties.

Third party commercially sensitive information will come into the possession of public authorities in a number of ways, for example:

- as a result of legal, regulatory, or licensing requirements;

---

[41] See Decision Notice FS50063478, June 20, 2005. The National Maritime Museum (NMM) refused to disclose information about payments to an artist, Conrad Shawcross, for his exhibition, on the ground that disclosure could prejudice their negotiations with the proposed next artist in the series. The Commissioner agreed that the public interest in protecting NMMs bargaining position "during active and contemporaneous negotiations for a project of a similar nature" overrode, for the time being, the public interest in releasing the financial details of the negotiations which immediately preceded those active negotiations because disclosure might have prejudiced NMMs ability to ensure value for public money. The Commissioner noted, however, that the likelihood of prejudice would diminish with time and with the conclusion of the active negotiations to the point where the balance of the public interest would shift towards disclosure.

- in the course of policy development—for example, information obtained, usually voluntarily, to inform and influence the development of policy, or changes to law or regulation;

- through providing support for business—for example, information provided by a company or trade association to a public authority to obtain advice, help with a specific project, and/or financial assistance; and

- through contracts for products, services or research.

Authorities may also procure commercial information as a product of their own research, for example when conducting assessments of performance and financial viability.

Public procurement

1–245 All public authorities buy goods and services. A great deal of the information which changes hands during the procurement process will be commercially sensitive. Certain areas of activity which all autorities carry out are likely to carry particular risks in the procurement context:

- **Information relating to general/preliminary procurement activities**: *e.g.* market sounding information; information relating to programme, project and procurement strategies; and contextual information about the authority, its business objectives and plans;

- **Information relating to supplier selection**: *e.g.* qualification information for potential bidders; information about requirements including specifications; details of the qualification process; and details of qualified bidders;

- **Information relating to contract negotiation and award**: *e.g.* bids; papers about capabilities of bidders, evaluations of bids, negotiating briefs and recommendations; the contract; information about successful bid and bidder, and information about other bids and bidders; and

- **Information relating to contract performance and post-contract activities**: *e.g.* information about implementation; information about performance; information about contract amendments with supporting papers; and information which may be provided and reviewed by third parties (*e.g.* consultants/auditors).

The Procurement Regulations

1–246 The requirements of the public procurement regime also need to be taken into account in relation to the possible disclosure of information. The EC

Public Procurement Directives, implemented in the Public Works Contracts Regulations 1991, the Public Services Contracts Regulations 1993 and the Public Supply Contracts Regulations 1995 recognise that the interests of suppliers in sensitive information supplied by them in a procurement must be respected and that both the interests of suppliers and the public interest may mean that certain information relating to a contract award is withheld from publication.

The new Consolidated Public Procurement Directive (2004/18/EC), yet to be implemented in the UK, continues to recognise these interests and prohibits the disclosure of information which suppliers have designated as confidential in a procurement, except as provided by the Directive and by national law.

Office of Government Commerce (OGC) Guidance

OGC, the government agency which acts as trusted advisor to the public   **1–247** sector for high risk projects, published FOIA guidance in early 2005. The guidance offers advice on FOIA procurement issues, sets out OGC policy on the application of key aspects of FOIA, and summarises OGC's view on disclosure positions in relation to specific categories of infromation (most notably Gateway Reviews).

The guidance has two principle aims:

- to balance openness and accountability in procurement with the need to preserve competitiveness in the marketplace; and

- to promote consistency between authorities dealing with FOIA requests related to procurement information.

The guidance is available from the OGC website at *www.ogc.gov.uk*.[42] An extract is reproduced at Appendix 3.

Copyright and database rights

There has been considerable debate about the interaction of FOIA with the   **1–248** Copyright, Designs and Patents Act 1988 ("**CDPA**") and the Copyright and Rights in Databases Regulations 1997 ("**CRDR**"), and in particular about whether the CDPA and CRDR authorize the copying of copyright and database right works for the purposes of complying with FOIA requests.

Section 50(1) CDPA states: "Where the doing of a particular act is specifically authorized by an Act of Parliament, whenever passed, then, unless the Act provides otherwise, the doing of that act does not infringe

---

[42] At the time of writing the full guidance is available from *http://www.ogc.gov.uk/embedded_object.asp?docid=1002589.*

copyright." Schedule 1, s.6 of CRDR says exactly the same in relation to infringement of database right.

Although at first glance this might appear to allow the copying of copyright and database right material for the purposes of FOIA, the position is not so simple. Nevertheless, it is the author's view that these two sections must apply to FOIA disclosures because any other conclusion would severely undermine the access regime which FOIA imposes.

Theoretical problems with applying s.50(1) CDPA and Schedule 1, s.6 CRDR to FOIA

1–249   By a strict reading, the two sections do not apply to FOIA because FOIA does not "specifically authorize" copying. It requires information to be "communicated" on request, but it does not specify how communication must be made.

Under FOIA s.11, applicants can express a preference for information to be communicated either by way of a copy, the opportunity to inspect a record containing the information, or a digest or summary of the information. However, authorities need only give effect to such a preference where "reasonably practicable", and in determining this, they are entitled by s.11(2) to take into account "all the circumstances". It would seem legitimate to argue that it is not reasonably practicable to supply a copy of a document if it is protected by copyright or database right, because to do so could be an infringing act. On this basis, an authority would instead have to allow the applicant to inspect the original material, or produce a summary of it (assuming that this would not also be an infringing act).

The better view

1–250   Notwithstanding the theoretical problems, it cannot in the author's view be correct to say that FOIA is subordinate *per se* to the law of copyright. This is because in some cases an authority will be unable to satisfy its FOIA obligations by summarizing information as opposed to providing copies, and in other cases it will be able to avoid its FOIA obligations altogether by effectively hiding behind copyright.

In the first case, the provision of a summary will not necessarily satisfy the FOIA obligation to "communicate" information. This is because the definition of "information" in FOIA is "information recorded in any form" and in many cases the form or medium will be inseparable from the information itself. For example:

- information which comprises tables of figures may be impossible to summarise without in some way changing it (*e.g.* because the summarizer will summarise subjectively, or because a summary will simply not convey all the pertinent elements of the original).

- Some information, and particularly information which is quantitative, cannot easily be distilled. An analogous example might be a transcript of a video which, while conveying the text of a speech, does not convey the inflection or facial expressions of the speaker, and therefore does not accurately convey all the information in the original.

There is also the problem that providing a summary may itself infringe copyright and database right.

In the second case (where authorities might seek to avoid their FOIA obligations by hiding behind copyright), the task of summarizing information will usually be much more time consuming than producing copies. So, a request which might be answered in a couple of hours by photocopying may take much longer to answer by summary. In many cases, this will take the request over the £600/450 cost threshold, which means that the authority will be entitled to refuse it simply because of the necessity of summarizing to avoid copyright or database right infringement. It cannot be right that individual's FOIA rights are circumvented as a result of the need to avoid copyright and database right infringement, particularly as these rights will continue to subsist in a work even if disclosed as part of a FOIA request—an applicant who copied a copyright or database right work obtained under FOIA would still be liable for infringement if he copied the work without lawful authority.

It is the author's view, therefore, that exceptions under s.50(1) CDPA and Sch.1, s.6 CRDR are likely to permit copying for the purposes of complying with FOIA, but the point remains untested by the courts. Either way, nothing in these provisions would put the disclosed material into the public domain or confer any right on any other person to copy or otherwise infringe a third party's rights in the material.

Copyright material produced by central government is covered by Crown copyright which is administered by Her Majesty's Stationery Office. Further information about the supply and re-use of Crown copyright information can be found on HMSOnline.[43]

Department for Constitutional Affairs Guidance[44]

There is a public interest in protecting the commercial interests of both the **1–251** private sector (which plays an important role in the general health of the economy) and the public sector (whose commercially-related functions need in any event to be exercised in the wider context of the public interest).

---

[43] See *www.hmso.gov.uk/copyright/guidance/gn_19.htm* which explains more fully the distinction between the supply of information held by public authorities under FOIA and the re-use of that information, and those circumstances where formal licnesing is required.
[44] See *www.foi.gov.uk/guidance/exguide/sec43/index.htm*.

Conversely, there is a general public interest in the disclosure of commercial information in order to ensure that:

- there is transparency in the accountability for use of public funds;

- there is proper scrutiny of government actions in carrying out licensing functions in accordance with published policy;

- public money is being used effectively, and that departments are getting value for money when purchasing goods and services;

- departments' commercial activities, including the procurement process, are conducted in an open and honest way; and

- business can respond better to government opportunities.

Factors that might weigh in favour of the public interest in withholding information in this area include:

- where disclosure would make it less likely that companies or individuals would provide the department with commercially sensitive information in the future and consequently undermine the ability of the department/agency to fulfil its role;

- where disclosure would be likely to prejudice the commercial interests of the department by affecting adversely its bargaining position during contractual negotiations which would result in the less effective use of public money;

- where disclosure would, as a consequence, make it more difficult for individuals to be able to conduct commercial transactions or have other dealings with public bodies which are not a typical commercial transaction—for example, where an organisation obtains a grant or financial assistance from a public authority—without fear of suffering commercially as a result. It would not, for example, be in the public interest to disclose information about a particular commercial body if that information was not common knowledge and would be likely to be used by competitors in a particular market to gain a competitive advantage.

44 Prohibitions on disclosure

1–252

(1) **Information is exempt information if its disclosure (otherwise than under this Act) by the public authority holding it—**

(a) **is prohibited by or under any enactment,**

(b) **is incompatible with any Community obligation, or**

(c) **would constitute or be punishable as a contempt of court.**

(2) **The duty to confirm or deny does not arise if the confirmation or denial that would have to be given to comply with section 1(1)(a) would (apart from this Act) fall within any of paragraphs (a) to (c) of subsection (1).**

NOTES

Initial Commencement

Specified date

Specified date: 30 November 2005 (unless the Secretary of State by order appoints this section before that date): see s 87(3) (as amended by SI 2001/3500, art 8, Sch 2, Pt I, para 8(1)(o) and SI 2003/1887, art 9, Sch 2, para 12(1)(c)). (See appointment note below.)

Appointment

Appointment: 1 January 2005: see SI 2004/3122, art 2.

GENERAL NOTE[45]

Disclosures which are prohibited by other legal rules are also exempt from FOIA. FOIA does not cut across existing legal regimes which restrict access to information, nor does it provide alternative means of access to information which is expressly protected.[46]

1–253

There are three types of existing legal provisions which will apply in this context:

(a) disclosures prohibited by statute;

(b) disclosures which would be incompatible with EU law[47]; or

---

[45] Section 44 is an absolute exemption. It applies to the duty to communicate information and the duty to confirm or deny.

[46] In 1998 the DCA initiated a review of every statutory provision capable of preventing disclosure of information, to determine its consistency with FOIA. It published its findings in June 2005, as a result of which 49 provisions are to be repealed or amended. See the commentary on s.75 for further analysis of the DCA review. At the time of writing, only one statutory instrument, dealing with eight repeals and amendments has been passed: SI 2004/3363, The Freedom of Information (Removal and Relaxation of Statutory Prohibitions on Disclosure of Information) Order 2004.

[47] The term "Community obligation" in s.44(1)(b) includes EU Regulations, Treaties, Directives and Decisions. All of these have direct effect in the UK which means that they create individual rights which national courts must protect. Individuals can rely on these rights against the state or an emanation of the state even if they have not been enacted in UK law. Recommendations and Opinions have no binding force and therefore do not fall within s.44(1)(b).

(c) disclosures which would be a contempt of court.

It will be immediately apparent that the exemption applies to any disclosure which is a criminal offence, or subject to regulatory, public or civil law restriction. It does not, however, extend to disclosures which are unlawful at common law (except by reason of contempt of court), so FOIA is no basis for avoiding a disclosure which might be a tort or breach of contract. Breaches of common law are dealt with where appropriate by specific exemptions, such as those covering breach of confidence (s.41) and defamation (s.79).

There will be many bars to disclosure falling within s.44, far too numerous to list.[48] The fundamental principle is that FOIA does not cut across other legal restrictions on disclosure. So, where disclosure is prohibited by the Official Secrets Act, the Data Protection Act or the Human Rights Act, for example, FOIA will not compel a public authority to make information available. There are similarly many restrictions relating to tax and social security, and various prohibitions on disclosure of information obtained in the course of investigations by bodies such as the Equal Opportunities Commission, the Commission for Racial Equality and the Parliamentary Commissioner for Administration. Certain information obtained by regulators such as the Financial Services Authority, the General Medical Council and utilities watchdogs like Ofgem, Ofwat and Ofcom will also be exempt, although the extent of any prohibition on disclosure will always depend on the circumstances in which the information was obtained and the precise scope of the relevant body's powers. It is worth noting also that in relation to self-regulating professions whose regulators are caught by FOIA, such regulators now operate (post-Shipman Enquiry) under greater than ever scrutiny and expectation of openness.

Contempt of court

1–254   Contempt of court serves primarily to protect the integrity of court proceedings. Contempt of court is extremely serious and carries a penalty of up to two years' imprisonment or an unlimited fine. The law relating to contempt is governed by the Contempt of Court Act 1981. The procedural formalities are set out in the Civil Procedure Rules 1998, Sch.1, RSC Order 52.

A court order requiring an authority not to disclose particular information would fall within s.44(1)(c) as would information the disclosure of which might prejudice the outcome of court proceedings. As a general guide,

---

[48] At the time of writing, only one complaint has been brought before the Commissioner in relation to s.44. This concerned a request for access to complaints handled originally by the Independent Police Complaints Authority (now the Independent Police Complaints Commission or IPCC). The IPCC refused to disclose on the ground that s.80 of the Police Act 1996, which expressly prohibits disclosure of information connected with the IPCC's complaints handling functions, engaged FOIA's s.44 exemption. The Commissioner agreed: Decision Notice FS50069386, July 20, 2005.

where an authority responds to a request for information and has no reason to believe that proceedings are imminent or that any relevant court order is extant, the disclosure will not constitute a contempt of court. Similarly, it is not a contempt if the risk of prejudice created by disclosure is merely incidental to a discussion of matters of general public interest.[49] There may be, for example, a request for disclosure of a document which is of public importance but contains material which may prejudice the defendant in particular proceedings. If the information is incidental to the main thrust of the report, the disclosure will not constitute a contempt.

If in doubt, authorities should take specialist legal advice.

Department for Constitutional Affairs Guidance[50]

Disclosure of any of the following will normally carry a significant risk of contempt:

1–255

- Material that assumes explicitly or implicitly the guilt of an accused.

- Material that assumes the outcome of a preliminary issue which should be determined by a jury.

- Material that may hamper a police investigation.

- Material which contains a detailed account of the circumstances leading to criminal charges, where this is not already in the public domain.

- Statements presented as fact or based on assertions of fact in advance of the evidence in a trial.

- Material which is likely to be inadmissible in court but which could be retained by a juror (*e.g.* previous convictions).

- Material concerning other proceedings in which a defendant or witness is involved.

- Material containing comment or information about witnesses which may undermine their integrity or credibility.

- Information that is disclosed in breach of restrictions imposed by court orders.

---

[49] Contempt of Court Act 1981, s.5.
[50] See *www.foi.gov.uk/guidance/exguide/sec44/index.htm*.

Part III

General Functions of Secretary of State, Lord Chancellor and Information Commissioner

45 Issue of code of practice . . .

1–256

(1) The [Secretary of State] shall issue, and may from time to time revise, a code of practice providing guidance to public authorities as to the practice which it would, in his opinion, be desirable for them to follow in connection with the discharge of the authorities' functions under Part I.

(2) The code of practice must, in particular, include provision relating to—

(a) the provision of advice and assistance by public authorities to persons who propose to make, or have made, requests for information to them,

(b) the transfer of requests by one public authority to another public authority by which the information requested is or may be held,

(c) consultation with persons to whom the information requested relates or persons whose interests are likely to be affected by the disclosure of information,

(d) the inclusion in contracts entered into by public authorities of terms relating to the disclosure of information, and

(e) the provision by public authorities of procedures for dealing with complaints about the handling by them of requests for information.

(3) The code may make different provision for different public authorities.

(4) Before issuing or revising any code under this section, the [Secretary of State] shall consult the Commissioner.

(5) The [Secretary of State] shall lay before each House of Parliament any code or revised code made under this section.

NOTES

1–257   Initial Commencement

Royal Assent

Royal Assent (for the purpose of exercising the power to make codes of practice): 30 November 2000: see s 87(1)(m).

Appointment

Appointment (for remaining purposes): 30 November 2002: see SI 2002/2812, art 2(b).

GENERAL NOTE

Section 45 provides for the Lord Chancellor to issue a code of practice   1–258
dealing with the matters listed in s.45(2)(a)–(e). The code, referred to
throughout this book as the **"Section 45 Code"**, was laid before
Parliament on November 20, 2002. It is reproduced here in Appendix 5.

The Section 45 Code is an important document for two reasons. First, it
sets out good practice guidelines for public authorities. Secondly, it is an
excellent source of information for FOIA applicants about how public
authorities are supposed to behave.

The Section 45 Code covers the following areas:

- the provision of advice and assistance to applicants[51];

- handling requests which are part of an organised campaign[52];

- timeliness in dealing with requests[53];

- charging fees[54];

- transferring requests[55];

- consulting with third parties[56];

- contracts, and accepting information in confidence[57];

- consulting with devolved administrations[58];

- refusing requests[59]; and

- complaints.[60]

---

[51] See also the commentary to s.16 in this book.
[52] See also the commentary to s.12 in this book.
[53] See also the commentary to s.10 in this book.
[54] See also the commentary to ss.12 and 13 in this book.
[55] See also the commentary to s.1 in this book
[56] See also the commentary to ss.3 and 28 in this book.
[57] See also the commentary to s.41 in this book.
[58] See also the commentary to s.28 in this book.
[59] See also the commentary to s.17 in this book.
[60] See also the commentary to s.50 in this book.

46 Issue of code of practice by Lord Chancellor

(1) The Lord Chancellor shall issue, and may from time to time revise, a code of practice providing guidance to relevant authorities as to the practice which it would, in his opinion, be desirable for them to follow in connection with the keeping, management and destruction of their records.

(2) For the purpose of facilitating the performance by the Public Record Office, the Public Record Office of Northern Ireland and other public authorities of their functions under this Act in relation to records which are public records for the purposes of the Public Records Act 1958 or the Public Records Act (Northern Ireland) 1923, the code may also include guidance as to—

(a) the practice to be adopted in relation to the transfer of records under section 3(4) of the Public Records Act 1958 or section 3 of the Public Records Act (Northern Ireland) 1923, and

(b) the practice of reviewing records before they are transferred under those provisions.

(3) In exercising his functions under this section, the Lord Chancellor shall have regard to the public interest in allowing public access to information held by relevant authorities.

(4) The code may make different provision for different relevant authorities.

(5) Before issuing or revising any code under this section the Lord Chancellor shall consult—

[(a) the Secretary of State,]

(b) the Commissioner, and

(c) in relation to Northern Ireland, the appropriate Northern Ireland Minister.

(6) The Lord Chancellor shall lay before each House of Parliament any code or revised code made under this section.

(7) In this section "relevant authority" means—

(a) any public authority, and

(b) any office or body which is not a public authority but whose administrative and departmental records are

public records for the purposes of the Public Records Act 1958 or the Public Records Act (Northern Ireland) 1923.

NOTES

Initial Commencement   **1–260**

Royal Assent

Royal Assent (for the purpose of exercising the power to make codes of practice): 30 November 2000: see s 87(1)(m).

Appointment

Appointment (for remaining purposes): 30 November 2002: see SI 2002/2812, art 2(b).

GENERAL NOTE

Section 46 provides for the Lord Chancellor to issue a code of practice for   **1–261**
the keeping, management and destruction of records. The code, referred to
throughout this book as the "**Section 46 Code**", was laid before
Parliament on November 20, 2002. It is reproduced here in Appendix 6.

The Section 46 Code is an important document because, as noted in the
White Paper, *Your Right to Know*[61]: "*A Freedom of Information Act can only
be as good as the quality of the records which are subject to its provisions. Statutory
rights of access are of little use if reliable records are not created in the first place,
if they cannot be found when needed, or if the arrangements for their eventual
archiving or destruction are inadequate*".

The Section 46 Code covers the following areas:

- functional responsibility;

- policy;

- human resources;

- active records management;

- disposal arrangements;

- management of electronic records; and

- review and transfer of public records.

---

[61] At para.6.12.

The Information Commissioner's "Awareness Guidance No.8: Records Management FAQs" is a related useful source of information.

Note that s.46(7) extends the application of the Section 46 Code beyond public authorities to include any other office or body whose "administrative and departmental records" are "public records" for the purposes of the Public Records Act 1958 (or its Northern Irish equivalent).

47 General functions of Commissioner

1–262

(1) It shall be the duty of the Commissioner to promote the following of good practice by public authorities and, in particular, so to perform his functions under this Act as to promote the observance by public authorities of—

(a) the requirements of this Act, and

(b) the provisions of the codes of practice under sections 45 and 46.

(2) The Commissioner shall arrange for the dissemination in such form and manner as he considers appropriate of such information as it may appear to him expedient to give to the public—

(a) about the operation of this Act,

(b) about good practice, and

(c) about other matters within the scope of his functions under this Act,

and may give advice to any person as to any of those matters.

(3) The Commissioner may, with the consent of any public authority, assess whether that authority is following good practice.

(4) The Commissioner may charge such sums as he may with the consent of the [Secretary of State] determine for any services provided by the Commissioner under this section.

(5) The Commissioner shall from time to time as he considers appropriate—

(a) consult the Keeper of Public Records about the promotion by the Commissioner of the observance by public authorities of the provisions of the code of practice under section 46 in relation to records which are public records for the purposes of the Public Records Act 1958, and

(b) consult the Deputy Keeper of the Records of Northern Ireland about the promotion by the Commissioner of the observance by public authorities of those provisions in relation to records which are public records for the purposes of the Public Records Act (Northern Ireland) 1923.

(6) In this section "good practice", in relation to a public authority, means such practice in the discharge of its functions under this Act as appears to the Commissioner to be desirable, and includes (but is not limited to) compliance with the requirements of this Act and the provisions of the codes of practice under sections 45 and 46.

NOTES

Initial Commencement   1–263

Royal Assent

Sub-ss (2)–(6): Royal Assent: 30 November 2000: see s 87(1)(d).

Specified date

Sub-s (1): Specified date: 30 November 2005 (unless the Secretary of State by order appoints this subsection before that date): see s 87(3) (as amended by SI 2001/3500, art 8, Sch 2, Pt I, para 8(1)(o) and SI 2003/1887, art 9, Sch 2, para 12(1)(c)). (See appointment note below.)

Appointment

Sub-s (1): Appointment: 30 November 2002: see SI 2002/2812, art 2(c).

Amendment

Sub-s (4): words "Secretary of State" in square brackets substituted by SI 2003/1887, art 9, Sch 2, para 12(1)(a).
    Date in force: 19 August 2003: see SI 2003/1887, art 1(2).

48 Recommendations as to good practice

(1) If it appears to the Commissioner that the practice of a   1–264
public authority in relation to the exercise of its functions under this Act does not conform with that proposed in the codes of practice under sections 45 and 46, he may give to the authority a recommendation (in this section referred to as a "practice recommendation") specifying the steps which ought in his opinion to be taken for promoting such conformity.

(2) A practice recommendation must be given in writing and must refer to the particular provisions of the code of practice with which, in the Commissioner's opinion, the public authority's practice does not conform.

(3) Before giving to a public authority other than the Public Record Office a practice recommendation which relates to conformity with the code of practice under section 46 in respect of records which are public records for the purposes of the Public Records Act 1958, the Commissioner shall consult the Keeper of Public Records.

(4) Before giving to a public authority other than the Public Record Office of Northern Ireland a practice recommendation which relates to conformity with the code of practice under section 46 in respect of records which are public records for the purposes of the Public Records Act (Northern Ireland) 1923, the Commissioner shall consult the Deputy Keeper of the Records of Northern Ireland.

NOTES

1–265   **Initial Commencement**

Specified date

Specified date: 30 November 2005 (unless the Secretary of State by order appoints this section before that date): see s 87(3) (as amended by SI 2001/3500, art 8, Sch 2, Pt I, para 8(1)(o) and SI 2003/1887, art 9, Sch 2, para 12(1)(c)). (See appointment note below.)

Appointment

Sub-ss (1), (2): Appointment (in relation to the issue of practice recommendations relating to the conformity with the code of practice under s 45 hereof of the practice of public authorities in relation to the exercise of their functions under the publication scheme provisions): 30 November 2002: see SI 2002/2812, art 2(d).
Sub-ss (1), (2): Appointment (for remaining purposes): 1 January 2005: see SI 2004/1909, art 2(1), (2)(b), (3).
Sub-ss (3), (4): Appointment: 1 January 2005: see SI 2004/1909, art 2(1), (2)(b), (3).

GENERAL NOTE

1–266 The Information Commissioner's remit is not limited to enforcement. He is also responsible for actively monitoring compliance with FOIA and with the Section 45 and 46 Codes of Practice. Accordingly, s.48 empowers him to make practice recommendations to authorities which do not pass muster.

Recommendations must be in writing and must specify the provisions of the Codes which the authority has failed to meet.

There are no formal sanctions for failing to comply with a practice recommendation. Authorities can expect to be named and shamed in the Commissioner's Annual Report (published under s.49) but it remains to be seen whether this will be a sufficient deterrent. More importantly, a failure which constitutes a breach of Pt 1 of the Act could lead to the Commissioner serving an enforcement notice. Failure to comply with an enforcement notice is equivalent to contempt of court.[62]

49 Reports to be laid before Parliament

(1) **The Commissioner shall lay annually before each House of Parliament a general report on the exercise of his functions under this Act.**   1–267

(2) **The Commissioner may from time to time lay before each House of Parliament such other reports with respect to those functions as he thinks fit.**

NOTES

Initial Commencement

Royal Assent

Royal Assent: 30 November 2000: see s 87(1)(e).

---

[62] See the commentary on ss.52, 53 and 54 in relation to enforcement notices and contempt of court.

Part IV

Enforcement

50 Application for decision by Commissioner

(1) Any person (in this section referred to as "the complainant") may apply to the Commissioner for a decision whether, in any specified respect, a request for information made by the complainant to a public authority has been dealt with in accordance with the requirements of Part I.

(2) On receiving an application under this section, the Commissioner shall make a decision unless it appears to him—

    (a) that the complainant has not exhausted any complaints procedure which is provided by the public authority in conformity with the code of practice under section 45,

    (b) that there has been undue delay in making the application,

    (c) that the application is frivolous or vexatious, or

    (d) that the application has been withdrawn or abandoned.

(3) Where the Commissioner has received an application under this section, he shall either—

    (a) notify the complainant that he has not made any decision under this section as a result of the application and of his grounds for not doing so, or

    (b) serve notice of his decision (in this Act referred to as a "decision notice") on the complainant and the public authority.

(4) Where the Commissioner decides that a public authority—

    (a) has failed to communicate information, or to provide confirmation or denial, in a case where it is required to do so by section 1(1), or

    (b) has failed to comply with any of the requirements of sections 11 and 17,

the decision notice must specify the steps which must be taken by the authority for complying with that requirement and the period within which they must be taken.

(5) A decision notice must contain particulars of the right of appeal conferred by section 57.

(6) Where a decision notice requires steps to be taken by the public authority within a specified period, the time specified in the notice must not expire before the end of the period within which an appeal can be brought against the notice and, if such an appeal is brought, no step which is affected by the appeal need be taken pending the determination or withdrawal of the appeal.

(7) This section has effect subject to section 53.

NOTES

Initial Commencement

Specified date

Specified date: 30 November 2005 (unless the Secretary of State by order appoints this section before that date): see s 87(3) (as amended by SI 2001/3500, art 8, Sch 2, Pt I, para 8(1)(o) and SI 2003/1887, art 9, Sch 2, para 12(1)(c)). (See appointment note below.)

Appointment

Appointment: 1 January 2005: see SI 2004/1909, art 2(1), (2)(c), (3).

GENERAL NOTE

Whether or not freedom of information proves effective in the UK will depend to a significant degree on the effectiveness of the Information Commissioner, for it is he who is charged with policing the new law. Thankfully, FOIA gives him real powers to do so, subject only to the ministerial veto under s.53.   1–269

Section 50 entitles anyone dissatisfied with an authority's response to a request to complain to the Commissioner. The process for bringing complaints is very simple: there are no procedural requirements and no fee. On receipt of a complaint the Commissioner is obliged to investigate it, provided the complainant has already exhausted the relevant authority's internal complaints process (and provided there has not been undue delay and the complaint is not frivolous or vexatious).[63] If he decides that the

---

[63] Note that s.50 does not entitle the Commissioner to investigate the *quality* of information held by public authorities, only their compliance with Pt 1 of the Act: see Decision Notice FS50076626, June 10, 2005.

authority has failed to comply with its duties under Pt 1, then the Commissioner must serve a decision notice specifying what steps the authority must take, and when.[64] The notice must also set out the authority's right to appeal under s.57.

In order to carry out his assessment, the Commissioner may serve on an authority an information notice (under s.51), and by service of an enforcement notice (under s.52) he can direct an authority to carry out his decision. Failure by the authority to comply is treated as a contempt of court.

There is one significant anomaly in the complaints process—namely, that it is only available to FOIA *applicants*. Others who may be affected by disclosure have no right to complain, even where an authority discloses in error. In particular, this precludes businesses from complaining where an authority has failed to apply an exemption correctly or failed to apply it altogether. As noted under s.3, this has important implications for the private sector.

Note that s.56 prevents the bringing of civil proceedings where an individual believes an authority has failed to comply with its FOIA obligations. This is to ensure that all complaints are brought using the enforcement mechanisms in FOIA.

51 Information notices

1–270

(1) **If the Commissioner—**

    (a) **has received an application under section 50, or**

    (b) **reasonably requires any information—**

        (i) **for the purpose of determining whether a public authority has complied or is complying with any of the requirements of Part I, or**

        (ii) **for the purpose of determining whether the practice of a public authority in relation to the exercise of its functions under this Act conforms with that proposed in the codes of practice under sections 45 and 46,**

    he may serve the authority with a notice (in this Act referred to as "an information notice") requiring it, within such time as is specified in the notice, to furnish the Commissioner, in such form as may be so specified, with such information relating to the application, to

---

[64] The Commissioner publishes all decision notices monthly on the ICO website: see *www.informationcommissioner.gov.uk/eventual.aspx?id=8617.*

compliance with Part I or to conformity with the code of practice as is so specified.

(2) An information notice must contain—

    (a) in a case falling within subsection (1)(a), a statement that the Commissioner has received an application under section 50, or

    (b) in a case falling within subsection (1)(b), a statement—

        (i) that the Commissioner regards the specified information as relevant for either of the purposes referred to in subsection (1)(b), and

        (ii) of his reasons for regarding that information as relevant for that purpose.

(3) An information notice must also contain particulars of the right of appeal conferred by section 57.

(4) The time specified in an information notice must not expire before the end of the period within which an appeal can be brought against the notice and, if such an appeal is brought, the information need not be furnished pending the determination or withdrawal of the appeal.

(5) An authority shall not be required by virtue of this section to furnish the Commissioner with any information in respect of—

    (a) any communication between a professional legal adviser and his client in connection with the giving of legal advice to the client with respect to his obligations, liabilities or rights under this Act, or

    (b) any communication between a professional legal adviser and his client, or between such an adviser or his client and any other person, made in connection with or in contemplation of proceedings under or arising out of this Act (including proceedings before the Tribunal) and for the purposes of such proceedings.

(6) In subsection (5) references to the client of a professional legal adviser include references to any person representing such a client.

(7) The Commissioner may cancel an information notice by written notice to the authority on which it was served.

(8) In this section "information" includes unrecorded information.

NOTES

1-271   **Initial Commencement**

Specified date

Specified date: 30 November 2005 (unless the Secretary of State by order appoints this section before that date): see s 87(3) (as amended by SI 2001/3500, art 8, Sch 2, Pt I, para 8(1)(o) and SI 2003/1887, art 9, Sch 2, para 12(1)(c)). (See appointment notes below.)

Appointment

1-272   Appointment (in relation to the issue and enforcement of information notices relating to the conformity with the code of practice under s 45 hereof of the practice of public authorities in relation to the exercise of their functions under the publication scheme provisions): 30 November 2002: see SI 2002/2812, art 2(d), (e).
Appointment (for remaining purposes): 1 January 2005: see SI 2004/1909, art 2(1), (2)(c), (3).

GENERAL NOTE

1-273   Where necessary, either to carry out an assessment of a complaint or to carry out an investigation of his own, the Commissioner may serve an information notice requiring an authority to furnish specific information. The notice must explain why the information is required (s.51(2)) and give a deadline for a response (s.51(1)). It must also detail the authority's right to appeal against the notice (s.51(3)). Self evidently, the deadline for a response must be at least as long as the deadline for an appeal against the notice itself (s.51(4)).

Information falling within s.51(5) need not be supplied in response to an information notice. Note, however, that this does not cover all legally privileged material which an authority may hold—it applies only to client-lawyer communications relating to the Act. The Commissioner is entitled to see (indeed, may positively need to see) privileged material in order to assess whether information which an authority has withheld should in fact be disclosed.

Note also that the definition of "information" under s.51 goes further than the definition in s.84. Section 51 extends to "unrecorded information" which means that the Commissioner may require an authority to provide evidence of, for example, its employees' recollection of events.

52 Enforcement notices

1-274   (1) If the Commissioner is satisfied that a public authority has failed to comply with any of the requirements of Part

I, the Commissioner may serve the authority with a notice (in this Act referred to as "an enforcement notice") requiring the authority to take, within such time as may be specified in the notice, such steps as may be so specified for complying with those requirements.

(2) An enforcement notice must contain—

(a) a statement of the requirement or requirements of Part I with which the Commissioner is satisfied that the public authority has failed to comply and his reasons for reaching that conclusion, and

(b) particulars of the right of appeal conferred by section 57.

(3) An enforcement notice must not require any of the provisions of the notice to be complied with before the end of the period within which an appeal can be brought against the notice and, if such an appeal is brought, the notice need not be complied with pending the determination or withdrawal of the appeal.

(4) The Commissioner may cancel an enforcement notice by written notice to the authority on which it was served.

(5) This section has effect subject to section 53.

NOTES

Initial Commencement   1–275

Specified date

Specified date: 30 November 2005 (unless the Secretary of State by order appoints this section before that date): see s 87(3) (as amended by SI 2001/3500, art 8, Sch 2, Pt I, para 8(1)(o) and SI 2003/1887, art 9, Sch 2, para 12(1)(c)). (See appointment notes below.)

Appointment

Appointment (in relation to the enforcement of the requirements on public authorities under the publication scheme provisions): 30 November 2002: see SI 2002/2812, art 2(e).
Appointment (for remaining purposes): 1 January 2005: see SI 2004/1909, art 2(1), (2)(c), (3).

GENERAL NOTE

If an authority has failed to comply with any requirement of Pt 1 of FOIA   **1–276** (the right of access) then the Commissioner may serve an enforcement notice requiring the authority to take specific steps to comply within a specific time. The notice must explain which Pt 1 requirement(s) the authority has failed to meet and the basis on which the Commissioner has come to this conclusion.

As with an information notice under s.51, an enforcement notice must detail the authority's right to appeal, and the deadline for responding to the notice must be at least as long as the deadline for an appeal.

The difference between decision notices and enforcement notices is that the former deal with authority decisions under Pt 1, whereas the latter compel authorities either to make a decision where they have failed or refused (in other words, to answer a request) or to comply with a decision of the Commissioner (where the Commissioner has issued a decision notice with which an authority has refused to comply).

53 Exception from duty to comply with decision notice or enforcement notice

1–277

(1) **This section applies to a decision notice or enforcement notice which—**

    (a) **is served on—**

        (i) **a government department,**

        (ii) **the National Assembly for Wales, or**

        (iii) **any public authority designated for the purposes of this section by an order made by the [Secretary of State], and**

    (b) **relates to a failure, in respect of one or more requests for information—**

        (i) **to comply with section 1(1)(a) in respect of information which falls within any provision of Part II stating that the duty to confirm or deny does not arise, or**

        (ii) **to comply with section 1(1)(b) in respect of exempt information.**

(2) **A decision notice or enforcement notice to which this section applies shall cease to have effect if, not later than the twentieth working day following the effective date, the accountable person in relation to that authority gives the Commissioner a certificate signed by him stating that he has on reasonable grounds formed the opinion that, in respect of the request or requests concerned, there was no failure falling within subsection (1)(b).**

(3) **Where the accountable person gives a certificate to the Commissioner under subsection (2) he shall as soon as**

practicable thereafter lay a copy of the certificate before—

(a) each House of Parliament,

(b) the Northern Ireland Assembly, in any case where the certificate relates to a decision notice or enforcement notice which has been served on a Northern Ireland department or any Northern Ireland public authority, or

(c) the National Assembly for Wales, in any case where the certificate relates to a decision notice or enforcement notice which has been served on the National Assembly for Wales or any Welsh public authority.

(4) In subsection (2) "the effective date", in relation to a decision notice or enforcement notice, means—

(a) the day on which the notice was given to the public authority, or

(b) where an appeal under section 57 is brought, the day on which that appeal (or any further appeal arising out of it) is determined or withdrawn.

(5) Before making an order under subsection (1)(a)(iii), the [Secretary of State] shall—

(a) if the order relates to a Welsh public authority, consult the National Assembly for Wales,

(b) if the order relates to the Northern Ireland Assembly, consult the Presiding Officer of that Assembly, and

(c) if the order relates to a Northern Ireland public authority, consult the First Minister and deputy First Minister in Northern Ireland.

(6) Where the accountable person gives a certificate to the Commissioner under subsection (2) in relation to a decision notice, the accountable person shall, on doing so or as soon as reasonably practicable after doing so, inform the person who is the complainant for the purposes of section 50 of the reasons for his opinion.

(7) The accountable person is not obliged to provide information under subsection (6) if, or to the extent that, compliance with that subsection would involve the disclosure of exempt information.

(8) In this section "the accountable person"—

(a) in relation to a Northern Ireland department or any Northern Ireland public authority, means the First

> Minister and deputy First Minister in Northern Ireland acting jointly,
>
> (b) in relation to the National Assembly for Wales or any Welsh public authority, means the Assembly First Secretary, and
>
> (c) in relation to any other public authority, means—
>
>> (i) a Minister of the Crown who is a member of the Cabinet, or
>>
>> (ii) the Attorney General, the Advocate General for Scotland or the Attorney General for Northern Ireland.
>
> (9) In this section "working day" has the same meaning as in section 10.

NOTES

1–278   **Initial Commencement**

Royal Assent

Royal Assent (in so far as this section confers powers to make any order, regulations or code of practice): 30 November 2000: see s 87(1)(m).

Specified date

Specified date (for remaining purposes): 30 November 2005 (unless the Secretary of State by order appoints this section before that date): see s 87(3) (as amended by SI 2001/3500, art 8, Sch 2, Pt I, para 8(1)(o) and SI 2003/1887, art 9, Sch 2, para 12(1)(c)). (See appointment note below.)

Appointment

Appointment (for remaining purposes): 1 January 2005: see SI 2004/1909, art 2(1), (2)(c), (3).

GENERAL NOTE

1–279   Section 53 gives Cabinet Ministers and the Attorney General the power to veto a decision or enforcement notice.[65] The "executive override", as the

---

[65] At the time of writing, the veto applies only to requests to government departments (including departments in Northern Ireland, where it can be exercised by the First Minister and deputy First Minister acting jointly) and the Welsh National Assembly (where the Assembly First Secretary has the power) (s53(1)(a)(i) and (ii)). The Lord Chancellor may extend this to other public authorities by order under s.53(1)(a)(iii).

Commissioner has called it, is exercised by means of a certificate stating that the relevant official has formed the view "on reasonable grounds" that the authority acted correctly in refusing to disclose information. The certificate must be given not later than the twentieth working day following the day on which the decision or enforcement notice was given or, where an appeal is brought, the day on which the appeal is determined or withdrawn.

The ministerial veto is controversial for the obvious reason that it allows ministers to overrule the Commissioner. It is worth stressing, however, that there are two safeguards against abuse. First, the person giving the certificate must lay it before both Houses of Parliament (s.53(3)) which will mean explaining publicly why he or she disagrees with the Commissioner. This should ensure that ministers are accountable for certificates, which in turn ought to prevent (or at least limit) misuse.[66] Secondly, where a certificate relates to a decision notice, the certifying official must notify the complainant of the reason for his opinion (s.53(6)). It is open to the Commissioner or the complainant to apply for judicial review based on this notification.[67]

Judicial review

A claim for judicial review must be made promptly and normally not later than three months after the grounds for the claim first arose, although the court may extend the time if it feels that it ought to.   1–280

There are three grounds for judicial review: illegality, irrationality and procedural impropriety. In relation to the ministerial veto, irrationality is the most likely basis for an application. Exercise of the veto could be judged irrational if held to have been so unreasonable that no reasonable person could have come to the same decision, or if the opinion underlying the veto is unsupported by evidence.

54 Failure to comply with notice

(1) If a public authority has failed to comply with—   1–281

    (a) so much of a decision notice as requires steps to be taken,

    (b) an information notice, or

    (c) an enforcement notice,

---

[66] In Australia, the Ministerial veto was exercised 55 times in the first four years of the Freedom of Information Act 1982. This seems quite high, given that it amounts to more than one veto every month.

[67] The government made it clear during the passage of the Bill through Parliament that the veto should be subject to judicial review: *Hansard*, HL (series 5) vol.612, col.828 (April 20, 2000).

the Commissioner may certify in writing to the court that the public authority has failed to comply with that notice.

(2) For the purposes of this section, a public authority which, in purported compliance with an information notice—

(a) makes a statement which it knows to be false in a material respect, or

(b) recklessly makes a statement which is false in a material respect,

is to be taken to have failed to comply with the notice.

(3) Where a failure to comply is certified under subsection (1), the court may inquire into the matter and, after hearing any witness who may be produced against or on behalf of the public authority, and after hearing any statement that may be offered in defence, deal with the authority as if it had committed a contempt of court.

(4) In this section "the court" means the High Court or, in Scotland, the Court of Session.

NOTES

1–282 **Initial Commencement**

Specified date

Specified date: 30 November 2005 (unless the Secretary of State by order appoints this section before that date): see s 87(3) (as amended by SI 2001/3500, art 8, Sch 2, Pt I, para 8(1)(o) and SI 2003/1887, art 9, Sch 2, para 12(1)(c)). (See appointment notes below.)

Appointment

Appointment (in relation to the enforcement of information notices relating to the conformity with the code of practice under s 45 hereof of the practice of public authorities in relation to the exercise of their functions under the publication scheme provisions): 30 November 2002: see SI 2002/2812, art 2(d), (e).
Appointment (for remaining purposes): 1 January 2005: see SI 2004/1909, art 2(1), (2)(c), (3).

GENERAL NOTE

1–283 Section 54 describes the procedure by which the Commissioner and the court should deal with an authority which fails to comply with a notice: the

Commissioner certifies the failure to the court, whereupon the court can treat it as a contempt.[68]

Section 54 gives the court discretion whether to examine a case of non-compliance, and also to hear argument from both sides (*i.e.* the Commissioner and the authority). The court could also seek evidence from the requestor of information in a case where an authority has defied a decision notice, but the requestor cannot initiate s.54 proceedings. That right lies solely with the Commissioner.

Contempt of court

Contempt of court is extremely serious and carries a penalty of up to two years imprisonment or an unlimited fine. Imprisonment would usually only apply where a public official had knowingly participated in a breach[69] but the possibility of an unlimited fine ought by itself to be sufficient deterrent. **1–284**

The law relating to contempt of court is governed by the Contempt of Court Act 1981. The procedural formalities are set out in the Civil Procedure Rules 1998, Schedule 1, RSC Order 52.

55 Powers of entry and inspection

Schedule 3 (powers of entry and inspection) has effect. **1–285**

NOTES

Initial Commencement

Specified date

Specified date: 30 November 2005 (unless the Secretary of State by order appoints this section before that date): see s 87(3) (as amended by SI 2001/3500, art 8, Sch 2, Pt I, para 8(1)(o) and SI 2003/1887, art 9, Sch 2, para 12(1)(c)). (See appointment notes below.)

Appointment

Appointment (for certain purposes): 30 November 2002: see SI 2002/2812, art 2(d)–(f).

---

[68] Any finding of contempt will of course be contingent on the notice being clear. As noted in *Miller Mead v Minister of Housing and Local Government* [1963] 2 QB 196, "does the notice tell (the person on whom it is served) fairly what he has done wrong and what he must do to remedy it?"

[69] Contempt of Court Act 1981, s.14. Generally, employees and officers of a public authority will not be personally liable for contempt unless they knowingly assist the breach (*i.e.* they will not be liable purely by virtue of their office: *Marengo v Daily Sketch and Sunday Graphic Limited* [1948] 1 All ER 406; *Director General of Fair Trading v Buckland* [1990] 1 WLR 920).

Appointment (for remaining purposes): 1 January 2005: see SI 2004/1909, art 2(1), (2)(c), (3).

GENERAL NOTE

1-286 The Information Commissioner can apply to a circuit judge for a warrant to enter premises and inspect documents. This would normally only be exercised where public officials are suspected of deliberately altering, destroying or withholding records.

The procedure for applying for a warrant is set out in Sch.3.

It is an offence to obstruct the Commissioner in the execution of a warrant or to fail, without reasonable excuse, to give assistance which he reasonably requires.

56 No action against public authority

1-287
(1) **This Act does not confer any right of action in civil proceedings in respect of any failure to comply with any duty imposed by or under this Act.**

(2) **Subsection (1) does not affect the powers of the Commissioner under section 54.**

NOTES

Initial Commencement

Specified date

Specified date: 30 November 2005 (unless the Secretary of State by order appoints this section before that date): see s 87(3) (as amended by SI 2001/3500, art 8, Sch 2, Pt I, para 8(1)(o) and SI 2003/1887, art 9, Sch 2, para 12(1)(c)). (See appointment note below.)

Appointment

Appointment: 30 November 2002: see SI 2002/2812, art 2(g).

GENERAL NOTE

1-288 Section 56 precludes civil claims against a public authority or the Information Commissioner for damages (*e.g.* for negligence or breach of statutory duty). An individual dissatisfied with an authority's response to a request is therefore compelled to invoke the enforcement procedures within FOIA.

Part V

Appeals

57 Appeal against notices served under Part IV

(1) Where a decision notice has been served, the complainant or the public authority may appeal to the Tribunal against the notice.

1–289

(2) A public authority on which an information notice or an enforcement notice has been served by the Commissioner may appeal to the Tribunal against the notice.

(3) In relation to a decision notice or enforcement notice which relates—

(a) to information to which section 66 applies, and

(b) to a matter which by virtue of subsection (3) or (4) of that section falls to be determined by the responsible authority instead of the appropriate records authority,

subsections (1) and (2) shall have effect as if the reference to the public authority were a reference to the public authority or the responsible authority.

NOTES

Initial Commencement

Specified date

Specified date: 30 November 2005 (unless the Secretary of State by order appoints this section before that date): see s 87(3) (as amended by SI 2001/3500, art 8, Sch 2, Pt I, para 8(1)(o) and SI 2003/1887, art 9, Sch 2, para 12(1)(c)). (See appointment notes below.)

Appointment

Sub-ss (1), (3): Appointment: 1 January 2005: see SI 2004/1909, art 2(1), (2)(d), (3).
Sub-s (2): Appointment: 30 November 2002: see SI 2002/2812, art 2(g).

GENERAL NOTE

Part V of FOIA sets out the appeals process. Appeals would normally be made first to the Information Tribunal and then to the court, although there is nothing to prevent an appeal to the court direct.

1–290

Under s.57 a FOIA applicant or a public authority can appeal to the Information Tribunal against a decision notice. Public authorities can also appeal information and enforcement notices.

As noted above in relation to ss.50, 51 and 52, notices served by the Commissioner must detail rights of, and deadlines for, appeal.

The appeals process itself is set out in ss.58–61.

58 Determination of appeals

1–291

(1) **If on an appeal under section 57 the Tribunal considers—**

    (a) **that the notice against which the appeal is brought is not in accordance with the law, or**

    (b) **to the extent that the notice involved an exercise of discretion by the Commissioner, that he ought to have exercised his discretion differently,**

the Tribunal shall allow the appeal or substitute such other notice as could have been served by the Commissioner; and in any other case the Tribunal shall dismiss the appeal.

(2) **On such an appeal, the Tribunal may review any finding of fact on which the notice in question was based.**

NOTES

Initial Commencement

Specified date

Specified date: 30 November 2005 (unless the Secretary of State by order appoints this section before that date): see s 87(3) (as amended by SI 2001/3500, art 8, Sch 2, Pt I, para 8(1)(o) and SI 2003/1887, art 9, Sch 2, para 12(1)(c)). (See appointment note below.)

Appointment

Appointment: 30 November 2002: see SI 2002/2812, art 2(g).

GENERAL NOTE

1–292   The Information Tribunal can allow appeals only on the grounds set out in s.58(a) and (b). These cover all questions of fact and discretion, which will therefore include assessments of the balance of the public interest. Appeals to the court on Tribunal decisions are permitted only on points of law (s.59). The Tribunal is therefore the final arbiter (subject to the ministerial veto)[70] on all questions of fact and discretion brought before it.

59 Appeals from decision of Tribunal

Any party to an appeal to the Tribunal under section 57 may appeal from the decision of the Tribunal on a point of law to the appropriate court; and that court shall be— **1–293**

    (a) the High Court of Justice in England if the address of the public authority is in England or Wales,

    (b) the Court of Session if that address is in Scotland, and

    (c) the High Court of Justice in Northern Ireland if that address is in Northern Ireland.

NOTES

Initial Commencement

Specified date

Specified date: 30 November 2005 (unless the Secretary of State by order appoints this section before that date): see s 87(3) (as amended by SI 2001/3500, art 8, Sch 2, Pt I, para 8(1)(o) and SI 2003/1887, art 9, Sch 2, para 12(1)(c)). (See appointment note below.)

Appointment

Appointment: 30 November 2002: see SI 2002/2812, art 2(g).

60 Appeals against national security certificate

    (1) Where a certificate under section 23(2) or 24(3) has been issued— **1–294**

        (a) the Commissioner, or

        (b) any applicant whose request for information is affected by the issue of the certificate,

    may appeal to the Tribunal against the certificate.

    (2) If on an appeal under subsection (1) relating to a certificate under section 23(2), the Tribunal finds that the information referred to in the certificate was not exempt information by virtue of section 23(1), the Tribunal may allow the appeal and quash the certificate.

---

[70] Freedom of Information Act 2000, s.53.

(3) **If on an appeal under subsection (1) relating to a certificate under section 24(3), the Tribunal finds that, applying the principles applied by the court on an application for judicial review, the Minister did not have reasonable grounds for issuing the certificate, the Tribunal may allow the appeal and quash the certificate.**

(4) **Where in any proceedings under this Act it is claimed by a public authority that a certificate under section 24(3) which identifies the information to which it applies by means of a general description applies to particular information, any other party to the proceedings may appeal to the Tribunal on the ground that the certificate does not apply to the information in question and, subject to any determination under subsection (5), the certificate shall be conclusively presumed so to apply.**

(5) **On any appeal under subsection (4), the Tribunal may determine that the certificate does not so apply.**

NOTES

1–295   **Initial Commencement**

Specified date

Specified date: 30 November 2005 (unless the Secretary of State by order appoints this section before that date): see s 87(3) (as amended by SI 2001/3500, art 8, Sch 2, Pt I, para 8(1)(o) and SI 2003/1887, art 9, Sch 2, para 12(1)(c)). (See appointment note below.)

Appointment

Appointment: 1 January 2005: see SI 2004/1909, art 2(1), (2)(d), (3).

GENERAL NOTE

1–296   The FOIA exemptions under s.23 (security matters) and s.24 (national security) are considerably enhanced by the fact that a certificate signed by a minister is conclusive evidence that information falls within them. Some may view this as a necessary weapon in the war on terror but it is also of course open to abuse. To counterbalance this risk there are two safeguards. First, certificates must be signed by a cabinet minister, the Attorney General or Solicitor General. Secondly, s.60 provides a mechanism for challenging certificates.

Both the Information Commissioner and the requestor of information can appeal a certificate to the Information Tribunal. The Tribunal may quash it if it concludes:

- in relation to a s.23 certificate, that the information in question does not fall within the exemption; or

- in relation to a s.24 certificate, that the certifying official did not have reasonable grounds for issuing it.

Sections 60(4) and (5) give the Tribunal power to determine whether a s.24 certificate of general description covers the information in a particular request.[71]

Baker v Secretary of State for the Home Department[72]

In 2001, Liberal Democrat MP Norman Baker applied for access to personal data which he believed MI5 held relating to him. The Home Secretary issued a certificate to prevent this which Mr Baker appealed to the Data Protection Tribunal. The Tribunal held that the certificate was too widely drawn and quashed it. Two other certificates, relating to MI6 and GCHQ, were also quashed as a result.

1–297

61 Appeal proceedings

(1) **Schedule 4 (which contains amendments of Schedule 6 to the Data Protection Act 1998 relating to appeal proceedings) has effect.**

1–298

(2) **Accordingly, the provisions of Schedule 6 to the Data Protection Act 1998 have effect (so far as applicable) in relation to appeals under this Part.**

NOTES

Initial Commencement

1–299

Specified date

Specified date: 30 November 2005 (unless the Secretary of State by order appoints this section before that date): see s 87(3) (as amended by SI 2001/3500, art 8, Sch 2, Pt I, para 8(1)(o) and SI 2003/1887, art 9, Sch 2, para 12(1)(c)). (See appointment notes below.)

---

[71] Sections 23 and 24 do not expressly require Ministers to give reasons for certifying information as exempt. However, since in practice it would be impossible for the Tribunal to adjudicate on certificates for which reasons are not provided, it is likely the courts will not allow certificates without them (see *Alexander Machinery (Dudley) Ltd v Crabtree* [1974] ICR 120, NIRC where the court stated that "in the absence of reasons it is impossible to determine whether or not there has been an error of law. Failure to give reasons therefore amounts to a denial of justice and is itself an error of law").

[72] [2001] UKHRR 1275.

Appointment

Sub-s (1): Appointment (for certain purposes): 14 May 2001: see SI 2001/1637, art 2(c).
Sub-s (1): Appointment (for certain purposes): 30 November 2002: see SI 2002/2812, art 2(i).
Sub-s (1): Appointment (for remaining purposes): 1 January 2005: see SI 2004/1909, art 2(1), (2)(d), (3).
Sub-s (2): Appointment: 30 November 2002: see SI 2002/2812, art 2(g).

Part VI

Historical Records and Records in Public Record Office or Public Record Office of Northern Ireland

62 Interpretation of Part VI

(1) For the purposes of this Part, a record becomes a "historical record" at the end of the period of thirty years beginning with the year following that in which it was created.

1–300

(2) Where records created at different dates are for administrative purposes kept together in one file or other assembly, all the records in that file or other assembly are to be treated for the purposes of this Part as having been created when the latest of those records was created.

(3) In this Part "year" means a calendar year.

NOTES

Initial Commencement

Specified date

Specified date: 30 November 2005 (unless the Secretary of State by order appoints this section before that date): see s 87(3) (as amended by SI 2001/3500, art 8, Sch 2, Pt I, para 8(1)(o) and SI 2003/1887, art 9, Sch 2, para 12(1)(c)). (See appointment note below.)

Appointment

Appointment: 1 January 2005: see SI 2004/1909, art 2(1), (2)(e), (3).

GENERAL NOTE

See commentary on s.67 below.

1–301

63 Removal of exemptions: historical records generally

(1) Information contained in a historical record cannot be exempt information by virtue of section 28, 30(1), 32, 33, 35, 36, 37(1)(a), 42 or 43.

1–302

(2) Compliance with section 1(1)(a) in relation to a historical record is not to be taken to be capable of having any of the effects referred to in section 28(3), 33(3), 36(3), 42(2) or 43(3).

(3) Information cannot be exempt information by virtue of section 37(1)(b) after the end of the period of sixty years beginning with the year following that in which the record containing the information was created.

(4) Information cannot be exempt information by virtue of section 31 after the end of the period of one hundred years beginning with the year following that in which the record containing the information was created.

(5) Compliance with section 1(1)(a) in relation to any record is not to be taken, at any time after the end of the period of one hundred years beginning with the year following that in which the record was created, to be capable of prejudicing any of the matters referred to in section 31(1).

NOTES

Initial Commencement

Specified date

Specified date: 30 November 2005 (unless the Secretary of State by order appoints this section before that date): see s 87(3) (as amended by SI 2001/3500, art 8, Sch 2, Pt I, para 8(1)(o) and SI 2003/1887, art 9, Sch 2, para 12(1)(c)). (See appointment note below.)

Appointment

Appointment: 1 January 2005: see SI 2004/3122, art 2.

GENERAL NOTE

1–303   See commentary on s.67 below.

64 Removal of exemptions: historical records in public record offices

1–304

(1) Information contained in a historical record in the Public Record Office or the Public Record Office of Northern Ireland cannot be exempt information by virtue of section 21 or 22.

(2) In relation to any information falling within section 23(1) which is contained in a historical record in the Public Record Office or the Public Record Office of Northern Ireland, section 2(3) shall have effect with the omission of the reference to section 23.

NOTES

Initial Commencement

Specified date

Specified date: 30 November 2005 (unless the Secretary of State by order appoints this section before that date): see s 87(3) (as amended by SI 2001/3500, art 8, Sch 2, Pt I, para 8(1)(o) and SI 2003/1887, art 9, Sch 2, para 12(1)(c)). (See appointment note below.)

Appointment

Appointment: 1 January 2005: see SI 2004/3122, art 2.

GENERAL NOTE

See commentary on s.67 below.   1–305

65 Decisions as to refusal of discretionary disclosure of historical records

(1) Before refusing a request for information relating to   1–306
information which is contained in a historical record and
is exempt information only by virtue of a provision not
specified in section 2(3), a public authority shall—

    (a) if the historical record is a public record within the
meaning of the Public Records Act 1958, consult the
Lord Chancellor, or

    (b) if the historical record is a public record to which the
Public Records Act (Northern Ireland) 1923 applies,
consult the appropriate Northern Ireland Minister.

(2) This section does not apply to information to which
section 66 applies.

NOTES

Initial Commencement

Specified date

Specified date: 30 November 2005 (unless the Secretary of State by order appoints this section before that date): see s 87(3) (as amended by SI 2001/3500, art 8, Sch 2, Pt I, para 8(1)(o) and SI 2003/1887, art 9, Sch 2, para 12(1)(c)). (See appointment note below.)

Appointment

Appointment: 1 January 2005: see SI 2004/3122, art 2.

GENERAL NOTE

1–307   See commentary on s.67 below.

66 Decisions relating to certain transferred public records

1–308

(1) This section applies to any information which is (or, if it existed, would be) contained in a transferred public record, other than information which the responsible authority has designated as open information for the purposes of this section.

(2) Before determining whether—

(a) information to which this section applies falls within any provision of Part II relating to the duty to confirm or deny, or

(b) information to which this section applies is exempt information,

the appropriate records authority shall consult the responsible authority.

(3) Where information to which this section applies falls within a provision of Part II relating to the duty to confirm or deny but does not fall within any of the provisions of that Part relating to that duty which are specified in subsection (3) of section 2, any question as to the application of subsection (1)(b) of that section is to be determined by the responsible authority instead of the appropriate records authority.

(4) Where any information to which this section applies is exempt information only by virtue of any provision of Part II not specified in subsection (3) of section 2, any question as to the application of subsection (2)(b) of that section is to be determined by the responsible authority instead of the appropriate records authority.

(5) Before making by virtue of subsection (3) or (4) any determination that subsection (1)(b) or (2)(b) of section 2 applies, the responsible authority shall consult—

(a) where the transferred public record is a public record within the meaning of the Public Records Act 1958, the Lord Chancellor, and

(b) where the transferred public record is a public record to which the Public Records Act (Northern Ireland) 1923 applies, the appropriate Northern Ireland Minister.

(6) Where the responsible authority in relation to information to which this section applies is not (apart

from this subsection) a public authority, it shall be treated as being a public authority for the purposes of Parts III, IV and V of this Act so far as relating to—

(a) the duty imposed by section 15(3), and

(b) the imposition of any requirement to furnish information relating to compliance with Part I in connection with the information to which this section applies.

NOTES

Initial Commencement

Specified date

Specified date: 30 November 2005 (unless the Secretary of State by order appoints this section before that date): see s 87(3) (as amended by SI 2001/3500, art 8, Sch 2, Pt I, para 8(1)(o) and SI 2003/1887, art 9, Sch 2, para 12(1)(c)). (See appointment note below.)

Appointment

Appointment: 1 January 2005: see SI 2004/3122, art 2.

GENERAL NOTE

See commentary on s.15 above and s.67 below.   1–309

67 Amendments of public records legislation

Schedule 5 (which amends the Public Records Act 1958 and the   1–310
Public Records Act (Northern Ireland) 1923) has effect.

NOTES

Initial Commencement   1–311

Royal Assent

Royal Assent (for certain purposes): 30 November 2000: see s 87(1)(j).

Specified date

Specified date (for remaining purposes): 30 November 2005 (unless the Secretary of State by order appoints this section before that date): see s 87(3) (as amended by SI 2001/3500, art 8, Sch 2, Pt I, para 8(1)(o) and SI 2003/1887, art 9, Sch 2, para 12(1)(c)). (See appointment notes below.)

Appointment

Appointment (for certain purposes): 30 November 2002: see SI 2002/2812, art 2(j).
Appointment (for remaining purposes): 1 January 2005: see SI 2004/3122, art 2.

GENERAL NOTE

1–312   Until January 1, 2005, access to the historical records of government was controlled by the Public Records Act 1958 ("**PRA**"). The PRA system was based on the "30-year-rule", by which public records were transferred to the Public Records Office (PRO) and then made available on the 30th anniversary of their creation. FOIA has significantly modified this system. Although the *transfer* of records is still governed by the PRA, the PRO is treated like any other public authority and therefore access to information held by it now falls under FOIA.

Historical records

1–313   By virtue of s.62(1), records become "historical records" 30 years from the end of the year in which they were created. Information contained in *any* historical record (whether or not subject to the PRA) is deemed less likely to require exemption from FOIA after 30 years, on the basis that any sensitivity associated with it will have diminished in that time.

Section 63

1–314   The rules in s.63 appear complicated. In fact they mean simply that as soon as a record becomes historical it ceases (irrespective of whether it is subject to the PRA) to be eligible for exemption under the following sections:

- s.28 (relations within the UK);

- s.30(1) (investigations and proceedings, but note that only subs.(1) is disapplied);

- s.32 (court records);

- s.33 (audit functions);

- s.35 (formulation of government policy);

- s.36 (prejudice to the effective conduct of public affairs);

- s.37(1)(a) (communications with Her Majesty etc.);

- s.42 (legal privilege); and

- s.43 (commercial interests).

In addition, s.63(3) states that the exemption under s.37(1)(b) (conferring of honours) applies for 60 years (rather than 30), and ss.63(4) and (5) state that s.31 (law enforcement) applies for 100 years.

Section 64

Historical records which are held at the PRO are not eligible for exemption **1–315** under:

- s.21 (information accessible by other means); and

- s.22 (information intended for future publication).

Section 23 continues to apply to historical records held at the PRO but only as a qualified exemption.

All the other FOIA exemptions remain applicable without time limit.

See also the commentary on ss.15 and 21 in relation to public archives and public records.

Section 65—duty to consult before refusing access to information contained in certain historical records

The PRA requires those responsible for "public records"[73] to select records **1–316** suitable for safekeeping and transfer them to the PRO not later than 30 years after their creation. Selection and transfer is carried out under the guidance of the Keeper of Public Records[74] and overall responsibility for the public records regime lies with the Lord Chancellor.[75] Some records—for example those necessary for administrative purposes, such as property deeds—can be withheld from transfer to the PRO. There is a similar exception for records whose sensitivity is such that it is impossible to estimate when they should be released. In either case, however, records may only be withheld from transfer following approval of a formal application to the Lord Chancellor's Advisory Body on Public Records.

Section 65 applies to historical records which have not been transferred to the PRO. If following a FOIA request a public authority believes that a qualified exemption applies to such information, then it must consult either the Lord Chancellor or a Northern Ireland Minister before refusing access. This is to ensure that any assessment of the public interest in withholding older documents is properly scrutinised.

---

[73] The principal categories of "public records" are (a) records of government departments and bodies controlled by them (*e.g.* the Legal Services Commission and National Health Service Authorities), (b) records of various other bodies such as the Criminal Cases Review Commission, the Imperial War Museum and the Information Commissioner, and (c) records of courts and tribunals (Public Records Act 1958, Sch.1).
[74] Public Records Act 1958, s.2.
[75] Public Records Act 1958, s.1.

Section 66—decisions relating to certain transferred records

1–317   Section 66 applies to records transferred to the PRO which have not been designated as "open records" and are therefore not yet open to public scrutiny. Such records will usually be records which at the time of transfer the transferring body believed should remain FOIA exempt, and therefore requested remain closed to the public.[76]

Where the PRO receives a FOIA request for information which has been transferred to it but which is not an open record, then before deciding whether the information is exempt it must consult the department or body which transferred the record.[77] Where consultation concerns an absolute exemption, the final decision whether the information is exempt rests with the PRO. Where consultation concerns a qualified exemption, both the PRO and the transferring authority must make a decision, as follows:

- the PRO has the final decision whether the information falls within a particular qualified exemption;

- the transferring authority has the final decision on where the balance of the public interest lies.

Finally, the PRO must consult the Lord Chancellor or a Northern Ireland Minister before refusing a request on qualified exemption grounds. As with s.65, this is to ensure that any assessment of the public interest in withholding older documents is properly scrutinised.

Note that bodies such as MI5 and MI6 which are not public authorities for FOIA purposes must still be consulted under the s.66 procedure where the PRO receives a request for information transferred to it by such a body.

To facilitate the s.66 procedure s.15 requires the PRO to send a copy of any relevant request to the body which transferred the record. This applies whether or not the transferred record is a historical record (this is necessary to ensure the process operates correctly for records transferred in advance of the 30 year deadline). On receipt of the copy request, the body which transferred the record must make a decision about release within "such time as is reasonable in the circumstances".[78] This mirrors the general time limit available for public interest decisions.

---

[76] In these circumstances the Lord Chancellor's Code of Practice on the Management of Records requires the authority to produce a schedule explaining why particular information should not be released. The schedule is scrutinised by the Lord Chancellor's Advisory Council on Public Records and the Lord Chancellor himself is ultimately responsible for deciding whether to grant the request for continued closure.

[77] The body to be consulted is called the "responsible authority", defined in s.15(5).

[78] Freedom of Information Act 2000, s.15(3).

Part VII

Amendments of Data Protection Act 1998

Amendments relating to personal information held by public authorities

68 Extension of meaning of "data"

(1) Section 1 of the Data Protection Act 1998 (basic interpretative provisions) is amended in accordance with subsections (2) and (3).   1–318

(2) In subsection (1)—

    (a) in the definition of "data", the word "or" at the end of paragraph (c) is omitted and after paragraph (d) there is inserted

       "or

          (e) is recorded information held by a public authority and does not fall within any of paragraphs (a) to (d);", and

    (b) after the definition of "processing" there is inserted—

       " "public authority" has the same meaning as in the Freedom of Information Act 2000;".

(3) After subsection (4) there is inserted—

    "(5) In paragraph (e) of the definition of "data" in subsection (1), the reference to information "held" by a public authority shall be construed in accordance with section 3(2) of the Freedom of Information Act 2000.

    (6) Where section 7 of the Freedom of Information Act 2000 prevents Parts I to V of that Act from applying to certain information held by a public authority, that information is not to be treated for the purposes of paragraph (e) of the definition of "data" in subsection (1) as held by a public authority."

(4) In section 56 of that Act (prohibition of requirement as to production of certain records), after subsection (6) there is inserted—

    "(6A) A record is not a relevant record to the extent that it relates, or is to relate, only to personal data falling within paragraph (e) of the definition of "data" in section 1(1)."

211

(5) In the Table in section 71 of that Act (index of defined expressions) after the entry relating to processing there is inserted—

"public authority section 1(1)".

NOTES

Initial Commencement

Specified date

Specified date: 30 November 2005 (unless the Secretary of State by order appoints this section before that date): see s 87(3) (as amended by SI 2001/3500, art 8, Sch 2, Pt I, para 8(1)(o) and SI 2003/1887, art 9, Sch 2, para 12(1)(c)). (See appointment note below.)

Appointment

Appointment: 1 January 2005: see SI 2004/1909, art 2(1), (2)(f), (3).

GENERAL NOTE

1–319   See commentary on s.40 above.

69 Right of access to unstructured personal data held by public authorities

1–320

(1) In section 7(1) of the Data Protection Act 1998 (right of access to personal data), for "sections 8 and 9" there is substituted "sections 8, 9 and 9A".

(2) After section 9 of that Act there is inserted—

"**9A Unstructured personal data held by public authorities**

(1) In this section "unstructured personal data" means any personal data falling within paragraph (e) of the definition of "data" in section 1(1), other than information which is recorded as part of, or with the intention that it should form part of, any set of information relating to individuals to the extent that the set is structured by reference to individuals or by reference to criteria relating to individuals.

(2) A public authority is not obliged to comply with subsection (1) of section 7 in relation to any unstructured personal data unless the request under that section contains a description of the data.

212

(3) Even if the data are described by the data subject in his request, a public authority is not obliged to comply with subsection (1) of section 7 in relation to unstructured personal data if the authority estimates that the cost of complying with the request so far as relating to those data would exceed the appropriate limit.

(4) Subsection (3) does not exempt the public authority from its obligation to comply with paragraph (a) of section 7(1) in relation to the unstructured personal data unless the estimated cost of complying with that paragraph alone in relation to those data would exceed the appropriate limit.

(5) In subsections (3) and (4) "the appropriate limit" means such amount as may be prescribed by the Secretary of State by regulations, and different amounts may be prescribed in relation to different cases.

(6) Any estimate for the purposes of this section must be made in accordance with regulations under section 12(5) of the Freedom of Information Act 2000.".

(3) In section 67(5) of that Act (statutory instruments subject to negative resolution procedure), in paragraph (c), for "or 9(3)" there is substituted ", 9(3) or 9A(5)".

NOTES

Initial Commencement

Royal Assent

Royal Assent (in so far as this section confers powers to make any order, regulations or code of practice): 30 November 2000: see s 87(1)(m).

1–321

Specified date

Specified date (for remaining purposes): 30 November 2005 (unless the Secretary of State by order appoints this section before that date): see s 87(3) (as amended by SI 2001/3500, art 8, Sch 2, Pt I, para 8(1)(o) and SI 2003/1887, art 9, Sch 2, para 12(1)(c)). (See appointment note below.)

Appointment

Appointment (for remaining purposes): 1 January 2005: see SI 2004/1909, art 2(1), (2)(f), (3).

GENERAL NOTE

1–322   See commentary on s.40 above.

Section 69 introduces a new s.9A into the Data Protection Act 1998 which provides for access to unstructured personal data held by public authorities.

70 Exemptions applicable to certain manual data held by public authorities

1–323   (1) **After section 33 of the Data Protection Act 1998 there is inserted—**

"**33A Manual data held by public authorities**

(1) **Personal data falling within paragraph (e) of the definition of "data" in section 1(1) are exempt from—**

(a) **the first, second, third, fifth, seventh and eighth data protection principles,**

(b) **the sixth data protection principle except so far as it relates to the rights conferred on data subjects by sections 7 and 14,**

(c) **sections 10 to 12,**

(d) **section 13, except so far as it relates to damage caused by a contravention of section 7 or of the fourth data protection principle and to any distress which is also suffered by reason of that contravention,**

(e) **Part III, and**

(f) **section 55.**

(2) **Personal data which fall within paragraph (e) of the definition of "data" in section 1(1) and relate to appointments or removals, pay, discipline, superannuation or other personnel matters, in relation to—**

(a) **service in any of the armed forces of the Crown,**

(b) **service in any office or employment under the Crown or under any public authority, or**

(c) **service in any office or employment, or under any contract for services, in respect of which**

214

power to take action, or to determine or approve the action taken, in such matters is vested in Her Majesty, any Minister of the Crown, the National Assembly for Wales, any Northern Ireland Minister (within the meaning of the Freedom of Information Act 2000) or any public authority,

are also exempt from the remaining data protection principles and the remaining provisions of Part II."

(2) In section 55 of that Act (unlawful obtaining etc of personal data) in subsection (8) after "section 28" there is inserted "or 33A".

(3) In Part III of Schedule 8 to that Act (exemptions available after 23rd October 2001 but before 24th October 2007) after paragraph 14 there is inserted—

"14A

(1) This paragraph applies to personal data which fall within paragraph (e) of the definition of "data" in section 1(1) and do not fall within paragraph 14(1)(a), but does not apply to eligible manual data to which the exemption in paragraph 16 applies.

(2) During the second transitional period, data to which this paragraph applies are exempt from—

(a) the fourth data protection principle, and

(b) section 14(1) to (3)."

(4) In Schedule 13 to that Act (modifications of Act having effect before 24th October 2007) in subsection (4)(b) of section 12A to that Act as set out in paragraph 1, after "paragraph 14" there is inserted "or 14A".

NOTES

Initial Commencement

Specified date

Specified date: 30 November 2005 (unless the Secretary of State by order appoints this section before that date): see s 87(3) (as amended by SI 2001/3500, art 8, Sch 2, Pt I, para 8(1)(o) and SI 2003/1887, art 9, Sch 2, para 12(1)(c)). (See appointment note below.)

Appointment

Appointment: 1 January 2005: see SI 2004/1909, art 2(1), (2)(f), (3).

GENERAL NOTE

1–324   Section 70 introduces a new s.33A into the Data Protection 1998. Section 33A exempts unstructured manual records held by public authorities from most of the DPA rules.

71 Particulars registrable under Part III of Data Protection Act 1998

1–325   In section 16(1) of the Data Protection Act 1998 (the registrable particulars), before the word "and" at the end of paragraph (f) there is inserted—

> "(ff) where the data controller is a public authority, a statement of that fact,".

NOTES

Initial Commencement

Specified date

Specified date: 30 November 2005 (unless the Secretary of State by order appoints this section before that date): see s 87(3) (as amended by SI 2001/3500, art 8, Sch 2, Pt I, para 8(1)(o) and SI 2003/1887, art 9, Sch 2, para 12(1)(c)). (See appointment note below.)

Appointment

Appointment: 1 January 2005: see SI 2004/1909, art 2(1), (2)(f), (3).

72 Availability under Act disregarded for purpose of exemption

1–326   In section 34 of the Data Protection Act 1998 (information available to the public by or under enactment), after the word "enactment" there is inserted "other than an enactment contained in the Freedom of Information Act 2000".

NOTES

Initial Commencement

Specified date

Specified date: 30 November 2005 (unless the Secretary of State by order appoints this section before that date): see s 87(3) (as amended by SI 2001/3500, art 8, Sch 2, Pt I, para 8(1)(o) and SI 2003/1887, art 9, Sch 2, para 12(1)(c)). (See appointment note below.)

Appointment

Appointment: 30 November 2002: see SI 2002/2812, art 2(k).

73 Further amendments of Data Protection Act 1998

Schedule 6 (which contains further amendments of the Data Protection Act 1998) has effect.

1–327

NOTES

Initial Commencement

Royal Assent

Royal Assent (for certain purposes): 30 November 2000: see s 87(1)(k).

Specified date

Specified date (for remaining purposes): 30 November 2005 (unless the Secretary of State by order appoints this section before that date): see s 87(3) (as amended by SI 2001/3500, art 8, Sch 2, Pt I, para 8(1)(o) and SI 2003/1887, art 9, Sch 2, para 12(1)(c)). (See appointment notes below.)

Appointment

Appointment (for certain purposes): 14 May 2001: see SI 2001/1637, art 2(d). Appointment (for remaining purposes): 1 January 2005: see SI 2004/1909, art 2(1), (2)(f), (3).

Part VIII

Miscellaneous and Supplemental

74 Power to make provision relating to environmental information

(1) In this section "the Aarhus Convention" means the Convention on Access to Information, Public Participation in Decision-making and Access to Justice in Environmental Matters signed at Aarhus on 25th June 1998.

(2) For the purposes of this section "the information provisions" of the Aarhus Convention are Article 4, together with Articles 3 and 9 so far as relating to that Article.

(3) The Secretary of State may by regulations make such provision as he considers appropriate—

(a) for the purpose of implementing the information provisions of the Aarhus Convention or any amendment of those provisions made in accordance with Article 14 of the Convention, and

(b) for the purpose of dealing with matters arising out of or related to the implementation of those provisions or of any such amendment.

(4) Regulations under subsection (3) may in particular—

(a) enable charges to be made for making information available in accordance with the regulations,

(b) provide that any obligation imposed by the regulations in relation to the disclosure of information is to have effect notwithstanding any enactment or rule of law,

(c) make provision for the issue by the Secretary of State of a code of practice,

(d) provide for sections 47 and 48 to apply in relation to such a code with such modifications as may be specified,

(e) provide for any of the provisions of Parts IV and V to apply, with such modifications as may be specified in the regulations, in relation to compliance with any requirement of the regulations, and

(f) contain such transitional or consequential provision (including provision modifying any enactment) as the Secretary of State considers appropriate.

(5) This section has effect subject to section 80.

NOTES

Initial Commencement

Royal Assent

Royal Assent: 30 November 2000: see s 87(1)(f).

75 Power to amend or repeal enactments prohibiting disclosure of information

(1) If, with respect to any enactment which prohibits the disclosure of information held by a public authority, it appears to the [Secretary of State] that by virtue of section 44(1)(a) the enactment is capable of preventing the disclosure of information under section 1, he may by order repeal or amend the enactment for the purpose of removing or relaxing the prohibition.

1–329

(2) In subsection (1)—

"enactment" means—

(a) any enactment contained in an Act passed before or in the same Session as this Act, or

(b) any enactment contained in Northern Ireland legislation or subordinate legislation passed or made before the passing of this Act;

"information" includes unrecorded information.

(3) An order under this section may do all or any of the following—

(a) make such modifications of enactments as, in the opinion of the [Secretary of State], are consequential upon, or incidental to, the amendment or repeal of the enactment containing the prohibition;

(b) contain such transitional provisions and savings as appear to the [Secretary of State] to be appropriate;

(c) make different provision for different cases.

NOTES

Initial Commencement

1–330

Royal Assent

Royal Assent: 30 November 2000: see s 87(1)(g).

Amendment

Sub-s (1): words "Secretary of State" in square brackets substituted by SI 2003/1887, art 9, Sch 2, para 12(1)(c).
Date in force: 19 August 2003: see SI 2003/1887, art 1(2).
Sub-s (3): in paras (a), (b) words "Secretary of State" in square brackets substituted by SI 2003/1887, art 9, Sch 2, para 12(1)(c).
Date in force: 19 August 2003: see SI 2003/1887, art 1(2).

Subordinate Legislation

Freedom of Information (Removal and Relaxation of Statutory Prohibitions on Disclosure of Information) Order 2004, SI 2004/3363.

GENERAL NOTE

1–331   Section 75 gives the Lord Chancellor power to repeal or amend any existing statute or statutory instrument which is capable of preventing disclosure of information under FOIA. The DCA commenced a review of statutory provisions in 1998. Its report, published on June 16, 2005, identified 448 provisions which limit disclosure of information in some way. However, of these, only 210 were deemed to merit consideration under s.75. Forty-nine will be amended or repealed, of which less than half will be repealed in their entirety. At the time of writing, only one statutory instrument, dealing with eight repeals and amendments has been passed: SI 2004/3363, The Freedom of Information (Removal and Relaxation of Statutory Prohibitions on Disclosure of Information) Order 2004.

A copy of the DCA report is available at:
http://www.dca.gov.uk/StatutoryBarsReport2005.pdf.

Practitioners should ensure they check up-to-date versions of any statutory provision where they believe a restriction on disclosure may exist.

76 Disclosure of information between Commissioner and ombudsmen

1–332   (1) The Commissioner may disclose to a person specified in the first column of the Table below any information obtained by, or furnished to, the Commissioner under or for the purposes of this Act or the Data Protection Act 1998 if it appears to the Commissioner that the information relates to a matter which could be the subject of an investigation by that person under the enactment specified in relation to that person in the second column of that Table.

TABLE

Ombudsman	Enactment
The Parliamentary Commissioner for Administration.	The Parliamentary Commissioner Act 1967 (c 13).
The Health Service Commissioner for England.	The Health Service Commissioners Act 1993 (c 46).
The Health Service Commissioner for Wales.	The Health Service Commissioners Act 1993 (c 46).
...	...
A Local Commissioner as defined by section 23(3) of the Local Government Act 1974.	Part III of the Local Government Act 1974 (c 7).
[The Scottish Public Services Ombudsman	The Scottish Public Services Ombudsman Act 2002 (asp 11)]
...	...
...	...
The Welsh Administration Ombudsman.	Schedule 9 to the Government of Wales Act 1998 (c 38).
[The Social Housing Ombudsman for Wales	Part 1, Chapter 5 of the Housing Act 1996 (c 52).]
The Northern Ireland Commissioner for Complaints.	The Commissioner for Complaints (Northern Ireland) Order 1996 (SI 1996/1297 (NI 7)).
The Assembly Ombudsman for Northern Ireland.	The Ombudsman (Northern Ireland) Order 1996 (SI 1996/1298 (NI 8)).

(2) Schedule 7 (which contains amendments relating to information disclosed to ombudsmen under subsection (1) and to the disclosure of information by ombudsmen to the Commissioner) has effect.

NOTES

Initial Commencement

1–333

Specified date

Specified date: 30 January 2001: see s 87(2)(b).

Amendment

Sub-s (1): Table: entries relating to "The Health Service Commissioner for Scotland", "The Commissioner for Local Administration in Scotland" and "The Scottish Parliamentary Commissioner for Administration" (omitted) repealed by the Scottish Public Services Ombudsman Act 2002, s 25(1), Sch 6, para 23(1), (2)(a).

Date in force: 23 October 2002: see SSI 2002/467, art 2.

Sub-s (1): Table: entry relating to "The Scottish Public Services Ombudsman" inserted by the Scottish Public Services Ombudsman Act 2002, s 25(1), Sch 6, para 23(1), (2)(b).

Date in force: 23 October 2002: see SSI 2002/467, art 2.

Sub-s (1): Table: entry relating to "The Social Housing Ombudsman for Wales" inserted by the Housing Act 2004, s 265(1), Sch 15, para 46.

Date in force: to be appointed: see the Housing Act 2004, s 270(4), (5)(c), (f).

[76A Disclosure between Commissioner and Scottish Information Commissioner]

1–334

[The Commissioner may disclose to the Scottish Information Commissioner any information obtained or furnished as mentioned in section 76(1) of this Act if it appears to the Commissioner that the information is of the same type that could be obtained by, or furnished to, the Scottish Information Commissioner under or for the purposes of the Freedom of Information (Scotland) Act 2002.]

NOTES

Amendment

Inserted by SI 2004/3089, art 3(1), (2).

Date in force: 1 January 2005: see SI 2004/3089, art 1.

77 Offence of altering etc records with intent to prevent disclosure

1–335

(1) Where—

(a) a request for information has been made to a public authority, and

(b) under section 1 of this Act or section 7 of the Data Protection Act 1998, the applicant would have been entitled (subject to payment of any fee) to communication of any information in accordance with that section,

any person to whom this subsection applies is guilty of an offence if he alters, defaces, blocks, erases, destroys or conceals any record held by the public authority, with the intention of preventing the disclosure by that authority of all, or any part, of the information to the communication of which the applicant would have been entitled.

(2) Subsection (1) applies to the public authority and to any person who is employed by, is an officer of, or is subject to the direction of, the public authority.

(3) A person guilty of an offence under this section is liable on summary conviction to a fine not exceeding level 5 on the standard scale.

(4) No proceedings for an offence under this section shall be instituted—

(a) in England or Wales, except by the Commissioner or by or with the consent of the Director of Public Prosecutions;

(b) in Northern Ireland, except by the Commissioner or by or with the consent of the Director of Public Prosecutions for Northern Ireland.

NOTES

Initial Commencement

Specified date

Specified date: 30 November 2005 (unless the Secretary of State by order appoints this section before that date): see s 87(3) (as amended by SI 2001/3500, art 8, Sch 2, Pt I, para 8(1)(o) and SI 2003/1887, art 9, Sch 2, para 12(1)(c)). (See appointment note below.)

Appointment

Appointment: 1 January 2005: see SI 2004/1909, art 2(1), (2)(g), (3).

GENERAL NOTE

Section 77 makes it a criminal offence to alter, deface, block, erase, destroy **1–336** or conceal any record with the intention of preventing FOIA disclosure. The offence applies to any employee or officer of a public authority or to anyone subject to the direction of a public authority.

The wording of subs.1 means that:

- it is not an offence to alter, deface etc. if the applicant is/was not entitled to the information anyway (either because an exemption applies or because ss.12 or 14 apply); but

- it is an offence merely to *attempt* to alter, deface etc. if there was an intention to defeat the legitimate exercise of the right of access (so even bungled attempts to do so are an offence).

See also the commentary on s.1(4) above.

78 Saving for existing powers

1–337   **Nothing in this Act is to be taken to limit the powers of a public authority to disclose information held by it.**

NOTES

Initial Commencement

Royal Assent

Royal Assent: 30 November 2000: see s 87(1)(h).

79 Defamation

1–338   **Where any information communicated by a public authority to a person ("the applicant") under section 1 was supplied to the public authority by a third person, the publication to the applicant of any defamatory matter contained in the information shall be privileged unless the publication is shown to have been made with malice.**

NOTES

Initial Commencement

Royal Assent

Royal Assent: 30 November 2000: see s 87(1)(h).

GENERAL NOTE

1–339   Note that while s.79 precludes a claim of defamation against an authority as a result of any non-malicious disclosure in accordance with s.1 of FOIA, the protection only applies to information supplied to the authority by third parties. Information created by the authority itself is not protected.

Defamation

1–340   Defamation is the publishing of a statement which either lowers an individual or a company in the estimation of the public, exposes them to hatred, contempt or ridicule, or causes them to be shunned or avoided.

There are two forms of defamation. These are libel (which is the permanent form, being contained in a document or film) and slander (which is the transient or verbal form). Since FOIA is concerned with the disclosure of information recorded in permanent form, s.79 is concerned with possible claims for libel.

A claim of defamation must be made to the High Court.

Meaning of "publishing" of a statement

For a statement to be actionable, it must have been communicated to a   1–341
third party, *i.e.* someone other than the person claiming to have been libelled. A person will be liable for any publication which he intends or can reasonably anticipate, and also for a publication which is unintentional but occurred because of a want of care.

Defamatory meaning

To be defamatory, the words used in a statement must bear a defamatory   1–342
meaning and also refer to the claimant. In interpreting this, the courts assess the natural and ordinary meaning of the words, together with any inference that the words may convey to an ordinary, reasonable and fair minded reader.[79]

Defences

The principle defences are based on justification (truth), fair comment on   1–343
a matter of public interest, parliamentary privilege (absolute and qualified), innocent dissemination, offer of amends, and consent to publication.

Remedies

The principal remedy is damages. An interim injunction may be awarded   1–344
where a claimant can prove that the defendant is intending to publish material which is clearly untrue and to which there is no arguable defence.

80 Scotland

(1) No order may be made under section 4(1) or 5 in relation   1–345
to any of the bodies specified in subsection (2); and the power conferred by section 74(3) does not include power to make provision in relation to information held by any of those bodies.

(2) The bodies referred to in subsection (1) are—

(a) the Scottish Parliament,

(b) any part of the Scottish Administration,

---

[79] Lord Bridge in *Charleston and Another v News Group Newspapers Ltd* [1995] 2 AC 65.

(c) the Scottish Parliamentary Corporate Body, or

(d) any Scottish public authority with mixed functions or no reserved functions (within the meaning of the Scotland Act 1998).

[(3) Section 50 of the Copyright, Designs and Patents Act 1988 and paragraph 6 of Schedule 1 to the Copyright and Rights in Databases Regulations 1997 apply in relation to the Freedom of Information (Scotland) Act 2002 as they apply in relation to this Act.]

NOTES

Initial Commencement

Royal Assent

Royal Assent: 30 November 2000: see s 87(1)(h).

Amendment

Sub-s (3): inserted by SI 2004/3089, art 3(1), (3).
    Date in force: 1 January 2005: see SI 2004/3089, art 1.

81 Application to government departments, etc

1–346

(1) For the purposes of this Act each government department is to be treated as a person separate from any other government department.

(2) Subsection (1) does not enable—

(a) a government department which is not a Northern Ireland department to claim for the purposes of section 41(1)(b) that the disclosure of any information by it would constitute a breach of confidence actionable by any other government department (not being a Northern Ireland department), or

(b) a Northern Ireland department to claim for those purposes that the disclosure of information by it would constitute a breach of confidence actionable by any other Northern Ireland department.

(3) A government department is not liable to prosecution under this Act, but section 77 and paragraph 12 of Schedule 3 apply to a person in the public service of the Crown as they apply to any other person.

(4) The provisions specified in subsection (3) also apply to a person acting on behalf of either House of Parliament or

on behalf of the Northern Ireland Assembly as they apply to any other person.

NOTES

Initial Commencement

Royal Assent

Royal Assent: 30 November 2000: see s 87(1)(h).

82 Orders and regulations

(1) Any power of the [. . .] Secretary of State to make an order or regulations under this Act shall be exercisable by statutory instrument. 1–347

(2) A statutory instrument containing (whether alone or with other provisions)—

(a) an order under section 5, 7(3) or (8), 53(1)(a)(iii) or 75, or

(b) regulations under section 10(4) or 74(3),

shall not be made unless a draft of the instrument has been laid before, and approved by a resolution of, each House of Parliament.

(3) A statutory instrument which contains (whether alone or with other provisions)—

(a) an order under section 4(1), or

(b) regulations under any provision of this Act not specified in subsection (2)(b),

and which is not subject to the requirement in subsection (2) that a draft of the instrument be laid before and approved by a resolution of each House of Parliament, shall be subject to annulment in pursuance of a resolution of either House of Parliament.

(4) An order under section 4(5) shall be laid before Parliament after being made.

(5) If a draft of an order under section 5 or 7(8) would, apart from this subsection, be treated for the purposes of the Standing Orders of either House of Parliament as a hybrid instrument, it shall proceed in that House as if it were not such an instrument.

NOTES

Initial Commencement

Royal Assent

Royal Assent: 30 November 2000: see s 87(1)(h).

Amendment

Sub-s (1): words (omitted) inserted by SI 2001/3500, art 8, Sch 2, Pt I, para 8(3).
    Date in force: 26 November 2001: see SI 2001/3500, art 1(2).
Sub-s (1): words omitted repealed by SI 2003/1887, art 9, Sch 2, para 12(3).
    Date in force: 19 August 2003: see SI 2003/1887, art 1(2).

83 Meaning of "Welsh public authority"

1–348

(1) In this Act "Welsh public authority" means—

(a) any public authority which is listed in Part II, III, IV or VI of Schedule 1 and whose functions are exercisable only or mainly in or as regards Wales, other than an excluded authority, or

(b) any public authority which is an Assembly subsidiary as defined by section 99(4) of the Government of Wales Act 1998.

(2) In paragraph (a) of subsection (1) "excluded authority" means a public authority which is designated by the [Secretary of State] by order as an excluded authority for the purposes of that paragraph.

(3) Before making an order under subsection (2), the [Secretary of State] shall consult the National Assembly for Wales.

NOTES

1–349   Initial Commencement

Royal Assent

Royal Assent: 30 November 2000: see s 87(1)(h).

Subordinate Legislation

Freedom of Information (Excluded Welsh Authorities) Order 2002, SI 2002/2832 (made under sub-s (2)).

84 Interpretation

1–350   In this Act, unless the context otherwise requires—
"applicant", in relation to a request for information, means the person who made the request;

"appropriate Northern Ireland Minister" means the Northern Ireland Minister in charge of the Department of Culture, Arts and Leisure in Northern Ireland;

"appropriate records authority", in relation to a transferred public record, has the meaning given by section 15(5);

"body" includes an unincorporated association;

"the Commissioner" means the Information Commissioner;

"decision notice" has the meaning given by section 50;

"the duty to confirm or deny" has the meaning given by section 1(6);

"enactment" includes an enactment contained in Northern Ireland legislation;

"enforcement notice" has the meaning given by section 52;

"executive committee", in relation to the National Assembly for Wales, has the same meaning as in the Government of Wales Act 1998;

"exempt information" means information which is exempt information by virtue of any provision of Part II;

"fees notice" has the meaning given by section 9(1);

"government department" includes a Northern Ireland department, the Northern Ireland Court Service and any other body or authority exercising statutory functions on behalf of the Crown, but does not include—

(a) any of the bodies specified in section 80(2),

(b) the Security Service, the Secret Intelligence Service or the Government Communications Headquarters, or

(c) the National Assembly for Wales;

"information" (subject to sections 51(8) and 75(2)) means information recorded in any form;

"information notice" has the meaning given by section 51;

"Minister of the Crown" has the same meaning as in the Ministers of the Crown Act 1975;

"Northern Ireland Minister" includes the First Minister and deputy First Minister in Northern Ireland;

"Northern Ireland public authority" means any public authority, other than the Northern Ireland Assembly or a Northern

Ireland department, whose functions are exercisable only or mainly in or as regards Northern Ireland and relate only or mainly to transferred matters;

"prescribed" means prescribed by regulations made by the [Secretary of State];

"public authority" has the meaning given by section 3(1);

"public record" means a public record within the meaning of the Public Records Act 1958 or a public record to which the Public Records Act (Northern Ireland) 1923 applies;

"publication scheme" has the meaning given by section 19;

"request for information" has the meaning given by section 8;

"responsible authority", in relation to a transferred public record, has the meaning given by section 15(5);

"the special forces" means those units of the armed forces of the Crown the maintenance of whose capabilities is the responsibility of the Director of Special Forces or which are for the time being subject to the operational command of that Director;

"subordinate legislation" has the meaning given by subsection (1) of section 21 of the Interpretation Act 1978, except that the definition of that term in that subsection shall have effect as if "Act" included Northern Ireland legislation;

"transferred matter", in relation to Northern Ireland, has the meaning given by section 4(1) of the Northern Ireland Act 1998;

"transferred public record" has the meaning given by section 15(4);

"the Tribunal" means the Information Tribunal;

"Welsh public authority" has the meaning given by section 83.

NOTES

Initial Commencement

Royal Assent

Royal Assent: 30 November 2000: see s 87(1)(h).

Amendment

In definition "prescribed" words "Secretary of State" in square brackets substituted by SI 2003/1887, art 9, Sch 2, para 12(1)(c).
Date in force: 19 August 2003: see SI 2003/1887, art 1(2).

85 Expenses

There shall be paid out of money provided by Parliament— 1–351

(a) any increase attributable to this Act in the expenses of the [Secretary of State] in respect of the Commissioner, the Tribunal or the members of the Tribunal,

(b) any administrative expenses of the [Secretary of State] attributable to this Act,

(c) any other expenses incurred in consequence of this Act by a Minister of the Crown or government department or by either House of Parliament, and

(d) any increase attributable to this Act in the sums which under any other Act are payable out of money so provided.

NOTES

Initial Commencement

Royal Assent

Royal Assent: 30 November 2000: see s 87(1)(h).

86 Repeals

Schedule 8 (repeals) has effect. 1–352

NOTES

Initial Commencement

Royal Assent

Royal Assent (for certain purposes): 30 November 2000: see s 87(1)(l).

Specified date

Specified date (for certain purposes): 30 January 2001: see s 87(2)(d). Specified date (for remaining purposes): 30 November 2005 (unless the Secretary of State by order appoints this section before that date): see s 87(3) (as amended by SI 2001/3500, art 8, Sch 2, Pt I, para 8(1)(o) and SI 2003/1887, art 9, Sch 2, para 12(1)(c)). (See appointment note below.)

Appointment

Appointment: 1 January 2005: by virtue of SI 2004/1909, art 2(1), (2)(f), (3).

87 Commencement

(1) The following provisions of this Act shall come into force on the day on which this Act is passed—

    (a) sections 3 to 8 and Schedule 1,

    (b) section 19 so far as relating to the approval of publication schemes,

    (c) section 20 so far as relating to the approval and preparation by the Commissioner of model publication schemes,

    (d) section 47(2) to (6),

    (e) section 49,

    (f) section 74,

    (g) section 75,

    (h) sections 78 to 85 and this section,

    (i) paragraphs 2 and 17 to 22 of Schedule 2 (and section 18(4) so far as relating to those paragraphs),

    (j) paragraph 4 of Schedule 5 (and section 67 so far as relating to that paragraph),

    (k) paragraph 8 of Schedule 6 (and section 73 so far as relating to that paragraph),

    (l) Part I of Schedule 8 (and section 86 so far as relating to that Part), and

    (m) so much of any other provision of this Act as confers power to make any order, regulations or code of practice.

(2) The following provisions of this Act shall come into force at the end of the period of two months beginning with the day on which this Act is passed—

    (a) section 18(1),

    (b) section 76 and Schedule 7,

    (c) paragraphs 1(1), 3(1), 4, 6, 7, 8(2), 9(2), 10(a), 13(1) and (2), 14(a) and 15(1) and (2) of Schedule 2 (and section 18(4) so far as relating to those provisions), and

    (d) Part II of Schedule 8 (and section 86 so far as relating to that Part).

(3) Except as provided by subsections (1) and (2), this Act shall come into force at the end of the period of five years beginning with the day on which this Act is passed or on such day before the end of that period as the [Secretary of State] may by order appoint; and different days may be appointed for different purposes.

(4) An order under subsection (3) may contain such transitional provisions and savings (including provisions capable of having effect after the end of the period referred to in that subsection) as the [Secretary of State] considers appropriate.

(5) During the twelve months beginning with the day on which this Act is passed, and during each subsequent complete period of twelve months in the period beginning with that day and ending with the first day on which all the provisions of this Act are fully in force, the [Secretary of State] shall—

(a) prepare a report on his proposals for bringing fully into force those provisions of this Act which are not yet fully in force, and

(b) lay a copy of the report before each House of Parliament.

NOTES

Initial Commencement   1–354

Royal Assent

Royal Assent: 30 November 2000: see s 87(1)(h).

Subordinate Legislation

Freedom of Information Act 2000 (Commencement No 1) Order 2001, SI 2001/1637 (made under sub-s (3)).
Freedom of Information Act 2000 (Commencement No 2) Order 2002, SI 2002/2812 (made under sub-s (3)).
Freedom of Information Act 2000 (Commencement No 3) Order 2003, SI 2003/2603 (made under sub-s (3)).
Freedom of Information Act 2000 (Commencement No 4) Order 2004, SI 2004/1909 (made under sub-s (3)).
Freedom of Information Act 2000 (Commencement No 5) Order 2004, SI 2004/3122 (made under sub-s (3)).

88 Short title and extent

(1) This Act may be cited as the Freedom of Information Act   1–355
2000.

(2) Subject to subsection (3), this Act extends to Northern Ireland.

(3) The amendment or repeal of any enactment by this Act has the same extent as that enactment.

NOTES

Initial Commencement

Specified date

Specified date: 30 November 2005 (unless the Secretary of State by order appoints this section before that date): see s 87(3) (as amended by SI 2001/3500, art 8, Sch 2, Pt I, para 8(1)(o) and SI 2003/1887, art 9, Sch 2, para 12(1)(c)). (See appointment note below.)

Appointment

Appointment: 30 November 2002: see SI 2002/2812, art 2(l).

SCHEDULE 1

PUBLIC AUTHORITIES

SECTION 3(1)(A)(I)

PART I

GENERAL

1 Any government department.   1–356

2 The House of Commons.

3 The House of Lords.

4 The Northern Ireland Assembly.

5 The National Assembly for Wales.

6 The armed forces of the Crown, except—

    (a) the special forces, and

    (b) any unit or part of a unit which is for the time being required by the Secretary of State to assist the Government Communications Headquarters in the exercise of its functions.

NOTES

Initial Commencement

Royal Assent

Royal Assent: 30 November 2000: see s 87(1)(a).

PART II

LOCAL GOVERNMENT

England and Wales

7 A local authority within the meaning of the Local   1–357
Government Act 1972, namely—

(a) in England, a county council, a London borough council, a district council or a parish council,

(b) in Wales, a county council, a county borough council or a community council.

8 The Greater London Authority.

9 The Common Council of the City of London, in respect of information held in its capacity as a local authority, police authority or port health authority.

10 The Sub-Treasurer of the Inner Temple or the Under-Treasurer of the Middle Temple, in respect of information held in his capacity as a local authority.

11 The Council of the Isles of Scilly.

12 A parish meeting constituted under section 13 of the Local Government Act 1972.

13 Any charter trustees constituted under section 246 of the Local Government Act 1972.

[14 A fire and rescue authority constituted by a scheme under section 2 of the Fire and Rescue Services Act 2004 or a scheme to which section 4 of that Act applies.]

15 A waste disposal authority established by virtue of an order under section 10(1) of the Local Government Act 1985.

16 A port health authority constituted by an order under section 2 of the Public Health (Control of Disease) Act 1984.

17 *A licensing planning committee constituted under section 119* of the Licensing Act 1964.

18 An internal drainage board which is continued in being by virtue of section 1 of the Land Drainage Act 1991.

19 A joint authority established under Part IV of the Local Government Act 1985 [(fire and rescue services and transport)].

20 The London Fire and Emergency Planning Authority.

21 A joint fire authority established by virtue of an order under section 42(2) of the Local Government Act 1985 (reorganisation of functions).

22 A body corporate established pursuant to an order under section 67 of the Local Government Act 1985 (transfer of functions to successors of residuary bodies, etc).

23 A body corporate established pursuant to an order under section 22 of the Local Government Act 1992 (residuary bodies).

24 The Broads Authority established by section 1 of the Norfolk and Suffolk Broads Act 1988.

25 A joint committee constituted in accordance with section 102(1)(b) of the Local Government Act 1972.

26 A joint board which is continued in being by virtue of section 263(1) of the Local Government Act 1972.

27 A joint authority established under section 21 of the Local Government Act 1992.

28 A Passenger Transport Executive for a passenger transport area within the meaning of Part II of the Transport Act 1968.

29 Transport for London.

30 The London Transport Users Committee.

31 A joint board the constituent members of which consist of any of the public authorities described in paragraphs 8, 9, 10, 12, 15, 16, 20 to 31, 57 and 58.

32 A National Park authority established by an order under section 63 of the Environment Act 1995.

33 A joint planning board constituted for an area in Wales outside a National Park by an order under section 2(1B) of the Town and Country Planning Act 1990.

34 . . .

35 The London Development Agency.

[35A A local fisheries committee for a sea fisheries district established under section 1 of the Sea Fisheries Regulation Act 1966.]

Northern Ireland

36 A district council within the meaning of the Local Government Act (Northern Ireland) 1972.

NOTES

Initial Commencement   1–358

Royal Assent

Royal Assent: 30 November 2000: see s 87(1)(a).

Amendment

Para 14: substituted by the Fire and Rescue Services Act 2004, s 53(1), Sch 1, para 95.

> Date in force (in relation to England): 1 October 2004: see SI 2004/2304, art 2(2).
> Date in force (in relation to Wales): 10 November 2004: see SI 2004/2917, art 2.

Para 17: repealed by the Licensing Act 2003, s 199, Sch 7.

> Date in force: to be appointed: see the Licensing Act 2003, s 201(2).

Para 19: words "(fire and rescue services and transport)" in square brackets substituted by the Civil Contingencies Act 2004, s 32(1), Sch 2, Pt 1, para 10(3)(d).

> Date in force: 1 April 2005: see SI 2005/772, art 2(b).

Para 34: repealed by the Courts Act 2003, s 109(1), (3), Sch 8, para 392, Sch 10.

> Date in force: 1 April 2005: see SI 2005/910, art 3(y), (aa); for transitional provisions see SI 2005/911, arts 2–5.

Para 35A: inserted by virtue of SI 2004/938, art 2, Sch 1 (as amended by SI 2004/1870, art 2).

> Date in force: 19 April 2004: see SI 2004/938, art 1(1).

PART III

THE NATIONAL HEALTH SERVICE

England and Wales

1–359

[36A A Strategic Health Authority established under section 8 of the National Health Service Act 1977.]

37 A Health Authority established under section 8 of the National Health Service Act 1977.

38 A special health authority established under section 11 of the National Health Service Act 1977.

39 A primary care trust established under section 16A of the National Health Service Act 1977.

[39A A Local Health Board established under section 16BA of the National Health Service Act 1977.]

40 A National Health Service trust established under section 5 of the National Health Service and Community Care Act 1990.

[40A An NHS foundation trust.]

41 A Community Health Council [continued in existence by or established under section 20A] of the National Health Service Act 1977.

[41A A Patients' Forum established under section 15 of the National Health Service Reform and Health Care Professions Act 2002.]

42 *The Dental Practice Board constituted under regulations made under section 37* of the National Health Service Act 1977.

43 ...

[43A Any person providing primary medical services or primary dental services—

    (a) in accordance with arrangements made under section 28C of the National Health Service Act 1977; or

    (b) under a contract under section 28K or 28Q of that Act;

in respect of information relating to the provision of those services.]

44 Any person providing *general medical services, general dental services,* general ophthalmic services or pharmaceutical services under Part II of the National Health Service Act 1977, in respect of information relating to the provision of those services.

45 *Any person providing personal medical services or personal dental services under arrangements made under section 28C* of the National Health Service Act 1977, in respect of information relating to the provision of those services.

[45A Any person providing local pharmaceutical services under—

    (a) a pilot scheme established under section 28 of the Health and Social Care Act 2001; or

    (b) an LPS scheme established under Schedule 8A to the National Health Service Act 1977 (c 49),

in respect of information relating to the provision of those services.]

[45B The Commission for Patient and Public Involvement in Health.]

Northern Ireland

1–360

46 A Health and Social Services Board established under Article 16 of the Health and Personal Social Services (Northern Ireland) Order 1972.

47 A Health and Social Services Council established under Article 4 of the Health and Personal Social Services (Northern Ireland) Order 1991.

48 A Health and Social Services Trust established under Article 10 of the Health and Personal Social Services (Northern Ireland) Order 1991.

49 A special agency established under Article 3 of the Health and Personal Social Services (Special Agencies) (Northern Ireland) Order 1990.

50 The Northern Ireland Central Services Agency for the Health and Social Services established under Article 26 of the Health and Personal Social Services (Northern Ireland) Order 1972.

51 Any person providing [primary medical services], general dental services, general ophthalmic services or pharmaceutical services under Part VI of the Health and Personal Social Services (Northern Ireland) Order 1972, in respect of information relating to the provision of those services.

NOTES

Initial Commencement

1–361

Royal Assent

Royal Assent: 30 November 2000: see s 87(1)(a).

Amendment

Para 36A: inserted by SI 2002/2469, reg 4, Sch 1, Pt 1, para 29.
    Date in force: 1 October 2002: see SI 2002/2469, reg 1.
Para 39A: inserted by the National Health Service Reform and Health Care Professions Act 2002, s 6(2), Sch 5, para 48.
    Date in force: 10 October 2002: see SI 2002/2532, art 2, Schedule.
Para 40A: inserted by the Health and Social Care (Community Health and Standards) Act 2003, s 34, Sch 4, paras 113, 114.
    Date in force: 1 April 2004: see SI 2004/759, art 2.
Para 41: words "continued in existence by or established under section 20A" in square brackets substituted by the Health (Wales) Act 2003, s 7(1), Sch 3, para 14.
    Date in force (in relation to Wales): 20 October 2003: see SI 2003/2660, art 2(1)(ii), (2).

Date in force (in relation to England): 1 December 2003: see SI 2003/3064, art 2(1)(ii), (2).

Para 41A: inserted by the National Health Service Reform and Health Care Professions Act 2002, s 19(7).

Date in force: 1 September 2003: see SI 2003/2246, art 2(a).

Para 42: repealed by the Health and Social Care (Community Health and Standards) Act 2003, s 196, Sch 14, Pt 4.

Date in force: to be appointed: see the Health and Social Care (Community Health and Standards) Act 2003, s 199(1)–(3).

Para 43: repealed by the Health and Social Care (Community Health and Standards) Act 2003, ss 190(2), 196, Sch 13, para 10, Sch 14, Pt 7.

Date in force: 1 April 2005: see SI 2005/457, art 2(1)(a), (b).

Para 43A: inserted by the Health and Social Care (Community Health and Standards) Act 2003, s 184, Sch 11, para 68.

Date in force (in relation to England): 17 January 2005: see SI 2005/38, art 2(c); for transitional provisions applying until the coming into force of the Health and Social Care (Community Health and Standards) Act 2003, s 172(1) in relation to general dental services contracts see art 3(a) thereof.

Date in force (in relation to Wales): to be appointed: see the Health and Social Care (Community Health and Standards) Act 2003, s 199(1)–(3).

Para 44: words "general medical services, general dental services," in italics repealed by the Health and Social Care (Community Health and Standards) Act 2003, s 196, Sch 14, Pt 4.

Date in force (in relation to England): 17 January 2005: see SI 2005/38, art 2(d)(i); for transitional provisions applying until the coming into force of the Health and Social Care (Community Health and Standards) Act 2003, s 172(1) in relation to general dental services contracts see art 3(b) thereof.

Date in force (in relation to Wales): to be appointed: see the Health and Social Care (Community Health and Standards) Act 2003, s 199(1)–(3).

Para 45: repealed by the Health and Social Care (Community Health and Standards) Act 2003, s 196, Sch 14, Pt 4.

Date in force (in relation to England in so far as it relates to personal medical services): 17 January 2005: see SI 2005/38, art 2(d)(ii).

Date in force (in relation to England for remaining purposes and in relation to Wales): to be appointed: see the Health and Social Care (Community Health and Standards) Act 2003, s 199(1)–(3).

Para 45A: inserted by the Health and Social Care Act 2001, s 67(1), Sch 5, Pt 1, para 14(1).

Date in force (in relation to Wales): 1 July 2002: see SI 2002/1475, art 2(1), Schedule, Pt 1.

Date in force (in relation to England): 1 January 2003: see SI 2003/53, art 2(a).

Para 45B: inserted by the National Health Service Reform and Health Care Professions Act 2002, s 20(11), Sch 6, para 19.

Date in force: 1 January 2003: see SI 2002/3190, art 2(1), (2)(a).

Para 51: words "primary medical services" in square brackets substituted by the Primary Medical Services (Northern Ireland) Order 2004, SI 2004/311, art 10, Sch 1, para 18.

Date in force: 1 April 2004: see the Primary Medical Services (2004 Order) (Commencement) Order (Northern Ireland) 2004, SR 2004/123, art 2(2).

PART IV

MAINTAINED SCHOOLS AND OTHER EDUCATIONAL INSTITUTIONS

England and Wales

1–362

52 *The governing body of a maintained school, within the meaning of the School Standards and Framework Act 1998.*

[52 The governing body of—

(a) a maintained school, as defined by section 20(7) of the School Standards and Framework Act 1998, or

(b) a maintained nursery school, as defined by section 22(9) of that Act.]

53 (1) The governing body of—

(a) an institution within the further education sector,

(b) a university receiving financial support under section 65 of the Further and Higher Education Act 1992,

(c) an institution conducted by a higher education corporation,

(d) a designated institution for the purposes of Part II of the Further and Higher Education Act 1992 as defined by section 72(3) of that Act, or

(e) any college, school, hall or other institution of a university which falls within paragraph (b).

(2) In sub-paragraph (1)—

(a) "governing body" is to be interpreted in accordance with subsection (1) of section 90 of the Further and Higher Education Act 1992 but without regard to subsection (2) of that section,

(b) in paragraph (a), the reference to an institution within the further education sector is to be construed in accordance with section 91(3) of the Further and Higher Education Act 1992,

(c) in paragraph (c), "higher education corporation" has the meaning given by section 90(1) of that Act, and

(d) in paragraph (e) "college" includes any institution in the nature of a college.

Northern Ireland

54 (1) The managers of—   1–363

(a) a controlled school, voluntary school or grant-maintained integrated school within the meaning of Article 2(2) of the Education and Libraries (Northern Ireland) Order 1986, or

(b) a pupil referral unit as defined by Article 87(1) of the Education (Northern Ireland) Order 1998.

(2) In sub-paragraph (1) "managers" has the meaning given by Article 2(2) of the Education and Libraries (Northern Ireland) Order 1986.

55 (1) The governing body of—

(a) a university receiving financial support under Article 30 of the Education and Libraries (Northern Ireland) Order 1993,

(b) a college of education . . . in respect of which grants are paid under Article 66(2) or (3) of the Education and Libraries (Northern Ireland) Order 1986, or

(c) an institution of further education within the meaning of the Further Education (Northern Ireland) Order 1997.

(2) In sub-paragraph (1) "governing body" has the meaning given by Article 30(3) of the Education and Libraries (Northern Ireland) Order 1993.

56 Any person providing further education to whom grants, loans or other payments are made under Article 5(1)(b) of the Further Education (Northern Ireland) Order 1997.

NOTES

Initial Commencement
                                                                           1–364
Royal Assent

Royal Assent: 30 November 2000: see s 87(1)(a).

Amendment

Para 52: substituted by the Education Act 2002, s 215(1), Sch 21, para 127.

Date in force (in relation to England): 1 September 2003: see SI 2003/1667, art 4.

Date in force (in relation to Wales): to be appointed: see the Education Act 2002, s 216(4).

Para 55: in sub-para (1)(b) words omitted repealed by the Colleges of Education (Northern Ireland) Order 2005, SI 2005/1963, art 14, Sch 3, para 4, Sch 4.

Date in force: 1 October 2005: see the Colleges of Education (Northern Ireland) Order 2005, SI 2005/1963, art 1(3).

PART V

POLICE

England and Wales

1–365

57 A police authority established under section 3 of the Police Act 1996.

58 The Metropolitan Police Authority established under section 5B of the Police Act 1996.

59 A chief officer of police of a police force in England or Wales.

Northern Ireland

1–366

60 The [Northern Ireland Policing Board].

61 The Chief Constable of the [Police Service of Northern Ireland].

Miscellaneous

1–367

62 The British Transport Police.

63 The Ministry of Defence Police established by section 1 of the Ministry of Defence Police Act 1987.

[63A The Civil Nuclear Police Authority.

63B The chief constable of the Civil Nuclear Constabulary.]

64 Any person who—

(a) by virtue of any enactment has the function of nominating individuals who may be appointed as special constables by justices of the peace, and

(b) is not a public authority by virtue of any other provision of this Act,

in respect of information relating to the exercise by any person appointed on his nomination of the functions of a special constable.

NOTES

Initial Commencement

Royal Assent

Royal Assent: 30 November 2000: see s 87(1)(a).

Amendment

Para 60: words "Northern Ireland Policing Board" in square brackets substituted by the Police (Northern Ireland) Act 2000, s 78(1), Sch 6, para 25(1), (2)(a).
   Date in force: 4 November 2001: see the Police (Northern Ireland) Act 2000 (Commencement No 3 and Transitional Provisions) Order 2001, SR 2001/396, art 2, Schedule.
Para 61: words "Police Service of Northern Ireland" in square brackets substituted by the Police (Northern Ireland) Act 2000, s 78(1), Sch 6, para 25(1), (2)(b).
   Date in force: 4 November 2001: see the Police (Northern Ireland) Act 2000 (Commencement No 3 and Transitional Provisions) Order 2001, SR 2001/396, art 2, Schedule.
Paras 63A, 63B: inserted by the Energy Act 2004, s 51(2), Sch 10, Pt 5, para 18.
   Date in force: 1 March 2005: see SI 2005/442, art 2(1), Sch 1.

See Further

See further, in relation to reference to the British Transport Police: the Railways and Transport Safety Act 2003, Sch 5, para 4(1).

PART VI

OTHER PUBLIC BODIES AND OFFICES: GENERAL

[The Adjudication Panel for Wales.]   1–368

The Adjudicator for the Inland Revenue and Customs and Excise.

The Administration of Radioactive Substances Advisory Committee.

[The Adult Learning Inspectorate.]

. . .

The Advisory Board on Restricted Patients.

The Advisory Board on the Registration of Homoeopathic Products.

. . .

The Advisory Committee for Disabled People in Employment and Training.

The Advisory Committee for the Public Lending Right.

. . .

The Advisory Committee on Advertising.

The Advisory Committee on Animal Feedingstuffs.

The Advisory Committee on Borderline Substances.

The Advisory Committee on Business and the Environment.

The Advisory Committee on Business Appointments.

The Advisory Committee on Conscientious Objectors.

The Advisory Committee on Consumer Products and the Environment.

The Advisory Committee on Dangerous Pathogens.

The Advisory Committee on Distinction Awards.

An Advisory Committee on General Commissioners of Income Tax.

The Advisory Committee on the Government Art Collection.

The Advisory Committee on Hazardous Substances.

The Advisory Committee on Historic Wreck Sites.

An Advisory Committee on Justices of the Peace in England and Wales.

The Advisory Committee on the Microbiological Safety of Food.

. . .

The Advisory Committee on Novel Foods and Processes.

[The Advisory Committee on Organic Standards.]

The Advisory Committee on Overseas Economic and Social Research.

The Advisory Committee on Packaging.

The Advisory Committee on Pesticides.

The Advisory Committee on Releases to the Environment.

[The Advisory Committee on Statute Law.]

[The Advisory Committee on Telecommunications for the Disabled and Elderly.]

[The Advisory Council on Historical Manuscripts.]

The Advisory Council on Libraries.

The Advisory Council on the Misuse of Drugs.

[The Advisory Council on National Records and Archives.]

The Advisory Council on Public Records.

The Advisory Group on Hepatitis.

[The Advisory Group on Medical Countermeasures.]

[The Advisory Panel on Beacon Councils.]

The Advisory Panel on Standards for the Planning Inspectorate.

The Aerospace Committee.

An Agricultural Dwelling House Advisory Committee.

An Agricultural Wages Board for England and Wales.

An Agricultural Wages Committee.

The Agriculture and Environment Biotechnology Commission.

[The Air Quality Expert Group.]

The Airborne Particles Expert Group.

The Alcohol Education and Research Council.

[The All-Wales Medicines Strategy Group.]

The Ancient Monuments Board for Wales.

The Animal Procedures Committee.

The Animal Welfare Advisory Committee.

. . .

[The Architects Registration Board.]

The Armed Forces Pay Review Body.

[The Arts and Humanities Research Council.]

The Arts Council of England.

The Arts Council of Wales.

The Audit Commission for Local Authorities and the National Health Service in England and Wales.

The Auditor General for Wales.

The Authorised Conveyancing Practitioners Board.

The Bank of England, in respect of information held for purposes other than those of its functions with respect to—

1–369

    (a) monetary policy,

    (b) financial operations intended to support financial institutions for the purposes of maintaining stability, and

    (c) the provision of private banking services and related services.

The Better Regulation Task Force.

The Biotechnology and Biological Sciences Research Council.

[The Board of the Pension Protection Fund.]

Any Board of Visitors established under section 6(2) of the Prison Act 1952.

The Britain-Russia Centre and East-West Centre.

The British Association for Central and Eastern Europe.

The British Broadcasting Corporation, in respect of information held for purposes other than those of journalism, art or literature.

The British Coal Corporation.

The British Council.

The British Educational Communications and Technology Agency.

The British Hallmarking Council.

The British Library.

The British Museum.

The British Pharmacopoeia Commission.

The British Potato Council.

The British Railways Board.

British Shipbuilders.

The British Tourist Authority.

The British Waterways Board.

The British Wool Marketing Board.

The Broadcasting Standards Commission.

The Building Regulations Advisory Committee.

[The Business Incubation Fund Investment Panel.]

[The Care Council for Wales.]

The Central Advisory Committee on War Pensions.

. . .

[The Central Police Training and Development Authority.]

The Central Rail Users' Consultative Committee.

[The Certification Officer.]

The Channel Four Television Corporation, in respect of information held for purposes other than those of journalism, art or literature.

[The Chemical Weapons Convention National Authority Advisory Committee.]

The Children and Family Court Advisory and Support Service.

[The Children's Commissioner for Wales.]

The Civil Aviation Authority.

The Civil Justice Council.

The Civil Procedure Rule Committee.

The Civil Service Appeal Board.

The Civil Service Commissioners.

The Coal Authority.

The Commission for Architecture and the Built Environment.

. . .

[The Commission for Healthcare Audit and Inspection, in respect of information held for purposes other than those of its functions exercisable by virtue of paragraph 5(a)(i) of the Care Standards Act 2000.]

The Commission for Local Administration in England.

The Commission for Local Administration in Wales.

The Commission for Racial Equality.

1–370   [The Commission for Social Care Inspection, in respect of information held for purposes other than those of its functions exercisable by virtue of paragraph 5(a)(ii) of the Care Standards Act 2000.]

The Commission for the New Towns.

The Commissioner for Integrated Transport.

The Commissioner for Public Appointments.

[The Commissioners of Northern Lighthouses.]

The Committee for Monitoring Agreements on Tobacco Advertising and Sponsorship.

The Committee of Investigation for Great Britain.

The Committee on Agricultural Valuation.

The Committee on Carcinogenicity of Chemicals in Food, Consumer Products and the Environment.

The Committee on Chemicals and Materials of Construction For Use in Public Water Supply and Swimming Pools.

The Committee on Medical Aspects of Food and Nutrition Policy.

The Committee on Medical Aspects of Radiation in the Environment.

The Committee on Mutagenicity of Chemicals in Food, Consumer Products and the Environment.

[The Committee on Radioactive Waste Management.]

[The Committee on Safety of Devices.]

The Committee on Standards in Public Life.

The Committee on Toxicity of Chemicals in Food, Consumer Products and the Environment.

The Committee on the Medical Effects of Air Pollutants.

The Committee on the Safety of Medicines.

The Commonwealth Scholarship Commission in the United Kingdom.

[Communications for Business.]

The Community Development Foundation.

The Competition Commission, in relation to information held by it otherwise than as a tribunal.

[The Competition Service.]

The Construction Industry Training Board.

Consumer Communications for England.

[The Consumer Council for Postal Services.]

. . .

[The Consumer Panel established under section 16 of the Communications Act 2003.]

The consumers' committee for Great Britain appointed under section 19 of the Agricultural Marketing Act 1958.

. . .

[The Council for the Regulation of Health Care Professionals.]

The Council for the Central Laboratory of the Research Councils.

The Council for Science and Technology.

The Council on Tribunals.

The Countryside Agency.

The Countryside Council for Wales.

The Covent Garden Market Authority.

The Criminal Cases Review Commission.

[The Criminal Injuries Compensation Appeals Panel, in relation to information held by it otherwise than as a tribunal.]

[The Criminal Injuries Compensation Authority.]

The Criminal Justice Consultative Council.

The Crown Court Rule Committee.

The Dartmoor Steering Group and Working Party.

The Darwin Advisory Committee.

The Defence Nuclear Safety Committee.

The Defence Scientific Advisory Council.

The Design Council.

. . .

1–371   The Diplomatic Service Appeal Board.

[The Director of Fair Access to Higher Education.]

[The Disability Employment Advisory Committee.]

The Disability Living Allowance Advisory Board.

The Disability Rights Commission.

The Disabled Persons Transport Advisory Committee.

[The Distributed Generation Co-Ordinating Group.

The East of England Industrial Development Board.]

The Economic and Social Research Council.

. . .

[The Electoral Commission.]

. . .

The Engineering Construction Industry Training Board.

The Engineering and Physical Sciences Research Council.

. . .

English Nature.

The English Sports Council.

The English Tourist Board.

The Environment Agency.

The Equal Opportunities Commission.

[The Ethnic Minority Business Forum.]

The Expert Advisory Group on AIDS.

The Expert Group on Cryptosporidium in Water Supplies.

An Expert Panel on Air Quality Standards.

The Export Guarantees Advisory Council.

The Family Proceedings Rules Committee.

The Farm Animal Welfare Council.

[The Financial Reporting Advisory Board.]

[The Financial Services Authority.]

The Fire Services Examination Board.

The Firearms Consultative Committee.

The Food Advisory Committee.

Food from Britain.

The Football Licensing Authority.

The Fuel Cell Advisory Panel.

[The Fuel Poverty Advisory Group.]

. . .

[The Gambling Commission.]

[Gangmasters Licensing Authority.]

. . .

[The Gas and Electricity Consumer Council.]

The Gene Therapy Advisory Committee.

The General Chiropractic Council.

The General Dental Council.

The General Medical Council.

The General Osteopathic Council.

[The General Social Care Council.]

[The General Teaching Council for England.]

[The General Teaching Council for Wales.]

The Genetic Testing and Insurance Committee.

The Government Hospitality Advisory Committee for the Purchase of Wine.

[The Government-Industry Forum on Non-Food Use of Crops.]

1–372   The Government Chemist.

The Great Britain-China Centre.

[The Health Professions Council]

[The Health Protection Agency.]

The Health and Safety Commission.

The Health and Safety Executive.

The Health Service Commissioner for England.

The Health Service Commissioner for Wales.

[The Hearing Aid Council.]

[Her Majesty's Chief Inspector of Education and Training in Wales or Prif Arolygydd Ei Mawrhydi dros Addysg a Hyfforddiant yng Nghymru].

[Her Majesty's Commissioners for Judicial Appointments.]

The Higher Education Funding Council for England.

The Higher Education Funding Council for Wales.

. . .

The Historic Buildings Council for Wales.

The Historic Buildings and Monuments Commission for England.

The Historic Royal Palaces Trust.

The Home-Grown Cereals Authority.

. . .

The Horserace Betting Levy Board.

The Horserace Totalisator Board.

The Horticultural Development Council.

Horticulture Research International.

The House of Lords Appointments Commission.

Any housing action trust established under Part III of the Housing Act 1988.

The Housing Corporation.

The Human Fertilisation and Embryology Authority.

[The Human Tissue Authority.]

The Human Genetics Commission.

The Immigration Services Commissioner.

The Imperial War Museum.

[The Independent Advisory Group on Teenage Pregnancy.]

The Independent Board of Visitors for Military Corrective Training Centres.

The Independent Case Examiner for the Child Support Agency.

The Independent Living Funds.

[The Independent Police Complaints Commission.]

[The Independent Review Panel for Advertising.

The Independent Review Panel for Borderline Products.]

[The Independent Scientific Group on Cattle Tuberculosis.]

The Independent Television Commission.

. . .

The Industrial Development Advisory Board.

The Industrial Injuries Advisory Council.

The Information Commissioner.

The Inland Waterways Amenity Advisory Council.

The Insolvency Rules Committee.

. . .

[The Integrated Administration and Controls System Appeals Panel.]

[The Intellectual Property Advisory Committee.]

Investors in People UK.

The Joint Committee on Vaccination and Immunisation.

The Joint Nature Conservation Committee.

The Joint Prison/Probation Accreditation Panel.

[The Judicial Appointments Commission.]

[The Judicial Appointments and Conduct Ombudsman.]

The Judicial Studies Board.

The Know-How Fund Advisory Board.

The Land Registration Rule Committee.

The Law Commission.

[The Learning and Skills Council for England.]

The Legal Services Commission.

1–373   [The Legal Services Complaints Commissioner.]

The Legal Services Consultative Panel.

The Legal Services Ombudsman.

. . .

The Local Government Boundary Commission for Wales.

The Local Government Commission for England.

A local probation board established under section 4 of the Criminal Justice and Court Services Act 2000.

[The London and South East Industrial Development Board.]

The London Pensions Fund Authority.

The Low Pay Commission.

The Magistrates' Courts Rules Committee.

The Marshall Aid Commemoration Commission.

The Measurement Advisory Committee.

The Meat and Livestock Commission.

. . .

The Medical Research Council.

. . .

The Medicines Commission.

The Milk Development Council.

The Millennium Commission.

The Museum of London.

The National Army Museum.

The National Audit Office.

The National Biological Standards Board (UK).

[The National Care Standards Commission.]

The National Consumer Council.

[The National Council for Education and Training for Wales.]

The National Crime Squad.

The National Employers' Liaison Committee.

[The National Employment Panel.]

The National Endowment for Science, Technology and the Arts.

The National Expert Group on Transboundary Air Pollution.

[The National Forest Company.]

The National Gallery.

The National Heritage Memorial Fund.

The National Library of Wales.

The National Lottery Charities Board.

The National Lottery Commission.

The National Maritime Museum.

The National Museum of Science and Industry.

The National Museums and Galleries of Wales.

The National Museums and Galleries on Merseyside.

The National Portrait Gallery.

. . .

1–374   The Natural Environment Research Council.

The Natural History Museum.

The New Deal Task Force.

The New Opportunities Fund.

[The North East Industrial Development Board.

The North West Industrial Development Board.]

[The Northern Ireland Judicial Appointments Ombudsman.]

[The Nuclear Decommissioning Authority.]

[The Nuclear Research Advisory Council.]

[The Nursing and Midwifery Council.]

. . .

[The Office of Communications.]

[The Office of Government Commerce.]

[The Office of Manpower Economics.]

The Oil and Pipelines Agency.

[The Ombudsman for the Board of the Pension Protection Fund.]

The OSO Board.

The Overseas Service Pensions Scheme Advisory Board.

The Panel on Standards for the Planning Inspectorate.

The Parliamentary Boundary Commission for England.

The Parliamentary Boundary Commission for Scotland.

The Parliamentary Boundary Commission for Wales.

The Parliamentary Commissioner for Administration.

The Parole Board.

The Particle Physics and Astronomy Research Council.

[The Patient Information Advisory Group.]

. . .

The Pensions Ombudsman.

[The Pensions Regulator.]

[The Pesticide Residues Committee.]

[The Pesticides Forum.]

The Pharmacists' Review Panel.

. . .

The Poisons Board.

[The Police Advisory Board for England and Wales.]

. . .

The Police Information Technology Organisation.

The Police Negotiating Board.

The Political Honours Scrutiny Committee.

[The Postgraduate Medical Education and Training Board.]

The Post Office.

. . .

. . .

[The Prison Service Pay Review Body.]   1–375

. . .

[The Public Private Partnership Agreement Arbiter.]

[The Public Services Ombudsman for Wales]

The Qualifications, Curriculum and Assessment Authority for Wales.

The Qualifications Curriculum Authority.

The Race Education and Employment Forum.

The Race Relations Forum.

The Radio Authority.

The Radioactive Waste Management Advisory Committee.

[. . .]

A Regional Cultural Consortium.

Any regional development agency established under the Regional Development Agencies Act 1998, other than the London Development Agency.

Any regional flood defence committee.

. . .

The Registrar of Public Lending Right.

Remploy Ltd.

The Renewable Energy Advisory Committee.

[The Renewables Advisory Board.]

Resource: The Council for Museums, Archives and Libraries.

The Review Board for Government Contracts.

The Review Body for Nursing Staff, Midwives, Health Visitors and Professions Allied to Medicine.

The Review Body on Doctors and Dentists Remuneration.

The Reviewing Committee on the Export of Works of Art.

The Royal Air Force Museum.

The Royal Armouries.

The Royal Botanic Gardens, Kew.

The Royal Commission on Ancient and Historical Monuments of Wales.

The Royal Commission on Environmental Pollution.

The Royal Commission on Historical Manuscripts.

[The Royal Hospital at Chelsea.]

. . .

The Royal Mint Advisory Committee on the Design of Coins, Medals, Seals and Decorations.

The School Teachers' Review Body.

[The Scientific Advisory Committee on Nutrition.]

The Scientific Committee on Tobacco and Health.

. . .

The Scottish Committee of the Council on Tribunals.   1–376

The Sea Fish Industry Authority.

[The Security Industry Authority.]

The Senior Salaries Review Body.

The Sentencing Advisory Panel.

The Service Authority for the National Crime Squad.

Sianel Pedwar Cymru, in respect of information held for purposes other than those of journalism, art or literature.

Sir John Soane's Museum.

. . .

[The Small Business Council.]

[The Small Business Investment Task Force.]

[The Social Care Institute for Excellence.]

The social fund Commissioner appointed under section 65 of the Social Security Administration Act 1992.

The Social Security Advisory Committee.

The Social Services Inspectorate for Wales Advisory Group.

[The South West Industrial Development Board.]

[The Specialist Advisory Committee on Antimicrobial Research.]

The Spongiform Encephalopathy Advisory Committee.

The Sports Council for Wales.

[The Standards Board for England.]

The Standing Advisory Committee on Industrial Property.

The Standing Advisory Committee on Trunk Road Assessment.

The Standing Dental Advisory Committee.

The Standing Nursing and Midwifery Advisory Committee.

The Standing Medical Advisory Committee.

The Standing Pharmaceutical Advisory Committee.

[The Statistics Commission.]

The Steering Committee on Pharmacy Postgraduate Education.

[The Strategic Investment Board.]

[*Strategic Rail Authority.*]

The subsidence adviser appointed under section 46 of the Coal Industry Act 1994.

The Substance Misuse Advisory Panel.

The Sustainable Development Commission.

. . .

[The Sustainable Energy Policy Advisory Board.]

The Tate Gallery.

The Teacher Training Agency.

[The Technical Advisory Board.]

The Theatres Trust.

The Traffic Commissioners, in respect of information held by them otherwise than as a tribunal.

[The Training and Development Agency for Schools.]

The Treasure Valuation Committee.

The UK Advisory Panel for Health Care Workers Infected with Bloodborne Viruses.

[The UK Chemicals Stakeholder Forum.]

The UK Sports Council.

1–377   The United Kingdom Atomic Energy Authority.

. . .

. . .

The United Kingdom Xenotransplantation Interim Regulatory Authority.

The Unlinked Anonymous Serosurveys Steering Group.

The Unrelated Live Transplant Regulatory Authority.

The Urban Regeneration Agency.

[The Valuation Tribunal Service.]

The Veterinary Products Committee.

[The Veterinary Residues Committee.]

The Victoria and Albert Museum.

[The Wales Centre for Health.]

. . .

The Wales Tourist Board.

The Wallace Collection.

The War Pensions Committees.

The Water Regulations Advisory Committee.

The Welsh Administration Ombudsman.

. . .

The Welsh Committee for Professional Development of Pharmacy.

The Welsh Dental Committee.

The Welsh Development Agency.

The Welsh Industrial Development Advisory Board.

The Welsh Language Board.

The Welsh Medical Committee.

. . .

The Welsh Nursing and Midwifery Committee.

The Welsh Optometric Committee.

The Welsh Pharmaceutical Committee.

The Welsh Scientific Advisory Committee.

The Westminster Foundation for Democracy.

[The West Midlands Industrial Development Board.]

The Wilton Park Academic Council.

The Wine Standards Board of the Vintners' Company.

The Women's National Commission.

[The Yorkshire and the Humber and the East Midlands Industrial Development Board.]

The Youth Justice Board for England and Wales.

The Zoos Forum.

NOTES

1–378   Initial Commencement

Royal Assent

Royal Assent: 30 November 2000: see s 87(1)(a).

Amendment

Entry "The Adjudication Panel for Wales." inserted by SI 2002/2623, art 2, Sch 1.
   Date in force: 11 November 2002: see SI 2002/2623, art 1(1).
Entry "The Adult Learning Inspectorate." inserted by SI 2003/1882, art 2, Sch 1.
   Date in force: 11 August 2003: see SI 2003/1882, art 1(1).
Entry "The Advisory Board on Family Law." (omitted) repealed by SI 2003/1883, art 2, Sch 1.
   Date in force: 11 August 2003: see SI 2003/1883, art 1(1).
Entry "The Advisory Committee for Cleaner Coal Technology." (omitted) repealed by SI 2004/1641, art 2, Sch 1.
   Date in force: 29 June 2004: see SI 2004/1641, art 1(1).
Entry "The Advisory Committee for Wales, (in relation to the Environment Agency)." (omitted) repealed by SI 2003/1883, art 2, Sch 1.
   Date in force: 11 August 2003: see SI 2003/1883, art 1(1).
Entry "The Advisory Committee on NHS Drugs." (omitted) repealed by SI 2003/1883, art 2, Sch 1.
   Date in force: 11 August 2003: see SI 2003/1883, art 1(1).
Entry "The Advisory Committee on Organic Standards." inserted by SI 2004/938, art 3, Sch 2.
   Date in force: 19 April 2004: see SI 2004/938, art 1(1).
Entry "The Advisory Committee on Statute Law." inserted by SI 2004/938, art 3, Sch 2.
   Date in force: 19 April 2004: see SI 2004/938, art 1(1).
Entry "The Advisory Committee on Telecommunications for the Disabled and Elderly." inserted by SI 2003/1882, art 2, Sch 1.
   Date in force: 11 August 2003: see SI 2003/1882, art 1(1).
Entry "The Advisory Council on Historical Manuscripts." inserted by SI 2003/1882, art 2, Sch 1.
   Date in force: 11 August 2003: see SI 2003/1882, art 1(1).
Entry "The Advisory Council on National Records and Archives." inserted by SI 2003/1882, art 2, Sch 1.
   Date in force: 11 August 2003: see SI 2003/1882, art 1(1).
Entry "The Advisory Group on Medical Countermeasures." inserted by SI 2003/1882, art 2, Sch 1.
   Date in force: 11 August 2003: see SI 2003/1882, art 1(1).
Entry "The Advisory Panel on Beacon Councils." inserted by SI 2003/1882, art 2, Sch 1.

Date in force: 11 August 2003: see SI 2003/1882, art 1(1).

Entry "The Air Quality Expert Group." inserted by SI 2003/1882, art 2, Sch 1.

Date in force: 11 August 2003: see SI 2003/1882, art 1(1).

Entry "The All-Wales Medicines Strategy Group." inserted by SI 2002/2623, art 2, Sch 1.

Date in force: 11 November 2002: see SI 2002/2623, art 1(1).

Entry "The Apple and Pear Research Council." (omitted) repealed by SI 2003/1883, art 2, Sch 1.

Date in force: 11 August 2003: see SI 2003/1883, art 1(1).

Entry "The Architects Registration Board." inserted by SI 2004/938, art 3, Sch 2.

Date in force: 19 April 2004: see SI 2004/938, art 1(1).

Entry "The Arts and Humanities Research Council." inserted by the Higher Education Act 2004, s 49, Sch 6, para 10.

Date in force: 16 December 2004: see SI 2004/3255, art 2.

Entry "The Board of the Pension Protection Fund." inserted by the Pensions Act 2004, s 319(1), Sch 12, para 79.

Date in force: 6 April 2005: see SI 2005/275, art 2(7), Schedule, Pt 7.

Entry "The British Railways Board" repealed by the Transport Act 2000, s 274, Sch 31, Pt IV.

Date in force: to be appointed: see the Transport Act 2000, s 275(1).

Entry "The Broadcasting Standards Commission." repealed by the Communications Act 2003, s 406(7), Sch 19(1).

Date in force: to be appointed: see the Communications Act 2003, s 411(2).

Entry "The Business Incubation Fund Investment Panel." inserted by SI 2003/1882, art 2, Sch 1.

Date in force: 11 August 2003: see SI 2003/1882, art 1(1).

Entry "The Care Council for Wales." inserted by SI 2002/2623, art 2, Sch 1.

Date in force: 11 November 2002: see SI 2002/2623, art 1(1).

Entry "The Central Council for Education and Training in Social Work (UK)" (omitted) repealed by SI 2002/797, art 2(c).

Date in force: 1 April 2002: see SI 2002/797, art 1(3).

Entry "The Central Police Training and Development Authority" inserted by the Criminal Justice and Police Act 2001, s 102, Sch 4, para 8.

Date in force: 1 April 2002: see SI 2002/533, art 2(d).

Entry "The Certification Officer." inserted by SI 2002/2623, art 2, Sch 1.

Date in force: 11 November 2002: see SI 2002/2623, art 1(1).

Entry "The Chemical Weapons Convention National Authority Advisory Committee." inserted by SI 2004/938, art 3, Sch 2.

Date in force: 19 April 2004: see SI 2004/938, art 1(1).

Entry "The Children's Commissioner for Wales." inserted by SI 2002/2623, art 2, Sch 1.

Date in force: 11 November 2002: see SI 2002/2623, art 1(1).

Entry "The Commission for Health Improvement." (omitted) repealed by the Health and Social Care (Community Health and Standards) Act 2003, s 196, Sch 14, Pt 2.

Date in force: 1 April 2004: see SI 2004/759, art 13(1), (2)(k).

Entry relating to "The Commission for Healthcare Audit and Inspection" inserted by the Health and Social Care (Community Health and Standards) Act 2003, s 147, Sch 9, para 31.

Date in force: 8 January 2004: see SI 2003/3346, art 5(b).

Entry "The Commission for Local Administration in Wales" repealed by the Public Services Ombudsman (Wales) Act 2005, s 39, Sch 6, paras 70, 72(a), Sch 7.

Date in force: to be appointed: see the Public Services Ombudsman (Wales) Act 2005, s 40.

Entry relating to "The Commission for Social Care Inspection" inserted by the Health and Social Care (Community Health and Standards) Act 2003, s 147, Sch 9, para 31.

Date in force: 1 January 2004: see SI 2003/3346, art 3(b).

Entry "The Commissioners of Northern Lighthouses." inserted by SI 2002/2623, art 2, Sch 1.

Date in force: 11 November 2002: see SI 2002/2623, art 1(1).

Entry "The Committee on Radioactive Waste Management." inserted by SI 2004/938, art 3, Sch 2.

Date in force: 19 April 2004: see SI 2004/938, art 1(1).

Entry "The Committee on Safety of Devices." inserted by SI 2003/1882, art 2, Sch 1.

Date in force: 11 August 2003: see SI 2003/1882, art 1(1).

Entry "Communications for Business." inserted by SI 2003/1882, art 2, Sch 1.

Date in force: 11 August 2003: see SI 2003/1882, art 1(1).

Entry "The Competition Service." inserted by SI 2003/1882, art 2, Sch 1.

Date in force: 11 August 2003: see SI 2003/1882, art 1(1).

Entry "The Consumer Council for Postal Services." inserted by SI 2002/2623, art 2, Sch 1.

Date in force: 11 November 2002: see SI 2002/2623, art 1(1).

Entry "The Consumer Panel." (omitted) repealed by SI 2003/1883, art 2, Sch 1.

Date in force: 11 August 2003: see SI 2003/1883, art 1(1).

Entry "The Consumer Panel established under section 16 of the Communications Act 2003." inserted by the Communications Act 2003, s 406(1), Sch 17, para 164.

Date in force: 29 December 2003: see SI 2003/3142, art 3(1), Sch 1.

Entry "The Council for Professions Supplementary to Medicine" (omitted) repealed by SI 2002/254, art 48(3), Sch 4, para 9; for transitional provisions see Sch 2 thereto.

Date in force: 1 April 2002: see SI 2002/254, art 1(2), (3), and the London Gazette, 25 March 2002.

Entry "The Council for the Regulation of Health Care Professionals." inserted by the National Health Service Reform and Health Care Professions Act 2002, s 25(4), Sch 7, para 24.

Date in force: 1 December 2002: see SI 2002/2202, art 2(2)(b).

Entry relating to "The Criminal Injuries Compensation Appeals Panel" inserted by SI 2002/2623, art 2, Sch 1.

Date in force: 11 November 2002: see SI 2002/2623, art 1(1).

Entry "The Criminal Injuries Compensation Authority." inserted by SI 2002/2623, art 2, Sch 1.

Date in force: 11 November 2002: see SI 2002/2623, art 1(1).

Entry "The Development Awareness Working Group." (omitted) repealed by SI 2003/1883, art 2, Sch 1.

Date in force: 11 August 2003: see SI 2003/1883, art 1(1).

Entry "The Director of Fair Access to Higher Education." inserted by the Higher Education Act 2004, s 49, Sch 6, para 10.

Date in force: 1 July 2004: see the Higher Education Act 2004, s 52(1).

Entry "The Disability Employment Advisory Committee." inserted by SI 2003/1882, art 2, Sch 1.

Date in force: 11 August 2003: see SI 2003/1882, art 1(1).

Entries "The Distributed Generation Co-Ordinating Group." and "The East of England Industrial Development Board." inserted by SI 2004/938, art 3, Sch 2.

Date in force: 19 April 2004: see SI 2004/938, art 1(1).

Entry "The Education Transfer Council." (omitted) repealed by SI 2003/1883, art 2, Sch 1.

Date in force: 11 August 2003: see SI 2003/1883, art 1(1).

Entry "The Electoral Commission." inserted by SI 2002/2623, art 2, Sch 1.

Date in force: 11 November 2002: see SI 2002/2623, art 1(1).

Entry "The Energy Advisory Panel." (omitted) repealed by SI 2003/1883, art 2, Sch 1.

Date in force: 11 August 2003: see SI 2003/1883, art 1(1).

1–379

Entries "The English National Board for Nursing, Midwifery and Health Visiting", "The United Kingdom Central Council for Nursing, Midwifery and Health Visiting" and "The Welsh National Board for Nursing, Midwifery and Health Visiting" (omitted) repealed by SI 2002/253, art 54(3), Sch 5, para 17; for transitional provisions see Sch 2 thereto.

Date in force: 1 April 2002: see SI 2002/253, art 1(2), (3), and the London Gazette, 25 March 2002.

Entry "The Ethnic Minority Business Forum." inserted by SI 2003/1882, art 2, Sch 1.

Date in force: 11 August 2003: see SI 2003/1882, art 1(1).

Entry "The Financial Reporting Advisory Board." inserted by SI 2003/1882, art 2, Sch 1.

Date in force: 11 August 2003: see SI 2003/1882, art 1(1).

Entry "The Financial Services Authority." inserted by SI 2003/1882, art 2, Sch 1.

Date in force: 11 August 2003: see SI 2003/1882, art 1(1).

Entry "The Fuel Poverty Advisory Group." inserted by SI 2004/938, art 3, Sch 2.

Date in force: 19 April 2004: see SI 2004/938, art 1(1).

Entry "The Further Education Funding Council for Wales." (omitted) repealed by SI 2003/1883, art 2, Sch 1.

Date in force: 11 August 2003: see SI 2003/1883, art 1(1).

Entry "The Gambling Commission." substituted, for entry "The Gaming Board for Great Britain." as originally enacted, by the Gambling Act 2005, s 356(1), Sch 16, Pt 2, para 16.

Date in force: 1 October 2005: see SI 2005/2455, art 2(1), Schedule.

Entry "Gangmasters Licensing Authority." inserted by the Gangmasters (Licensing) Act 2004, s 1(6), Sch 1, para 6.

Date in force: 1 December 2004: see SI 2004/2857, arts 1(1), 2(l).

Entry "The Gas Consumers' Council." (omitted) repealed by SI 2003/1883, art 2, Sch 1.

Date in force: 11 August 2003: see SI 2003/1883, art 1(1).

Entry "The Gas and Electricity Consumer Council." inserted by SI 2002/2623, art 2, Sch 1.

Date in force: 11 November 2002: see SI 2002/2623, art 1(1).

Entry "The General Social Care Council." inserted by SI 2002/2623, art 2, Sch 1.

Date in force: 11 November 2002: see SI 2002/2623, art 1(1).

Entry "The General Teaching Council for England." inserted by SI 2003/1882, art 2, Sch 1.

Date in force: 11 August 2003: see SI 2003/1882, art 1(1).

Entry "The General Teaching Council for Wales." inserted by SI 2002/2623, art 2, Sch 1.

Date in force: 11 November 2002: see SI 2002/2623, art 1(1).

Entry "The Government-Industry Forum on Non-Food Use of Crops." inserted by SI 2003/1882, art 2, Sch 1.

Date in force: 11 August 2003: see SI 2003/1882, art 1(1).

Entry "The Health Professions Council" inserted by SI 2002/254, art 48(3), Sch 4, para 9; for transitional provisions see Sch 2 thereto.

Date in force: 1 April 2002: see SI 2002/254, art 1(2), (3), and the London Gazette, 25 March 2002.

Entry "The Health Protection Agency." inserted by the Health Protection Agency Act 2004, s 11(1), Sch 3, para 15.

Date in force: 1 April 2005: see SI 2005/121, art 2(2).

Entry "The Health Service Commissioner for Wales" repealed by the Public Services Ombudsman (Wales) Act 2005, s 39, Sch 6, paras 70, 72(a), Sch 7.

Date in force: to be appointed: see the Public Services Ombudsman (Wales) Act 2005, s 40.

Entry "The Hearing Aid Council." inserted by SI 2003/1882, art 2, Sch 1.

Date in force: 11 August 2003: see SI 2003/1882, art 1(1).

Entry "Her Majesty's Chief Inspector of Education and Training in Wales or Prif Arolygydd Ei Mawrhydi dros Addysg a Hyfforddiant yng Nghymru" in square brackets substituted by the Learning and Skills Act 2000, s 73(1), (3)(a).

Date in force: 1 January 2001: see SI 2000/3230, art 2, Schedule.

Entry "Her Majesty's Commissioners for Judicial Appointments." inserted by SI 2004/938, art 3, Sch 2.

Date in force: 19 April 2004: see SI 2004/938, art 1(1).

Entries "The Hill Farming Advisory Committee." and "The Hill Farming Advisory Sub-committee for Wales." (omitted) repealed by SI 2004/1641, art 2, Sch 1.

Date in force: 29 June 2004: see SI 2004/1641, art 1(1).

Entry "The Honorary Investment Advisory Council." (omitted) repealed by SI 2003/1883, art 2, Sch 1.

Date in force: 11 August 2003: see SI 2003/1883, art 1(1).

Entry "The Horserace Betting Levy Board" repealed by the

Horserace Betting and Olympic Lottery Act 2004, s 17(2), Sch 4, para 9.

   Date in force: to be appointed: see the Horserace Betting and Olympic Lottery Act 2004, s 40(1).

Entry "The Horserace Totalisator Board" repealed by the Horserace Betting and Olympic Lottery Act 2004, ss 13, 38, Sch 2, para 22, Sch 6.

   Date in force: to be appointed: see the Horserace Betting and Olympic Lottery Act 2004, s 40(1).

Entry "The Human Tissue Authority." inserted by the Human Tissue Act 2004, s 13(2), Sch 2, para 27.

   Date in force: 1 April 2005: see SI 2005/919, arts 2, 3, Schedule.

Entry "The Independent Advisory Group on Teenage Pregnancy." inserted by SI 2003/1882, art 2, Sch 1.

   Date in force: 11 August 2003: see SI 2003/1882, art 1(1).

Entry "The Independent Police Complaints Commission." inserted by the Police Reform Act 2002, s 107(1), Sch 7, para 23(a).

   Date in force: 1 April 2004: see SI 2004/913, art 2(e).

Entries "The Independent Review Panel for Advertising." and "The Independent Review Panel for Borderline Products." inserted by SI 2004/938, art 3, Sch 2.

   Date in force: 19 April 2004: see SI 2004/938, art 1(1).

Entry "The Independent Scientific Group on Cattle Tuberculosis." inserted by SI 2003/1882, art 2, Sch 1.

   Date in force: 11 August 2003: see SI 2003/1882, art 1(1).

Entry "The Independent Television Commission." repealed by the Communications Act 2003, s 406(7), Sch 19(1).

   Date in force: to be appointed: see the Communications Act 2003, s 411(2).

Entry "The Indian Family Pensions Funds Body of Commissioners." (omitted) repealed by SI 2003/1883, art 2, Sch 1.

   Date in force: 11 August 2003: see SI 2003/1883, art 1(1).

Entry "The Insurance Brokers Registration Council" (omitted) repealed by SI 2001/1283, art 3(7).

   Date in force: 30 April 2001: see SI 2001/1283, art 1(1).

Entry "The Integrated Administration and Controls System Appeals Panel." inserted by SI 2003/1882, art 2, Sch 1.

   Date in force: 11 August 2003: see SI 2003/1882, art 1(1).

Entry "The Intellectual Property Advisory Committee." inserted by SI 2003/1882, art 2, Sch 1.

   Date in force: 11 August 2003: see SI 2003/1882, art 1(1).

Entry "The Judicial Appointments Commission." inserted by the Constitutional Reform Act 2005, s 61(2), Sch 12, Pt 2, para 36(3).

   Date in force: to be appointed: see the Constitutional Reform Act 2005, s 148(1).

Entry "The Judicial Appointments and Conduct Ombudsman." inserted by the Constitutional Reform Act 2005, s 62(2), Sch 13, para 17(3).

   Date in force: to be appointed: see the Constitutional Reform Act 2005, s 148(1).

Entry "The Learning and Skills Council for England." inserted by SI 2003/1882, art 2, Sch 1.

Date in force: 11 August 2003: see SI 2003/1882, art 1(1).

Entry "The Legal Services Complaints Commissioner." inserted by SI 2004/938, art 3, Sch 2.

Date in force: 19 April 2004: see SI 2004/938, art 1(1).

Entry "The Library and Information Services Council (Wales)." (omitted) repealed by SI 2004/803, art 3(3).

Date in force: 1 April 2004: see SI 2004/803, art 1(2).

Entry "The London and South East Industrial Development Board." inserted by SI 2004/938, art 3, Sch 2.

Date in force: 19 April 2004: see SI 2004/938, art 1(1).

Entry "The Medical Practices Committee." (omitted) repealed by SI 2003/1883, art 2, Sch 1.

Date in force: 11 August 2003: see SI 2003/1883, art 1(1).

Entry "The Medical Workforce Standing Advisory Committee." (omitted) repealed by SI 2003/1883, art 2, Sch 1.

Date in force: 11 August 2003: see SI 2003/1883, art 1(1).

Entry "The National Care Standards Commission." inserted by SI 2002/2623, art 2, Sch 1.

Date in force: 11 November 2002: see SI 2002/2623, art 1(1).

Entry "The National Council for Education and Training for Wales." inserted by SI 2002/2623, art 2, Sch 1.

Date in force: 11 November 2002: see SI 2002/2623, art 1(1).

1–380   Entry "The National Crime Squad." repealed by the Serious Organised Crime and Police Act 2005, ss 59, 174(2), Sch 4, paras 158, 160, Sch 17, Pt 2.

Date in force: to be appointed: see the Serious Organised Crime and Police Act 2005, s 178(8).

Entry "The National Employment Panel." inserted by SI 2003/1882, art 2, Sch 1.

Date in force: 11 August 2003: see SI 2003/1882, art 1(1).

Entry "The National Forest Company." inserted by SI 2003/1882, art 2, Sch 1.

Date in force: 11 August 2003: see SI 2003/1882, art 1(1).

Entry "The National Radiological Protection Board." (omitted) repealed by the Health Protection Agency Act 2004, s 11(2), Sch 4.

Date in force: 1 April 2005: see SI 2005/121, art 2(2).

Entries "The North East Industrial Development Board." and "The North West Industrial Development Board." inserted by SI 2004/938, art 3, Sch 2.

Date in force: 19 April 2004: see SI 2004/938, art 1(1).

Entry "The Northern Ireland Judicial Appointments Ombudsman." inserted by the Justice (Northern Ireland) Act 2002, s 9A(3), Sch 3A, para 17(3) (as inserted by the Constitutional Reform Act 2005, s 124(3), Sch 15).

Date in force: to be appointed: see the Constitutional Reform Act 2005, s 148(1).

Entry "The Nuclear Decommissioning Authority." inserted by the Energy Act 2004, s 2(10), Sch 1, Pt 3, para 18.

Date in force: 27 July 2004: see SI 2004/1973, art 2, Schedule.

Entry "The Nuclear Research Advisory Council." inserted by SI 2003/1882, art 2, Sch 1.

Date in force: 11 August 2003: see SI 2003/1882, art 1(1).

Entry "The Nursing and Midwifery Council" inserted by SI 2002/253, art 54(3), Sch 5, para 17(b); for transitional provisions see Sch 2 thereto.

Date in force: 1 April 2002: see SI 2002/253, art 1(2), (3), and the London Gazette, 25 March 2002.

Entries "The Occupational Pensions Regulatory Authority.", "The Pensions Compensation Board." and "The Registrar of Occupational and Personal Pension Schemes." (omitted) repealed by the Pensions Act 2004, s 320, Sch 13, Pt 1.

Date in force: 6 April 2005: see SI 2005/275, art 2(7), Schedule, Pt 7.

Entry "The Office of Communications." inserted by the Office of Communications Act 2002, s 1(10), Schedule, para 22.

Date in force: 1 July 2002: see SI 2002/1483, art 2.

Entry "The Office of Government Commerce." inserted by SI 2003/1882, art 2, Sch 1.

Date in force: 11 August 2003: see SI 2003/1882, art 1(1).

Entry "The Office of Manpower Economics." inserted by SI 2003/1882, art 2, Sch 1.

Date in force: 11 August 2003: see SI 2003/1882, art 1(1).

Entry "The Ombudsman for the Board of the Pension Protection Fund." inserted by the Pensions Act 2004, s 319(1), Sch 12, para 79.

Date in force: 6 April 2005: see SI 2005/275, art 2(7), Schedule, Pt 7.

Entry "The Patient Information Advisory Group." inserted by the Health and Social Care Act 2001, s 67(1), Sch 5, Pt 3, para 18.

Date in force: 11 May 2001: (no specific commencement provision).

Entry "The Pensions Regulator." inserted by the Pensions Act 2004, s 319(1), Sch 12, para 79.

Date in force: 6 April 2005: see SI 2005/275, art 2(7), Schedule, Pt 7.

Entry "The Pesticide Residues Committee." inserted by SI 2003/1882, art 2, Sch 1.

Date in force: 11 August 2003: see SI 2003/1882, art 1(1).

Entry "The Pesticides Forum." inserted by SI 2004/938, art 3, Sch 2.

Date in force: 19 April 2004: see SI 2004/938, art 1(1).

Entry "The Place Names Advisory Committee." (omitted) repealed by SI 2003/1883, art 2, Sch 1.

Date in force: 11 August 2003: see SI 2003/1883, art 1(1).

Entry "The Police Advisory Board for England and Wales." inserted by SI 2004/938, art 3, Sch 2.

Date in force: 19 April 2004: see SI 2004/938, art 1(1).

Entry "The Police Complaints Authority." (omitted) repealed by the Police Reform Act 2002, s 107, Sch 7, para 23(b), Sch 8.

Date in force: 1 April 2004: see SI 2004/913, art 2(e), (f)(ix).

Entry "The Postgraduate Medical Education and Training Board." inserted by SI 2004/938, art 3, Sch 2.

Date in force: 19 April 2004: see SI 2004/938, art 1(1).

Entry "The Post Office Users' Councils for Scotland, Wales and Northern Ireland." (omitted) repealed by SI 2003/1883, art 2, Sch 1.

Date in force: 11 August 2003: see SI 2003/1883, art 1(1).

Entry "The Post Office Users' National Council." (omitted) repealed by SI 2003/1883, art 2, Sch 1.

Date in force: 11 August 2003: see SI 2003/1883, art 1(1).

Entry "The Prison Service Pay Review Body." inserted by SI 2004/938, art 3, Sch 2.

Date in force: 19 April 2004: see SI 2004/938, art 1(1).

Entry "The Property Advisory Group." (omitted) repealed by SI 2004/1641, art 2, Sch 1.

Date in force: 29 June 2004: see SI 2004/1641, art 1(1).

Entry "The Public Private Partnership Agreement Arbiter." inserted by SI 2004/938, art 3, Sch 2.

Date in force: 19 April 2004: see SI 2004/938, art 1(1).

Entry "The Public Services Ombudsman for Wales" inserted by the Public Services Ombudsman (Wales) Act 2005, s 39(1), Sch 6, paras 70, 72(b).

Date in force: to be appointed: see the Public Services Ombudsman (Wales) Act 2005, s 40.

Entry "The Radio Authority." repealed by the Communications Act 2003, s 406(7), Sch 19(1).

Date in force: to be appointed: see the Communications Act 2003, s 411(2).

Entry relating to "Any Rail Passengers' Committee" (omitted) inserted by SI 2002/2623, art 2, Sch 1.

Date in force: 11 November 2002: see SI 2002/2623, art 1(1).

Entry relating to "Any Rail Passengers' Committee" (omitted) repealed by the Railways Act 2005, s 59(6), Sch 13, Pt 1.

Date in force: 24 July 2005: see SI 2005/1909, art 2, Schedule.

Entry "The Renewables Advisory Board." inserted by SI 2004/938, art 3, Sch 2.

Date in force: 19 April 2004: see SI 2004/938, art 1(1).

Entry "The Royal Hospital at Chelsea." inserted by SI 2004/938, art 3, Sch 2.

Date in force: 19 April 2004: see SI 2004/938, art 1(1).

Entry "The Royal Military College of Science Advisory Council." (omitted) repealed by SI 2004/1641, art 2, Sch 1.

Date in force: 29 June 2004: see SI 2004/1641, art 1(1).

Entry "The Scientific Advisory Committee on Nutrition." inserted by SI 2003/1882, art 2, Sch 1.

Date in force: 11 August 2003: see SI 2003/1882, art 1(1).

Entry "The Scottish Advisory Committee on Telecommunications." (omitted) repealed by the Communications Act 2003, s 406(7), Sch 19(1).

Date in force: 29 December 2003: see SI 2003/3142, art 3(1), Sch 1.

Entry "The Security Industry Authority" inserted by the Private Security Industry Act 2001, s 1(6), Sch 1, para 23.

Date in force: 1 April 2003: see SI 2002/3125, art 3(a), (d).

Entry "The Service Authority for the National Crime Squad." repealed by the Serious Organised Crime and Police Act 2005, ss 59, 174(2), Sch 4, paras 158, 160, Sch 17, Pt 2.

Date in force: to be appointed: see the Serious Organised Crime and Police Act 2005, s 178(8).
Entry "The Skills Task Force." (omitted) repealed by SI 2004/1641, art 2, Sch 1.
Date in force: 29 June 2004: see SI 2004/1641, art 1(1).
Entry "The Small Business Council." inserted by SI 2003/1882, art 2, Sch 1.
Date in force: 11 August 2003: see SI 2003/1882, art 1(1).
Entry "The Small Business Investment Task Force." inserted by SI 2003/1882, art 2, Sch 1.
Date in force: 11 August 2003: see SI 2003/1882, art 1(1).
Entry "The Social Care Institute for Excellence." inserted by SI 2003/1882, art 2, Sch 1.
Date in force: 11 August 2003: see SI 2003/1882, art 1(1).
Entry "The South West Industrial Development Board." inserted by SI 2004/938, art 3, Sch 2.
Date in force: 19 April 2004: see SI 2004/938, art 1(1).
Entry "The Specialist Advisory Committee on Antimicrobial Research." inserted by SI 2003/1882, art 2, Sch 1.
Date in force: 11 August 2003: see SI 2003/1882, art 1(1).
Entry "The Standards Board for England." inserted by SI 2002/2623, art 2, Sch 1.
Date in force: 11 November 2002: see SI 2002/2623, art 1(1).

Entry "The Statistics Commission." inserted by SI 2003/1882, art 2, Sch 1.

1–381

Date in force: 11 August 2003: see SI 2003/1882, art 1(1).
Entry "The Strategic Investment Board." inserted by SI 2003/1882, art 2, Sch 1.
Date in force: 11 August 2003: see SI 2003/1882, art 1(1).
Entry "Strategic Rail Authority." in square brackets inserted by the Transport Act 2000, s 204, Sch 14, Pt V, para 30.
Date in force: 15 January 2001: see SI 2000/3376, art 2.
Entry "Strategic Rail Authority." repealed by the Railways Act 2005, s 59(6), Sch 13, Pt 1.
Date in force: to be appointed: see the Railways Act 2005, s 60(2).
Entry "The Sustainable Development Education Panel." (omitted) repealed by SI 2003/1883, art 2, Sch 1.
Date in force: 11 August 2003: see SI 2003/1883, art 1(1).
Entry "The Sustainable Energy Policy Advisory Board." inserted by SI 2004/938, art 3, Sch 2.
Date in force: 19 April 2004: see SI 2004/938, art 1(1).
Entry "The Technical Advisory Board." inserted by SI 2003/1882, art 2, Sch 1.
Date in force: 11 August 2003: see SI 2003/1882, art 1(1).
Entry "The Training and Development Agency for Schools." inserted by the Education Act 2005, s 98, Sch 14, para 22.
Date in force: 1 September 2005: see the Education Act 2005, s 125(3)(a).
Entry "The UK Chemicals Stakeholder Forum." inserted by SI 2003/1882, art 2, Sch 1.
Date in force: 11 August 2003: see SI 2003/1882, art 1(1).

Entry "The United Kingdom Register of Organic Food Standards." (omitted) repealed by SI 2004/1641, art 2, Sch 1.
    Date in force: 29 June 2004: see SI 2004/1641, art 1(1).
Entry "The Valuation Tribunal Service." inserted by the Local Government Act 2003, s 105(9), Sch 4, para 24.
    Date in force: 1 April 2004: see SI 2003/2938, art 6.
Entry "The Veterinary Residues Committee." inserted by SI 2003/1882, art 2, Sch 1.
    Date in force: 11 August 2003: see SI 2003/1882, art 1(1).
Entry "The Wales Centre for Health." inserted by the Health (Wales) Act 2003, s 7(1), Sch 3, para 15.
    Date in force: 1 April 2005: see SI 2003/2660, art 3(2).
Entry "The Wales New Deal Advisory Task Force." (omitted) repealed by SI 2003/1883, art 2, Sch 1.
    Date in force: 11 August 2003: see SI 2003/1883, art 1(1).
Entry "The Welsh Administration Ombudsman" repealed by the Public Services Ombudsman (Wales) Act 2005, s 39, Sch 6, paras 70, 72(a), Sch 7.
    Date in force: to be appointed: see the Public Services Ombudsman (Wales) Act 2005, s 40.
Entry "The Welsh Advisory Committee on Telecommunications." (omitted) repealed by the Communications Act 2003, s 406(7), Sch 19(1).
    Date in force: 29 December 2003: see SI 2003/3142, art 3(1), Sch 1.
Entry "The West Midlands Industrial Development Board." inserted by SI 2004/938, art 3, Sch 2.
    Date in force: 19 April 2004: see SI 2004/938, art 1(1).
Entry "The Yorkshire and the Humber and the East Midlands Industrial Development Board." inserted by SI 2004/938, art 3, Sch 2.
    Date in force: 19 April 2004: see SI 2004/938, art 1(1).

PART VII

OTHER PUBLIC BODIES AND OFFICES: NORTHERN IRELAND

1–382   An Advisory Committee on General Commissioners of Income Tax (Northern Ireland).

[An advisory committee established under paragraph 25 of the Health and Personal Social Services (Northern Ireland) Order 1972.]

The Advisory Committee on Justices of the Peace in Northern Ireland.

    . . .

The Advisory Committee on Pesticides for Northern Ireland.

[The Agri-food and Biosciences Institute.]

The Agricultural Research Institute of Northern Ireland.

The Agricultural Wages Board for Northern Ireland.

The Arts Council of Northern Ireland.

The Assembly Ombudsman for Northern Ireland.

[The Attorney General for Northern Ireland.]

[The Belfast Harbour Commissioners.]

The Board of Trustees of National Museums and Galleries of Northern Ireland.

. . .

The Boundary Commission for Northern Ireland.

[A central advisory committee established under paragraph 24 of the Health and Personal Social Services (Northern Ireland) Order 1972.]

[The Certification Officer for Northern Ireland.]

The Charities Advisory Committee.

The Chief Electoral Officer for Northern Ireland.

[The Chief Inspector of Criminal Justice in Northern Ireland.]

The Civil Service Commissioners for Northern Ireland.

[Comhairle na Gaelscolaíochta.]

[Commissioner for Children and Young People for Northern Ireland.]

The Commissioner for Public Appointments for Northern Ireland.

The Construction Industry Training Board.

The consultative Civic Forum referred to in section 56(4) of the Northern Ireland Act 1998.

The Council for Catholic Maintained Schools.

The Council for Nature Conservation and the Countryside.

The County Court Rules Committee (Northern Ireland).

[The Criminal Injuries Compensation Appeals Panel for Northern Ireland, in relation to information held by it otherwise than as a tribunal.]

[A development corporation established under Part III of the Strategic Investment and Regeneration of Sites (Northern Ireland) Order 2003.]

The Disability Living Allowance Advisory Board for Northern Ireland.

The Distinction and Meritorious Service Awards Committee.

[A district policing partnership.]

The Drainage Council for Northern Ireland.

An Education and Library Board established under Article 3 of the Education and Libraries (Northern Ireland) Order 1986.

Enterprise Ulster.

The Equality Commission for Northern Ireland.

The Family Proceedings Rules Committee (Northern Ireland).

The Fire Authority for Northern Ireland.

The Fisheries Conservancy Board for Northern Ireland.

The General Consumer Council for Northern Ireland.

[The General Teaching Council for Northern Ireland.]

[The Governors of the Armargh Observatory and Planetarium.]

[The Harbour of Donaghadee Commissioners.]

1–383   The Health and Safety Agency for Northern Ireland.

The Historic Buildings Council.

The Historic Monuments Council.

The Independent Assessor of Military Complaints Procedures in Northern Ireland.

[An independent monitoring board appointed under section 10 of the Prison Act (Northern Ireland) 1953.]

The Independent Reviewer of the Northern Ireland (Emergency Provisions) Act.

The Independent Commissioner for Holding Centres.

. . .

. . .

[Invest Northern Ireland.]

. . .

The Labour Relations Agency.

The Laganside Corporation.

The Law Reform Advisory Committee for Northern Ireland.

The Lay Observer for Northern Ireland.

[. . .]

The Legal Aid Advisory Committee (Northern Ireland).

[The Life Sentence Review Commissioners appointed under Article 3 of the Life Sentences (Northern Ireland) Order 2001.]

The Livestock & Meat Commission for Northern Ireland.

. . .

The Local Government Staff Commission.

[The Londonderry Port and Harbour Commissioners.]

The Magistrates' Courts Rules Committee (Northern Ireland).

The Mental Health Commission for Northern Ireland.

. . .

The Northern Ireland Audit Office.

The Northern Ireland Building Regulations Advisory Committee.

The Northern Ireland Civil Service Appeal Board.

The Northern Ireland Commissioner for Complaints.

The Northern Ireland Community Relations Council.

. . .

The Northern Ireland Council for the Curriculum, Examinations and Assessment.

. . .

[The Northern Ireland Court of Judicature Rules Committee.]

The Northern Ireland Crown Court Rules Committee.

The Northern Ireland Economic Council.

The Northern Ireland Fishery Harbour Authority.

The Northern Ireland Higher Education Council.

The Northern Ireland Housing Executive.

The Northern Ireland Human Rights Commission.

The Northern Ireland Insolvency Rules Committee.

[The Northern Ireland Judicial Appointments Commission.]

[The Northern Ireland Law Commission.]

[The Northern Ireland Legal Services Commission.]

1–384   The Northern Ireland Local Government Officers' Superannuation Committee.

The Northern Ireland Museums Council.

The Northern Ireland Pig Production Development Committee.

[The Northern Ireland Practice and Education Council for Nursing and Midwifery.]

[The Northern Ireland Social Care Council.]

The Northern Ireland Supreme Court Rules Committee.

The Northern Ireland Tourist Board.

The Northern Ireland Transport Holding Company.

The Northern Ireland Water Council.

[Obstetrics Committee.]

The Parades Commission.

The Police Ombudsman for Northern Ireland.

The Probation Board for Northern Ireland.

The Rural Development Council for Northern Ireland.

The Sentence Review Commissioners appointed under section 1 of the Northern Ireland (Sentences) Act 1998.

The social fund Commissioner appointed under Article 37 of the Social Security (Northern Ireland) Order 1998.

The Sports Council for Northern Ireland.

The Staff Commission for Education and Library Boards.

The Statistics Advisory Committee.

The Statute Law Committee for Northern Ireland.

[A sub-group established under section 21 of the Police (Northern Ireland) Act 2000.]

. . .

Ulster Supported Employment Ltd.

[The Warrenpoint Harbour Authority.]

[The Waste Management Advisory Board.]

The Youth Council for Northern Ireland.

NOTES

Initial Commencement   1–385

Royal Assent

Royal Assent: 30 November 2000: see s 87(1)(a).

Amendment

Entry "An advisory committee established under paragraph 25 of the Health and Personal Social Services (Northern Ireland) Order 1972." inserted by SI 2004/938, art 4, Sch 3.
  Date in force: 19 April 2004: see SI 2004/938, art 1(1).
Entry "Advisory Committee on Juvenile Court Lay Panel (Northern Ireland)." (omitted) repealed by the Justice (Northern Ireland) Act 2002, s 86, Sch 13.
  Date in force: 1 April 2005: see the Justice (Northern Ireland) Act 2002 (Commencment No 8) Order 2005, SR 2005/109, art 2, Schedule.
Entry "The Agri-food and Biosciences Institute." inserted by SI 2004/3327, art 3(5), Sch 1, para 21.
  Date in force: to be appointed: see SI 2004/3327, art 1(3).
Entry "The Agricultural Research Institute of Northern Ireland." repealed by SI 2004/3327, art 13, Sch 4.
  Date in force: to be appointed: see SI 2004/3327, art 1(3).
Entry "The Attorney General for Northern Ireland." inserted by the Justice (Northern Ireland) Act 2002, s 23(9).
  Date in force: to be appointed: see the Justice (Northern Ireland) Act 2002, s 87(1).
Entry "The Belfast Harbour Commissioners." inserted by SI 2002/2623, art 3, Sch 2.
  Date in force: 11 November 2002: see SI 2002/2623, art 1(1).

Entry "Boards of Visitors and Visiting Committees." (omitted) repealed by the Criminal Justice (Northern Ireland) Order 2005, SI 2005/1965, art 10(2), Sch 1, para 10(a).
 Date in force: 19 August 2005: see the Criminal Justice (Northern Ireland) Order 2005, SI 2005/1965, art 1(4).
Entry "A central advisory committee established under paragraph 24 of the Health and Personal Social Services (Northern Ireland) Order 1972." inserted by SI 2004/938, art 4, Sch 3.
 Date in force: 19 April 2004: see SI 2004/938, art 1(1).
Entry "The Certification Officer for Northern Ireland." inserted by SI 2002/2623, art 3, Sch 2.
 Date in force: 11 November 2002: see SI 2002/2623, art 1(1).
Entry "The Chief Inspector of Criminal Justice in Northern Ireland." inserted by the Justice (Northern Ireland) Act 2002, s 45(3), Sch 8, para 16.
 Date in force: 26 May 2003: see the Justice (Northern Ireland) Act 2002 (Commencement No 3) Order 2003, SR 2003/265, art 2.
Entry "Comhairle na Gaelscolaíochta." inserted by SI 2003/1882, art 3, Sch 2.
 Date in force: 11 August 2003: see SI 2003/1882, art 1(1).
Entry "Commissioner for Children and Young People for Northern Ireland." inserted by SI 2003/439, art 5(3), Sch 2, para 15.
 Date in force: 13 March 2003: see SI 2003/439, art 1(2)(b).
Entry "The Criminal Injuries Compensation Appeals Panel for Northern Ireland, in relation to information held by it otherwise than as a tribunal." inserted by SI 2003/1882, art 3, Sch 2.
 Date in force: 11 August 2003: see SI 2003/1882, art 1(1).
Entry beginning "A development corporation" inserted by SI 2003/410, art 15(3), Sch 1, para 23.
 Date in force: 7 March 2003: see SI 2003/410, art 1(2).
Entry "A district policing partnership." inserted by the Police (Northern Ireland) Act 2000, s 78(1), Sch 6, para 25(1), (3).
 Date in force: 4 November 2001: see the Police (Northern Ireland) Act 2000 (Commencement No 3 and Transitional Provisions) Order 2001, SR 2001/396, art 2, Schedule.
Entry "The General Teaching Council for Northern Ireland." inserted by SI 2003/1882, art 3, Sch 2.
 Date in force: 11 August 2003: see SI 2003/1882, art 1(1).
Entry "The Governors of the Armargh Observatory and Planetarium." inserted by SI 2003/1882, art 3, Sch 2.
 Date in force: 11 August 2003: see SI 2003/1882, art 1(1).
Entry "The Harbour of Donaghadee Commissioners." inserted by SI 2003/1882, art 3, Sch 2.
 Date in force: 11 August 2003: see SI 2003/1882, art 1(1).
Entry "An independent monitoring board appointed under section 10 of the Prison Act (Northern Ireland) 1953" inserted by the Criminal Justice (Northern Ireland) Order 2005, SI 2005/1965, art 10(2), Sch 1, para 10(b).
 Date in force: 19 August 2005: see the Criminal Justice (Northern Ireland) Order 2005, SI 2005/1965, art 1(4).
Entry "The Industrial Development Board for Northern Ireland." (omitted) repealed by the Industrial Development Act (Northern Ireland) 2002, s 5(4), Sch 4.

Date in force: 1 April 2002: see the Industrial Development (2002 Act) (Commencement) Order (Northern Ireland) 2002, SR 2002/134, art 2.

Entry "The Industrial Research and Technology Unit." (omitted) repealed by the Industrial Development Act (Northern Ireland) 2002, s 5(4), Sch 4.

Date in force: 1 April 2002: see the Industrial Development (2002 Act) (Commencement) Order (Northern Ireland) 2002, SR 2002/134, art 2.

Entry "Invest Northern Ireland." inserted by the Industrial Development Act (Northern Ireland) 2002, s 1(2), Sch 1, para 21.

Date in force: 1 April 2002: see the Industrial Development (2002 Act) (Commencement) Order (Northern Ireland) 2002, SR 2002/134, art 2.

Entry "The Juvenile Justice Board." (omitted) repealed by SI 2004/1641, art 3, Sch 2.

Date in force: 29 June 2004: see SI 2004/1641, art 1(1).

Entry "Law Reform Advisory Committee for Northern Ireland." repealed by the Justice (Northern Ireland) Act 2002, s 86, Sch 13.

Date in force: to be appointed: see the Justice (Northern Ireland) Act 2002, s 87(1).

Entry "The Learning and Skills Advisory Board." inserted by SI 2003/1882, art 3, Sch 2.

Date in force: 11 August 2003: see SI 2003/1882, art 1(1).

Entry "The Learning and Skills Advisory Board." (omitted) repealed by SI 2004/1641, art 3, Sch 2.

Date in force: 29 June 2004: see SI 2004/1641, art 1(1).

Entry "The Life Sentence Review Commissioners appointed under Article 3 of the Life Sentences (Northern Ireland) Order 2001." inserted by SI 2001/2565, art 4.

Date in force: 8 October 2001 (being the date on which the Life Sentences (Northern Ireland) Order 2001, SI 2001/2564 came into force): see SI 2001/337, art 2, SI 2001/2564, art 1(2) andSI 2001/2565, art 1(2).

Entry "The Local Enterprise Development Unit." (omitted) repealed by the Industrial Development Act (Northern Ireland) 2002, s 5(4), Sch 4.

Date in force: 1 April 2002: see the Industrial Development (2002 Act) (Commencement) Order (Northern Ireland) 2002, SR 2002/134, art 2.

Entry "The Londonderry Port and Harbour Commissioners." inserted by SI 2002/2623, art 3, Sch 2.

Date in force: 11 November 2002: see SI 2002/2623, art 1(1).

Entry "The Northern Ireland Advisory Committee on Telecommunications." (omitted) repealed by the Communications Act 2003, s 406(7), Sch 19(1).

Date in force: 29 December 2003: see SI 2003/3142, art 3(1), Sch 1.

Entry "The Northern Ireland Consumer Committee for Electricity." (omitted) repealed by SI 2004/1641, art 3, Sch 2.

Date in force: 29 June 2004: see SI 2004/1641, art 1(1).

Entry "The Northern Ireland Council for Postgraduate Medical and Dental Education." (omitted) repealed by SI 2004/1641, art 3, Sch 2.

Date in force: 29 June 2004: see SI 2004/1641, art 1(1).
Entry "The Northern Ireland Court of Judicature Rules Committee." inserted by the Constitutional Reform Act 2005, s 59(5), Sch 11, Pt 4, para 34(b).
Date in force: to be appointed: see the Constitutional Reform Act 2005, s 148(1).

1–386   Entry "The Northern Ireland Judicial Appointments Commission." inserted by the Justice (Northern Ireland) Act 2002, s 3(3), Sch 2, para 20.
Date in force: 15 June 2005: see the Justice (Northern Ireland) Act 2002 (Commencement No 9 and Transitional Provisions) Order 2005, SR 2005/281, art 3(1), Sch 2, para 6.
Entry "The Northern Ireland Law Commission." inserted by the Justice (Northern Ireland) Act 2002, s 50(7), Sch 9, para 15.
Date in force: to be appointed: see the Justice (Northern Ireland) Act 2002, s 87(1).
Entry "The Northern Ireland Legal Services Commission." inserted by SI 2003/435, art 49(1), Sch 4, para 15.
Date in force: to be appointed: see SI 2003/435, art 1(2).
Entry "The Northern Ireland Practice and Education Council for Nursing and Midwifery." inserted by SI 2003/1882, art 3, Sch 2.
Date in force: 11 August 2003: see SI 2003/1882, art 1(1).
Entry "The Northern Ireland Social Care Council." inserted by SI 2003/1882, art 3, Sch 2.
Date in force: 11 August 2003: see SI 2003/1882, art 1(1).
Entry "The Northern Ireland Supreme Court Rules Committee." repealed by the Constitutional Reform Act 2005, ss 59(5), 146, Sch 11, Pt 4, para 34(a), Sch 18, Pt 5.
Date in force: to be appointed: see the Constitutional Reform Act 2005, s 148(1).
Entry "Obstetrics Committee." inserted by SI 2004/938, art 4, Sch 3.
Date in force: 19 April 2004: see SI 2004/938, art 1(1).
Entry "A sub-group established under section 21 of the Police (Northern Ireland) Act 2000." inserted by the Police (Northern Ireland) Act 2003, s 19(1), Sch 1, paras 1, 15.
Date in force: to be appointed: see the Police (Northern Ireland) Act 2003, s 19(2).
Entry "The Training and Employment Agency." (omitted) repealed by SI 2004/1641, art 3, Sch 2.
Date in force: 29 June 2004: see SI 2004/1641, art 1(1).
Entry "The Warrenpoint Harbour Authority." inserted by SI 2002/2623, art 3, Sch 2.
Date in force: 11 November 2002: see SI 2002/2623, art 1(1).
Entry "The Waste Management Advisory Board." inserted by SI 2003/1882, art 3, Sch 2.
Date in force: 11 August 2003: see SI 2003/1882, art 1(1).

SCHEDULE 2

THE COMMISSIONER AND THE TRIBUNAL

SECTION 18(4)

PART I

PROVISION CONSEQUENTIAL ON S 18(1) AND (2)

General

1 (1) Any reference in any enactment, instrument or document to the Data Protection Commissioner or the Data Protection Registrar shall be construed, in relation to any time after the commencement of section 18(1), as a reference to the Information Commissioner.

 1–387

(2) Any reference in any enactment, instrument or document to the Data Protection Tribunal shall be construed, in relation to any time after the commencement of section 18(2), as a reference to the Information Tribunal.

2 (1) Any reference in this Act or in any instrument under this Act to the Commissioner shall be construed, in relation to any time before the commencement of section 18(1), as a reference to the Data Protection Commissioner.

(2) Any reference in this Act or in any instrument under this Act to the Tribunal shall be construed, in relation to any time before the commencement of section 18(2), as a reference to the Data Protection Tribunal.

Public Records Act 1958 (c 51)

3 (1) In Part II of the Table in paragraph 3 of Schedule 1 to the Public Records Act 1958 (definition of public records), the entry relating to the Data Protection Commissioner is omitted and there is inserted at the appropriate place—

 1–388

"Information Commissioner.".

(2) In paragraph 4(1) of that Schedule, for paragraph (nn) there is substituted—

"(nn) records of the Information Tribunal;".

Parliamentary Commissioner Act 1967 (c 13)

1–389

4 In Schedule 2 to the Parliamentary Commissioner Act 1967 (departments etc subject to investigation), the entry relating to the Data Protection Commissioner is omitted and there is inserted at the appropriate place—

"Information Commissioner".

5 In Schedule 4 to that Act (tribunals exercising administrative functions), for the entry relating to the Data Protection Tribunal there is substituted—

"Information Tribunal constituted under section 6 of the Data Protection Act 1998.".

Superannuation Act 1972 (c 11)

1–390

6 In Schedule 1 to the Superannuation Act 1972 (employment with superannuation scheme), for "Data Protection Commissioner" there is substituted "Information Commissioner".

Consumer Credit Act 1974 (c 39)

1–391

7 In section 159 of the Consumer Credit Act 1974 (correction of wrong information), in subsections (7) and (8)(b), for "Data Protection Commissioner", in both places where it occurs, there is substituted "Information Commissioner".

House of Commons Disqualification Act 1975 (c 24)

1–392

8 (1) In Part II of Schedule 1 to the House of Commons Disqualification Act 1975 (bodies whose members are disqualified), the entry relating to the Data Protection Tribunal is omitted and there is inserted at the appropriate place—

"The Information Tribunal".

(2) In Part III of that Schedule (disqualifying offices), the entry relating to the Data Protection Commissioner is omitted and there is inserted at the appropriate place—

"The Information Commissioner".

Northern Ireland Assembly Disqualification Act 1975 (c 25)

1–393

9 (1) In Part II of Schedule 1 to the Northern Ireland Assembly Disqualification Act 1975 (bodies whose members are disqualified), the entry relating to the Data

Protection Tribunal is omitted and there is inserted at the appropriate place—

"The Information Tribunal".

(2) In Part III of that Schedule (disqualifying offices), the entry relating to the Data Protection Commissioner is omitted and there is inserted at the appropriate place—

"The Information Commissioner".

Tribunals and Inquiries Act 1992 (c 53)

10 In paragraph 14 of Part I of Schedule 1 to the Tribunals   1–394
and Inquiries Act 1992 (tribunals under direct supervision of Council on Tribunals)—

    (a) in sub-paragraph (a), for "The Data Protection Commissioner" there is substituted "The Information Commissioner", and

    (b) for sub-paragraph (b) there is substituted—

        "(b) the Information Tribunal constituted under that section, in respect of its jurisdiction under—

           (i) section 48 of that Act, and

           (ii) section 57 of the Freedom of Information Act 2000.".

Judicial Pensions and Retirement Act 1993 (c 8)

11 In Schedule 5 to the Judicial Pensions and Retirement Act 1993 (retirement provisions: the relevant offices), in the entry relating to the chairman and deputy chairman of the Data Protection Tribunal, for "the Data Protection Tribunal" there is substituted "the Information Tribunal".

12 In Schedule 7 to that Act (retirement dates: transitional provisions), in paragraph 5(5)(xxvi) for "the Data Protection Tribunal" there is substituted "the Information Tribunal".

Data Protection Act 1998 (c 29)

13 (1) Section 6 of the Data Protection Act 1998 (the Data Protection Commissioner and the Data Protection Tribunal) is amended as follows.

(2) For subsection (1) there is substituted—

"(1) For the purposes of this Act and of the Freedom of Information Act 2000 there shall be an officer known as the

Information Commissioner (in this Act referred to as "the Commissioner").".

(3) For subsection (3) there is substituted—

"(3) For the purposes of this Act and of the Freedom of Information Act 2000 there shall be a tribunal known as the Information Tribunal (in this Act referred to as "the Tribunal").".

14 In section 70(1) of that Act (supplementary definitions)—

    (a) in the definition of "the Commissioner", for "the Data Protection Commissioner" there is substituted "the Information Commissioner", and

    (b) in the definition of "the Tribunal", for "the Data Protection Tribunal" there is substituted "the Information Tribunal".

15 (1) Schedule 5 to that Act (the Data Protection Commissioner and the Data Protection Tribunal) is amended as follows.

(2) In paragraph 1(1), for "Data Protection Commissioner" there is substituted "Information Commissioner".

(3) Part III shall cease to have effect.

NOTES

1–397 **Initial Commencement**

Royal Assent

Para 2: Royal Assent: 30 November 2000: see s 87(1)(i).

Specified date

Paras 1(1), 3(1), 4, 6, 7, 8(2), 9(2), 10(a), 13(1), (2), 14(a), 15(1), (2): Specified date: 30 January 2001: see s 87(2)(c).
Paras 1(2), 3(2), 5, 8(1), 9(1), 10(b), 11, 12, 13(3), 14(b), 15(3): Specified date: 30 November 2005 (unless the Secretary of State by order appoints these paras before that date): see s 87(3) (as amended by SI 2001/3500, art 8, Sch 2, Pt I, para 8(1)(o) and SI 2003/1887, art 9, Sch 2, para 12(1)(c)). (See appointment notes below.)

Appointment

Paras 1(2), 3(2), 5, 8(1), 9(1), 11, 12, 13(3), 14(b), 15(3): Appointment: 14 May 2001: see SI 2001/1637, art 2(b).

Para 10(b): Appointment: 30 November 2002: see SI 2002/2812, art 2(h).

PART II

AMENDMENTS RELATING TO EXTENSION OF FUNCTIONS OF COMMISSIONER AND TRIBUNAL

Interests represented by lay members of Tribunal

16 In section 6(6) of the Data Protection Act 1998 (lay members of Tribunal)—   1–398

  (a) for the word "and" at the end of paragraph (a) there is substituted—

  "(aa) persons to represent the interests of those who make requests for information under the Freedom of Information Act 2000," and

  (b) after paragraph (b) there is inserted

  "and

  (bb) persons to represent the interests of public authorities".

Expenses incurred under this Act excluded in calculating fees

17 In section 26(2) of that Act (fees regulations), in paragraph (a)—

  (a) after "functions" there is inserted "under this Act", and

  (b) after "Tribunal" there is inserted "so far as attributable to their functions under this Act".

Information provided to Commissioner or Tribunal

18 In section 58 of that Act (disclosure of information to Commissioner or Tribunal), after "this Act" there is inserted "or the Freedom of Information Act 2000".   1–399

19 (1) Section 59 of that Act (confidentiality of information) is amended as follows.

  (2) In subsections (1) and (2), for "this Act", wherever occurring, there is substituted "the information Acts".

  (3) After subsection (3) there is inserted—

  "(4) In this section "the information Acts" means this Act and the Freedom of Information Act 2000.".

Deputy commissioners

1–400   20 (1) **Paragraph 4 of Schedule 5 to that Act (officers and staff) is amended as follows.**

(2) **In sub-paragraph (1)(a), after "a deputy commissioner" there is inserted "or two deputy commissioners".**

(3) **After sub-paragraph (1) there is inserted—**

"(1A) The Commissioner shall, when appointing any second deputy commissioner, specify which of the Commissioner's functions are to be performed, in the circumstances referred to in paragraph 5(1), by each of the deputy commissioners.".

Exercise of Commissioner's functions by others

1–401   21 (1) **Paragraph 5 of Schedule 5 to that Act (exercise of functions of Commissioner during vacancy etc) is amended as follows.**

(2) **In sub-paragraph (1)—**

  (a) **after "deputy commissioner" there is inserted "or deputy commissioners", and**

  (b) **after "this Act" there is inserted "or the Freedom of Information Act 2000".**

(3) **In sub-paragraph (2) after "this Act" there is inserted "or the Freedom of Information Act 2000".**

Money

1–402   22 **In paragraph 9(1) of Schedule 5 to that Act (money) for "or section 159 of the Consumer Credit Act 1974" there is substituted ", under section 159 of the Consumer Credit Act 1974 or under the Freedom of Information Act 2000".**

NOTES

Initial Commencement

Royal Assent

Paras 17–22: Royal Assent: 30 November 2000: see s 87(1)(i).

Specified date

Para 16: Specified date: 30 November 2005 (unless the Secretary of State by order appoints this para before that date): see s 87(3) (as

amended by SI 2001/3500, art 8, Sch 2, Pt I, para 8(1)(o) and SI 2003/1887, art 9, Sch 2, para 12(1)(c)). (See appointment note below.)

Appointment

Para 16: Appointment: 14 May 2001: see SI 2001/1637, art 2(b).

SCHEDULE 3

POWERS OF ENTRY AND INSPECTION

SECTION 55

Issue of warrants

1-403

1 (1) If a circuit judge [or a District Judge (Magistrates' Courts)] is satisfied by information on oath supplied by the Commissioner that there are reasonable grounds for suspecting—

    (a) that a public authority has failed or is failing to comply with—

        (i) any of the requirements of Part I of this Act,

        (ii) so much of a decision notice as requires steps to be taken, or

        (iii) an information notice or an enforcement notice, or

    (b) that an offence under section 77 has been or is being committed,

and that evidence of such a failure to comply or of the commission of the offence is to be found on any premises specified in the information, he may, subject to paragraph 2, grant a warrant to the Commissioner.

(2) A warrant issued under sub-paragraph (1) shall authorise the Commissioner or any of his officers or staff at any time within seven days of the date of the warrant—

    (a) to enter and search the premises,

    (b) to inspect and seize any documents or other material found there which may be such evidence as is mentioned in that sub-paragraph, and

    (c) to inspect, examine, operate and test any equipment found there in which information held by the public authority may be recorded.

2 (1) A judge shall not issue a warrant under this Schedule unless he is satisfied—

    (a) that the Commissioner has given seven days' notice in writing to the occupier of the premises in question demanding access to the premises, and

    (b) that either—

        (i) access was demanded at a reasonable hour and was unreasonably refused, or

        (ii) although entry to the premises was granted, the occupier unreasonably refused to comply with a request by the Commissioner or any of the Commissioner's officers or staff to permit the Commissioner or the officer or member of staff to do any of the things referred to in paragraph 1(2), and

    (c) that the occupier, has, after the refusal, been notified by the Commissioner of the application for the warrant and has had an opportunity of being heard by the judge on the question whether or not it should be issued.

(2) Sub-paragraph (1) shall not apply if the judge is satisfied that the case is one of urgency or that compliance with those provisions would defeat the object of the entry.

3 A judge who issues a warrant under this Schedule shall also issue two copies of it and certify them clearly as copies.

Execution of warrants

4 A person executing a warrant issued under this Schedule may use such reasonable force as may be necessary.

5 A warrant issued under this Schedule shall be executed at a reasonable hour unless it appears to the person executing it that there are grounds for suspecting that the evidence in question would not be found if it were so executed.

6 (1) If the premises in respect of which a warrant is issued under this Schedule are occupied by a public authority and any officer or employee of the authority is present when the warrant is executed, he shall be shown the warrant and supplied with a copy of it; and if no such officer or employee is present a copy of the warrant shall be left in a prominent place on the premises.

(2) If the premises in respect of which a warrant is issued under this Schedule are occupied by a person other than a

1–404

public authority and he is present when the warrant is executed, he shall be shown the warrant and supplied with a copy of it; and if that person is not present a copy of the warrant shall be left in a prominent place on the premises.

7 (1) A person seizing anything in pursuance of a warrant under this Schedule shall give a receipt for it if asked to do so.

(2) Anything so seized may be retained for so long as is necessary in all the circumstances but the person in occupation of the premises in question shall be given a copy of anything that is seized if he so requests and the person executing the warrant considers that it can be done without undue delay.

Matters exempt from inspection and seizure

8 The powers of inspection and seizure conferred by a warrant issued under this Schedule shall not be exercisable in respect of information which is exempt information by virtue of section 23(1) or 24(1).

9 (1) Subject to the provisions of this paragraph, the powers of inspection and seizure conferred by a warrant issued under this Schedule shall not be exercisable in respect of—

   (a) any communication between a professional legal adviser and his client in connection with the giving of legal advice to the client with respect to his obligations, liabilities or rights under this Act, or

   (b) any communication between a professional legal adviser and his client, or between such an adviser or his client and any other person, made in connection with or in contemplation of proceedings under or arising out of this Act (including proceedings before the Tribunal) and for the purposes of such proceedings.

(2) Sub-paragraph (1) applies also to—

   (a) any copy or other record of any such communication as is there mentioned, and

   (b) any document or article enclosed with or referred to in any such communication if made in connection with the giving of any advice or, as the case may be, in connection with or in contemplation of and for the purposes of such proceedings as are there mentioned.

(3) This paragraph does not apply to anything in the possession of any person other than the professional legal

1–405

adviser or his client or to anything held with the intention of furthering a criminal purpose.

(4) In this paragraph references to the client of a professional legal adviser include references to any person representing such a client.

10 If the person in occupation of any premises in respect of which a warrant is issued under this Schedule objects to the inspection or seizure under the warrant of any material on the grounds that it consists partly of matters in respect of which those powers are not exercisable, he shall, if the person executing the warrant so requests, furnish that person with a copy of so much of the material in relation to which the powers are exercisable.

Return of warrants

11 A warrant issued under this Schedule shall be returned to the court from which it was issued—

    (a) after being executed, or

    (b) if not executed within the time authorised for its execution;

and the person by whom any such warrant is executed shall make an endorsement on it stating what powers have been exercised by him under the warrant.

1–406

Offences

12 Any person who—

    (a) intentionally obstructs a person in the execution of a warrant issued under this Schedule, or

    (b) fails without reasonable excuse to give any person executing such a warrant such assistance as he may reasonably require for the execution of the warrant,

is guilty of an offence.

1–407

Vessels, vehicles etc

13 In this Schedule "premises" includes any vessel, vehicle, aircraft or hovercraft, and references to the occupier of any premises include references to the person in charge of any vessel, vehicle, aircraft or hovercraft.

1–408

Scotland and Northern Ireland

14 In the application of this Schedule to Scotland—

    (a) for any reference to a circuit judge there is substituted a reference to the sheriff, and

1–409

(b) for any reference to information on oath there is substituted a reference to evidence on oath.

15 In the application of this Schedule to Northern Ireland—

(a) for any reference to a circuit judge there is substituted a reference to a county court judge, and

(b) for any reference to information on oath there is substituted a reference to a complaint on oath.

NOTES

1–410   **Initial Commencement**

Specified date

Specified date: 30 November 2005 (unless the Secretary of State by order appoints this Schedule before that date): see s 87(3) (as amended by SI 2001/3500, art 8, Sch 2, Pt I, para 8(1)(o) and SI 2003/1887, art 9, Sch 2, para 12(1)(c)). (See appointment notes below.)

Appointment

Appointment (in relation to the enforcement of information notices relating to the conformity with the code of practice under s 45 hereof of the practice of public authorities in relation to the exercise of their functions under the publication scheme provisions): 30 November 2002: see SI 2002/2812, art 2(d), (e). Appointment (for remaining purposes): 1 January 2005: see SI 2004/1909, art 2(1), (2)(c), (3).

Amendment

Para 1: in sub-para (1) words "or a District Judge (Magistrates' Courts)" in square brackets inserted by the Courts Act 2003, s 65, Sch 4, para 13.
    Date in force: to be appointed: see the Courts Act 2003, s 110(1).

See Further

See further, in relation to additional powers of seizure from premises: the Criminal Justice and Police Act 2001, s 50, Sch 1, Pt 1, para 73.

SCHEDULE 4

APPEAL PROCEEDINGS: AMENDMENTS OF SCHEDULE 6 TO DATA PROTECTION ACT 1998

SECTION 61(1)

Constitution of Tribunal in national security cases

1 In paragraph 2(1) of Schedule 6 to the Data Protection Act 1998 (constitution of Tribunal in national security cases), at the end there is inserted "or under section 60(1) or (4) of the Freedom of Information Act 2000". 1–411

2 For paragraph 3 of that Schedule there is substituted—

"3 The Tribunal shall be duly constituted—

    (a) for an appeal under section 28(4) or (6) in any case where the application of paragraph 6(1) is excluded by rules under paragraph 7, or

    (b) for an appeal under section 60(1) or (4) of the Freedom of Information Act 2000,

if it consists of three of the persons designated under paragraph 2(1), of whom one shall be designated by the Lord Chancellor to preside.".

Constitution of Tribunal in other cases

3 (1) Paragraph 4 of that Schedule (constitution of Tribunal in other cases) is amended as follows. 1–412

(2) After sub-paragraph (1) there is inserted—

"(1A) Subject to any rules made under paragraph 7, the Tribunal shall be duly constituted for an appeal under section 57(1) or (2) of the Freedom of Information Act 2000 if it consists of—

    (a) the chairman or a deputy chairman (who shall preside), and

(b) an equal number of the members appointed respectively in accordance with paragraphs (aa) and (bb) of section 6(6).".

(3) In sub-paragraph (2), after "(1)" there is inserted "or (1A)".

Rules of procedure

1–413

4 (1) Paragraph 7 of that Schedule (rules of procedure) is amended as follows.

(2) In sub-paragraph (1), for the words from "regulating" onwards there is substituted—

"regulating—

(a) the exercise of the rights of appeal conferred—

(i) by sections 28(4) and (6) and 48, and

(ii) by sections 57(1) and (2) and section 60(1) and (4) of the Freedom of Information Act 2000, and

(b) the practice and procedure of the Tribunal.".

(3) In sub-paragraph (2), after paragraph (a) there is inserted—

"(aa) for the joinder of any other person as a party to any proceedings on an appeal under the Freedom of Information Act 2000,

(ab) for the hearing of an appeal under this Act with an appeal under the Freedom of Information Act 2000,".

NOTES

Initial Commencement

Specified date

Specified date: 30 November 2005 (unless the Secretary of State by order appoints this Schedule before that date): see s 87(3) (as amended by SI 2001/3500, art 8, Sch 2, Pt I, para 8(1)(o) and SI 2003/1887, art 9, Sch 2, para 12(1)(c)). (See appointment notes below.)

Appointment

Paras 1, 4: Appointment: 14 May 2001: see SI 2001/1637, art 2(c). Para 2: Appointment: 1 January 2005: see SI 2004/1909, art 2(1), (2)(d), (3). Para 3: Appointment: 30 November 2002: see SI 2002/2812, art 2(i).

SCHEDULE 5

AMENDMENTS OF PUBLIC RECORDS LEGISLATION

SECTION 67

PART I

AMENDMENTS OF PUBLIC RECORDS ACT 1958

Functions of Advisory Council on Public Records

1 In section 1 of the Public Records Act 1958 (general responsibility of the Lord Chancellor for public records), after subsection (2) there is inserted—

1–414

"(2A) The matters on which the Advisory Council on Public Records may advise the Lord Chancellor include matters relating to the application of the Freedom of Information Act 2000 to information contained in public records which are historical records within the meaning of Part VI of that Act."

Access to public records

2 (1) Section 5 of that Act (access to public records) is amended in accordance with this paragraph.

1–415

(2) Subsections (1) and (2) are omitted.

(3) For subsection (3) there is substituted—

"(3) It shall be the duty of the Keeper of Public Records to arrange that reasonable facilities are available to the public for inspecting and obtaining copies of those public records in the Public Record Office which fall to be disclosed in accordance with the Freedom of Information Act 2000."

(4) Subsection (4) and, in subsection (5), the words from "and subject to" to the end are omitted.

3 Schedule 2 of that Act (enactments prohibiting disclosure of information obtained from the public) is omitted.

Power to extend meaning of "public records"

1–416

4 In Schedule 1 to that Act (definition of public records) after the Table at the end of paragraph 3 there is inserted—

"3A (1) Her Majesty may by Order in Council amend the Table at the end of paragraph 3 of this Schedule by adding to either Part of the Table an entry relating to any body or establishment—

(a) which, at the time when the Order is made, is specified in Schedule 2 to the Parliamentary Commissioner Act 1967 (departments, etc subject to investigation), or

(b) in respect of which an entry could, at that time, be added to Schedule 2 to that Act by an Order in Council under section 4 of that Act (which confers power to amend that Schedule).

(2) An Order in Council under this paragraph may relate to a specified body or establishment or to bodies or establishments falling within a specified description.

(3) An Order in Council under this paragraph shall be subject to annulment in pursuance of a resolution of either House of Parliament."

NOTES

Initial Commencement

Royal Assent

Para 4: Royal Assent: 30 November 2000: see s 87(1)(j).

Specified date

Paras 1–3: Specified date: 30 November 2005 (unless the Secretary of State by order appoints these paras before that date): see s 87(3) (as amended by SI 2001/3500, art 8, Sch 2, Pt I, para 8(1)(o) and SI 2003/1887, art 9, Sch 2, para 12(1)(c)). (See appointment notes below.)

Appointment

Para 1: Appointment: 30 November 2002: see SI 2002/2812, art 2(j).
Paras 2, 3: Appointment: 1 January 2005: see SI 2004/3122, art 2.

PART II

AMENDMENT OF PUBLIC RECORDS ACT (NORTHERN IRELAND) 1923

5 After section 5 of the Public Records Act (Northern Ireland) 1923 (deposit of documents in Record Office by trustees or other persons) there is inserted—

1–417

"**5A Access to public records**

It shall be the duty of the Deputy Keeper of the Records of Northern Ireland to arrange that reasonable facilities are available to the public for inspecting and obtaining copies of those public records in the Public Record Office of Northern Ireland which fall to be disclosed in accordance with the Freedom of Information Act 2000."

NOTES

Initial Commencement

Specified date

Specified date: 30 November 2005 (unless the Secretary of State by order appoints this Part before that date): see s 87(3) (as amended by SI 2001/3500, art 8, Sch 2, Pt I, para 8(1)(o) and SI 2003/1887, art 9, Sch 2, para 12(1)(c)). (See appointment note below.)

Appointment

Appointment: 1 January 2005: see SI 2004/3122, art 2.

SCHEDULE 6

FURTHER AMENDMENTS OF DATA PROTECTION ACT 1998

SECTION 73

Request by data controller for further information

1–418

1 In section 7 of the Data Protection Act 1998 (right of access to personal data), for subsection (3) there is substituted—

"(3) Where a data controller—

    (a) reasonably requires further information in order to satisfy himself as to the identity of the person making a request under this section and to locate the information which that person seeks, and

    (b) has informed him of that requirement,

the data controller is not obliged to comply with the request unless he is supplied with that further information."

Parliament

1–419

2 After section 35 of that Act there is inserted—

"35A Parliamentary privilege

Personal data are exempt from—

    (a) the first data protection principle, except to the extent to which it requires compliance with the conditions in Schedules 2 and 3,

    (b) the second, third, fourth and fifth data protection principles,

    (c) section 7, and

    (d) sections 10 and 14(1) to (3),

if the exemption is required for the purpose of avoiding an infringement of the privileges of either House of Parliament."

3 After section 63 of that Act there is inserted—

"63A Application to Parliament

(1) Subject to the following provisions of this section and to section 35A, this Act applies to the processing of personal data by or on behalf of either House of Parliament as it applies to the processing of personal data by other persons.

(2) Where the purposes for which and the manner in which any personal data are, or are to be, processed are determined by or on behalf of the House of Commons, the data controller in respect of those data for the purposes of this Act shall be the Corporate Officer of that House.

(3) Where the purposes for which and the manner in which any personal data are, or are to be, processed are determined by or on behalf of the House of Lords, the data controller in respect of those data for the purposes of this Act shall be the Corporate Officer of that House.

(4) Nothing in subsection (2) or (3) is to be taken to render the Corporate Officer of the House of Commons or the Corporate Officer of the House of Lords liable to prosecution under this Act, but section 55 and paragraph 12 of Schedule 9 shall apply to a person acting on behalf of either House as they apply to any other person."

4 In Schedule 2 to that Act (conditions relevant for the purposes of the first data protection principle: processing of any personal data) in paragraph 5 after paragraph (a) there is inserted—

"(aa) for the exercise of any functions of either House of Parliament,".

5 In Schedule 3 to that Act (conditions relevant for the purposes of the first data protection principle: processing of sensitive personal data) in paragraph 7 after paragraph (a) there is inserted—

"(aa) for the exercise of any functions of either House of Parliament,".

Honours

6 In Schedule 7 to that Act (miscellaneous exemptions) in paragraph 3(b) (honours) after "honour" there is inserted "or dignity".

1–420

Legal professional privilege

1–421

7 In paragraph 10 of that Schedule (legal professional privilege), for the words "or, in Scotland, to confidentiality as between client and professional legal adviser," there is substituted "or, in Scotland, to confidentiality of communications".

Extension of transitional exemption

1–422

8 In Schedule 14 to that Act (transitional provisions), in paragraph 2(1) (which confers transitional exemption from the prohibition on processing without registration on those registered under the Data Protection Act 1984) the words "or, if earlier, 24th October 2001" are omitted.

NOTES

Initial Commencement

Royal Assent

Para 8: Royal Assent: 30 November 2000: see s 87(1)(k).

Specified date

Paras 1–7: Specified date: 30 November 2005 (unless the Secretary of State by order appoints these paras before that date): see s 87(3) (as amended by SI 2001/3500, art 8, Sch 2, Pt I, para 8(1)(o) and SI 2003/1887, art 9, Sch 2, para 12(1)(c)). (See appointment notes below.)

Appointment

Paras 1, 6, 7: Appointment: 14 May 2001: see SI 2001/1637, art 2(d).
Paras 2–5: Appointment: 1 January 2005: see SI 2004/1909, art 2(1), (2)(f), (3).

SCHEDULE 7

DISCLOSURE OF INFORMATION BY OMBUDSMEN

SECTION 76(2)

The Parliamentary Commissioner for Administration

1 At the end of section 11 of the Parliamentary Commissioner Act 1967 (provision for secrecy of information) there is inserted—

1–423

"(5) Information obtained from the Information Commissioner by virtue of section 76(1) of the Freedom of Information Act 2000 shall be treated for the purposes of subsection (2) of this section as obtained for the purposes of an investigation under this Act and, in relation to such information, the reference in paragraph (a) of that subsection to the investigation shall have effect as a reference to any investigation."

2 After section 11A of that Act there is inserted—

"11AA Disclosure of information by Parliamentary Commissioner to Information Commissioner

(1) The Commissioner may disclose to the Information Commissioner any information obtained by, or furnished to, the Commissioner under or for the purposes of this Act if the information appears to the Commissioner to relate to—

    (a) a matter in respect of which the Information Commissioner could exercise any power conferred by—

        (i) Part V of the Data Protection Act 1998 (enforcement),

        (ii) section 48 of the Freedom of Information Act 2000 (practice recommendations), or

        (iii) Part IV of that Act (enforcement), or

    (b) the commission of an offence under—

    (i) **any provision of the Data Protection Act 1998 other than paragraph 12 of Schedule 9 (obstruction of execution of warrant), or**

    (ii) **section 77 of the Freedom of Information Act 2000 (offence of altering etc records with intent to prevent disclosure).**

(2) **Nothing in section 11(2) of this Act shall apply in relation to the disclosure of information in accordance with this section."**

The Commissions for Local Administration in England and Wales

1–424

3 In section 32 of the Local Government Act 1974 (law of defamation, and disclosure of information) after subsection (6) there is inserted—

"(7) Information obtained from the Information Commissioner by virtue of section 76 of the Freedom of Information Act 2000 shall be treated for the purposes of subsection (2) above as obtained for the purposes of an investigation under this Part of this Act and, in relation to such information, the reference in paragraph (a) of that subsection to the investigation shall have effect as a reference to any investigation."

4 After section 33 of that Act there is inserted—

"**33A Disclosure of information by Local Commissioner to Information Commissioner**

(1) A Local Commissioner may disclose to the Information Commissioner any information obtained by, or furnished to, the Local Commissioner under or for the purposes of this Part of this Act if the information appears to the Local Commissioner to relate to—

    (a) a matter in respect of which the Information Commissioner could exercise any power conferred by—

        (i) Part V of the Data Protection Act 1998 (enforcement),

        (ii) section 48 of the Freedom of Information Act 2000 (practice recommendations), or

        (iii) Part IV of that Act (enforcement), or

    (b) the commission of an offence under—

        (i) any provision of the Data Protection Act 1998 other than paragraph 12 of Schedule 9 (obstruction of execution of warrant), or

  (ii) section 77 of the Freedom of Information Act 2000 (offence of altering etc records with intent to prevent disclosure).

(2) Nothing in section 32(2) of this Act shall apply in relation to the disclosure of information in accordance with this section."

The Health Service Commissioners

5 At the end of section 15 of the Health Service 1–425
Commissioners Act 1993 (confidentiality of information) there is inserted—

"(4) Information obtained from the Information Commissioner by virtue of section 76 of the Freedom of Information Act 2000 shall be treated for the purposes of subsection (1) as obtained for the purposes of an investigation and, in relation to such information, the reference in paragraph (a) of that subsection to the investigation shall have effect as a reference to any investigation."

6 After section 18 of that Act there is inserted—

"18A Disclosure of information to Information Commissioner

(1) The Health Service Commissioner for England or the Health Service Commissioner for Wales may disclose to the Information Commissioner any information obtained by, or furnished to, the Health Service Commissioner under or for the purposes of this Act if the information appears to the Health Service Commissioner to relate to—

  (a) a matter in respect of which the Information Commissioner could exercise any power conferred by—

    (i) Part V of the Data Protection Act 1998 (enforcement),

    (ii) section 48 of the Freedom of Information Act 2000 (practice recommendations), or

    (iii) Part IV of that Act (enforcement), or

  (b) the commission of an offence under—

    (i) any provision of the Data Protection Act 1998 other than paragraph 12 of Schedule 9 (obstruction of execution of warrant), or

(ii) section 77 of the Freedom of Information Act 2000 (offence of altering etc records with intent to prevent disclosure).

(3) Nothing in section 15 (confidentiality of information) applies in relation to the disclosure of information in accordance with this section."

The Welsh Administration Ombudsman

1–426

7 *In Schedule 9 to the Government of Wales Act 1998 (the Welsh Administration Ombudsman), at the end of paragraph 25 (confidentiality of information) there is inserted—*

"(5) Information obtained from the Information Commissioner by virtue of section 76 of the Freedom of Information Act 2000 shall be treated for the purposes of sub-paragraph (1) as obtained for the purposes of an investigation and, in relation to such information, the reference in paragraph (a) of that subsection to the investigation shall have effect as a reference to any investigation."

8 *After paragraph 27 of that Schedule there is inserted—*
"Disclosure of information to Information Commissioner

1–427

28 *(1) The Welsh Administration Ombudsman may disclose to the Information Commissioner any information obtained by, or furnished to, the Welsh Administration Ombudsman under or for the purposes of this Schedule if the information appears to the Welsh Administration Ombudsman to relate to—*

(a) a matter in respect of which the Information Commissioner could exercise any power conferred by—

(i) Part V of the Data Protection Act 1998 (enforcement),

(ii) section 48 of the Freedom of Information Act 2000 (practice recommendations), or

(iii) Part IV of that Act (enforcement), or

(b) the commission of an offence under—

(i) any provision of the Data Protection Act 1998 other than paragraph 12 of Schedule 9 (obstruction of execution of warrant), or

(ii) section 77 of the Freedom of Information Ac 2000 (offence of altering etc records with intent to prevent disclosure).

(2) Nothing in paragraph 25(1) applies in relation to the disclosure of information in accordance with this paragraph."

The Northern Ireland Commissioner for Complaints

9 At the end of Article 21 of the Commissioner for Complaints (Northern Ireland) Order 1996 (disclosure of information by Commissioner) there is inserted—

1–428

"(5) Information obtained from the Information Commissioner by virtue of section 76 of the Freedom of Information Act 2000 shall be treated for the purposes of paragraph (1) as obtained for the purposes of an investigation under this Order and, in relation to such information, the reference in paragraph (1)(a) to the investigation shall have effect as a reference to any investigation."

10 After that Article there is inserted—

"Disclosure of information to Information Commissioner

21A (1) The Commissioner may disclose to the Information Commissioner any information obtained by, or furnished to, the Commissioner under or for the purposes of this Order if the information appears to the Commissioner to relate to—

    (a) a matter in respect of which the Information Commissioner could exercise any power conferred by—

        (i) Part V of the Data Protection Act 1998 (enforcement),

        (ii) section 48 of the Freedom of Information Act 2000 (practice recommendations), or

        (iii) Part IV of that Act (enforcement), or

    (b) the commission of an offence under—

        (i) any provision of the Data Protection Act 1998 other than paragraph 12 of Schedule 9 (obstruction of execution of warrant), or

        (ii) section 77 of the Freedom of Information Act 2000 (offence of altering etc records with intent to prevent disclosure).

(2) Nothing in Article 21(1) applies in relation to the disclosure of information in accordance with this Article."

The Assembly Ombudsman for Northern Ireland

1–429

11 **At the end of Article 19 of the Ombudsman (Northern Ireland) Order 1996 there is inserted—**

"(5) Information obtained from the Information Commissioner by virtue of section 76 of the Freedom of Information Act 2000 shall be treated for the purposes of paragraph (1) as obtained for the purposes of an investigation under this Order and, in relation to such information, the reference in paragraph (1)(a) to the investigation shall have effect as a reference to any investigation."

12 **After that Article there is inserted—**

"Disclosure of information to Information Commissioner

19A (1) The Ombudsman may disclose to the Information Commissioner any information obtained by, or furnished to, the Omubudsman under or for the purposes of this Order if the information appears to the Ombudsman to relate to—

(a) a matter in respect of which the Information Commissioner could exercise any power conferred by—

(i) Part V of the Data Protection Act 1998 (enforcement),

(ii) section 48 of the Freedom of Information Act 2000 (practice recommendations), or

(iii) Part IV of that Act (enforcement), or

(b) the commission of an offence under—

(i) any provision of the Data Protection Act 1998 other than paragraph 12 of Schedule 9 (obstruction of execution of warrant), or

(ii) section 77 of the Freedom of Information Act 2000 (offence of altering etc records with intent to prevent disclosure).

(2) Nothing in Article 19(1) applies in relation to the disclosure of information in accordance with this Article."

. . .

13 . . .

NOTES

Initial Commencement

Specified date

Specified date: 30 January 2001: see s 87(2)(b).

Amendment

Paras 7, 8: repealed by the Public Services Ombudsman (Wales) Act 2005, s 39(2), Sch 7.
    Date in force: to be appointed: see the Public Services Ombudsman (Wales) Act 2005, s 40.
Para 13: repealed by the Scottish Public Services Ombudsman Act 2002, s 25(1), Sch 6, para 23(1), (3).
    Date in force: 23 October 2002: see SSI 2002/467, art 2.

SCHEDULE 8

REPEALS

SECTION 86

PART I

REPEAL COMING INTO FORCE ON PASSING OF ACT

Chapter	Short title	Extent of repeal
1998 c 29	The Data Protection Act 1998	In Schedule 14, in paragraph 2(1), the words "or, if earlier, 24th October 2001".

NOTES

Initial Commencement

Royal Assent

Royal Assent: 30 November 2000: see s 87(1)(l).

PART II

REPEALS COMING INTO FORCE IN ACCORDANCE WITH SECTION 87(2)

Chapter	Short title	Extent of repeal
1958 c 51	The Public Records Act 1958	In Schedule 1, in Part II of the Table in paragraph 3, the entry relating to the Data Protection Commissioner.
1967 c 13	The Parliamentary Commissioner Act 1967	In Schedule 2, the entry relating to the Data Protection Commissioner.
1975 c 24	The House of Commons Disqualification Act 1975	In Schedule 1, in Part III, the entry relating to the Data Protection Commissioner.
1975 c 25	The Northern Ireland Assembly Disqualification Act 1975	In Schedule 1, in Part III, the entry relating to the Data Protection Commissioner.
1998 c 29	The Data Protection Act 1998	In Schedule 5, Part III.
		In Schedule 15, paragraphs 1(1), 2, 4, 5(2) and 6(2).

NOTES

Initial Commencement

Specified date

Specified date: 30 January 2001: see s 87(2)(d).

PART III

REPEALS COMING INTO FORCE IN ACCORDANCE WITH SECTION 87(3)

Chapter	Short title	Extent of repeal
1958 c 51	The Public Records Act 1958	In section 5, subsections (1), (2) and (4) and, in subsection (5), the words from "and subject to" to the end.
		Schedule 2.
1975 c 24	The House of Commons Disqualification Act 1975	In Schedule 1, in Part II, the entry relating to the Data Protection Tribunal.
1975 c 25	The Northern Ireland Assembly Disqualification Act 1975	In Schedule 1, in Part II, the entry relating to the Data Protection Tribunal.
1998 c 29	The Data Protection Act 1998	In section 1(1), in the definition of "data", the word "or" at the end of paragraph (c).
		In Schedule 15, paragraphs 1(2) and (3), 3, 5(1) and 6(1).

NOTES

Initial Commencement

Specified date

Specified date: 30 November 2005 (unless the Secretary of State by order appoints this Part before that date): see s 87(3) (as amended by SI 2001/3500, art 8, Sch 2, Pt I, para 8(1)(o) and SI 2003/1887, art 9, Sch 2, para 12(1)(c)). (See appointment note below.)

Appointment

Appointment: 1 January 2005: by virtue of SI 2004/1909, art 2(1), (2)(f), (3).

I

CHAPTER 2

ENVIRONMENTAL INFORMATION REGULATIONS 2004

FREEDOM OF INFORMATION ENVIRONMENTAL PROTECTION

Made   21st December 2004

Coming into force   1st January 2005

313

PART III

EXCEPTIONS TO THE DUTY TO DISCLOSE ENVIRONMENTAL INFORMATION

PART IV

CODE OF PRACTICE AND HISTORICAL RECORDS

PART V

ENFORCEMENT AND APPEALS, OFFENCES, AMENDMENT AND REVOCATION

Whereas a draft of these Regulations has been approved by resolution of each House of Parliament in pursuance of paragraph 2(2) of Schedule 2 to the European Communities Act 1972;

Now, therefore, the Secretary of State, being a Minister designated for the purposes of section 2(2) of the European Communities Act 1972 in relation to freedom of access to, and dissemination of, information on the environment held by or for public authorities or other bodies, in exercise of the powers conferred on her by that section, makes the following Regulations:

Part I

Introductory

1 Citation and commencement

These Regulations may be cited as the Environmental Information Regulations 2004 and shall come into force on 1st January 2005.

NOTES

Initial Commencement

Specified date

Specified date: 1 January 2005: see above.

GENERAL NOTE

Unlike freedom of information generally—for which legislation has developed piecemeal across Europe and the rest of the world—in the specific area of environmental information the European Union has taken the lead in developing access rights to records held by public authorities. As a result, an environmental information access regime has existed in the UK for more than a decade, in the form of the Environmental Information Regulations 1992 (the "**1992 Regulations**").[1]   2–002

As of January 1, 2005 (but with retrospective effect) the 1992 Regulations were superseded by the Environmental Information Regulations 2004 (referred to throughout this book as the "**EIRs**").[2] The EIRs bring UK law into line with the UNECE Convention on Access to Information, Public Participation and Access to Justice in Environmental Matters 1998 (known as the "**Aarhus Convention**")[3] and Directive 2003/4/EC on Public Access to Environmental Information (the "**Directive**").[4] The EIRs are also intended to help deliver government policy on sustainable development[5]

[1] The 1992 Regulations implemented Directive 90/313/EEC on Freedom of Access to Information on the Environment.
[2] Environmental Information Regulations 2004, Reg.21.
[3] The Aarhus Convention (adopted at a European Environmental Ministers' meeting in Aarhus, Denmark) came into force on October 30, 2001. The UK ratified the Convention on February 23, 2005 and became a full party to it on May 23, 2005. It covers three areas: access to information, public participation, and access to justice on environmental matters. The UNECE is the United Nations Economic Commission for Europe.
[4] The Directive brings Community law into line with the Aarhus Convention. Article 1 of the Directive states its two objectives as: "(a) to grant a right of access to environmental information held by or for public authorities and to set out the basic terms and conditions of its exercise; and (b) to promote, as a matter of course, the widest possible systematic availability of and dissemination to the public of environmental information."
[5] See *www.sustainable-development.gov.uk*.

and to assimilate procedures and processes for both environmental information and the broader rights of access under FOIA. The environmental information regime is entirely separate from the freedom of information regime,[6] but there are close similarities between them.

Differences between the 1992 Regulations and the EIRs

2–003 The principal differences between the 1992 Regulations and the EIRs are as follows:

(a) the definition of "environmental information", and the list of bodies caught by the EIRs, have been clarified;

(b) the time limit for responding to requests is now reduced in most cases to 20 working days;

(c) a public interest test now applies to any potential refusal of a request; and

(d) the Information Commissioner and the Information Tribunal provide a much enhanced enforcement and appeal regime.

Interaction of the EIRs and FOIA

2–004 The EIRs and FOIA are mutually exclusive by virtue of s.39 of FOIA which says that insofar as a request relates to environmental information it will be governed by the EIRs. Requests which comprise both environmental and non-environmental information fall under both regimes respectively, and requests relating to personal data fall within the regime under the Data Protection Act 1998.

As noted above, the existence of separate regimes for access to environmental and other information is a result of the two having grown up separately. There are nevertheless strong similarities between the two and where differences exist they arise from European legislation and other international obligations. The principal differences are as follows:

(a) requests for environmental information are not required to be in writing;

(b) the EIRs cover a wider range of organisations, including some private organisations;

(c) the public interest test applies to *all* the grounds under the EIRs for refusing a request; and

---

[6] Brought in by the Freedom of Information Act 2000.

(d) the EIR exceptions differ in some respects from the FOIA exemptions.

2 Interpretation

(1) **In these Regulations—**

"**the Act**" means the Freedom of Information Act 2000;

"**applicant**", in relation to a request for environmental information, means the person who made the request;

"**appropriate records authority**", in relation to a transferred public record, has the same meaning as in section 15(5) of the Act;

"**the Commissioner**" means the Information Commissioner;

"**the Directive**" means Council Directive 2003/4/EC on public access to environmental information and repealing Council Directive 90/313/EEC;

"**environmental information**" has the same meaning as in Article 2(1) of the Directive, namely any information in written, visual, aural, electronic or any other material form on—

(a) the state of the elements of the environment, such as air and atmosphere, water, soil, land, landscape and natural sites including wetlands, coastal and marine areas, biological diversity and its components, including genetically modified organisms, and the interaction among these elements;

(b) factors, such as substances, energy, noise, radiation or waste, including radioactive waste, emissions, discharges and other releases into the environment, affecting or likely to affect the elements of the environment referred to in (a);

(c) measures (including administrative measures), such as policies, legislation, plans, programmes, environmental agreements, and activities affecting or likely to affect the elements and factors referred to in (a) and (b) as well as measures or activities designed to protect those elements;

(d) reports on the implementation of environmental legislation;

(e) cost-benefit and other economic analyses and assumptions used within the framework of the measures and activities referred to in (c); and

(f) the state of human health and safety, including the contamination of the food chain, where relevant, conditions of human life, cultural sites and built structures inasmuch as they are or may be affected by the state of the elements of the environment referred to in (a) or, through those elements, by any of the matters referred to in (b) and (c);

"historical record" has the same meaning as in section 62(1) of the Act;

"public authority" has the meaning given by paragraph (2);

"public record" has the same meaning as in section 84 of the Act;

"responsible authority", in relation to a transferred public record, has the same meaning as in section 15(5) of the Act;

"Scottish public authority" means—

(a) a body referred to in section 80(2) of the Act; and

(b) insofar as not such a body, a Scottish public authority as defined in section 3 of the Freedom of Information (Scotland) Act 2002;

"transferred public record" has the same meaning as in section 15(4) of the Act; and

"working day" has the same meaning as in section 10(6) of the Act.

(2) Subject to paragraph (3), "public authority" means—

(a) government departments;

(b) any other public authority as defined in section 3(1) of the Act, disregarding for this purpose the exceptions in paragraph 6 of Schedule 1 to the Act, but excluding—

(i) any body or office-holder listed in Schedule 1 to the Act only in relation to information of a specified description; or

        (ii) any person designated by Order under section 5 of the Act;

    (c) any other body or other person, that carries out functions of public administration; or

    (d) any other body or other person, that is under the control of a person falling within sub-paragraphs (a), (b) or (c) and—

        (i) has public responsibilities relating to the environment;

        (ii) exercises functions of a public nature relating to the environment; or

        (iii) provides public services relating to the environment.

(3) Except as provided by regulation 12(10) a Scottish public authority is not a "public authority" for the purpose of these Regulations.

(4) The following expressions have the same meaning in these Regulations as they have in the Data Protection Act 1998, namely—

    (a) "data" except that for the purposes of regulation 12(3) and regulation 13 a public authority referred to in the definition of data in paragraph (e) of section 1(1) of that Act means a public authority within the meaning of these Regulations;

    (b) "the data protection principles";

    (c) "data subject"; and

    (d) "personal data".

(5) Except as provided by this regulation, expressions in these Regulations which appear in the Directive have the same meaning in these Regulations as they have in the Directive.

NOTES

Initial Commencement

Specified date

Specified date: 1 January 2005: see reg 1.

GENERAL NOTE

Because there are close similarities between the EIRs and FOIA there is a   **2–006** great deal of potential for overlap. Understanding and correctly applying the definition of "environmental information" is therefore critical to the correct operation of each.

It will be apparent from the wording of the definition that it goes well beyond merely the elements of the physical environment.

Department for Constitutional Affairs Guidance

2–007 The definition of environmental information operates without geographical restriction. So, for example, information on the estates of embassies will be covered, as will overseas aid programme grants for schemes which impact the environment.

There is no restriction on the "types" of information covered—information in any "material form" is caught. This will include information contained in documents, maps, pictures and records (records will include registers, reports, returns, computer records and other non-documentary records), all types of decision letters, applications, inspection reports, concession agreements, contracts, tables, databases, spreadsheets, e-mails, photographs, sketches and handwritten notes or drawings.

The definition covers opinions and advice as well as facts.

The EIRs do not require authorities to carry out research or analysis to produce information which does not exist when the request is made. The definition does not cover information which can only be created by manipulating existing information.

The definition does not include information destroyed in accordance with established records management procedures (but note s.19 which, consistent with FOIA, creates an offence of altering records to avoid disclosure).

The DCA guidance suggests that the definition *does* include information relating to the way information was obtained, and information about the accuracy of records, although there is nothing in the wording of the definition in these terms. Common sense suggests that it may be prudent for authorities to state that certain information is based on opinion rather than fact, or derived from forecasts or samples, or originated from a third party who may have submitted it in order to argue a particular point of view. In cases where the reliability of information is uncertain it may be sensible to issue a disclaimer to this effect, or to the effect that the use of information should be undertaken with due care as to its accuracy, source or other relevant characteristics. For example, where the information requested is derived from a very small statistical sample, it may be appropriate to make clear that this is the case and that it would be unwise to rely upon it.

The DCA has stated that the government treats all information relating to GM crop trials, to pesticide testing, to diseased cattle and to land-use planning (including the reasons for decisions to approve as well as to refuse planning permission) as environmental information. The definition will also include reports on the implementation of environmental legislation and any analysis resulting from an appraisal of policy, including any Regulatory Impact Assessment.

Case law under the 1992 Regulations

Case law relating to the now superseded 1992 Regulations gives some useful pointers to the scope of the definition of environmental information. In *R. v British Coal Corporation Ex p. Ibstock Builiding Products Ltd*[7] the High Court held that whether information is environmental information is a question of fact. The case involved an application for judicial review of the continuing refusal of the British Coal Corporation to disclose information relating to the alleged dumping of naval munitions in 1947 down mineshafts beneath the Ibstock Brick Works. The parties both accepted that the presence of munitions in the mineshafts was information within the definition of environmental information. The court held that the definition could also include the source of information relating to the state of the environment, including the identity of an individual, if necessary to assess the credibility of the information. Accordingly, the name of an informant who had told British Coal that the dumping had occurred was considered to be a part of the environmental information that should be released. The judge rejected arguments that the information was confidential because it related to the dumping of naval ordnance secretly and this was information relating to matters affecting national defence or public security.

2–008

In *R. v The Secretary of State for the Environment, Transport & The Regions and Midland Expressway Limited Ex p. Alliance Against the Birmingham Northern Relief Road*[8] the High Court decided that the content of a concession agreement relating to the construction of a motorway was environmental information for the purposes of the 1992 Regulations. The case arose out of an inquiry into the Birmingham northern relief road which was to be built, financed and operated as a toll road by Midland Expressway. A public inquiry concluded that the scheme should go ahead, but the Alliance was concerned that the Secretary of State's decision may have been influenced by the prospect of having to pay compensation to Midland under the terms of the agreement had he decided not to proceed. In August 1997 the Alliance requested a copy of the concession agreement under the 1992 Regulations. The Department refused, claiming that it was commercially confidential. The Alliance applied for judicial review of that decision. Having inspected the agreement, the court decided that only parts of if were confidential and therefore that the Alliance was entitled to see the other parts.

---

[7] [1995] JPL 836.
[8] [1999] JPL 231.

The European Court of Justice has also indicated that it will adopt a broad view of the definition of environmental information. In *Wilhelm Mecklenburg v Kreis Pinneberg*[9] a statement of views given by a countryside protection authority which was capable of influencing the outcome of development consent proceedings was found to be environmental information.

Defra Guidance

2–009   The Defra guidance sets out a list of definitions relating to words contained within the EIR definition of environmental information.

"**Air**" should be taken to include the air within buildings and other natural and man-made structures above or below ground and in air conditioning systems.

"**Water**" includes underground and surface water (both natural and in man-made structures), sewage and foul water, water tables and aquifers. Surface water includes inland waters (*e.g.* rivers, canals and lakes), estuaries and seas.

"**Soil**" includes the *in situ* upper layer of the mantle rock in which plants grow.

"**Land and landscape**" includes all land surfaces, buildings, caves and underground strata. Land covered by water is also included.

A "**natural site**" should be taken to include areas identified by reason of their flora, fauna, geological or physiographical features (*e.g.* Sites of Special Scientific Interest) or general environmental quality (*e.g.* Areas of Outstanding Natural Beauty).

"**Biological diversity**" should be taken to include species both living and dead.

"**Human health and safety**" and "**conditions of human life**" include human response to physical, chemical and biological agents delivered through environmental media of water, air, land, and biodiversity etc.

"**Built structures**" should be taken to include structures, roads and other infrastructure created by mankind and includes ancient and historic monuments.

The "**state**" should be taken to include physical, chemical, electromagnetic, radiological and biological conditions at any moment in time.

---

[9] Der Landrat, ECJ judgment of June 17, 1998 (Sixth Chamber) Pinneberg.

"Emissions, discharges and other releases into the environment wherever they occur" should be taken to include the direct or indirect release of substances, liquids, gases, radiation, vibrations, light or noise from individual or diffuse sources into or onto air, water or land.

"Measure (including administrative measures)" can include environmental management programmes, procurement plans and programmes, permit schemes, management contracts, housing maintenance programmes, land-use planning regimes and permits, regeneration and transport development plans and proposals as well as the policies of central and local government.

"Activities" should be taken to include the range of activities involved in achieving desired outcomes.

"Affecting or likely to affect" includes direct and indirect effect. Strategic Environmental Assessments, Environmental Impact Assessments, sustainability appraisals and Regulatory Impact Assessments help public authorities identify the potential impacts of policies, plans and programmes, including any unintended environmental effects as well as assessing desired outcomes. Examples include schools admissions policies that may have the effect of either increasing or reducing travel to school, congestion charging schemes that may result in a greater use of public transport, policies that relate to the locations of hospitals, GP surgeries, waste and recycling facilities, and the availability of funds for crime reduction work, cultural activities and the arts, or the provision of business infrastructure.

"Economic analyses" include financial analyses.

Meaning of "public authority"

The EIR definition covers all public authorities caught by FOIA, but it also goes further. It includes in addition: 2–010

- anyone carrying out functions of public administration;

- anyone "under the control of" a public authority who has public responsibilities to the environment, exercises public functions or provides public services; and

- the special forces and any unit assisting GCHQ.[10]

Meaning of "under the control of" a public authority

Guidance from Defra states that "control" for this purpose is taken to mean any relationship constituted by statute, regulations, rights, licence, contracts or other means which either separately or jointly confer the   2–011

---

[10] These are carved out of FOIA by the exceptions to para.6 of Schedule 1, but the exceptions do not apply under the EIRs.

possibility of directly or indirectly exercising a decisive influence on a body. Clearly, this is very broad. It means that control may exist even where it relates only to services provided by the body rather than to control of the body itself. This will bring within the scope of the EIRs any private company providing services on behalf of a public authority if the authority exercises the requisite degree of control. The Defra Guidance gives the following examples of circumstances where private companies may come within the rules:

- private companies and public private partnerships dealing with environmental functions such as waste disposal, water, energy and transport (*e.g.* the Civil Aviation Authority and port authorities);

- companies involved with the supply of essential public services, such as water,[11] electricity and gas[12];

- environmental consultants; and

- the Ambulance Service (which carries out a public service and collects statistics on road traffic accidents) and HM Revenue & Customs, which deals with the illegal import of endangered species.

Private voluntary organisations (whether charitable or not) which collect, collate and/or disseminate environmental information for their own interests will not generally be covered by the EIRs unless they are brought within the rules by virtue of a contract or license arrangement with a public authority.

By virtue of Reg.3(3), the rules do not apply to any public authority when acting in a judicial or legislative capacity. So, the judicial or legislative work of the courts, the Planning Inspectorate, Rent Assessment Panels, Licensing Panels and Social Services Complaints Panels is not subject to the EIRs, but their work in carrying out other functions—such as the management of their own estates and operations—will be. Records will, however, be subject to the EIRs if kept beyond the completion of any relevant judicial procedure or appeal period that applies.

Security and intelligence services are within the scope of the rules.

Historical information

2–012   There is no time limit on historical data. If environmental information currently exists it is covered by the Regulations, no matter when the information was created or gathered.[13]

---

[11] See *Griffin v South West Water Services Ltd* [1995] IRLR.
[12] See *Foster v British Gas plc*, Case C-188/89, [1990] 2 CMLR 833.
[13] See Reg.17 in relation to historical and transferred public records.

3 Application

    (1) **Subject to paragraphs (3) and (4), these Regulations**   2–013
    apply to public authorities.

    (2) **For the purposes of these Regulations, environmental information is held by a public authority if the information—**

        (a) **is in the authority's possession and has been produced or received by the authority; or**

        (b) **is held by another person on behalf of the authority.**

    (3) **These Regulations shall not apply to any public authority to the extent that it is acting in a judicial or legislative capacity.**

    (4) **These Regulations shall not apply to either House of Parliament to the extent required for the purpose of avoiding an infringement of the privileges of either House.**

    (5) **Each government department is to be treated as a person separate from any other government department for the purposes of Parts 2, 4 and 5 of these Regulations.**

NOTES

Initial Commencement

Specified date

Specified date: 1 January 2005: see reg 1.

GENERAL NOTE

As is the case under FOIA, the EIR right of access is engaged by mere   **2–014** possession of information by a public authority—the right does not depend on ownership or legal right of use. The regime is also retrospective, so catches information collected before January 1, 2005.

The EIRs apply whether or not information was obtained as a result of the authority's environmental responsibilities, and authoritites are treated as holding information even where the information is held by someone else on their behalf—for example where information is stored off-site. If a request is received for information which has been put into storage in the charge of another organisation, then the authority receiving the request is still responsible for responding to the request. Authorities must therefore make arrangements with organisations which hold information for them to ensure that they can retrieve it in time to comply with their EIR obligations.

Unlike under FOIA, the EIRs do not exclude information which a public authority holds on behalf of someone else.[14] Environmental information held by an authority on behalf of another person is accessible in the same way as the authority's other environmental information, although exceptions may apply under Reg.12. By way of example, some county archives offices hold district council records by arrangement with the district council, usually on a chargeable basis. An archives office must respond to any request it receives, assuming it holds the information requested.

Historical records

2–015 Environmental information includes information passed for safekeeping to the National Archives and other record offices. Records that are public records under the Public Records Act 1958 ("**PRA**") are Crown property but held by the National Archives in its own right as the government's archives under the PRA.[15]

---

[14] Freedom of Information Act 2000, s.3(2)(a).
[15] See Reg.17 in relation to historical and transferred public records.

Part II

Access to Environmental Information Held by Public Authorities

4 Dissemination of environmental information

(1) Subject to paragraph (3), a public authority shall in respect of environmental information that it holds— 2–016

   (a) progressively make the information available to the public by electronic means which are easily accessible; and

   (b) take reasonable steps to organize the information relevant to its functions with a view to the active and systematic dissemination to the public of the information.

(2) For the purposes of paragraph (1) the use of electronic means to make information available or to organize information shall not be required in relation to information collected before 1st January 2005 in non-electronic form.

(3) Paragraph (1) shall not extend to making available or disseminating information which a public authority would be entitled to refuse to disclose under regulation 12.

(4) The information under paragraph (1) shall include at least—

   (a) the information referred to in Article 7(2) of the Directive; and

   (b) facts and analyses of facts which the public authority considers relevant and important in framing major environmental policy proposals.

NOTES

Initial Commencement

Specified date

Specified date: 1 January 2005: see reg 1.

GENERAL NOTE

As well as the duty under Reg.5 to make information available on request, 2–017
Reg.4 obliges public authorities to be proactive in disseminating environmental information.

Organisations which are subject to FOIA are of course required to maintain a Publication Scheme,[16] and any such scheme will have to include environmental information as well as everything else. Provided an authority's publication scheme is FOIA-compliant (and that assumes the authority is proactive in keeping it up to date and progressively expanding its coverage), then it should meet the proactive dissemination requirements under Reg.4.

Organisations which are not subject to FOIA will need to consider what they need to do in order to comply with the proactive dissemination requirement. The first step will be to undertake an audit of all environmental information which they hold, whether on websites, through annual reports or other literature.

Regulation 4(4) identifies categories of information which should be given priority for publication unless they fall into an exempt category. Some of the categories are information most likely to be held by central government departments. These include texts of international treaties, conventions or agreements, and national legislation (all of which can be made available by means of links to the relevant international and domestic websites). See further below.

Priority should also be given to identifying and disseminating information which is most likely to be of interest to the public. This may, for example, include information on emissions and waste as a result of the authority's operations, and the way in which these are handled. Information on energy consumption may also be of particular interest.

Information on rights of redress should also be disseminated. These include information on where to make complaints when there is, or appears to be, a failure in the provision of environmental services or in regulatory monitoring of the environment, where to turn for legal advice on environmental matters and the appeal mechanisms available.

According to Defra *"proactive dissemination is particularly encouraged by means of computer telecommunications and/or electronic technology. Members of the public should be encouraged to check websites to see whether the information is in the public domain before they formulate requests. In order to demonstrate that the public authority is taking reasonable steps to organise and actively disseminate its environmental information, it is advised to draw up a plan, setting out the steps it proposes to take in order to meet these requirements and to make this available to the public, preferably on its public website."*

Archives offices are not expected to re-organise their archival collections as a result of Reg.4.

---

[16] Freedom of Information Act 2000, ss.19 and 20.

Regulations 4(1)(a)—meaning of "progressively make available . . . by electronic means"

Information which is already held in an electronic form should be made   2–018
available on a publicly accessible website, especially if it falls within the
categories listed in Reg.4(4). Environmental information which is gathered,
produced or commissioned after February 2005 should be in electronic
form wherever possible. This includes electronic information on permits,
applications for permits and monitoring data relating to those permits.
However, Defra does not expect information that is rarely requested, or of
little relevance to the quality and condition of the environment today, to be
methodically scanned. Nor does it expect archives offices to scan
environmental information in their archival collections, whether received by
them before or after implementation of the EIRs. The key question in
relation to historical environmental information will be whether it can be
found when requested.

Regulation 4(1)(b)—meaning of "reasonable steps"

In deciding what would constitute "reasonable steps", authorities must   2–019
consider whether and to what extent information is readily retrievable and
capable of being made available to the public. Priority should be given to
organising and disseminating the types of information specifically identified
in Reg.4(4). Thus, for example, if the body produces data or summaries of
data derived from monitoring activities that affect, or are likely to affect, the
environment, or holds permits and licenses with respect to activities likely
to have a significant impact upon the environment, these should be
organised and made available as soon as possible.

Regulation 4(4)

The information referred to in Art.7(2) of the Directive is: 2–020

(a) texts of international treaties, conventions or agreements, and of
Community, national, regional or local legislation, on the
environment or relating to it;

(b) policies, plans and programmes relating to the environment;

(c) progress reports on the implementation of the items referred to in
(a) and (b) when prepared or held in electronic form by public
authorities;

(d) the reports on the state of the environment referred to in (c);

(e) data or summaries of data derived from the monitoring of
activities affecting, or likely to affect, the environment;

(f) authorisations with a significant impact on the environment and
environmental agreements or a reference to the place where such

information can be requested or found in accordance with the EIR rules of access;

(g) environmental impact studies and risk assessments concerning the environmental elements referred to in part (a) of the definition of "environmental information" in Reg.2(1), or a reference to the place where the information can be requested or found in accordance with the EIR rules of access.

Many authorities at all levels of government, and other bodies which are subject to the EIRs, will hold information relating to policies, plans, programmes, progress reports, reports on the state of the environment and data on activities affecting the environment, and other topics listed in Art.7(2). Environmental impact studies include those on environmental health (which, by the World Health Organisation definition "*comprises those aspects of human health, including quality of life, that are determined by physical, biological, social and psychosocial factors in the environment. It also refers to the theory and practice of assessing, correcting, controlling and preventing those factors in the environment that can potentially affect adversely the health of present and future generations*").[17] Usually this information will be made available through the organisation's primary website, or be clearly and appropriately signposted. Defra provides information on the reporting of environmental information. The Sustainable Development Unit in particular has a number of documents relating to the environment.[18]

Defra guidance

2–021 Regulation 4 leaves it to each public authority to determine how best to organize its environmental information in order to comply with the proactive dissemination requirement. The nature of an authority's arrangements will turn on matters such as what proportion of the information it holds is environmental, and whether environmental information can be separated out from other information (increasingly, in most areas of government, policies and plans will be contained in policy appraisal documents which combine environmental considerations with social and economic issues—Regulatory Impact Assessments and integrated policy appraisals, for example, show how public authorities have explored the sustainable development impacts of a new initiative or policy and these will often include environmental information).

---

[17] See *www.who.int/phe/en*. Further information on topics relating to the protection of human health within the environment can be found at *www.who.int/phe/health_topics/en/*.
[18] Defra reports on Sustainable Development can be found at:
www.defra.gov.uk/corporate/sdstrategy/sdstrategy.pdf
www.sustainable-development.gov.uk/ar2002/index.htm
www.sustainable-development.gov.uk/uk_strategy/index.htm
www.sustainable-development.gov.uk/sdig/reports/index.htm.

Registers of environmental information[19]

Wherever other legislation requires a public authority to keep an accessible   **2–022**
register of environmental information (*e.g.* the Pollutant Release and
Transfers Register and local authority registers of planning applications),
these registers must be kept up to date.

The Environmental Information Unit now maintains a Central Register of
Environmental Registers showing where Environmental Registers can be
found, as required by Art.3(5)(c) of the Directive, and every public
authority which is subject to a legislative requirement to maintain a public
register should provide a link to this central Register. The Central Register
is available at *www.defra.gov.uk/corporate/opengov/eir/pdf/registers.pdf*.

A public authority may respond to a request by explaining where the
information may be obtained, provided it is available without a charge or
upon the payment of a reasonable charge which is available in a schedule of
charges.

The requirements of Reg.4 appear to bring the UK into line with the EU
Strategic Environmental Assessment (SEA) Directive, under which public
bodies are required to conduct a formal investigation of environmental
impacts of new policies and programmes prior to determining their final
shape.

5 **Duty to make available environmental information on
   request**

> (1) Subject to paragraph (3) and in accordance with   **2–023**
>   paragraphs (2), (4), (5) and (6) and the remaining
>   provisions of this Part and Part 3 of these Regulations, a
>   public authority that holds environmental information
>   shall make it available on request.
>
> (2) Information shall be made available under paragraph (1)
>   as soon as possible and no later than 20 working days after
>   the date of receipt of the request.
>
> (3) To the extent that the information requested includes
>   personal data of which the applicant is the data subject,
>   paragraph (1) shall not apply to those personal data.
>
> (4) For the purposes of paragraph (1), where the information
>   made available is compiled by or on behalf of the public
>   authority it shall be up to date, accurate and comparable,
>   so far as the public authority reasonably believes.
>
> (5) Where a public authority makes available information in
>   paragraph (b) of the definition of environmental

---

[19] See also the commentary on Reg.8.

information, and the applicant so requests, the public authority shall, insofar as it is able to do so, either inform the applicant of the place where information, if available, can be found on the measurement procedures, including methods of analysis, sampling and pre-treatment of samples, used in compiling the information, or refer the applicant to a standardised procedure used.

(6) Any enactment or rule of law that would prevent the disclosure of information in accordance with these Regulations shall not apply.

NOTES

Initial Commencement

Specified date

Specified date: 1 January 2005: see reg 1.

GENERAL NOTE

2–024 Any request, regardless of where it originates or the form it takes, will be a valid request for environmental information so long as the information requested is "environmental". In common with the rules under FOIA, the EIR regime is "purpose-blind", meaning that applicants do not have to give a reason for wanting information[20]; nor do they have to mention the EIRs themselves.

Oral requests

2–025 One significant difference from the rules under FOIA is that requests for environmental information need not be in writing—they can be made orally (whether face-to-face or by telephone), and can even be made using sign language.

The Defra guidance points out that authorities should seek to have oral requests confirmed in writing where the request appears to be complex or relates to information which is seldom requested (and which therefore may need to be retrieved from an off-site storage facility). Refusal by the applicant to confirm an oral request in writing is not a ground for the authority to refuse it, however.

---

[20] There may be circumstances where it could be useful to know the applicant's interest or reasons for the request. For example, the request may be made in connection with a planning application and the information may be needed very quickly to enable the applicant to take action on the information within the time frames set out under planning legislation. If the applicant is willing to provide this information, then every effort should be made to supply the information in time. However, if the applicant does not give their reason, the authority should still respond to the request as soon as possible in accordance with the rules.

Authorities should take care to ensure that the date of oral requests are recorded accurately because the 20-day time limit runs from the date of the telephone call or face-to-face meeting.

Unless an authority can give a response to an oral request immediately, it will need contact details from the applicant in order to reply and so it will usually be sensible for applicants to provide these in writing to avoid risk of them being taken down incorrectly.

The Defra guidance observes that authorities will need to be clear about the impact oral requests could have on the practice of using answer-phones or voicemail. Because of the responsibility to review a case when any complaint is received and because of the Information Commissioner's powers of investigation under s.54 of FOIA, every public authority needs effective systems both to keep track of requests while they are being handled and also to give conclusive answers to anyone reviewing the handling of a case at a later date.

Time limits for responding to requests

The general duty is to make information available "as soon as possible" and in any event within 20 working days. Regulation 7 permits an extension to 40 working days where the complexity and volume of information makes this reasonable. In contrast to the rules under FOIA, these time limits apply even where the authority is considering the application of an exemption or the balance of the public interest.   **2–026**

Defra guidance states that *"the aim . . . should be to provide a quick and efficient service to those requesting information and to do so without incurring unnecessary costs. Requests for information can be satisfied in a variety of ways. Where the request is for information that is readily available (i.e. does not require collating or editing), it should be possible to give a quick verbal or written response or allow an inspection of records to personal callers on an ad hoc basis. Where a request for information involves the collating and editing of documents, significant staff time may be involved, so the request is probably best handled through correspondence."* It goes on: *"An authority may decide that it is more efficient to set aside reception facilities for the public and staff to handle the information to be inspected free of charge. Where the level of demand warrants it, the authority may also provide access to a photocopier or computer printer. Charges for the use of the copying machine or printer should be limited to the actual cost of providing a copy."*

Regulation 5(4)—quality of information

A novel feature of the regulations is the obligation on authorities to ensure that where information to be released has been compiled by or for the public authority, it must be "up to date, accurate and comparable." This effectively imposes an obligation on authorities to ensure the quality of information which they provide—something which does not exist under the FOIA regime.   **2–027**

6 Form and format of information

2–028

(1) Where an applicant requests that the information be made available in a particular form or format, a public authority shall make it so available, unless—

    (a) it is reasonable for it to make the information available in another form or format; or

    (b) the information is already publicly available and easily accessible to the applicant in another form or format.

(2) If the information is not made available in the form or format requested, the public authority shall—

    (a) explain the reason for its decision as soon as possible and no later than 20 working days after the date of receipt of the request for the information;

    (b) provide the explanation in writing if the applicant so requests; and

    (c) inform the applicant of the provisions of regulation 11 and of the enforcement and appeal provisions of the Act applied by regulation 18.

NOTES

Initial Commencement

Specified date

Specified date: 1 January 2005: see reg 1.

GENERAL NOTE

2–029   Regulation 6 entitles applicants to specify the format in which they would like information to be provided. Authorities are entitled to refuse where reasonable, or where the information is already available to the public in another format.[21]

Unlike under FOIA, there is no specific reference in the EIRs to the provision of information in the form of a summary or digest.[22] Where a request for environmental information includes such a preference, a summary should generally be provided so long as reasonably practical, taking into account the cost.

---

[21] Note also that the Defra guidance makes it clear that the EIR provisions for requesting environmental information in a particular form or format are not intended to enable applicants to avoid payment for published information.

[22] Freedom of Information Act 2000, s.11(1).

The Defra guidance states that authorities should aim be to be flexible with respect to form and format, for example taking into account the fact that some applicants may not be able to read attachments in certain formats, and that some members of the public may prefer paper to electronic copies.

7 Extension of time

(1) **Where a request is made under regulation 5, the public authority may extend the period of 20 working days referred to in the provisions in paragraph (2) to 40 working days if it reasonably believes that the complexity and volume of the information requested means that it is impracticable either to comply with the request within the earlier period or to make a decision to refuse to do so.**   2–030

(2) **The provisions referred to in paragraph (1) are—**

(a) **regulation 5(2);**

(b) **regulation 6(2)(a); and**

(c) **regulation 14(2).**

(3) **Where paragraph (1) applies the public authority shall notify the applicant accordingly as soon as possible and no later than 20 working days after the date of receipt of the request.**

NOTES

Initial Commencement

Specified date

Specified date: 1 January 2005: see reg 1.

GENERAL NOTE

Where the complexity and volume of information requested may make it impracticable to respond within 20 working days (and note that both complexity *and* volume must make it impractical), then the period for responding may be extended to 40 working days (but note that authorities must still provide a substantive response as soon as possible). There is no right to extend the period for response beyond 40 working days. If an authority decides that an extension is needed, then the applicant should be informed as soon as possible and in any event within 20 working days, together with the reasons for it.   2–031

A typical circumstance where an extension of time may be appropriate is where a request necessitates an extensive search to gather the data and this makes a 20 working day turnaround impossible.

8 Charging

2–032

(1) Subject to paragraphs (2) to (8), where a public authority makes environmental information available in accordance with regulation 5(1) the authority may charge the applicant for making the information available.

(2) A public authority shall not make any charge for allowing an applicant—

(a) to access any public registers or lists of environmental information held by the public authority; or

(b) to examine the information requested at the place which the public authority makes available for that examination.

(3) A charge under paragraph (1) shall not exceed an amount which the public authority is satisfied is a reasonable amount.

(4) A public authority may require advance payment of a charge for making environmental information available and if it does it shall, no later than 20 working days after the date of receipt of the request for the information, notify the applicant of this requirement and of the amount of the advance payment.

(5) Where a public authority has notified an applicant under paragraph (4) that advance payment is required, the public authority is not required—

(a) to make available the information requested; or

(b) to comply with regulations 6 or 14,

unless the charge is paid no later than 60 working days after the date on which it gave the notification.

(6) The period beginning with the day on which the notification of a requirement for an advance payment is made and ending on the day on which that payment is received by the public authority is to be disregarded for the purposes of determining the period of 20 working days referred to in the provisions in paragraph (7), including any extension to those periods under regulation 7(1).

(7) The provisions referred to in paragraph (6) are—

(a) regulation 5(2);

(b) regulation 6(2)(a); and

(c) regulation 14(2).

(8) **A public authority shall publish and make available to applicants—**

(a) **a schedule of its charges; and**

(b) **information on the circumstances in which a charge may be made or waived.**

NOTES

Initial Commencement

Specified date

Specified date: 1 January 2005: see reg 1.

GENERAL NOTE[23]

Authorities may levy a charge for making information available, provided that the amount is reasonable. For this purpose authorities are required to make a schedule of charges available. This might include a price list of publications, or the charge per unit of work which will be incurred to meet the request.

2–033

Generally, charges must not exceed the actual cost of producing the information. Authorities cannot charge for legal advice sought on whether or not to disclose, nor for the cost of explaining grounds for the refusal of a request.

The Regulation 16 Code states that authorities should seek to minimize costs where possible, for example by using CD-Rom or electronic communications in preference to paper where the information requested is voluminous (although the preference of the applicant must still be taken into account). Where historical records exist then the cost of digitising material must also be taken into consideration when deciding what is the most effective approach.

One exception to the rule about costs not exceeding actual costs applies to authorities who are entitled to levy market-based charges (*e.g.* trading funds). The EIRs allow the levy of a market-based charge for information where the data is collected and published on a commercial basis in order to ensure its continued supply. A market-based charge may be levied in advance of the supply of the information where it is reasonable to impose this requirement. The schedule of charges must make clear the basis on which the charges are calculated.

---

[23] Note that from July 1, 2005 the Re-Use of Public Sector Information Regulations 2005 (SI 1515/2005) entitle authorities to charge for the re-use of documents in certain circumstances.

The European Court of Justice has imposed strict limits on public authorities seeking to recover the cost of their time in responding to requests.[24] It has ruled that authorities are not allowed to recover all of their costs of responding to a request, and states that costs which have the effect of preventing people from trying to access information are unlawful.

Charges are not permitted where the applicant is given access to a public register of information, or for examination of information on-site. In effect, therefore, charges are only permitted for copying and transmission.

Charges are also not permitted simply for advising on the availability of information (unless research into historical records is needed to provide that advice).

Part V of the Regulation 16 Code deals with charges.

Payment in advance

2–034 Whenever an authority makes the supply of information subject to an advance charge, it must notify the applicant how the charge will be applied and how advanced payment is justified in the context of the EIR regime. Since, in the majority of cases, charges cannot exceed the cost of actually producing the information, advance payment will only be legitimate in limited circumstances. Examples are where:

- it is the normal practice of the public authority's publisher; or

- the public authority may have to incur costs that would be excessive as compared to its own business needs.

When an advance payment is required, the applicant should be notified and the public authority should invite the applicant to say whether they wish to proceed with the request, or whether the request can be met in some other way (*e.g.* by a visit to the authority's offices to inspect the information, or by making use of more easily identifiable data).

Where a requirement for advance payment has been notified, the period between the notification and the receipt of payment will be disregarded when determining the response time for meeting requests.[25] The request will remain active for up to 60 working days from the date of notification and if no payment is received during that time, then the request lapses. When a fee payment is received the authority should release the information promptly and within the appropriate time limit.

Defra guidance

The Defra guidance points out that it is often not cost effective to charge for supplying information that can readily be made available (*e.g.* information

---

[24] *Commission v Germany* (Case C-217/97).
[25] Environmental Information Regulations 2004, Reg.8(5).

held in working files or databases). Moreover, where charges are small they may cost more to collect than the revenue they yield. Some public authorities may therefore adopt a policy of not charging for the supply of environmental information below a certain threshold. Other authorities may operate concessions for certain groups (*e.g.* pupils, students and charitable organisations). If this is the case, then guidance on the concessions available should be included in the Schedule of Charges.

Charging by authorities which are subject to FOIA as well as the EIRs

Public authorities which are subject to both FOIA and the EIRs will usually want to harmonise charges for the supply of information. Using the same charging approach for both FOIA and EIR requests up to the "appropriate limit" under FOIA should mean the public benefit from a unified, simple and transparent approach to charging.

2–035

FOIA gives authorities discretion whether to respond to requests the cost of which exceed thresholds of £600 (for central government) or £450 (for everyone else). No such discretion exists under the EIRs. Requests for environmental information which involve considerable staff time in identifying and gathering the information may entitle the authority to a time extension under Reg.7(1) but they still have to be answered, subject to the payment of reasonable charges.

If a request relates to information only part of which is environmental, and the calculation of the whole request results in a figure in excess of the appropriate FOIA threshold, then the authority should separate out the constituent parts of the request and recalculate to determine whether fees may still be charged under FOIA. Fees should then be determined according to each separate regime.

9 Advice and assistance

(1) **A public authority shall provide advice and assistance, so far as it would be reasonable to expect the authority to do so, to applicants and prospective applicants.**

2–036

(2) **Where a public authority decides that an applicant has formulated a request in too general a manner, it shall—**

    (a) **ask the applicant as soon as possible and in any event no later than 20 working days after the date of receipt of the request, to provide more particulars in relation to the request; and**

    (b) **assist the applicant in providing those particulars.**

(3) **Where a code of practice has been made under regulation 16, and to the extent that a public authority conforms to**

that code in relation to the provision of advice and assistance in a particular case, it shall be taken to have complied with paragraph (1) in relation to that case.

(4) Where paragraph (2) applies, in respect of the provisions in paragraph (5), the date on which the further particulars are received by the public authority shall be treated as the date after which the period of 20 working days referred to in those provisions shall be calculated.

(5) The provisions referred to in paragraph (4) are—

(a) regulation 5(2);

(b) regulation 6(2)(a); and

(c) regulation 14(2).

NOTES

Initial Commencement

Specified date

Specified date: 1 January 2005: see reg 1.

GENERAL NOTE

2–037 The general duty to provide advice and assistance is the same as under FOIA and readers should refer to the commentary on s.16 of FOIA in Ch.1.

The Regulation 16 Code (reproduced here in Appendix 5) sets out the practice required of public authorities when providing advice and assistance. The Code covers:

- Publishing information about the procedures a body has adopted for handling requests for information.

- Explaining to an applicant their rights under the EIRs.

- Transferring requests to other public authorities or bodies.

- Clarification of a request.

- What constitutes appropriate assistance.

- Relevant differences between EIR and FOIA.

Examples of what authorities might be expected to do in offering advice and assistance are:

- providing an outline of the different kinds of information that might meet the terms of the request;

- providing access to detailed catalogues and indexes, where these are available, to help the applicant ascertain the nature and extent of the information held by the authority;

- providing a general response to the request setting out options for further information that could be provided on request; and

- advising the person that another person or agency (such as a Citizens Advice Bureau) may be able to assist them with the application or make the application on their behalf.

10 Transfer of a request

(1) **Where a public authority that receives a request for environmental information does not hold the information requested but believes that another public authority or a Scottish public authority holds the information, the public authority shall either—**   2–038

    (a) **transfer the request to the other public authority or Scottish public authority; or**

    (b) **supply the applicant with the name and address of that authority,**

and inform the applicant accordingly with the refusal sent under regulation 14(1).

(2) **Where a request is transferred to a public authority, for the purposes of the provisions referred to in paragraph (3) the request is received by that public authority on the date on which it receives the transferred request.**

(3) **The provisions referred to in paragraph (2) are—**

    (a) **regulation 5(2);**

    (b) **regulation 6(2)(a); and**

    (c) **regulation 14(2).**

NOTES

Initial Commencement

Specified date

Specified date: 1 January 2005: see reg 1.

GENERAL NOTE

2–039 Regulation 10 only applies if the body receiving the request:

- does not hold the information; and

- does not use another person to hold the information on its behalf and would therefore have no other option but to provide advice and assistance and to refuse the request under Reg.12(4)(a).

In some circumstances, the applicant may not want their request transferred (they may, for example, prefer to make a new request). For this reason, the applicant should always be asked before any transfer is made.

Part VI of the Regulation 16 Code sets out best practice for ensuring that appropriate help and assistance is provided to the applicant when an authority proposes transferring a request. This includes:

- Providing a telephone number where appropriate so that the applicant can receive advice and assistance from the authority receiving the request.

- Ensuring that the practices followed by the authority when making transfers of requests are set out clearly in their Publication Scheme or on their web site.

- If information is freely available via a third party's public register, an authority may point to that register as part of providing advice and assistance, but this does not alter the authority's responsibility to respond to the request (although see the commentary in relation to Reg.12(4)(b)).

- When a request is transferred, the body transferring the request must complete its response to the original request by issuing a refusal notice within 20 days of receipt of the request. The refusal notice should contain:

  - An explanation of the fact that the information requested is not held by that body; and

  - Information about the reconsideration procedure and the applicant's right of appeal under Reg.11;

- When a request has been transferred from another body it becomes a new request. This means that a new start date is set for the request. This will be the date of receipt of the transferred request and the 20 working days allowed for handling that request will start then.

Transferred public records

Special provisions apply to historical records and other information that has **2–040** been transferred to the National Archives, the Public Records Office of Northern Ireland and to other record offices holding public records in England, Wales and Northern Ireland. These provide for consultation as necessary between the records office holding the records, the authority responsible for the information, and the Secretary of State responsible for public records. However, the requirements for handling environmental information requests, including those relating to timeliness, exceptions and appeals, are in all other respects the same as those for other environmental information.

11 Representations and reconsideration

(1) Subject to paragraph (2), an applicant may make **2–041** representations to a public authority in relation to the applicant's request for environmental information if it appears to the applicant that the authority has failed to comply with a requirement of these Regulations in relation to the request.

(2) Representations under paragraph (1) shall be made in writing to the public authority no later than 40 working days after the date on which the applicant believes that the public authority has failed to comply with the requirement.

(3) The public authority shall on receipt of the representations and free of charge—

(a) consider them and any supporting evidence produced by the applicant; and

(b) decide if it has complied with the requirement.

(4) A public authority shall notify the applicant of its decision under paragraph (3) as soon as possible and no later than 40 working days after the date of receipt of the representations.

(5) Where the public authority decides that it has failed to comply with these Regulations in relation to the request, the notification under paragraph (4) shall include a statement of—

(a) the failure to comply;

(b) the action the authority has decided to take to comply with the requirement; and

(c) the period within which that action is to be taken.

NOTES

Initial Commencement

Specified date

Specified date: 1 January 2005: see reg 1.

GENERAL NOTE

2–042 Regulation 11 entitles applicants to ask for an internal review of the handling of their request. The only procedural formality is to submit the request for internal review within 40 working days.

Internal review is available if a request is refused, but also for any of the following reasons:

- failure of the authority to respond "as soon as possible"[26];

- failure of the authority to respond within 20 working days[27];

- failure to respond at all[28];

- an unreasonable extension of the 20 day time limit[29];

- provision of information which is not "up to date, accurate and comparable"[30];

- the imposition of unreasonable or unlawful charges[31];

- failure of the authority to provide a schedule of charges[32];

- failure of the authority to provide adequate advice and assistance[33];

- failure to provide information in the form or format required[34];

- failure to provide reasons for refusing a request where reasons are required[35];

[26] Environmental Information Regulations 2004, Reg.5(2).
[27] *Ibid.*, Reg.5(2).
[28] *Ibid.*, Reg.5.
[29] *Ibid.*, Reg.7.
[30] *Ibid.*, Reg.5(4).
[31] Environmental Information Regulations 2004, Reg.8.
[32] *Ibid.*, Reg.8.
[33] *Ibid.*, Reg.9.
[34] *Ibid.*, Reg.6.
[35] *Ibid.*, Regs 6 and 14.

- failure to put a refusal in writing.[36]

Where an applicant is dissatisfied with the outcome of a Reg.11 complaint he or she may complain to the Information Commissioner under Reg.18, which effectively applies the FOIA enforcement and appeal procedures to EIR requests.[37]

Part XII of the Regulation 16 Code deals with review and complaints procedures. The Regulation 16 Code is reproduced in full at Appendix 5 to this book.

---

[36] *Ibid.*, Reg.14.
[37] Pt IV of FOIA deals with enforcement, Pt V with appeals.

Part III

Exceptions to the Duty to Disclose Environmental Information

12 Exceptions to the duty to disclose environmental information

2–043

(1) Subject to paragraphs (2), (3) and (9), a public authority may refuse to disclose environmental information requested if—

    (a) an exception to disclosure applies under paragraphs (4) or (5); and

    (b) in all the circumstances of the case, the public interest in maintaining the exception outweighs the public interest in disclosing the information.

(2) A public authority shall apply a presumption in favour of disclosure.

(3) To the extent that the information requested includes personal data of which the applicant is not the data subject, the personal data shall not be disclosed otherwise than in accordance with regulation 13.

(4) For the purposes of paragraph (1)(a), a public authority may refuse to disclose information to the extent that—

    (a) it does not hold that information when an applicant's request is received;

    (b) the request for information is manifestly unreasonable;

    (c) the request for information is formulated in too general a manner and the public authority has complied with regulation 9;

    (d) the request relates to material which is still in the course of completion, to unfinished documents or to incomplete data; or

    (e) the request involves the disclosure of internal communications.

(5) For the purposes of paragraph (1)(a), a public authority may refuse to disclose information to the extent that its disclosure would adversely affect—

    (a) international relations, defence, national security or public safety;

346

    (b) the course of justice, the ability of a person to receive a fair trial or the ability of a public authority to conduct an inquiry of a criminal or disciplinary nature;

    (c) intellectual property rights;

    (d) the confidentiality of the proceedings of that or any other public authority where such confidentiality is provided by law;

    (e) the confidentiality of commercial or industrial information where such confidentiality is provided by law to protect a legitimate economic interest;

    (f) the interests of the person who provided the information where that person—

        (i) was not under, and could not have been put under, any legal obligation to supply it to that or any other public authority;

        (ii) did not supply it in circumstances such that that or any other public authority is entitled apart from these Regulations to disclose it; and

        (iii) has not consented to its disclosure; or

    (g) the protection of the environment to which the information relates.

(6) For the purposes of paragraph (1), a public authority may respond to a request by neither confirming nor denying whether such information exists and is held by the public authority, whether or not it holds such information, if that confirmation or denial would involve the disclosure of information which would adversely affect any of the interests referred to in paragraph (5)(a) and would not be in the public interest under paragraph (1)(b).

(7) For the purposes of a response under paragraph (6), whether information exists and is held by the public authority is itself the disclosure of information.

(8) For the purposes of paragraph (4)(e), internal communications includes communications between government departments.

(9) To the extent that the environmental information to be disclosed relates to information on emissions, a public authority shall not be entitled to refuse to disclose that information under an exception referred to in paragraphs (5)(d) to (g).

(10) **For the purposes of paragraphs (5)(b), (d) and (f), references to a public authority shall include references to a Scottish public authority.**

(11) **Nothing in these Regulations shall authorise a refusal to make available any environmental information contained in or otherwise held with other information which is withheld by virtue of these Regulations unless it is not reasonably capable of being separated from the other information for the purpose of making available that information.**

NOTES

Initial Commencement

Specified date

Specified date: 1 January 2005: see reg 1.

GENERAL NOTE

2–044   The EIRs impose a duty to make information available on request, but with exceptions.

Every request for information under the EIRs must be processed on the basis of a presumption of disclosure.[38] Furthermore, the Directive expressly states that grounds for refusal must be interpreted restrictively.[39] Thirdly, *all* the exceptions under the EIRs are subject to the public interest.

An authority may only refuse a request under the EIRs if:

(a) when the request is received, the authority does not hold the information (but note Regulation 10 on transferring requests)[40];

(b) the request is manifestly unreasonable;

(c) the request is too general;

(d) it relates to material which is still work-in-progress;

(e) it would involve disclosing internal communications; or

(f) one of the exceptions under Regulation 12(5) applies (on which, see below).

---

[38] Environmental Information Regulations 2004, Reg.12(2).
[39] Directive 2003/4/EC, Art.4.
[40] For the purposes of the EIRs, an authority is treated as holding information even where the information is held by someone else on the authority's behalf.

The exceptions listed in (a)–(e) above stand alone. The exceptions listed in Regulation 12(5) are engaged only where disclosure would "adversely affect" the particular interest which each exception seeks to protect.

Meaning of "manifestly unreasonable"—Regulation 12(4)(b)

The Information Commissioner has stated that requests which would be 2–045 judged vexatious or repeated under s.14 of FOIA will fall within the exception to disclosure under Reg.12(4)(b).[41]

The word "manifestly" implies that no reasonable person would consider the request to be reasonable. In common with FOIA, however, the motive for a request is irrelevant.

The Defra guidance gives the following examples of requests which may be manifestly unreasonable:

- requests which place a substantial and unreasonable burden on a public authority or which require an unreasonable diversion of resources by the authority from its routine work providing public services;

- requests which require extensive scans of historical information;

- requests which require lengthy searching of large databases or files;

- requests which necessitate extensive redaction of information;

- requests for information which has been provided to an applicant already (there is no express equivalent in the EIRs to the FOIA exemption for "repeated" requests, but such requests may engage Reg.12(4)(b));

- the fact that information is publicly available from another source may be a relevant factor when considering whether to answer a request which would require a major exercise researching files and databases.

There are no cost limits in the EIRs but Reg.12(4)(b) could apply where a request would involve a manifestly unreasonable level of work and/or cost (subject to the authority providing advice and assistance with a view to the applicant narrowing their request to manageable parameters).

Meaning of "requests formulated in too general a manner"—Regulation 12(4)(c)

Authorities must exercise this exception with care, always bearing in mind 2–046 that they are obliged to provide advice and assistance under Regulation 9.

---

[41] Freedom of Information Act Awareness Guidance No.22: Vexatious and Repeated Requests.

Authorities cannot refuse requests simply because the applicant is unfamiliar with the relevant terminology or the way records are filed. For example, a request for "all the information you hold in relation to waste" may be too general if the authority in question is responsible both for public waste collection and disposal and also for its own internal operations within its own buildings and depots. The authority cannot simply refuse such a request, however. It must attempt to help the applicant refine his request so that it can be answered.

Meaning of "material which is still in the course of completion", "unfinished documents" and "incomplete data"—Regulation 12(4)(d)

2–047   Documents which are unfinished will be exempt only where they are genuinely "work-in-progress". In other words, it will need to be clear what work remains to be done, that the work is still planned, who will carry the work out and in what timescale. Authorities cannot avoid disclosure simply by labelling documents "draft". If for all practical purposes a document is finished, then it should be disclosed, whether or not it is actually complete. If necessary, the authority should provide an explanation stating that there may be additions at some point in the future.

As is the case under FOIA, there is a difference between "information" and "documents". Where environmental information can be extracted from an unfinished document and supplied in its own right, then this is the appropriate course, unless there are clear public interest reasons for not doing so.

Whether or not data is "incomplete" will depend on the circumstances. In *Maile v Wigan Metropolitan BC*[42] the court held that a database which comprised raw data concerning potentially contaminated sites did not have to be disclosed because evidence suggested the data was not complete and appeared to contain inaccuracies. Eady J commented that *"it would be highly unsatisfactory to reveal to the public material which had variously been described as inchoate, embryonic and hypothetical"*.

The Defra guidance gives several examples of circumstances which may or may not fall within Reg.12(4)(d):

- If a study depends on a scientifically selected sample of cases, then the data set will not be complete until the requisite level of responses has been achieved. The requisite level will normally have been specified as part of a study requirement, or it may be the level at which data collection is closed down for reasons of cost or practicality.

---

[42] [2001] Env LR 11.

- If a study depends on making a series of tests against a hypothesis, and the number of items tested cannot be specified in advance, then the data set will be complete once the results of the tests taken as whole are judged to have confirmed or rejected the hypothesis.

- In the case of a longitudinal survey, each stage of the survey should normally be treated as a separate survey and data released at the end of each stage. Data which is part of regular, routine monitoring should not be regarded as part of an unfinished set but should normally be released as soon as practicable after it is collected, or according to a planned and published timetable. For example, if readings are taken on an hourly or a daily basis, it might be reasonable to have a timetable to collate and release this information at least once a month. An authority might then respond to a request by treating the data as complete up to the time when it was last collated.

- Where public authorities are producing a study or report it may be reasonable that access to certain documents produced during the process (*e.g.* interim reports) should await completion of the whole process so that analysis and interpretation can proceed unhindered. However, if a study is abandoned, any interim reports should normally be released.

- A report cannot be refused on the ground that an authority plans to publish an edited version some time in the future.

- Time spent separating out the disclosable parts of a completed report does not mean the report itself is still in the course of completion. On the other hand, if in compiling the report, time is being taken to organise it so that the disclosable parts are separate from the non-disclosable parts, then the report will not be complete until it is in its final format.

Meaning of "internal communications"—Regulation 12(4)(e)

Regulation 12(4)(e) exists to protect authorities' internal deliberative 2–048 processes—that is to say, to give them "private thinking space". In this sense it has a similar application to the exemptions under FOIA for the formulation of government policy and the effective conduct of public affairs.[43] Accordingly, it will cover expressions of opinion and interpretation, particularly where these are not yet validated, as well as more factual information.

---

[43] Freedom of Information Act 2000, ss.35 and 36. The guidance in relation to these sections will be of relevance to any assessment of the application of Reg.12(4)(e).

The exception does not protect communications between a public authority and another person or body, because such communications are not "internal". However, Reg.12(8), which was added late in the legislative process, has the effect of bringing all communications between government departments within Reg.12(4)(e). This was controversial and the debate continues over whether it is compatible with the Directive.

There are many examples of the sorts of communications which might be protected by this exception, far too numerous to list exhaustively. However, the Defra guidance usefully sets out the following:

- correspondence between local authority council Members or board members of a government agency;

- information passed between officials in the course of their duties;

- internal minutes, briefs and submissions to Members;

- reports submitted by an Inspector to a Minister, or to a local authority committee, as part of the internal process for considering the report where it is necessary to maintain confidentiality pending a decision.

For government departments, the scope of the exception may extend to inter-agency correspondence or correspondence between one department and another where they are collectively formulating or developing policy. Defra guidance also suggests that the exception may function to protect information which is subject to collective ministerial responsibility.

The phrase "internal communications" is not qualified by any requirement that information should be confidential or commercially sensitive (and, where this is the case, other exceptions may apply anyway), nor does it require communications to take a particular form—the exception can apply to memoranda, notes of meetings, e-mails, Cabinet Committee papers, including correspondence between Ministers and between Ministers and officials, submissions to Ministers, correspondence between departments and public bodies in connection with policy development, minutes and proceedings of both ministerial and officials' committees and internal departmental correspondence. Drafts of such documents are also likely to be covered, as well as ancillary documents such as e-mails discussing points arising on drafts (although a document is not protected simply because it is labeled "draft").

The exception does not protect environmental information held within an internal communication if this can be extracted and released in its own right. Nor will it cover transactions of business that are merely administrative or routine.

Because the public interest must always be considered before applying any exception, in the case of Reg.12(4)(e) the fundamental issue will usually be why the public authority wishes to keep the information out of the public domain. Factors in favour of withholding might include:

- protecting the confidentiality of internal deliberations, papers and reports leading to a policy statement or decision;

- preventing or avoiding speculation, confusion or uncertainty which is not in the public interest,

- ensuring that the outcome of deliberations are not jeopardized by release.

There are no provisions in the EIRs requiring certification by a qualified person in order to use this exception. However, the Defra guidance recommends use of the FOIA s.36 procedure where possible in order to ensure consistent and sound decision-making.

Regulation 12(5)

The exceptions in Reg.12(5) can only apply where disclosure would   **2–049** "adversely affect" any of the interests listed. The test of adverse affect is similar to the prejudice test in FOIA and can be taken to operate as a test of harm.[44] The principal difference is that, under FOIA, prejudice resulting from disclosure need only be "likely" in order to engage the exemption. The EIR exceptions can only apply where disclosure "would" have an adverse affect, meaning that some certainty of harm must exist. Note also that the exceptions in Reg.12(5)(d)–(g) do not apply to information which relates to "emissions" and other information which is inseparable from such information.

It will be apparent that the EIR exceptions are broadly similar to the FOIA exemptions. One of the most notable differences, however, is that there is no exception under the EIRs for information which could be harmful to the economy, nor for information which is subject to legal professional privilege.[45]

Meaning of "international relations", "defence", "national security" and "public safety"—Regulation 12(5)(a)

These terms appear to have the same meanings under the EIRs as they do   **2–050** under FOIA. The guidance on FOIA ss.27, 26, 24 and 38 respectively is therefore of relevance.

The Defra guidance sets out the following explanations and examples in relation to these terms:

[44] Freedom of Information Act Awareness Guidance No.20: Prejudice & Adverse Affect.
[45] See FOIA ss.29 and 42 respectively.

- International relations may comprise confidential information obtained from (or which relates to) a foreign state, an international organisation or overseas territories where disclosure might compromise future co-operation with the UK in areas of our vital interests, or information which has the potential to undermine the relationship between UK and other countries (or international organisations).

- Defence information may include information which makes it possible to calculate military capacity (*e.g.* levels of discharges from a naval submarine) or that would undermine the ability of the armed forces to carry out their defence functions. It may also include information the disclosure of which would damage national security.

- National security information might have a defence context but it could also extend more widely. For example, information about the national utility infrastructure could require protection for reasons of national security. Public safety could also be a factor in withholding such information.

In all of these areas, the sensitivity of information will normally diminish over time. Since defence measures change, both in terms of technology and plans and strategy, passage of time will affect the relevance of the exception. For example, information about the environmental impact of defence equipment that is no longer in service will be intrinsically less sensitive than similar information about equipment that is still in use. In the *Ibstock* case, information relating to the dumping of munitions in mineshafts in 1947 was not considered to affect defence adversely in 1995.[46]

Regulation 15 provides for a Cabinet Minister, the Attorney-General or Advocate General (or a person designated by one of them) to certify that the exception under Reg.12(5)(a) applies. The application and effect of a Reg.12(5)(a) certificate is the same as for certificates issued under FOIA s.24 (although note that there is no blanket exemption under the EIRs for security bodies).

Regulation 12(5)(b)

2–051 Regulation 12(5)(b) can apply to any institution or public authority and to any level of institution, whether local, regional, national or international. It will cover actual or likely proceedings, and it may include information whose disclosure could prejudice the enforcement or proper administration of the law, whether the prevention, investigation or detection of crime, the apprehension or prosecution of offenders, or the proceedings of a coroner's court.

---

[46] *R. v British Coal Corporation ex p. Ibstock Building Products Ltd* [1995] JPL 836.

While each case will depend on its own facts, it is likely to be more difficult to justify withholding information once proceedings have concluded (although in circumstances where an appeal may be permitted long after the time of the original proceedings, it will be a matter of judgment when to treat papers relating to proceedings as no longer current).

When considering the application of Reg.12(5)(b), reference can usefully be made to FOIA s.30 (investigations and proceedings), s.31 (law enforcement) and s.32 (court records).

Regulation 12(5)(c)—intellectual property rights

Regulation 12(5)(b) covers any intellectual property rights, including   2–052
copyright material, a patented design or the constituents of a chemical which has yet to be marketed, or other trade secret. All may be protected by this exception where a potentially adverse effect can be reasonably anticipated and where the public interest in disclosure does not outweigh the adverse effects.

Reference to FOIA s.43 may be useful when considering Reg.12(5)(b).

Regulation 12(5)(d)—"confidentiality of the proceedings of . . . any public authority where such confidentiality is provided by law"

Regulation 12(5)(d) will only protect the proceedings of a public authority   2–053
where those proceedings are expressly designated as confidential by law. This means that the exception will normally be limited to an authority's formal board and council meetings. The application of the exception in any given case will depend on the legal framework within which a particular public authority operates, and on precisely which proceedings are designated confidential.[47]

Where the exception does apply, it applies to information relating to the confidential proceedings of *any* body, not just those of the authority receiving the request.

Regulation 12(5)(d) should normally be considered alongside Reg.12(4)(e). Note also the guidance in Ch.1 in relation to document designations.[48]

---

[47] Part VII of the Local Government Act 1972 (inserted by the Local Government (Access to Information) Act 1985) provides for public and press access to meetings and access to documents connected with those meetings. The Local Authorities (Executive Arrangements) (Access to Information) England Regulations provide for public and press access to meetings and papers where key executive and executive decisions are made. Not all information is accessible, however. There are exceptions for certain "confidential" and "exempt" information. Reg.5(6) of the EIRs disapplies the exemptions under the Local Government Act in relation to environmental information.

[48] See para.1–226.

Increasingly public authorities are choosing to release and disseminate summaries or full minutes of board meetings through their Publication Schemes. Wherever possible, any environmental information contained in these should also be released. Where publication is planned, it may be economic to ask applicants to wait until the information becomes available in the normal course of the publication timetable.

Regulation 12(5)(e)—"confidentiality of commercial or industrial information where . . . provided by law to protect a legitimate economic interest"

2–054   Regulation 12(5)(e) recognizes that the operation of the EIRs should take account of legitimate economic interests which are protected by confidentiality. Authorities may restrict access to information on this basis, but they must be careful not to restrict the release of information unreasonably. Case law under the 1992 Regulations suggested that authorities were tending to apply the equivalent exemption too broadly.

The confidentiality of commercial or industrial information must safeguard "a legitimate economic interest". Hence, economic interests in activities which are unlawful cannot be protected. A legitimate economic interest could cover information relating to entitlements to compensation, details of prices or payment, information that would give an insight into a company's general method of business, or its approach to certain types of contracts. In *Amway Corp. v Eurway International Ltd*[49] the court held (when looking at the equivalent provision in the 1992 Regulations) that legitimate economic interest implies that the exception may be invoked only if disclosure would significantly damage the interest in question and assist the relevant party's competitors. Similarly, in *R. v Secretary of State for the Environment, Transport etc and Midland Expressway Ltd ex p. Alliance Against the Birmingham Northern Relief Road*[50] the court held that the test was whether the person whose interests are protected would suffer a real commercial or competitive disadvantage if the information were released. The court also ruled that:

- Commercial and industrial confidentiality must refer to specific information that an enterprise needs to keep confidential in order to protect its competitive position.

- What is or is not confidential is an objective question.

- A number of provisions of the contract in question were clearly not commercially confidential, while certain specific provisions might be.

---

[49] BNRR Case No.CO/4553/98.
[50] [1999] Env LR 447.

- The confidentiality of a contract would depend on the time at which a request was made (at some times the contract might be confidential but at a later date it might not be).

Statutory provisions may sometimes help authorities to identify what might be protected under this exception, although Reg.5(6) requires that a decision to refuse a request must be on the basis of one of the EIR exceptions rather than any restriction contained elsewhere.

Confidentiality "provided by law" should be taken to mean confidentiality based on the common law rules of confidence rather than as may be imposed under a contract,[51] although commercially sensitive information can still include contract details where the contract relates to activities likely to affect the environment, such as the maintenance of buildings, parks and roads.[52]

Part VIII of the Regulation 16 Code covers public sector contracts in the context of the EIRs and Pt IX deals with accepting information in confidence from third parties. The content of these sections is very similar to the corresponding parts of the Section 45 Code issued under FOIA. Points to note:

- Sweeping confidentiality restrictions in contracts are considered incompatible with the spirit of the EIRs and authorities are directed not to sign up to them. Paragraph 49 of the Regulation 16 Code states that: *"Any acceptance of confidentiality provisions must be for good reasons and capable of being justified to the Commissioner."*

- When a supplier of information believes that its release would adversely affect his economic interests he should:

  – Identify the information to be protected;

  – Give cogent evidence of the need for the protection of such information on grounds of commercial or industrial confidentiality; and

  – Justify a period of time for which protection is sought.

- Bodies will need to exercise particular care when handling commercial information for businesses in which they have or had a controlling influence, or with which they are in partnership.

---

[51] See commentary on FOIA s.41, at para.1–223.
[52] Note that from December 1, 2005 all central government departments and their Executive Agencies in England are obliged to have an environmental purchasing policy, to integrate this with departmental procurement activities and to set up mechanisms for measuring and reporting on progress. This will require authorities to consider the environmental impacts and implications of all government contracts.

When considering Reg.12(5)(e), reference to s.41 (information provided in confidence) and s.43 (commercial interests) of FOIA may be helpful.[53]

Regulation 12(5)(f)—"interests of the person who provided the information"

2–055   The purpose of this exception is to preserve the free flow of volunteered information between citizens (including third parties and any other legal person) and regulators (for example for collecting statistical data and conducting sample surveys). The exception recognises that disclosure of such information via the EIR regime could inhibit open and constructive discussions between environmental control authorities and third parties.

The exception can also sometimes be relevant when members of the public and companies are applying for grants, permits and licenses. It will also protect whistle blowers.

The Defra guidance stresses that notwithstanding the existence of Reg.12(5)(f), suppliers of volunteered information should be encouraged to consent to release where appropriate. Such consent can be sought in advance (most obviously, when the information is collected) or it can be sought later, in response to a particular request or for the purpose of proactively disseminating the information. There may be circumstances where an authority wishes to provide reassurance that the information will not be made available to a third party once supplied. Such assurances should be avoided, on the basis that what might be in the public interest today may change tomorrow.

There is nothing to stop public authorities undertaking to consult with the volunteers of sensitive information in the event of receipt of a request for this information.

If the public authority could have required the information pursuant to a legal obligation had it not been provided voluntarily, then the information will not fall within this exception.

Where environmental information has been supplied to a public authority in pursuit or support of an application for a regulatory benefit, including any consent, licence or grant, then whether such a benefit would have been forthcoming if the information had not been supplied may be taken into account when considering the public interest.

If access rights to the information exist under another piece of legislation or there are other circumstances which entitle the public authority to disclose it, then the information will not fall within this exception.

---

[53] See para.1–221 onwards in relation to FOIA s.41 and para.1–240 onwards in relation to FOIA s.43.

In *Amway Corp. v Eurway International Ltd*[54] the court found that information contained in the main body of a concession agreement as a result of negotiations between the parties could not fairly be described as information "supplied" by one party to another.

It may be possible to distinguish environmental information from other information by putting data supplied by another party into annexes or schedules to an agreement rather than incorporating it into the main body. This will allow the documents to be handled separately in response to a request for information.

Regulation 12(5)(g)—"protection of the environment to which the information relates"

In some cases the availability of environmental information could lead to   **2–056**
harm or pollution of the environment. For example, information about the location of nesting sites, rare habitats, vulnerable archaeological sites or endangered/protected species may need to be withheld to avoid the risk of damage. Equally, information about possible sites of Special Scientific Interest should not normally be made available until a formal notice is served, especially if there is any risk that making information available prematurely could result in pre-emptive damage being caused to a site before it was protected.

Meaning of "emissions"—Regulation 12(9)

"Emissions" includes discharges and other releases into the environment   **2–057**
and should be taken to include the direct or indirect release of substances, gases, vibrations, light or noise from individual or diffuse sources into or onto air, water or land. It will include any trade effluent information or information on emissions from aerials that may be held by a public authority. It will also include any residues from veterinary medicines if these are released into the environment.

The public interest

As noted above, *all* the exceptions set out under Reg.12 are subject to the   **2–058**
public interest. The public interest operates for EIR purposes in exactly the same way as for FOIA.[55] In essence, public authorities must decide whether in any particular case it serves the interests of the public better to withhold or to disclose information. The presumption set out in Reg.12(2) in favour of disclosure means that where the arguments are equal on both sides, the information must be disclosed.

The Aarhus Convention sets out four fundamental principles underlying the public interest in access to environmental information. These should

---

[54] BNRR Case No.CO/4553/98.
[55] Readers are directed to Ch.3 for a detailed analysis of the public interest.

always be considered by authorities when assessing where the balance of the public interest lies:

- environmental decisions are best made with the full and effective participation of the public;

- access to environmental information is a prerequisite for citizens to be able to live in an environment adequate to their well being and health;

- individual citizens and non-governmental organisations have important roles in environmental protection;

- environmental education has a key role in environmental protection, and relies on access to environmental information.

Other public interest considerations might include:

- where resources have to be diverted in order to process a request and this might delay a pre-planned publication date, this will tip the balance in favour of refusing the request;

- if the public have information on potential contaminants they can influence decisions from a position of known facts rather than speculation;

- disclosure of information may contribute towards scientific advancements, and assist in access to justice and other fundamental rights;

- access to environmental information is particularly important as environmental issues affect the whole population;

- the length of time that has passed since a certain event may be relevant—and the balance of factors for and against disclosure may change over time;

- relevant questions to consider may include:

  - whether the information could reveal environmental impacts, or potential impacts, which could affect the public;

  - whether access to information is likely to support decision and policy-making (disclosure of certain information before or shortly after a policy decision is made may prejudice the formulation of policy, but this will not remain the case indefinitely).

Separation out or redaction of information—Regulation 12(11)

2–059 Wherever possible, information which is covered by an exception must be separated out or redacted, and the remaining part of any environmental information made available. This is the case even where it reduces the information being refused to a few paragraphs or sentences, or even to a letter heading and address which can be blacked out or removed.

Whether or not material is "incapable" of being separated is a simple practical test. The test does not turn on whether an authority has resources available to carry out the separation—authorities are now required to manage their records in a way which facilitates disclosure.

Refusing a request

See the commentary on Reg.14 in relation to the required process for refusing requests.   2–060

13 Personal data

(1) To the extent that the information requested includes personal data of which the applicant is not the data subject and as respects which either the first or second condition below is satisfied, a public authority shall not disclose the personal data.   2–061

(2) The first condition is—

(a) in a case where the information falls within any of paragraphs (a) to (d) of the definition of "data" in section 1(1) of the Data Protection Act 1998, that the disclosure of the information to a member of the public otherwise than under these Regulations would contravene—

(i) any of the data protection principles; or

(ii) section 10 of that Act (right to prevent processing likely to cause damage or distress) and in all the circumstances of the case, the public interest in not disclosing the information outweighs the public interest in disclosing it; and

(b) in any other case, that the disclosure of the information to a member of the public otherwise than under these Regulations would contravene any of the data protection principles if the exemptions in section 33A(1) of the Data Protection Act 1998 (which relate to manual data held by public authorities) were disregarded.

(3) The second condition is that by virtue of any provision of Part IV of the Data Protection Act 1998 the information is exempt from section 7(1) of that Act and, in all the circumstances of the case, the public interest in not

disclosing the information outweighs the public interest in disclosing it.

(4) In determining whether anything done before 24th October 2007 would contravene any of the data protection principles, the exemptions in Part III of Schedule 8 to the Data Protection Act 1998 shall be disregarded.

(5) For the purposes of this regulation a public authority may respond to a request by neither confirming nor denying whether such information exists and is held by the public authority, whether or not it holds such information, to the extent that—

(a) the giving to a member of the public of the confirmation or denial would contravene any of the data protection principles or section 10 of the Data Protection Act 1998 or would do so if the exemptions in section 33A(1) of that Act were disregarded; or

(b) by virtue of any provision of Part IV of the Data Protection Act 1998, the information is exempt from section 7(1)(a) of that Act.

NOTES

Initial Commencement

Specified date

Specified date: 1 January 2005: see reg 1.

GENERAL NOTE

2–062   An understanding of Regulation 13 is impossible without a basic understanding of the Data Protection Act 1998 (the "**DPA**"). A detailed explanation of the DPA is outside the scope of this book, but readers may refer to the commentary in Ch.1 on s.40 of FOIA for a brief summary.[56]

The Reg.13 exception operates broadly in the same way as the s.40 exemption under FOIA (and in common with the s.40 exemption, it is extremely convoluted). The treatment of EIR requests for information which is or contains personal data depends on whether that personal data relates to the person making the request, or to a third party.

Requests for information which is or contains personal data relating to the data subject himself

2–063   Insofar as the personal data relates to the applicant him or herself, then the position is simple: the request must be dealt with under the DPA subject

---

[56] At para.1–214 onwards.

access regime, contained in s.7 of the DPA. Requests of this type effectively fall outside the scope of the EIRs altogether. Note, however, that the EIR principles of separating out and redacting information will always apply, and so just because information contains personal data relating to the applicant does not automatically mean that it can be refused. Where the personal data can be removed and the remaining information disclosed, then this is the correct approach.

Requests for information which is or contains personal data relating to a third party

Requests for personal data which relate to third parties are more complicated. Such requests fall within the EIR regime and must be processed in accordance with Reg.13.

2–064

Regulation 13(1), (2) and (3)

FOIA extends the meaning of the term "personal data" (insofar as it applies to information held by public authorities) to include unstructured manual files. This category of data is known as "category (e)" data, because it appears in the DPA under a new s.1(1)(e). Previously, the DPA only applied to electronic records, and manual records held in filing systems which were structured in a way which enabled a user to find personal data held therein without having to flick through every page.

2–065

Section 70 of FOIA introduces a new s.33A into the DPA which exempts category (e) data from much of the DPA, but Reg.13(2)(b) effectively disapplies these exemptions for the purposes of requests under the EIRs.

The aggregate effect of all this is as follows:

(a) Personal data of which the applicant is not the data subject must *not* be disclosed if disclosure would breach any of the data protection principles. This is the case whether the personal data is electronic or manual, and whether or not it is in a structured file.

(b) Personal data other than category (e) data (that is to say, electronic data, and manual data held in structured files only) must *not* be disclosed if:

- the data subject has given notice under s.10 of the DPA that disclosure would cause unwarranted damage or distress, and there is no public interest override which applies under the EIRs; or

- the data subject himself would not be entitled to access that data under s.7 of the DPA, and there is no public interest override which applies under the EIRs.

Because these last two exceptions are subject to any countervailing public interest, authorities need to understand what interests may be served or harm avoided by nondisclosure, the interests served by disclosure, and why the applicant wants the personal data.

Regulation 13(4)

2–066 For the purposes of the EIRs, the transitional exemptions which apply under the DPA until October 24, 2007 must be ignored.

14 Refusal to disclose information

2–067

(1) **If a request for environmental information is refused by a public authority under regulations 12(1) or 13(1), the refusal shall be made in writing and comply with the following provisions of this regulation.**

(2) **The refusal shall be made as soon as possible and no later than 20 working days after the date of receipt of the request.**

(3) **The refusal shall specify the reasons not to disclose the information requested, including—**

(a) **any exception relied on under regulations 12(4), 12(5) or 13; and**

(b) **the matters the public authority considered in reaching its decision with respect to the public interest under regulation 12(1)(b) or, where these apply, regulations 13(2)(a)(ii) or 13(3).**

(4) **If the exception in regulation 12(4)(d) is specified in the refusal, the authority shall also specify, if known to the public authority, the name of any other public authority preparing the information and the estimated time in which the information will be finished or completed.**

(5) **The refusal shall inform the applicant—**

(a) **that he may make representations to the public authority under regulation 11; and**

(b) **of the enforcement and appeal provisions of the Act applied by regulation 18.**

NOTES

Initial Commencement

Specified date

Specified date: 1 January 2005: see reg 1.

GENERAL NOTE

Any refusal to disclose information must: 2–068

- be made in writing;

- be made within 20 working days (or 40 working days where an extension under Reg.7 applies) of receipt of the request;

- state the reasons for non-disclosure (with reference to particular exceptions and the matters underlying the assessment of the public interest); and

- give details of the mechanisms available for reconsideration of and appeal against the decision to refuse.

Where the information is work-in-progress, the authority must indicate (if known) the estimated time before completion.

Part X of the Regulation 16 Code deals with refusals of requests. See Appendix 5 for full text of the Code.

15 Ministerial certificates

(1) **A Minister of the Crown may certify that a refusal to**   2–069
disclose information under regulation 12(1) is because the
disclosure—

(a) **would adversely affect national security; and**

(b) **would not be in the public interest under regulation**
12(1)(b).

(2) **For the purposes of paragraph (1)—**

(a) **a Minister of the Crown may designate a person to**
certify the matters in that paragraph on his behalf;
and

(b) **a refusal to disclose information under regulation**
12(1) includes a response under regulation 12(6).

(3) **A certificate issued in accordance with paragraph (1)—**

(a) **shall be conclusive evidence of the matters in that**
paragraph; and

(b) **may identify the information to which it relates in**
general terms.

(4) **A document purporting to be a certificate under**
paragraph (1) shall be received in evidence and deemed to
be such a certificate unless the contrary is proved.

(5) A document which purports to be certified by or on behalf of a Minister of the Crown as a true copy of a certificate issued by that Minister under paragraph (1) shall in any legal proceedings be evidence (or, in Scotland, sufficient evidence) of that certificate.

(6) In paragraphs (1), (2) and (5), a "Minister of the Crown" has the same meaning as in section 25(3) of the Act.

NOTES

Initial Commencement

Specified date

Specified date: 1 January 2005: see reg 1.

Part IV

Code of Practice and Historical Records

16 Issue of a code of practice and functions of the Commissioner

(1) The Secretary of State may issue, and may from time to time revise, a code of practice providing guidance to public authorities as to the practice which it would, in the Secretary of State's opinion, be desirable for them to follow in connection with the discharge of their functions under these Regulations.

(2) The code may make different provision for different public authorities.

(3) Before issuing or revising any code under this regulation, the Secretary of State shall consult the Commissioner.

(4) The Secretary of State shall lay before each House of Parliament any code issued or revised under this regulation.

(5) The general functions of the Commissioner under section 47 of the Act and the power of the Commissioner to give a practice recommendation under section 48 of the Act shall apply for the purposes of these Regulations as they apply for the purposes of the Act but with the modifications specified in paragraph (6).

(6) For the purposes of the application of sections 47 and 48 of the Act to these Regulations, any reference to—

(a) a public authority is a reference to a public authority within the meaning of these Regulations;

(b) the requirements or operation of the Act, or functions under the Act, includes a reference to the requirements or operation of these Regulations, or functions under these Regulations; and

(c) a code of practice made under section 45 of the Act includes a reference to a code of practice made under this regulation.

2–070

NOTES

Initial Commencement

Specified date

Specified date: 1 January 2005: see reg 1.

367

GENERAL NOTE

2–071   Regulation 16 provides for the Secretary of State to issue a code of practice dealing with the matters described in Reg.16(1). The code, referred to throughout this book as the "**Regulation 16 Code**", was laid before Parliament on February 16, 2005. It is reproduced here in Appendix 5.

17 Historical and transferred public records

2–072

(1) **Where a request relates to information contained in a historical record other than one to which paragraph (2) applies and the public authority considers that it may be in the public interest to refuse to disclose that information under regulation 12(1)(b), the public authority shall consult—**

    (a) **the Lord Chancellor, if it is a public record within the meaning of the Public Records Act 1958; or**

    (b) **the appropriate Northern Ireland Minister, if it is a public record to which the Public Records Act (Northern Ireland) 1923 applies,**

before it decides whether the information may or may not be disclosed.

(2) **Where a request relates to information contained in a transferred public record, other than information which the responsible authority has designated as open information for the purposes of this regulation, the appropriate records authority shall consult the responsible authority on whether there may be an exception to disclosure of that information under regulation 12(5).**

(3) **If the appropriate records authority decides that such an exception applies—**

    (a) **subject to paragraph (4), a determination on whether it may be in the public interest to refuse to disclose that information under regulation 12(1)(b) shall be made by the responsible authority;**

    (b) **the responsible authority shall communicate its determination to the appropriate records authority within such time as is reasonable in all the circumstances; and**

    (c) **the appropriate records authority shall comply with regulation 5 in accordance with that determination.**

(4) **Where a responsible authority is required to make a determination under paragraph (3), it shall consult—**

(a) **the Lord Chancellor, if the transferred public record is a public record within the meaning of the Public Records Act 1958; or**

(b) **the appropriate Northern Ireland Minister, if the transferred public record is a public record to which the Public Records Act (Northern Ireland) 1923 applies,**

before it determines whether the information may or may not be disclosed.

(5) **A responsible authority which is not a public authority under these Regulations shall be treated as a public authority for the purposes of—**

(a) **the obligations of a responsible authority under paragraphs (3)(a) and (b) and (4); and**

(b) **the imposition of any requirement to furnish information relating to compliance with regulation 5.**

NOTES

Initial Commencement

Specified date

Specified date: 1 January 2005: see reg 1.

GENERAL NOTE

The EIR rules relating to historical records and transferred public records   2–073
are very similar to the rules under FOIA.

Regulation 17(1)

Regulation 17(1) deals with public records that are historical records and   2–074
which, instead of being transferred to the Public Records Office, have been
retained by the originating department. If the department has decided that
an exception applies, and believes that the public interest lies in not
disclosing the information, then before reaching a final decision it must
consult the Lord Chancellor or the appropriate Northern Ireland Minister.
The decision, however, remains at the discretion of the originating
department.

These provisions mirror those is s.65 of FOIA. Readers should refer to the
commentary on s.65 in Ch.1 (at para.1–316).

Regulations 17(2), (3), (4) and (5)

Regulations 17(2) and (3) deal with "transferred" public records, *i.e.*   2–075
records transferred to the Public Records Office, and apply to information

of any age. They divide the disclosure decision into two stages: first, the decision on the application of the exception is made by the "appropriate records authority" (see s.15 of FOIA), but the appropriate records authority must then consult the department (the "responsible authority") in relation to the public interest. Before reaching a final decision to refuse to disclose the information in the public interest, the responsible authority must consult the Lord Chancellor or the appropriate Northern Ireland Minister. The responsible authority must notify the appropriate records authority of its decision on the public interest as soon as possible so that the records authority can inform the applicant.

Regulation 17(5) applies this process to records for which the responsible authority is not a public authority.

These provisions mirror those in s.66 of FOIA. Readers should refer to the commentary on s.66 in Ch.1 (at para.1–317).

Part V

Enforcement and Appeals, Offences, Amendment and Revocation

18 Enforcement and appeal provisions

(1) The enforcement and appeals provisions of the Act shall apply for the purposes of these Regulations as they apply for the purposes of the Act but with the modifications specified in this regulation.

2–076

(2) In this regulation, "the enforcement and appeals provisions of the Act" means—

    (a) Part IV of the Act (enforcement), including Schedule 3 (powers of entry and inspection) which has effect by virtue of section 55 of the Act; and

    (b) Part V of the Act (appeals).

(3) Part IV of the Act shall not apply in any case where a certificate has been issued in accordance with regulation 15(1).

(4) For the purposes of the application of the enforcement and appeals provisions of the Act—

    (a) for any reference to—

        (i) "this Act" there shall be substituted a reference to "these Regulations"; and

        (ii) "Part I" there shall be substituted a reference to "Parts 2 and 3 of these Regulations";

    (b) any reference to a public authority is a reference to a public authority within the meaning of these Regulations;

    (c) for any reference to the code of practice under section 45 of the Act (issue of a code of practice by the Secretary of State) there shall be substituted a reference to any code of practice issued under regulation 16(1);

    (d) in section 50(4) of the Act (contents of decision notice)—

        (i) in paragraph (a) for the reference to "section 1(1)" there shall be substituted a reference to "regulation 5(1)"; and

        (ii) in paragraph (b) for the references to "sections 11 and 17" there shall be substituted references to "regulations 6, 11 or 14";

(e) in section 56(1) of the Act (no action against public authority) for the words "This Act does not confer" there shall be substituted the words "These Regulations do not confer";

(f) in section 57(3)(a) of the Act (appeal against notices served under Part IV) for the reference to "section 66" of the Act (decisions relating to certain transferred public records) there shall be substituted a reference to "regulations 17(2) to (5)";

(g) in paragraph 1 of Schedule 3 to the Act (issue of warrants) for the reference to "section 77" (offence of altering etc records with intent to prevent disclosure) there shall be substituted a reference to "regulation 19"; and

(h) in paragraph 8 of Schedule 3 to the Act (matters exempt from inspection and seizure) for the reference to "information which is exempt information by virtue of section 23(1) or 24(1)" (bodies and information relating to national security) there shall be substituted a reference to "information whose disclosure would adversely affect national security".

(5) In section 50(4)(a) of the Act (contents of decision notice) the reference to confirmation or denial applies to a response given by a public authority under regulation 12(6) or regulation 13(5).

(6) Section 53 of the Act (exception from duty to comply with decision notice or enforcement notice) applies to a decision notice or enforcement notice served under Part IV of the Act as applied to these Regulations on any of the public authorities referred to in section 53(1)(a); and in section 53(7) for the reference to "exempt information" there shall be substituted a reference to "information which may be refused under these Regulations".

(7) Section 60 of the Act (appeals against national security certificate) shall apply with the following modifications—

(a) for the reference to a certificate under section 24(3) of the Act (national security) there shall be substituted a reference to a certificate issued in accordance with regulation 15(1);

(b) subsection (2) shall be omitted; and

(c) in subsection (3), for the words, "the Minister did not have reasonable grounds for issuing the certificate" there shall be substituted the words "the Minister or

person designated by him did not have reasonable grounds for issuing the certificate under regulation 15(1)".

(8) **A person found guilty of an offence under paragraph 12 of Schedule 3 to the Act (offences relating to obstruction of the execution of a warrant) is liable on summary conviction to a fine not exceeding level 5 on the standard scale.**

(9) **A government department is not liable to prosecution in relation to an offence under paragraph 12 of Schedule 3 to the Act but that offence shall apply to a person in the public service of the Crown and to a person acting on behalf of either House of Parliament or on behalf of the Northern Ireland Assembly as it applies to any other person.**

(10) **Section 76(1) of the Act (disclosure of information between Commissioner and ombudsmen) shall apply to any information obtained by, or furnished to, the Commissioner under or for the purposes of these Regulations.**

NOTES

Initial Commencement

Specified date

Specified date: 1 January 2005: see reg 1.

GENERAL NOTE

Regulation 18 effectively applies the FOIA enforcement and appeal 2–077 procedures to EIR requests.[57] As is the case under the FOIA, the Information Commissioner will not investigate a complaint:

- unless the complainant has already completed the authority's own internal review procedure;

- if there has been "undue delay" in making the complaint; or

- if the application is frivolous or vexatious.

Part XII of the Regulation 16 Code deals with review and complaints procedures under the EIRs.

---

[57] Pt IV of FOIA deals with enforcement, Pt V with appeals.

19 Offence of altering records with intent to prevent disclosure

2–078

(1) Where—

    (a) a request for environmental information has been made to a public authority under regulation 5; and

    (b) the applicant would have been entitled (subject to payment of any charge) to that information in accordance with that regulation,

any person to whom this paragraph applies is guilty of an offence if he alters, defaces, blocks, erases, destroys or conceals any record held by the public authority, with the intention of preventing the disclosure by that authority of all, or any part, of the information to which the applicant would have been entitled.

(2) Subject to paragraph (5), paragraph (1) applies to the public authority and to any person who is employed by, is an officer of, or is subject to the direction of, the public authority.

(3) A person guilty of an offence under this regulation is liable on summary conviction to a fine not exceeding level 5 on the standard scale.

(4) No proceedings for an offence under this regulation shall be instituted—

    (a) in England and Wales, except by the Commissioner or by or with the consent of the Director of Public Prosecutions; or

    (b) in Northern Ireland, except by the Commissioner or by or with the consent of the Director of Public Prosecutions for Northern Ireland.

(5) A government department is not liable to prosecution in relation to an offence under paragraph (1) but that offence shall apply to a person in the public service of the Crown and to a person acting on behalf of either House of Parliament or on behalf of the Northern Ireland Assembly as it applies to any other person.

NOTES

Initial Commencement

Specified date

Specified date: 1 January 2005: see reg 1.

GENERAL NOTE

Regulation 19 makes it a criminal offence to alter, deface, block, erase, destroy or conceal any record with the intention of preventing FOIA disclosure. The wording of Reg.19 mirrors that in s.77 of FOIA, but note Reg.19(5) which states that a government department cannot be prosecuted in its capacity as a public authority under the EIRs, but a Crown servant can be. Similarly, Parliament and the Northern Ireland Assembly cannot be prosecuted. 2–079

20 Amendment

    (1) Section 39 of the Act is amended as follows. 2–080

    (2) In subsection (1)(a), for "regulations under section 74" there is substituted "environmental information regulations".

    (3) After subsection (1) there is inserted—

    "(1A) In subsection (1) "environmental information regulations" means—

        (a) regulations made under section 74, or

        (b) regulations made under section 2(2) of the European Communities Act 1972 for the purpose of implementing any Community obligation relating to public access to, and the dissemination of, information on the environment.".

NOTES

Initial Commencement

Specified date

Specified date: 1 January 2005: see reg 1.

21 Revocation

The following are revoked— 2–081

    (a) The Environmental Information Regulations 1992 and the Environmental Information (Amendment) Regulations 1998 except insofar as these apply to Scottish public authorities; and

    (b) The Environmental Information Regulations (Northern Ireland) 1993 and the Environmental Information (Amendment) Regulations (Northern Ireland) 1998.

NOTES

Initial Commencement

Specified date

Specified date: 1 January 2005: see reg 1.

II

CHAPTER 3

THE PUBLIC INTEREST TEST

Introduction

The public interest is not defined in FOIA. Nor is there anything which **3–001** usefully serves as a definition among the few specific areas of English law to which public interest considerations have applied since before January 1, 2005.[1] We should not assume, however, that this makes the law unclear. Nor is it the case that the absence of a definition makes assessing the public interest inherently difficult. The lack of a definition simply reflects the principle that the public interest in any given case will depend on the circumstances prevailing at the time. As the Department for Constitutional Affairs Guidance states, the public interest is *"an inherently dynamic concept"* which will *"develop by decisions made within government and by the Information Commissioner and the Courts"*.[2] To define it would be to limit it, which would not be in keeping with the spirit of the law.

We should also remember that even though no formal definition of the public interest exists, the canvass is not entirely blank. We have guidance from the Information Commissioner and from the Department for Constitutional Affairs. There is also much useful material from overseas, in the form of judicial and regulatory decisions on freedom of information in countries which have long established regimes of their own.

By drawing on these various sources, this chapter explains what we should understand the public interest to be, and explains how we can approach the task of assessing and balancing the public interest in practice.

---

[1] *Cf.* the public interest defence in claims for breach of confidence (see *Coco v AN Clarke (Engineers) Ltd* [1969] RPC 41; *Lion Laboratories v Evans* [1985] QB 526; *X v Y* [1988] 2 All ER 417; *Attorney-General v Guardian Newspapers (No.2)* [1990] 1 AC 109; *Campbell v MGN Ltd* [2004] 2 WLR 1232, HL; *A v B and C* [2002] EMLR 21); the public interest defence in claims of copyright infringement (see *Hyde Park Residence v Yelland* [2001] Ch 257; *Ashdown v Telegraph Group Ltd* [2002] QB 546); and the Public Interest Disclosure Act 1998 (see *Bladon v ALM Medical Services*, April 25, 2000 and *Fernandes v Netcom Consultants UK*, May 18, 2000 [2000] IRLB, No.648, p.2).

[2] See *www.foi.gov.uk/guidance/exintro/chap07.htm*.

The Concept of the Public Interest

3–002 Probably the best judicial summary of the public interest comes from an Australian case, *Commonwealth of Australia v John Fairfax Ltd*,[3] in which the court said:

> "*It is unacceptable in our democratic society that there should be a restraint on the publication of information relating to government when the only vice of that information is that it enables the public to discuss, review and criticise government action. Accordingly, the court will determine the Government's claim to confidentiality by reference to the public interest. Unless disclosure is likely to injure the public interest, it will not be protected. The court will not prevent the publication of information which merely throws light on the past workings of the government, even if it be not public property, so long as it does not prejudice the community in other respects. Then disclosure will itself serve the public interest in keeping the community informed and in promoting discussion of public affairs. If, however, it appears that disclosure will be inimical to the public interest because national security, relations with foreign countries or the ordinary business of government will be prejudiced, disclosure will be restrained.*"

When thinking about what we mean by the public interest, this is as good a place to start as any.

It is instructive to bear in mind that under the Freedom of Information Bill, public authorities were to be given discretion to consider whether information should be disclosed on public interest grounds. This changed at the report stage, when consideration of the public interest was made a duty. Parliament recognised that for freedom of information to work in the UK, there would have to be a fundamental shift from the historic Westminster culture of need-to-know to a new "open" era of right-to-know. As a result, "*information must be disclosed except where there is an overriding public interest in keeping specific information confidential*".[4]

The public interest in practice

3–003 The text of FOIA itself gives us nothing in the way of guidance on what the public interest means in practice. For that, we have to look overseas. A review of overseas jurisprudence indicates that in a freedom of information context the public interest generally means:

- promoting public debate of issues of the day;

- ensuring the public is not deceived about the way public authorities, or bodies which they regulate, operate;

---

[3] (1981) 32 A.L.R. 485, endorsed by the House of Lords in the Spycatcher case: *A-G v Guardian Newspapers (No.2)* [1990] AC 109.

[4] *Hansard*, HL (series 5) vol.619, col.143 (November 14, 2000), Lord Falconer.

- ensuring accountability in decision-making in public office;

- exposing misconduct;

- contributing to the maintenance of peace and order;

- keeping the public adequately informed of any danger to public health or safety or to the environment.

All of these principals support the case for disclosure of information. The main factors against disclosure are those set out in the FOIA exemptions—most obviously national security, defence, international relations, law enforcement, health and safety, and commercial interests. These represent specific interests which require special dispensation. Effectively, each of the qualified exemptions represents a hypothetical public interest in restricting access to information of a certain type, or in a certain context, but the hypothetical will only be permitted to prevail in practice where, in a particular case, the circumstances allow. So, the public interest 'test' is simply a matter of weighing competing interests in the context of the circumstances prevailing at a given time.

The Balancing Exercise

The public interest test described in s.2 of FOIA stipulates that a qualified   **3–004** exemption can only apply where the public interest in maintaining an exemption outweighs the public interest in disclosing information. This means that public authorities have a duty to consider the public interest for and against disclosure, always bearing in mind that there is a general presumption in favour of disclosure unless and until this is outweighed by factors to the contrary. It also means that if the arguments are evenly balanced, then the outcome must be disclosure.

This presumption in favour of disclosure means that a burden of proof rests with public authorities to show two things: first, that there is a pressing need for non-disclosure, and secondly, that to override the right of access is a necessary and proportionate way of meeting that need.

As such, whenever an authority makes an assessment of the public interest it should clearly document:

- all the circumstances that have been considered;

- the public interests in favour of withholding information and the weight given to each;

- the public interests in favour of disclosure of information and the weight given to each;

- the considerations given to timescales; and

- the considerations given to partial disclosure.

Aside from helping authorities to make assessments in the future, this will also provide a defence to any complaint or appeal.

Practical Guidance from the Information Commissioner

3–005 The Information Commissioner has put forward some examples of factors which might apply in favour of disclosure when considering the public interest, and factors which are irrelevant.

Factors in favour of disclosure:

1. Furthering the understanding of issues of the day, and facilitating participation in public debate of those issues.

2. Promoting accountability for and transparency of decisions taken by public authorities (because it will improve the quality of decisions and administration if authorities and officials have to provide reasoned explanations for their actions).

3. Promoting accountability for and transparency of public expenditure (for example, where public services are outsourced to the private sector there is a public interest in genuine competition and value for money; disclosure of information about gifts and expenses will also reassure the public of the probity of elected officials.)

4. Enabling individuals and companies to understand decisions made by public authorities which affect them, and where appropriate help them to challenge those decisions.

5. Bringing to light information affecting public health and safety (the prompt disclosure of information by scientific and other experts may prevent accidents or outbreaks of disease and may also increase public confidence in official scientific advice).[5]

Factors which are irrelevant:

1. A risk of information being misunderstood, either because it is technical or incomplete.

2. A risk of embarrassment or loss of confidence.

3. The "class" or "type" of information is not of itself an argument against disclosure (although "high level correspondence" may be more likely to have characteristics which make its disclosure contrary to the public interest).

4. Public curiosity—"the public interest" is not the same as "something which may be of interest to the public".

Other Sources of Guidance

The Code of Practice on Access to Government Information

3–006 Although the Code of Practice on Access to Government Information has now been replaced by FOIA it still offers useful authority on the UK

---

[5] It is instructive to recall that the Philips Inquiry in 2000 concluded that a Whitehall culture

interpretation of the public interest in relation to the disclosure of information. In common with the FOIA regime, there was a presumption under the Code in favour of disclosure unless the harm likely to arise outweighed the public interest in making information available.

The Parliamentary Ombudsman's decisions on the public interest as it applied to applications under the Code provide an indication of the sorts of issues which a decision-maker might have to consider when applying the public interest under FOIA. Some cases are considered below in relation to the principal categories of public interest already discussed.

Lessons from other Countries

Many other countries have well established freedom of information regimes 3–007 which can offer useful pointers to decision-makers in the UK. Indeed, the Information Commissioner has said that he will look at decisions from other countries where these are instructive. Of particular relevance are the regimes in Australia,[6] Canada,[7] New Zealand[8] and Ireland,[9] all of which have close similarities to the UK system.

of secrecy, interdepartmental conflict and complacency had contributed to the public health crisis which followed the discovery that BSE had jumped from cows to humans in the form of vCJD.

[6] The Australian Federal Freedom of Information Act 1982 requires decision-makers to consider public interest factors for and against disclosure. This operates in three different ways: (i) requiring the decision-maker to weigh factors for and against disclosure and decide where the balance lies; (ii) a presumption that disclosure of information would be contrary to the public interest if it would have an adverse effect on the management of the economy or disturb the ordinary course of business (the decision-maker has to consider whether this adverse effect exists); and (iii) deliberative internal documents must only be withheld where disclosure would be contrary to the public interest. See *McKinnon v Secretary, Department of Treasury* [2005] FCAFC 142 (August 2, 2005) for a detailed discussion of the public interest.

[7] Access to information in Canada is regulated at both federal and provincial levels. The Access to Information Act 1983 applies at federal level to all government departments and most agencies, including the police and Security Intelligence Service. Canadian legislation does not contain a general public interest override but the discretionary exemptions all imply a balancing of public interest considerations.

[8] In New Zealand the Official Information Act 1982 applies to central government agencies, the police, the Security Intelligence Service, and most public corporations. Unlike FOIA, the Official Information Act has a purpose clause, which sates that the purpose of the Act is "*To increase progressively the availability of official information to the people of New Zealand in order to enable their more effective participation in the making and administration of laws and policies, to promote the accountability of Ministers of the Crown and Officials and thereby to enhance respect for the law and promote the good government of New Zealand, to provide for proper access by each person to official information in relation to that person, to protect official information to the extent consistent with the public interest, and the preservation of personal privacy*". Cases where the public interest test has been an issue have tended to relate to access to personal information. In the majority of cases, it was held that the public interest in the accountability of public bodies overrode privacy interests, although when a journalist asked the Department of Corrections for details of a course on which a prisoner had enrolled, the Ombudsman held that the prisoner had a right to privacy and that there were no public interest considerations which outweighed this.

[9] In Ireland the Freedom of Information Act 1997 creates a broad presumption that the public can access all information held by government bodies. There are a number of exemptions and exclusions with different harm and public-interest tests. Records can be withheld if they relate to: (i) the deliberative process, unless the public interest is better

It is important to remember that the operation of the public interest in these jurisdictions is not identical to the system under FIOA.[10] Even where a public interest test is used, the terminology and emphasis is usually slightly different. Nevertheless, there have been a number of cases in the Australian, Canadian, New Zealand and Irish courts which do illuminate public interest test considerations and these are considered below in relation to the principal categories of public interest.

Assessing and balancing the public interest in practice

3–008 Looking at the evidence from decisions of the Parliamentary Ombudsman under the Code of Practice on Access to Government Information, and the experience of public authorities in overseas countries, there are something like nine principal circumstances which recur where the public interest plays a major role. Each of these is considered below, together with reference to Ombudsman decisions and overseas jurisprudence where these shed light on the principles at issue:

1. Enhancing the scrutiny of decision making to improve accountability and participation.

2. The administration of justice and the enforcement of the law.

3. The expenditure of public funds.

4. Keeping the public adequately informed of any danger to public health or safety.

5. Safeguarding national security or international relations.

served by releasing the document; (ii) cases where the release of information would prejudice the effectiveness of investigations or audits or the performance of government functions and negotiations unless the public interest is better served by releasing documents; or (iii) cases where disclosure would prejudice law enforcement, security, defence or international affairs. There is a public interest test for records obtained in confidence or those containing personal or commercially sensitive information. But the public interest argument cannot be made for records related to defence or international relations. The argument can be made in a limited way for law-enforcement records.

[10] In some statutes the public interest test applies to specific exemptions (*e.g.* New Zealand), whereas in others, it applies to all exemptions (*e.g.* British Columbia). Some Jurisdictions have defined what is meant by the public interest: "*as it relates to the public health, public safety or protection of the environment*" (Canada, Access to Information Act, R.s. 1985, c.A-1, as amended); "*an immediate hazard to the health or safety of persons or a serious or irreparable impediment to their right to a healthy environment*" (Quebec, Access to Documents held by Public Bodies and the Protection of Personal Information, R.S.Q. 1982, c, A-2.1, as amended); "a risk of significant harm to the environment or to the health or to the health or safety of the public or a group of people" (British Columbia—Freedom of Information and Protection of Privacy Act, RSBC 1996, c165, as amended). As these examples illustrate, there are differences between jurisdictions in both the terminology and the application of the public interest test. One reason for this is that the test is very often context specific. Therefore, what may be of concern for one country will not necessarily assimilate to another. In the US, for example, a new exemption to the freedom of information regime was created after 9/11 for "Critical infrastructure information".

6. Disclosure that contributes to a debate on a matter of public interest.

7. Disclosure that would prejudice the protection of an individual's right to privacy.

8. Non-disclosure necessary to avoid serious damage to the proper working of government.

9. Disclosures affecting the commercial interests of a third party.

Ombudsman decisions and overseas jurisprudence

1. Enhancing the scrutiny of decision making processes to improve accountability and participation

This goes to the heart of freedom of information legislation and the 3–009 principle that the public should have the opportunity to call public authorities to account.

In the Canadian case of *Dagg v Canada (Minister of Finance)*[11] the court stated that "*the overarching purpose of access to information legislation . . . is to facilitate democracy. It helps to ensure first, that citizens have the information required to participate meaningfully in the democratic process, and secondly, that politicians and bureaucrats remain accountable to the citizenry*".

On this basis, the Parliamentary Ombudsman decided that the public interest in knowing how legal aid money is spent is akin to ensuring government accountability.[12]

The Australian case of *Re Pearce and QRAA*[13] allowed for the disclosure of information about the administration of government grant schemes on the basis that disclosure would improve accountability.

2. The administration of justice and the enforcement of the law.

The public interest must be paramount where there are reasonable grounds 3–010 for believing that a failure to make information available would be likely to prejudice the prevention or detection of crime. That said, it is not enough merely to believe that an individual to whom the information applies has acted fraudulently—there must be a *substantial* chance that the harm would occur if the information was not disclosed.

In a Parliamentary Ombudsman decision, a request for information from the Benefits Agency found that the details of an investigation did not

[11] [1997] 2 S.C.R.
[12] Case No.A.5/97—The Marchioness disaster.
[13] Case No.99008.

contain reasonable evidence to suggest that the requester had committed a benefit fraud. The Benefits Agency Officers had exceeded their remit and went beyond acceptable behaviour, and demonstrated a lack of understanding of the legislation covering their investigations.[14]

An Australian case also highlights the public interest in disclosing information which provides justice to an individual. In *Re Villanueva and Queensland Nursing Council*[15] information that would assist a complainant to understand the steps taken by an agency in dealing with his complaint warranted disclosure in the public interest.

3. The Expenditure of Public Funds

3–011   On examination of the case examples of other jurisdictions, ensuring that the public obtain value for money is an evident public interest consideration.

The Irish Information Commissioner has stated that *"such openness is a significant aid to ensuring effective oversight of public expenditure, to ensure the public obtains value for money, to preventing fraud and corruption and to preventing the waste or misuse of public funds"*.[16]

A request to the Cardiff Bay Development Corporation for the cost estimates for a proposed wetland habitat was allowed by the Parliamentary Ombudsman on the grounds that it was in the public interest to have up-to-date information concerning cost estimates, and that this outweighed any likely prejudice to the Corporation's competitive position.[17]

In Ireland, in a case relating to a request for access to travel, office administration and telephone expenses paid to members of the Houses of Oireachtas, the Commissioner had to balance the right to privacy of those members with the public interest in ensuring accountability for the use of public funds. The public interest in accountability prevailed.[18]

4. Keeping the public adequately informed of any danger to public health or safety

3–012   A review of Canadian cases indicates that consideration of the public interest will very much depend on the circumstances in a particular case. This is illustrated by two relatively similar cases. In one case, where a journalist requested records from Transport Canada in order to investigate violations of the Aeronautics Act and Regulations by commercial pilots, the

---

[14] Case No.1513/00—Benefits Agency: Mishandling of a fraud investigation.
[15] Case No.02/2000.
[16] Case 98049, 98056, 98057—Henry Ford & Sons Ltd, Nissan Ireland and Motor Distributors Ltd and The Office of Public Works.
[17] Case No.A.1/97.
[18] Case No.99168—Mr Richard Oakley, *The Sunday Tribune* Newspaper and the Department of Enterprise, Trade and Employment.

Commissioner was not convinced that the public interest in disclosure would be outweighed by the invasion of privacy that would result. He accepted that there was no need to intrude into the privacy of the pilots, as public safety was adequately served by Transport Canada's regulatory role.[19] On the other hand, when a journalist requested information from the Transportation Safety Board concerning air traffic control tapes relating to a plane crash, the Commissioner decided that the public interest in air safety outweighed any privacy considerations.[20]

5. Safeguarding national security or international relations

Examples of potential harm to international relations include the risk that   **3–013**
disclosure would effect negotiations, undermine frankness in diplomatic communications or result in the impairment of confidential communications between governments.

Where information relates to ongoing activities, some of that information may remain sensitive for many months or even years after a decision is made (see, for example, the Ministry of Defence and the Foreign and Commonwealth Office refusal to release a National Audit Office report and other information related to the Al Yamamah project).[21] It is also important to note that sensitivity of such information generally reduces over time.[22]

Under the Code of Access to Government Information, the Ministry of Defence were asked for four internal reports relating to departmental performance. The Parliamentary Ombudsman held that the public interest did not outweigh the possible harm which might be caused by release of information relating to nuclear capability and security and intelligence matters.[23]

6. Disclosure that contributes to a debate on a matter of public interest

Where the information requested relates to a high profile issue that has   **3–014**
featured heavily in the media and involves accountability for public funds, there will be a strong public interest in releasing the information.

During the Ilisu Dam project in Turkey, the Chair of the House of Commons Select Committee on International Development asked the Minister for Europe to provide him with all relevant copies of correspondence between the Foreign and Commonwealth Office and the Department of Trade and Industry. The Parliamentary Ombudsman acknowledged concerns about the potential impact which release of the information could have on the frankness of debate on similar issues in the

---

[19] Case 13–98, Annual Report 1997–1998.
[20] Case 3100–14483/001 and 002, Annual Report 2000–2001.
[21] Case No.A.10/04.
[22] Case No.A.12/03.
[23] Case No.A.2/00.

future. However, the public interest overrode this harm, on the basis that the government had already recognised a public interest in the project by placing its assessments and judgments on the public record. It was also decided that there was a valid public interest in questions pertaining to human rights issues.

In the Australian case of *Re Cardwell Properties Pty Ltd and Department of the Premier, Economic and Trade Development*,[24] informing a community about details of a major development proposal that would affect them was considered to be in the public interest as it was information that encouraged a more informed debate about issues which were at the time under government consideration.

When applying the public interest test, the word "public" does not necessarily mean "the citizens of the whole of the UK". It could mean "the residents of Coventry" or "the majority of people living in Birmingham". In assessing where the balance of public interest lies in any given case it is necessary to identify which section or sections of society are affected.

The Irish Freedom of Information Manual states that "*usually the public interest pertains to a fairly large group of people but there is nothing to stop it applying to a single individual*". Factors which operate against disclosure include potential damage to community interests.

7. *Disclosure that would prejudice the protection of an individual's right to privacy*

3–015   In a New Zealand case, a photograph of an individual committing a crime was requested. It was rejected on the basis that the disclosure would prejudice the individual's privacy and that matters which may be interesting to the public are not necessarily matters that would be in the public interest to disclose.[25]

In a Canadian case where a whistle blower exposed contracting irregularities and the misuse of government funds, the Commissioner stated that there was a public interest in exposing instances of misappropriation of public funds and that this clearly outweighed any invasion of privacy.[26] The Commissioner was guided by Justice Muldoon in the case of *Bland v Canada (National Capital Commission)*[27] at the Federal Court:

> "*It is always in the public interest to dispel rumours of corruption or just plain mismanagement of the taxpayers' money and property. Naturally, if there has been negligence, somnolence or wrongdoing in the conduct of a government institution's operations it is by virtual definition in the public interest to disclose it and not to cover it up in wraps of secrecy.*"

[24] Case No.95019.
[25] Case No.W42789.
[26] Canada 16–95, Annual Report 1994–1995.
[27] [1993] 1 F.C. 541.

In a Canadian case, the Citizenship and Immigration Department were asked by the Legal Services Board to make available details of refugees held in detention so that it could take steps to improve its legal representation of those refugees. The Board claimed that any privacy interest of the refugees was outweighed by the public interest in effective legal representation. The Commissioner came to the conclusion that an invasion of privacy was not warranted, as there were other ways of dealing with the Board's concerns.[28]

A decision by the UK Ombudsman found that withholding the names of industry representatives, where details of the issue had already been released, did not succumb to a public interest override. The Ombudsman held that no exemption applied to details of what was discussed in a proposed code of practice, but accepted that the names of the industry representatives involved could be withheld.[29]

8. Non-disclosure is necessary to avoid serious damage to the proper working of government

In a case brought before the Irish Commissioner, a request was made by a journalist to the Department of Enterprise, Trade and Employment, for information listing high-risk companies which might be forced to make staff redundancies. The department refused access on the basis that they contained commercially sensitive information and information given in confidence. The Commissioner agreed that the balance of the public interest did not favour disclosure and stated that the premature release of this information could significantly limit the opportunities available to the state to take action that would prevent job losses.[30]   **3–016**

9. Disclosures affecting the commercial interests of a third party

Overseas jurisprudence suggests that commercial interests will often be paramount even where there is an obvious public interest in the release of information. Often, the issue in relation to commercial information will be the *timing* of its release.   **3–017**

Two examples (both are decisions made by the Irish Information Commissioner):

A public body was obliged to disclose copies of invoices paid to a supplier of IT services, even though the IT supplier argued that releasing such information could prejudice its ability to compete for future business from public and private bodies. Although the public interest in public bodies obtaining value for money, and openness about the expenditure of public

---

[28] Case 01 2000, Annual Report 2000–01.
[29] Case No.A.5/94.
[30] Case No.98100.

funds, was not absolute, in this case it outweighed any public interest in protecting the IT company's commercial interests.

The release of tender information, including the tenderer's name, the tender price and the quantity and type of goods involved was in the public interest in openness and accountability and outweighed any public interest in preventing commercial harm to tenderers and the tender process.

Where the commercial interests of the authority itself are at issue, the public interest is more likely to favour release because there is a clear public interest in accountability for public funds.

It may be that in some cases the only fair and reasonable way to balance public interest and corporate loss will be to undertake some measure of fact finding with the company concerned.

In situations involving public safety, the public interest is more likely to be strong enough to override the commercial interests of a third party.

II

CHAPTER 4

MAKING FREEDOM OF INFORMATION REQUESTS

Introduction

This chapter explains how to make requests using the Freedom of **4–001** Information Act 2000 and the Environmental Information Regulations 2004. It also offers practical advice on how to maximise the chances of getting the information you want and how to use the complaints process if you do not. Using the experience of information practitioners in the UK and abroad, it aims to help those seeking information make the most of the law.

The right of access is very wide and the rules require public authorities to advise and assist applicants at every stage of the process. This is good news for the citizen. At the same time, we should remain realistic. Many public authorities are under-resourced and some still lack anything approaching a sophisticated document management capability. It is also probably fair to say that for some of the hoarier members of the civil service, freedom of information may simply be too great a departure from the old ways of Westminster secrecy. None of these shortcomings serve as excuses, but the fact remains. We are all new to freedom of information and there will be teething troubles.

There follows a detailed explanation of how to make a FOIA request, how to complain if a request is not properly processed, and how to appeal decisions made in response to complaints. Examples letters of request are set out in the Annex to this Chapter. Throughout this Chapter "FOIA" refers to the Freedom of Information Act 2000 and the "EIRs" are the Environmental Information Regulations 2004. The legislation itself is covered in detail in Chs 1 and 2.

First steps

Who can make a request

4–002 Anyone, anywhere in the world can request information using FOIA or the EIRs. This includes companies and other organisations. The right of access applies irrespective of age, nationality or place of residence.

Formulating your information "strategy"

4–003 Unless your request is straightforward, it is usually worthwhile spending time formulating a strategy before you actually submit a request. The two fundamental questions which you should research before you do anything else are:

(a) what information do I actually want?

(b) who is likely to hold the information?

Identifying the information you want

4–004 When we talk about "information" we may mean one of two things. We may mean a particular document which contains the information, or we may mean simply an answer to a question. Before submitting a request, decide whether you want a particular document or extract, or whether you simply want an answer to a question (leaving it up to the authority to decide how exactly it answers). For example, if you wanted information relating to the building of Heathrow Terminal 5, you could ask for copies of the documents containing the Department of Transport's decision to approve the scheme, and any documents setting out the reasons for the decision. Alternatively, you could simply ask "when did the Department of Transport formally agree to permit the building of Heathrow Terminal 5, and why?"

Who is likely to hold the information?

4–005 In many cases, it will be obvious who holds the information. If you are not sure, then every public authority must now operate a Publication Scheme describing the categories of information which it routinely makes available. Publication schemes are accessible via the internet and should give an indication of whether an authority is likely to hold the information you want.

Central government departments all now operate an Information Asset Register (IAR) which lists unpublished information held by central government. The IAR is intended to help users identify, from a single source, the information held in a wide variety of government departments, agencies and other organisations. Further information is available at the Office of Public Sector Information website: *www.opsi.gov.uk/iar/ index.htm.*

Increasing numbers of authorities also now publish disclosure logs which detail all FOIA and EIR requests and the information supplied in response. If the information you want has been requested before, then it may be included in a disclosure log.

In more general terms, the rules apply to all public authorities within the following categories:

- central and local government,

- the health sector,

- the police and armed forces, and

- the education sector.

There is also a list of other public authorities in Schedule 1 of the Act. A full list is available on the Department for Constitutional Affairs' website.[1]

Companies which are wholly owned by a public authority are also caught by the rules, even if they are not listed.

Certain other bodies which perform functions of a public nature may also be caught if they have been designated as such for FOIA purposes by the Secretary of State.

Will the information I want be accessible using FOIA or the EIRs?

The right of access applies to *all* information which an authority holds, regardless of age, format, provenance or degree of accessibility. The rules also cover information held by someone on an authority's behalf. **4–006**

FOIA does not cover information held by a public authority only "on behalf of" someone else, but the EIRs do include such information.

As will be apparent, the entitlement is extremely wide, but the law does recognise that certain areas of government need to retain some measure of secrecy and that freedom of access to information by the public should be balanced with legitimate commercial and confidential interests. Accordingly, there are 23 exemptions under FOIA to the right of access, and various exceptions to the right under the EIRs.

The FOIA exemptions divide into two categories: "absolute exemptions" and "qualified exemptions". Absolute exemptions protect whole categories of information (such as records which relate to the security services), while

---

[1] At the time of writing, the up-to-date list is available at: *http://www.dca.gov.uk/foi/coverage.htm#V6*. This list is updated monthly.

qualified exemptions can apply only if disclosure would damage the particular interests which each is designed to protect and, even then, subject to the balance of the public interest. When assessing the application of a qualified exemption, a public authority must assess the public interest factors for and against disclosure of information. All of the exceptions under the EIRs are subject to the public interest. Chapter 3 discusses the application of the public interest in detail.

Making the request

Initial contact

4–007 It is often a good idea to make initial contact with an authority by phone, or in person, to discuss your request. You may want to contact someone in the particular department likely to be responsible for the information you want (*e.g.* the planning department) or the authority's Information Officer or Freedom of Information Unit. Sending your request to the wrong person can cause delay, so an initial conversation may ensure that when you make a formal request, you have exactly the right contact details.

Many authorities have Information Officers whose job it is to deal with requests for access to information. An Information Officer should be able to help you focus your request so that you can access the information you want as quickly and cost-effectively as possible. Knowing the name of the Information Officer will also ensure that your request gets dealt with speedily on receipt. A telephone conversation before sending a request may help the Information Officer understand the context of your request, which should help him or her to find the information.

Always keep a note of any conversations that you have with a public authority, including the name of the person you spoke to, the date and time, and what they told you. Any correspondence should refer back to your conversation. Do not be put off by unhelpful staff, or by staff who tell you that you will not be able to access the information you want.

A Code of Practice requires all public authorities to publish their procedures for dealing with requests and to supply details of who applicants should contact. Authorities must also provide a telephone helpline number. This information will normally be available on the authority's website.

Making a formal request

4–008 There are very few formalities for making a request.

For a request under FOIA, the request must:

- be in writing (which can include email),

- be legible (although it does not have to be in English—requests are permitted in any language),

- state the name and address of the applicant,

- describe the information requested, and

- be capable of being used for subsequent reference.

Requests made under the EIRs do not have to be in writing (they can be made orally or even using sign language) although written requests are usually preferable, to ensure that there is a record and to avoid confusion about the scope of the request and when it was made. If you do make a request orally, make sure you record the name of the person you spoke to, when you spoke to them and what you asked for. Ask them to read the request back to you to confirm they have understood what you want. Even then, it is sensible to follow up the request in writing.

It is not necessary to state that a request is a "freedom of information request" or an "environmental information request" or to refer to either piece of legislation. Nevertheless, it is always sensible to do so because this will make it clear to the authority how the request must be treated.

Where a request is made by email it is advisable to include a postal address as well as an email address. This is because an authority may have grounds for refusing a request if the information is held only in hard copy and would therefore have to be scanned for response by email. Moreover, even if an authority does have scanning capability it will probably want to pass on to you the cost of scanning documents.

Under FOIA (but not the EIRs) authorities are generally not obliged to answer requests by telephone, although in exceptional circumstances, where someone is not capable of making a request in writing, an authority may take a note of an application over the telephone. The rules require authorities to advise and assist you, so this should mean that telephone applications receive appropriate instructions for submitting the request in writing. Authorities are not permitted simply to dismiss telephone requests out of hand.

Sometimes it may be quicker and cheaper to go and inspect the information you want rather than (or before) asking for copies. Generally, it is more difficult for authorities to charge you for accessing information if you simply ask to inspect it. Although it may be more time consuming initially, a preliminary inspection may also enable you to decide what information you really do need, and to take copies only of the relevant parts.

Describing the information you want

Generally, requests should be as specific and comprehensive as possible. **4–009** Requests which say simply "all files relating to X" are still valid, but they may be costly to process and you may not be entitled to the information unless you are prepared to pay. Also, the larger the volume of information you request, the longer it will take to assemble.

If you know the document you want, then name it. Always include relevant dates or ranges of dates, document references, authors' and recipients' names and the names of committees or other relevant bodies. If possible, limit your request to particular formats of information, such as letters, reports or emails. If you think you know how an authority came into the possession of a piece of information, then this may assist the processing of your request.

Some basic examples of how to describe information:

- "the ABC Ltd contract let in February 2005 for the supply of waste management services in Chelsea and Westminster";

- "the tender documents submitted by XYZ Ltd in response to the Invitation to Tender dated 28 April 2005, reference number 1234567";

- "correspondence between the Grants Department of Bradford Metropolitan Council and the Agricultural Subsidy Committee of the Department for the Environment, Food and Rural Affairs in relation to the application of Mr John Smith of Bennet's Farm, Bradford, application number 89101112".

If you don't know the specific document you want, describe it as specifically as you can. It may help to refer to the source from which you learnt about the information, *e.g.* a newspaper article.

Remember that authorities are obliged by law to advise and assist you, and this includes helping you to identify and describe the information you want. Advice and assistance could include:

- providing an outline of the different kinds of information which might meet the terms of your request;

- providing access to detailed catalogues and indexes, where these are available, to help you ascertain the nature and extent of the information held by the authority;

- providing a general response to the request setting out options for further information which could be provided on request.

Authorities cannot expect you to have identifiers such as file reference numbers or descriptions of particular records, unless this information is made available by the authority itself for applicants' use. Where you don't have this, it is often worthwhile making your requests in "stages" or "layers".

(a) Staged requests

Staged requests ask initially for a list of the types of information which an **4–010** authority holds on a particular subject, followed by a further, more focused request based on this information.

A staged request might start with a request along the lines: "I am interested in the Mount Vernon apartments development. Please can you provide me with a list of the names of files that contain, or may contain, information about the development. Please provide me with the names (and references) of the files and tell me whether they are electronic or manual files. Please provide me with a description of the type of information contained in each file."

When you have this information, you can make a more focused request for specific pieces of information based on the file names and references you receive. This will often be less costly and more focussed than a general request. It will also help you to understand the way the authority manages its information.

(b) Layered requests

It can be effective to ask a series of requests in one letter, moving from the **4–011** more general to the more specific. Even if the more specific information is refused, you may still get access to the more general. Accessing the general information may be sufficient, and may help you challenge the refusal of the more specific information.

For example, you might ask for the following information in a single letter or email:

1. The number of traffic accidents on West End Lane in 2004;

2. The number of traffic accidents on West End Lane in 2004 in which a cyclist was involved;

3. Details of any traffic accidents on West End Lane in 2004 involving a cyclist; such details to include at least:

   (a) The date of the accident;

   (b) Details of the parties' vehicles;

   (c) Names of the parties.

Staged or layered requests are a valid means of eliciting the information you want. However, you should take care not simply to make the same request more than once. Although there is no particular limit to the number of requests you can make, if you make the same request more than once within a short period it is likely the authority will refuse it on the grounds you are simply asking for information which has already been disclosed or refused. Authorities are also entitled to refuse requests which they consider to be part of an organised campaign.

If after assistance has been provided you are still unable to describe the information you want sufficient to enable the public authority to identify and locate it, then the authority is not required to seek further clarification. Any information which the authority has found by that stage should be disclosed and it should also explain why it cannot take the request any further. It should also give you details of its complaints process and your rights of appeal against its response.

Costs for making requests

4–012 Under FOIA, requests are free, provided the cost of answering them does not exceed £600 (for central government) or £450 (for all other public authorities). The cost is calculated using a government published figure of £25 per hour per person identifying, locating, retrieving and extracting information. Based on the £600/£450 thresholds, this equates to around three-and-a-half or two-and-a-half days' work respectively.

If the cost exceeds the appropriate limit, then the authority can refuse the request. Alternatively, it can offer to respond for a fee. The fee must not exceed the total costs the authority reasonably expects to incur in answering the request. For this purpose, authorities are entitled to charge for photocopying and postage, and also for the costs of complying with an applicant's preferred means of communication (see below).

There are no cost thresholds for answering requests under the EIRs. Authorities may levy a charge for making information available, provided the amount is reasonable (and they must provide a schedule of charges if they propose making a charge). Generally, charges must not exceed the actual cost of producing the information. Authorities are not permitted to charge for providing access to environmental information which is available on a public register.

4–013 The more specific a request, the cheaper it will be for the authority to answer. For this reason, requests should be as specific as possible. It may be possible to reduce costs by asking the authority to provide information on a CD-Rom or by email.

Where an authority proposes making a charge, they must notify you in advance so that you can decide whether to continue with the request. They are not entitled to process the request and then simply bill you when they send the information.

Under FOIA, where a whole series of requests are made together or in quick succession, authorities may be entitled to treat them as a single request. This means that it will not normally be possible to keep a request below the cost thresholds by dividing it up into several smaller requests. The better approach is to be as specific as possible about a piece of information in order to help the authority find it quickly (see above in relation to describing the information you want in a request).

You should bear in mind that although a certain amount of work must be undertaken by authorities for free when processing requests, the amount is finite. Similarly, authorities are not required to collate and despatch large volumes of paper for nothing. The rules provide for a certain level of service, but also recognise that the burden on the taxpayer should be limited to reasonable levels.

Getting an answer

Time limits for a response

Under FOIA, when an authority receives a request it must respond within 20 working days, unless: **4–014**

- it needs more information about what you are requesting;

- it proposes to charge you a fee (see above); or

- the information requested is covered by a qualified exemption (see above), in which case the authority is entitled to take as much time as is reasonable to decide where the balance of the public interest lies.

If the authority proposes to charge you a fee then it must send you a fees notice. You will then have three months to pay, failing which the request will lapse.

Under the EIRs, authorities must respond to requests within 20 working days unless the complexity and volume of the request make it reasonable to extend the time limit, in which case it may be extended up to 40 working days. No extension beyond 40 days is permitted, and the time limits apply even where the authority is considering the application of an exemption or the balance of the public interest.

Format of the response

You can request that information be supplied in any form, but it is likely the authority will charge you for the cost of doing so if it will be expensive. You are, however, entitled to express a preference for a copy of the information, or a digest or summary of the information, or the opportunity to inspect a record containing the information. The authority must comply where this is reasonably practicable. When requesting large numbers of documents it may be cheaper to ask to be able to inspect them. **4–015**

It should be possible to have information supplied in Braille or audio format, in large type, or translated into another language.

Refusals of requests

4-016   Under FOIA, an authority may only refuse a request if:

- the information you want is exempt (see above);

- the cost of answering it would exceed the £600/£450 limit (see above);

- it is entitled to charge you a fee which you do not pay (see above); or

- your request "repeated" or "vexatious" (see below).

The EIRs permit requests to be refused only if:

- when the request is received, the authority does not hold the information;

- the request is manifestly unreasonable;

- the request is too general;

- it relates to material which is still work-in-progress;

- it would involve disclosing internal communications; or

- one of the exceptions applies (these are broadly similar to the FOIA exemptions).

If information is exempt and the authority refuses the request on this basis, it must identify which exemption applies and tell you how to apply for an internal review of this decision. If, after an internal review, the authority still refuses the request, then you are entitled to ask the Information Commissioner to review the decision.

Understanding and dealing with responses

4-017   All being well, the authority will respond to your request by supplying the information you requested. If it does not, then you will get one of the following responses:

(a) A holding letter

4-018   This may simply confirm receipt of the request and inform you that you will get a full response in due course. This is perfectly legitimate, but you should check for the following:

(i) A request for payment—this means that time stops running until you have paid.

(ii) A request for you to clarify your request, either because it is formulated too generally or because the authority does not understand it—again, time stops running until you have responded.

(iii) Reference only to FOIA when in fact the request should be dealt with under the EIRs—this is a common mistake made by authorities and you should respond by reminding them that they should process the request according to the EIR rules.

If the letter contains an estimated date of response, make a note of it and chase for a response if you have not received one by that date. Note down also any reference number provided by the authority—it will help you keep track of the request.

(b) A time extension letter

Sometimes authorities will tell you they need more time to deal with your request. They may be entitled to an extension but you should look out for the following, depending on what type of information you have requested:

4–019

(i) If your request is for environment information, an extension can only be made if the complexity and volume of the information requested make it impracticable to respond within 20 working days. Even in these circumstances, time can only be extended for a maximum of 20 working days.

(ii) Where your request is for non-environmental information, there can only usually be a time extension if the authority needs further time to consider the public interest. There is no absolute time limit for responding in such a case but you are entitled to ask for a clear statement of when the information will be provided.

(c) The fees notice

As noted above, in some circumstances an authority is entitled to charge you for releasing information. Any demand for payment automatically extends the time for responding to your request for the period between the demand and corresponding payment. You are not obliged to pay, but the authority can refuse your request if you do not.

4–020

Where you receive a request for payment and you think it is unreasonable, consider the following:

- Is the sum consistent with the authority's charging schedule (for EIR requests)?

- Does the authority explain clearly how it has calculated the amount demanded, and is this consistent with what it is allowed to charge for under FOIA or the EIRs?

- Has the authority proposed alternative ways of providing some of the information free of charge?

(d) The refusal

Where you receive a clear refusal to release information, you need to consider carefully the terms of the refusal.

- Has the authority complied with the procedural requirements for refusals (see para.4–016).

- Do you agree with the reasons for refusing to release information (*e.g.* does any exemption which the authority cites seem relevant and appropriate)? You can refer to the precise wording of the exemptions, and guidance on their scope issued by the Information Commissioner, the Department for Constitutional Affairs and the Department for the Environment, Food and Rural Affairs, in Chapters 1 and 2 of this book.

Do not assume that the authority is right. The exemptions are complex, and the people answering your request will often be no more expert than you are. In some ways (particularly in relation to the public interest), they may be less so, as you will probably know more about the subject matter and background of the request. This will put you in a strong position to argue the public interest in favour of disclosure in your particular case. If your request is for environmental information, make sure the authority has made its refusal on environmental information grounds, rather than FOIA grounds.

Just because an authority is legally entitled to withhold some of the information in a document does not necessarily mean it can withhold all of it. They must release any part of the document which is not exempt, provided it is possible to separate out the exempt and the non-exempt parts. The fact that removing the confidential information is a difficult job will not normally constitute an exemption.

(e) The partial refusal

4–021 Sometimes you will be sent some of the information that you asked for but not all. In such a case, your request may have been refused in part. You should satisfy yourself that the authority has complied with the requirements for refusing to release information (see para.4–016).

Sometimes, authorities will send documents with sections blacked out (this is known as "redaction"). This will often happen where a document contains personal information about individuals or certain types of commercially confidential information. Where a document has been redacted, you should ensure that the authority has given a clear explanation why. The explanation should cover every bit of information which has been redacted.

(f) The non-response

If your request specified a time by which you wanted the information and it has not arrived by that date, consider chasing it.　4–022

If you have not received a response within 20 working days, phone the person you wrote to (or perhaps the Information Officer within the authority) to complain and ask where the information is, and immediately follow up with a letter. There are no lawful excuses for failure to respond, as long as you provided the authority with the correct contact details.

A failure to respond within the legal time limits is unlawful and may result in censure by the Information Commissioner. Consider writing directly to the authority seeking a formal reconsideration of its failure to respond. If that fails to elicit a response, complain to the Commissioner.

(g) Mis-categorising your request

Where you have made a request for environmental information and the authority has processed your request under FOIA, you are entitled to require that they deal with your request properly. Your rights under the EIRs may be different to your rights under FOIA.　4–023

Depending on the precise nature of the response, you may need to apply for a formal reconsideration under Regulation 11 of the EIRs.

(h) The transfer letter

If an authority does not hold the information you have requested but knows that it is held by another authority, then it is entitled to transfer the request to that authority, or to tell you that the other authority holds the information. However, read the letter carefully to check that it is not transferring the request for any other reason. For example, the authority might try to transfer the request even if it does hold the information, simply because it would rather another authority dealt with the request. This might happen if the authority has received the information from another authority and is not sure how to deal with the request. This type of transfer is not lawful.　4–024

Using the information once you receive it

Disclosure of information under FOIA does not remove the copyright in it, so you must abide by any copyright restrictions on use.　4–025

Appeals

The right to dispute the way the authority handled your request

4–026   There are various grounds for disputing or complaining about an authority's response to a request:

> (a) You may dispute any refusal to disclose information, whether this is:
>
> > (i) under an exemption; or
> >
> > (ii) because the authority says you have not described it in a way which enables the authority to locate it; or
> >
> > (iii) because the authority says the request is repeated or vexatious.
>
> (b) You may complain if the information is supplied late (see above in relation to time limits for complying).
>
> (c) You may dispute any fees which the authority asks you to pay.

The process of complaining and appealing

4–027   Any complaint or appeal should first be made to the authority itself. When the authority refuses your request it is required to supply details of its internal complaints process, so use these details to complain in the first instance.

If you are dissatisfied with the outcome of the authority's internal review, you can ask the Information Commissioner, the UK's Freedom of Information Watchdog, to review the way your request was handled (see *www. informationcommissioner.gov.uk*). The Commissioner is obliged to investigate your complaint for free. When applying to the Information Commissioner, you should include:

> • a covering letter explaining what you would like the Commissioner to assess;
>
> • a copy of the initial request or, if the request was verbal, any details of the request which you recorded;
>
> • a copy of the authority's initial response;
>
> • a copy of the complaint you made to invoke the authority's internal review/complaints procedure;
>
> • a copy of the authority's response following reconsideration through the internal review/complaints procedure;

- any other information which you think is relevant;

- an indication of any particular urgency in your case (the Information Commissioner's Office does not guarantee to respond to complaints within a particular time but they will take into account any special circumstances); and

- your own contact details, to enable the Commissioner's Office to obtain any further information from you.

The Commissioner will notify you of the outcome of his investigation by sending you a Decision Notice. You are entitled to appeal a Decision Notice to the Information Tribunal (as is the public authority itself if it disagrees with the Commissioner's decision). Any appeal from the Information Tribunal must be to the High Court.

Annex

Pro-forma letters of request for information

The following letters are examples of how requests might be made. They are for guidance only.

Letter 1—basic letter of request

[Applicant's name and address]

[Date]

[Contact details for public authority]

Dear [*insert name of addressee or contact at addressee*]

Request for information under the Freedom of Information Act 2000

This is a request, made under the Freedom of Information Act 2000 ("**FOIA**") for the information set out below.

Should you consider that the cost of meeting this request will exceed £[450]/[600], please notify [me]/[us] of what information you are able to provide within the £[450]/[600] limit.

If you have any questions about any of the items below, please contact [me]/[us]/[A N Other] at [the above address]/[the following address: *insert address*].

Information requested

[Describe the information requested—be as specific and comprehensive as possible. If you know the document you want, then name it. Always include relevant dates, document references and authors' and recipients' names. If you don't know the specific document you want, describe it as specifically as you can. It may help to refer to the source from which you learnt about the information, *e.g.* a newspaper article.]

Yours faithfully

[name of applicant]

Letter 2—general request for information about files held   4–029

[Applicant's name and address]

[Date]

[Contact details for public authority]

Dear Sirs

Request for information under the Freedom of Information Act 2000

I am writing to request information about the proposed apartment development at Mount Vernon, Hampstead, London NW3.

Please would you provide me with the following details of any files held by [*insert name of public authority*] which contain information relating to the proposed development. For each file, I would like the following information:

- the file name;

- which department or unit within [*insert name of public authority*] holds it;

- whether the file is held in electronic or manual format; and

- a summary or description of the type of information contained in the file.

Please will you acknowledge receipt of this request. I look forward to hearing from you in due course.

Yours sincerely

[name of applicant]

4–030 Letter 3—request for environmental information

[Applicant's name and address]

[Date]

[Contact details for public authority]

Dear Sirs

Request for information under the Environmental Information Regulations 2004

This is a request, made under the Environment Information Regulations 2004 (the "**EIRs**") for the information set out below.

I refer to our telephone conversation yesterday in which I requested copies of any reports held by [*insert name of public authority*] in relation to the proposed redevelopment of [*insert details*].

I need this information urgently to allow me to comment on a related planning application. Please provide me with the information by not later than [*insert date*] (two weeks from today). If for any reason you are not able to do so, please write to me before then explaining why, and telling me when you expect to provide the information.

I note from your schedule of charges that you will not charge for sending documents in electronic form or for copies of less than 250 pages. If the reports are lengthy (more than 100 pages) please could you provide them to me on a CD.

Please will you acknowledge receipt of this request. I look forward to hearing from you in due course

Yours sincerely

[name of applicant]

II

CHAPTER 5

FOIA AND PUBLIC
AUTHORITIES—THE REQUEST
HANDLING PROCESS

Fundamentally, FOIA presents challenges for public bodies on three fronts: **5–001**
cultural and political change; the physical processing of information; and
dealings with external organisations, particularly the private sector. This
chapter deals with one aspect of the second of these, namely: how to
manage the information handling process in order to answer requests
correctly.

There is no prescribed formula for dealing with requests, and an authority's
method will reflect its corporate structure and internal culture.
Nevertheless, there are certain fundamental issues which are common to
every request, regardless of the size or diversity of the authority, and this
chapter sets out in a series of flow charts the request handling steps which
will always be necessary. Readers should refer to the appropriate sections of
Chs 1 and 2 for a detailed analysis of the rules relating to time limits, fees
and exemptions.

The Foundations of the Request Handling Process

All public bodies need to have systems in place which enable them to **5–002**
process FOIA and EIR requests in accordance with their legal obligations.
At its most basic, this means correctly identifying requests when they come
in, ensuring they end up on the right person's desk, collecting and sifting all
the information requested, and responding correctly within the relevant
time limit, taking account of all potential exemptions and exceptions.

The detailed methodology will vary from organisation to organisation, but
the key issues are the same:

1. Document filing and management

5–003   Public authorities need to know what types of information they hold, and where it is. Some form of document management or filing system is essential. At its most basic, this means naming and numbering files informatively and using systematic cross referencing. It is also imperative to keep filing up to date. There is no point working hard to process a request on time, only to find that important papers were omitted because they are sitting in someone's out-tray.

2. Responsibility for handling requests

5–004   Authorities should consider their organisational structure and how responsibility for information handling should be devolved. In all but the smallest public bodies, some measure of devolution will be inevitable.

Everyone in the FOIA/EIR chain needs a working understanding of the rules, and expertise sufficient to identify issues for escalation. Someone—and this will usually be the Information Officer or a member of the Legal Department—will need to know in detail how the various exemptions and exceptions work so that they can make decisions about disclosure in borderline cases.

3. The request lifecycle

5–005   The information request flow charts in the Annex to this Chapter map the key stages of the request lifecycle.

Authorities may benefit from establishing links with the Information Commissioner's Office, who will be able to offer support and advice. In addition, the government has now established a central "Clearing House" within the Department for Constitutional Affairs to which Whitehall departments may transfer FOIA requests in certain circumstances. The Clearing House's role is threefold:

- to ensure a consistent government-wide position on round robin and potentially precedent-setting cases;

- to provide guidance on sensitive cases with a high public profile and to align the response to such cases with government policy and guidance; and

- to revise government guidance in the light of emerging case law and new policy imperatives.

The Clearing House's remit only covers Whitehall Departments (including non-ministerial departments), and the Scottish Executive and the National

Assembly for Wales on issues which may have implications for the UK administration.[1]

Further information is available from the Access to Information Central Clearing House Toolkit, at *www.foi.gov.uk/guidance/pdf/toolkit.pdf*.

The Request Handling Process

The following section comprises an accompanying narrative to the key steps identified in the information request flow charts in the Annex.   5–006

1. Receipt of requests and request validation (Flowchart Steps 1 and 2)

As identified above, there are two key actions required when a request first   5–007
arrives. The first is to get it logged (including the date of receipt, so that the authority can track response deadlines), and the second is to ensure that it is passed immediately to the appropriate person for processing. Because requests do not have to refer to the Act or the Regulations, nor be addressed to a particular person within the organisation, it is imperative that everyone has a rudimentary grasp of the FOIA and EIR rules so that they can recognise a request if they get one.

Requests from the media

Some authorities will routinely receive requests from the media. Although   5–008
the time limit for a response is 20 days (with scope to extend where permitted under FOIA or the EIRs), the overriding obligation under FOIA is to respond "promptly", and under the EIRs "as soon as possible". Strictly speaking, therefore, authorities should endeavour to respond to media requests sooner than the 20 day deadline if the requestor specifies a particular date (*e.g.* because a journalist is working to a publication deadline).[2]

The interaction of FOIA, the EIRs and the Data Protection Act (DPA)

It is important to identify correctly the access regime under which a request   5–009
will fall. This is because the rules differ in each case. Requests for environmental information must be dealt with under the EIR rules, and requests by an individual for his or her own personal data must be dealt with under the DPA rules.

---

[1] Non Departmental Public Bodies, Executive Agencies and other bodies sponsored by government departments are expected to refer in the first instance to their sponsoring Whitehall departments.
[2] As noted in Ch.1, it is difficult to imagine circumstances in which a 20 working day response would lead to adverse consequences. In every case to date where complaints have been lodged as a result of delay, the Commissioner has identified the breach of the statutory time limit, but declined to impose further penalties or remedial steps.

Notifying third parties

5–010 Public sector contracts frequently impose obligations on public authorities to notify and/or consult suppliers whenever requests are made for information relating to them. It is important to comply with such obligations. Failure to do so may be a breach of contract, and also a breach of the Section 45 Code of Practice.

2. Charges (Flowchart Step 3)

5–011 Remember that although FOIA requires authorities to provide a certain amount of time and effort for free, the rules also recognise that the taxpayer should not have to bear the whole burden. It is important to calculate up front the cost of locating and retrieving information so that the authority can assess whether it is entitled to refuse the request or perhaps offer to answer it for a fee.

In practice the question of how to calculate costs is somewhat vexed. Under FOIA, authorities are entitled to include time spent identifying, locating, retrieving and extracting information. Time spent on these activities (whether by authority staff or by anyone on the authority's behalf) must be assessed at a rate of £25 per hour. Fees charged must not exceed the total costs which the authority reasonably expects to incur in complying with FOIA s.1. In assessing costs, authorities may include the cost of:

- compliance with FOIA s.11 (where an applicant expresses a preferred means of communication)

- production of any document; and

- postage and other forms of transmitting information.

It may be difficult to know how long it will take to locate and retrieve information without actually locating and retrieving it. If so, the best advice is to produce an estimate based on demonstrable calculations. Even if the calculations turn out to be inaccurate, it will help to rebut complaints if the authority can show that its estimate is a genuine attempt to quantify costs rather than simply a guess.

Under the EIRs authorities are entitled to levy a charge for making information available, provided the amount is "reasonable". Generally, charges must not exceed the actual cost of producing the information. The Regulation 16 Code requires authorities to minimize costs where possible, for example by using CD-Rom or electronic communications in preference to paper where the information requested is voluminous. A "market-based" charge is permitted in limited cases.

3. Retrieval of documents (Flowchart Step 4)

5–012 The process of retrieving and collating information will usually be the most time consuming element of the request handling process. Information

Officers rarely control the generation and storage of information, which has become increasingly disparate with the advent of electronic documents and email, so successfully retrieving and collating it will require the cooperation of all staff likely to be repositories of what has been requested.

Authorities are also expected to comply with the Section 46 Code of Practice under FOIA when processing requests, which deals with the management of records.

4. Applying the exemptions (Flowchart Step 5)

Once information has been retrieved and collated, the process begins of **5–013** deciding what may be eligible for exemption. The process should always start with the presumption that information must be disclosed, each record then being considered in the light of the exemptions or exceptions. Once the information has been separated into "non-exempt" and "potentially exempt", the latter should be considered more closely, and the public interest assessed for all information to which a qualified exemption applies.

5. Responding to requests (Flowchart Step 6)

The final stage involves the formal response to the request. There are some **5–014** useful pro-forma letters of response on the Defra website.[3] Although these are intended for use with EIR requests, they will serve just as well for FOIA applications, subject to a little tailoring.

Annex

The flow charts which follow provide a simple step-by-step guide to the **5–015** processing of FOIA requests.

---

[3] See *www.defra.gov.uk/corporate/opengov/eir/lettersappeals/letters.htm.*

Freedom of Information Request Handling Process

5–016 Receipt of Requests

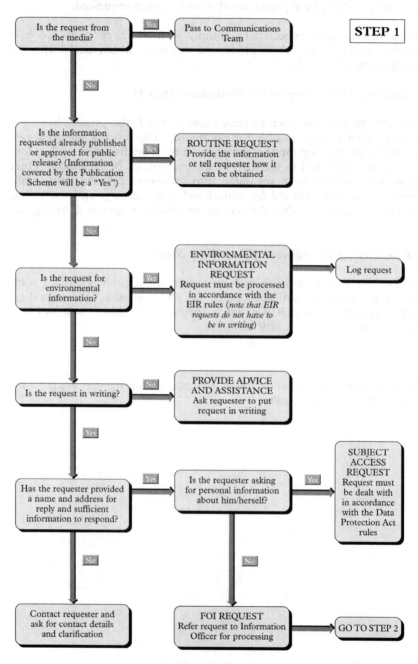

Request Validation

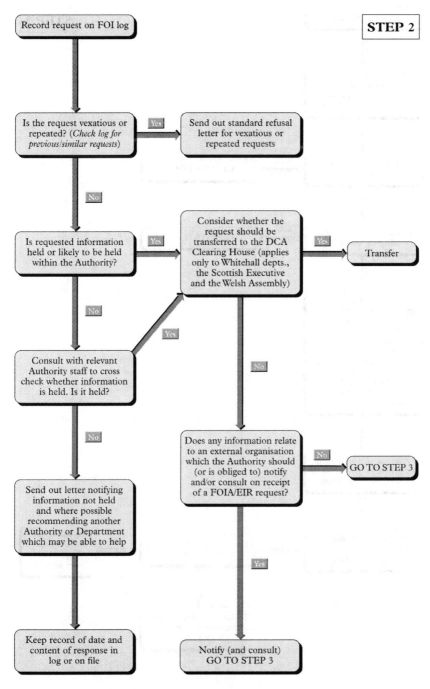

5–018

Charges

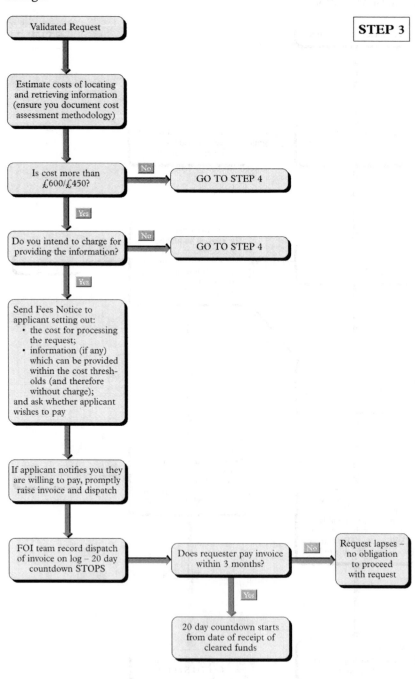

Retrieval of Information   5–019

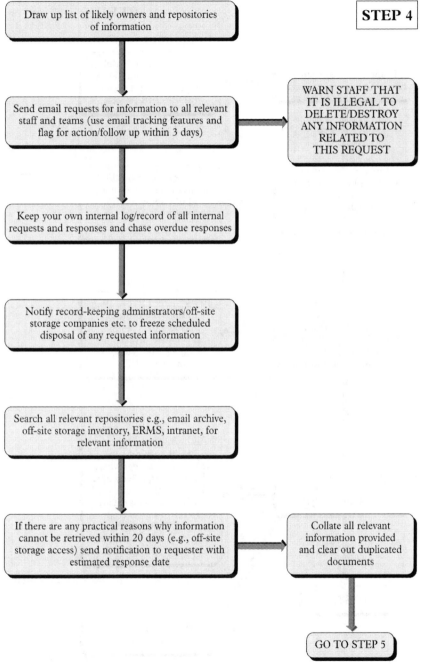

Draw up list of likely owners and repositories of information

STEP 4

Send email requests for information to all relevant staff and teams (use email tracking features and flag for action/follow up within 3 days)

WARN STAFF THAT IT IS ILLEGAL TO DELETE/DESTROY ANY INFORMATION RELATED TO THIS REQUEST

Keep your own internal log/record of all internal requests and responses and chase overdue responses

Notify record-keeping administrators/off-site storage companies etc. to freeze scheduled disposal of any requested information

Search all relevant repositories e.g., email archive, off-site storage inventory, ERMS, intranet, for relevant information

If there are any practical reasons why information cannot be retrieved within 20 days (e.g., off-site storage access) send notification to requester with estimated response date

Collate all relevant information provided and clear out duplicated documents

GO TO STEP 5

5–020 Exemptions

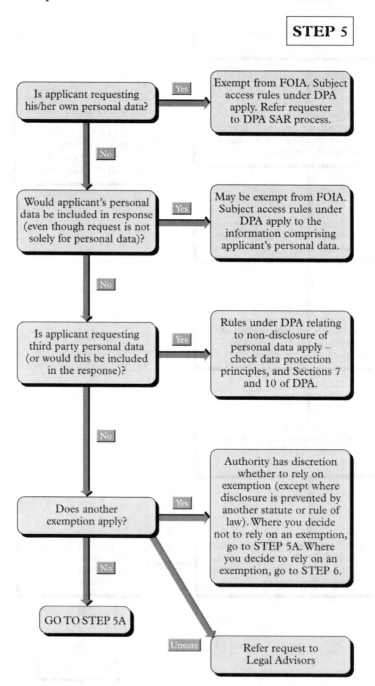

STEP 5

Is applicant requesting his/her own personal data?

Yes → Exempt from FOIA. Subject access rules under DPA apply. Refer requester to DPA SAR process.

No ↓

Would applicant's personal data be included in response (even though request is not solely for personal data)?

Yes → May be exempt from FOIA. Subject access rules under DPA apply to the information comprising applicant's personal data.

No ↓

Is applicant requesting third party personal data (or would this be included in the response)?

Yes → Rules under DPA relating to non-disclosure of personal data apply – check data protection principles, and Sections 7 and 10 of DPA.

No ↓

Does another exemption apply?

Yes → Authority has discretion whether to rely on exemption (except where disclosure is prevented by another statute or rule of law). Where you decide not to rely on an exemption, go to STEP 5A. Where you decide to rely on an exemption, go to STEP 6.

No ↓

GO TO STEP 5A

Unsure → Refer request to Legal Advisors

Consultation with third parties 5–021

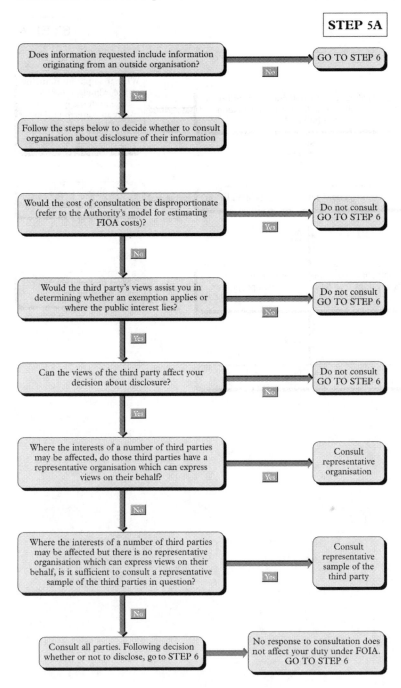

5–022 Responding to requests

STEP 6

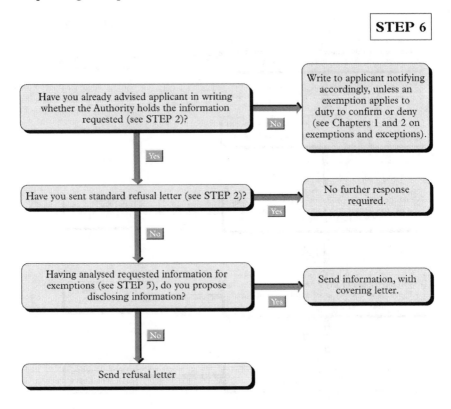

Have you already advised applicant in writing whether the Authority holds the information requested (see STEP 2)?

No → Write to applicant notifying accordingly, unless an exemption applies to duty to confirm or deny (see Chapters 1 and 2 on exemptions and exceptions).

Yes ↓

Have you sent standard refusal letter (see STEP 2)?

Yes → No further response required.

No ↓

Having analysed requested information for exemptions (see STEP 5), do you propose disclosing information?

Yes → Send information, with covering letter.

No ↓

Send refusal letter

II

CHAPTER 6

THE IMPLICATIONS OF FREEDOM OF INFORMATION FOR THE PRIVATE SECTOR

Everyone reading this book will understand why the Freedom of **6–001** Information Act 2000 (**FOIA**) has changed the way government has to operate. It is less obvious, however, and therefore frequently not understood, that FOIA represents profound benefits and risks to every company doing business with the public sector.

In 2000, the Information Commissioner, Richard Thomas, wrote[1] that FOIA represents both "opportunities and threats" to the private sector. On the one hand, "*as sophisticated companies know, a treasure trove of reports, surveys, statistics, analyses, opinions and recommendations has been amassed by various organs of government over the past decades . . . Provided their own genuine secrets remain secret, businesses have a strong interest in ensuring maximum access to the information held by government and public authorities.*"[2] At the same time, competitors will themselves be able to ask for information about other companies supplying to government, including, potentially, information which is confidential or commercially sensitive. The experience abroad illustrates this well. Research in the US indicates that nearly 60 per cent of access requests there come from commercial bodies seeking information on business competitors.[3] Disclosure of contracts, price and all, is now accepted in the US as the price of doing business with government.

---

[1] In his essay *Freedom of Information: the Implications for Business*, collected in *Freedom of Expression and Freedom of Information—Essays in Honour of Sir David Williams* (2000), J Beatson and Y Cripps (eds).

[2] *Ibid.*

[3] See ME Tankersley, *How the Electronic Freedom of Information Act Amendments of 1996 update public access for the information age* (1998) 50 Admin Law Review 421–458, reprinted in RG Vaughan (ed), *Freedom of Information* (2000).

1. Opportunities

6–002   There are principally four areas in which FOIA offers opportunities for business. These can be categorised as: customer intelligence and marketing; competitor intelligence; ensuring fair treatment; and legal claims.

Chapter 4 of this book describes how to make freedom of information requests and how to ensure that you make the most of the rights of access under FOIA and the EIRs. In the corporate context, the first step is to review the list of public authorities in Schedule 1 to FOIA and identify the public authorities relevant to your business from whom information can usefully be sourced. Bear in mind that, as well as the list in Schedule 1, the Lord Chancellor may designate organisations as public authorities if they cannot be added to the list by other means,[4] and publicly owned companies are also subject to FOIA.[5] Having identified your target authorities, the next step is to identify the sort of information which those targets may hold.

Customer Intelligence and Marketing

6–003   The most obvious benefit to the private sector of freedom of information is the access it provides to information about public services. Records showing how public services are delivered, and the cost of doing so, are a treasure trove of information for companies preparing tenders for the supply of those services. Public authorities will also hold information setting out what they want and expect from suppliers. This is an invaluable resource for companies looking to tailor their approach to selling products and services.

Prior to the tender process, information about policy, including policy development, the implementation of policy, and timetables and targets for the delivery of policy, is an invaluable predictor of future business opportunities. In the context of public procurement, companies looking for new business opportunities can access information on authorities' procurement histories, market intelligence, studies underlying proposed new projects, prices, service standards and customer needs. Public bodies hold a vast array of information which constitutes market intelligence in the form of the *"reports, surveys, statistics, analyses, opinions and recommendations"* cited by Richard Thomas, quoted above.

Competitor Intelligence

6–004   Information about competitors will be available from a variety of sources. Examples include:

- export licences;
- grant applications;
- applications for regulatory approval;

[4] Freedom of Information Act 2000, ss.4 and 5.
[5] *Ibid.*, s.6.

- contract bids;

- tender evaluations;

- contracts;

- performance reviews;

- planning applications;

- tax returns; and

- negotiated dispensations.

This is very much a double-edged sword of course, given that many authorities will hold similar information about competitor companies within the same sector, and what is available in relation to one, may, correspondingly, be available to others.

Ensuring Fair Treatment

Companies which have been subject to adverse regulatory or procurement decisions can use FOIA to uncover information which may help them gain redress. A great deal of information about regulatory bodies, including internal guidance, is now accessible under FOIA. **6–005**

Legal claims

Companies may use FOIA to obtain information which can assist in litigation or criminal cases. Because FOIA confers access to information *as of right*, applicants do not need to establish a need-to-know or other justification for wanting the information. It is perfectly permissible to seek information where this may facilitate a claim in litigation, whether against an authority or against a third party. **6–006**

2. Threats

FOIA impacts every company which supplies to government, including under any PPP[6] or PFI[7] scheme, the G-Cat[8] or S-Cat[9] regimes, and **6–007**

---

[6] The Public Private Partnership or PPP scheme is the mechanism used by government to finance and deliver public services at lower long term economic cost.

[7] The Private Finance Initiative or PFI offers one specific form of PPP scheme under which government can access new or improved capital assets such as buildings, roads, plant, apparatus and vehicles. Unlike traditional procurement, under PFI the public sector does not buy the assets, but rather pays for the use of assets held by the private sector, and the services associated with those assets.

[8] GCat is the Government catalogue for IT and Telecoms related goods and services. It comprises a number of Framework Agreements and is available to any UK contracting authority in the public and utilities sectors.

[9] S-Cat is a catalogue based procurement scheme established by CCTA in 1997 to provide public sector organisations with a simplified means of procuring, and contracting for, a wide range of IT related consultancy and specialist services from a variety of service providers.

whether as a prime or subcontractor. Put simply, whenever a company contracts with a government customer, competitors have the opportunity to establish:

- the contract price, and perhaps also information about costs and profit, and the supplier's service specification or methodology;

- service levels; and

- the reasons why that particular company won the contract.

The experience in Canada, Australia, New Zealand and Ireland, where freedom of information laws have been around for many years, suggests that FOIA requests to government here will focus on the private sector delivery of public services. This means that journalists, pressure groups and competitors will be asking public bodies for information which they hold originating from the private sector. This includes tender documents, contracts and even invoices, much of which will be commercially sensitive or confidential.

Identifying the risks

6–008 Put simply, the FOIA risk to companies lies in the fact that public authorities are obliged to make available on request *any* information they hold, irrespective of where that information originated, who owns it or who has rights of use. The rules are also retrospective so apply to records generated before, as well as after, January 1, 2005. The right of access applies to contracts, tender documents, invoices, correspondence and any other information which relates to suppliers or which originated from them, if held by the authority.

There are 23 potential exemptions to the right of access, but even if one of them is available, it will only prevent disclosure if the public body chooses to apply it. Information may be exempt where disclosure could prejudice a company's commercial interests, or where information is confidential. However, both of these exemptions are subject to public interest considerations. The public interest is a notoriously slippery concept and almost anything may be disclosable—regardless of sensitivity—if circumstances dictate. Overseas jurisprudence demonstrates that requests relating to contracts for the delivery of public services bring into play strong public interest considerations such as accountability for public spending and obtaining value for money—considerations which tend to tip the balance in favour of disclosure, even for information which might be confidential or commercially sensitive. This is ably illustrated by three examples where the public interest in disclosure will be particularly strong because of the context in which a request is made:

- requests relating to issues which are the subject of national or parliamentary debate—such as the implementation of an integrated IT system for police intelligence handling, as recommended by the Bichard Report;

- requests relating to an issue which affects a wide range of people—such as the introduction of a national identity card;

- requests for information where public safety may be at issue—such as the modernisation of the tube under the government's PPP scheme.

Protecting your sensitive information

Companies must think carefully about how to manage the risk of sensitive information being disclosed. In most cases this will involve working closely with government customers to manage the information handling process in a way which allows public authorities to meet their legal obligations, but also enables the company to mitigate the risk of secret information finding its way into the public domain. Unfortunately, the legal regime which requires government to make documents available contains no matching requirement for them to consult companies before disclosure, nor is there any mechanism within FOIA for companies to stop or prevent disclosure.

6–009

This means that companies have limited options when faced with the prospect of information about their business being disclosed under FOIA. There are essentially three options:

1. Attempting by consultation and discussion to persuade public authority customers not to disclose information.

2. Seeking to prevent disclosure by means of injunction.

3. Suing for damages after the event (perhaps with an injunction to prevent further disclosure in future), with all the difficulties of quantifying loss which this entails.

None of these offers certainty of outcome, and the second and third will be expensive. What is more, the first and second options will only be available if the public authority actually notifies the supplier before responding to the FOIA request.

With this is mind there are some important practical steps which companies should take to protect their businesses from the risks of FOIA disclosure.

Identifying responsibility for FOIA compliance

The best way to deal with FOIA risk is to prevent information being disclosed in the first place. There is no fool-proof way to prevent disclosure, but one thing is guaranteed: namely, that it will be impossible to manage

6–010

the risk if you are not even aware that a request for your company's information has been made. Companies should find out from public sector customers who has responsibility for processing and responding to FOIA requests. This may be the Information Officer or it may be someone specific to a particular project. Suppliers should endeavour to build relationships with the personnel responsible for FOIA applications and work with them to ensure that they notify the company as soon as a request comes in. When you know who the decision makers are and can be confident they will tell you when they receive a request, you will be in a position to influence the decisions they make about disclosure of your information.

For companies providing outsourcing services it is important to clarify who will bear the costs of finding and producing information which the supplier might be holding on the customer's behalf. The fact that you are holding a lot of information for your government customers does not mean that information falls outside FOIA. On the contrary, the Act specifically includes it. Although it is the public body which has to respond to any request, you can be sure your customers will want help—even if only in locating the information requested. Some government customers might even go further and ask you to deal with requests yourself on the authority's behalf. Either way, the important question is who pays for this? Searching and sifting information is time and labour intensive in all but the most routine cases.

Contractual protection

6–011   Following on from the previous section, it is a good idea to formalize arrangements for notification and consultation by including them in the contract. In essence, this means simply requiring public sector customers to notify and consult on requests for information under FOIA relating to company information. As a further step, it may be possible to require the customer to take account of representations made by the company in relation to such requests. The important thing is that the customer notifies and consults *before* disclosing anything in response to a request.

Another approach is to tell customers up front what information you consider exempt from FOIA disclosure, and document it in the contract. A schedule which lists information the parties agree is likely to be exempt may be workable, and ought to ensure that the customer considers relevant exemptions before deciding whether or not to disclose information.

The Annex to this Chapter sets out some examples of contract clauses covering these issues.

The private sector must understand that the default position now for public bodies is to disclose information unless there is a justifiable reason for withholding it. Only by working with their customers can companies adequately manage what will sometimes be conflicting risks—their own business risk, and their customer's FOIA compliance risk. Contracts under negotiation now and in future should incorporate this; contracts already signed may very well benefit from variation.

Annex

Precedent clauses for public sector contracts

The purpose of FOIA is to bring openness and transparency to the public **6–012** sector, one face of which means illuminating the way it does business. Accordingly, attempts to impose unreasonable and unjustifiable restrictions on a public authority's ability to disclose information will be unacceptable to most customers and may be open to challenge by the Information Commissioner and the Courts. The new regime means that some information which companies have been able to keep confidential in the past may now have to be disclosed. At the same time, FOIA does recognise the importance of balancing the right of access with the protection of legitimate business interests. It should therefore be possible to agree contractual provisions with government customers which reflect this.

There are numerous ways of dealing with FOIA in supply contracts and the right approach will depend on the nature of each project. In basic terms, the options can be summarised thus:

Option 1

The customer is either encouraged or obliged to consult the supplier before **6–013** it discloses information pursuant to a FOIA request, and to take account before disclosing anything of any representations the supplier makes. This approach is well suited to smaller projects. The extent to which the Authority is obliged to consult and take account of representations can be negotiated. Note however that some customers will agree only to *try* to consult, and many will insist that decisions about disclosure must be at their sole discretion.

This option will not be appropriate for larger contracts, nor for outsourcing arrangements.

Option 2

The customer must consult the supplier before disclosing any "exempt" **6–014** information, and the contract will have a FOIA schedule which lists all the information the supplier wishes to be exempt. This offers the best protection and has the advantage of identifying at the outset what the customer should not disclose. However, many customers are reluctant to accept contractual terms which control their FOIA processes. Also, identifying and listing exempt information in a schedule usually requires considerable work and is therefore impractical where project teams are stretched and deadlines looming.

Option 3

6–015   The contract will have a FOIA schedule which describes in broad terms the information which the supplier would normally expect to be exempt, but without imposing on the customer an obligation not to disclose. This is consistent with the statutory legal position, which imposes obligations on the public authority irrespective of any contractual restrictions. This will usually also be considerably less time consuming that Option 2.

An example of each option is set out below. These are only examples and should be tailored as necessary.

Outsourcing contracts

6–016   Regardless of whether and how the supplier tries to control or influence the customer's approach to FOIA, in any outsourcing arrangement which involves the supplier holding information on behalf of the customer, the customer will want (indeed will need) the supplier's assistance finding information when a request comes in. Outsourcing contracts should include provisions which make it clear what assistance the supplier will provide and who pays for this. Generally, there will be two options: (a) to include projected costs for FOIA assistance in the overall price, or (b) to price them separately. In either case, but particularly the latter, the contract must be clear about how costs are calculated.

Option 1

6–017   ***1. Definitions***

"Exempt Information"	means any information or class of information (including but not limited to any document, report, contract or other material containing information) relating to this Agreement or otherwise relating to the Supplier which the Supplier has designated by notice in writing to the Authority as potentially falling within an FOIA Exemption.
"FOIA"	means the Freedom of Information Act 2000 and all regulations made thereunder from time to time or any superseding or amending enactment and regulations.
"FOIA Exemption"	means any applicable exemption to FOIA including but not limited to confidentiality (section 41), trade secrets (section 43) and

426

prejudice to commercial interests (section 43).

2. Freedom of Information

2.1 The Supplier acknowledges that the Authority is subject to legal **6–018** duties under FOIA which may require the Authority to disclose on request information relating to this Agreement or which otherwise relates to the Supplier.

2.2 The Authority acknowledges and agrees that certain information provided by the Supplier to the Authority under this Agreement constitutes information which is confidential to the Supplier or comprises personal information about the Supplier's personnel or third party personnel or which is information which would be prejudicial to the Supplier's commercial interests if disclosed to a third party.

2.3 The Authority shall promptly notify the Supplier of any request received by the Authority for Exempt Information and before making any disclosure of Exempt Information the Authority shall take account of representations made by the Supplier within a reasonable time about the applicability of the FOIA Exemptions to such Exempt Information.

2.4 The Authority shall not:

(a) confirm or deny that information is held by the Authority; or

(b) disclose information requested

to the extent that in the Authority's opinion the information is eligible in the circumstances for a FOIA Exemption and therefore that the Authority may lawfully refrain from doing either of the things described in pts (a) and (b) of this Clause 2.4.

2.5 The Authority shall indemnify the Supplier for any and all costs (including legal fees) incurred by the Supplier:

(a) in any successful application for an injunction to prevent disclosure by the Authority of Exempt Information; and

(b) in any application for judicial review of a decision of the Authority to disclose information where disclosure by the Authority is held by such judicial review to have been unnecessary, unwarranted or unlawful.

Option 2

1. Definitions

6–019   **"Exempt Information"** means any information or class of information (including but not limited to any document, report, contract or other material containing information) relating to this Agreement or otherwise relating to the Supplier which has been designated by the Supplier as potentially falling within an exemption to FOIA (as set out therein) and which is listed in [Schedule [X]].

    "FOIA" means the Freedom of Information Act 2000 and all regulations made thereunder from time to time or any superseding or amending enactment and regulations.

    "FOIA notice" means a decision notice, enforcement notice and/or an information notice.

2. Freedom of Information

6–020   2.1   The Supplier acknowledges that the Authority is subject to legal duties under FOIA which may require the Authority to disclose on request information relating to this Agreement or otherwise relating to the Supplier.

    2.2   The Authority acknowledges that certain information provided by the Supplier to the Authority under this Agreement constitutes information which is confidential to the Supplier or comprises personal information about the Supplier's personnel or third party personnel or which is information which would be prejudicial to the Supplier's commercial interests if disclosed to a third party.

    2.3   The Authority shall not disclose Exempt Information (in whatever form) pursuant to a request made under FOIA unless and until it has consulted the Supplier and taken into account representations made by the Supplier.

    2.4   The Authority shall not:

       (a) confirm or deny that information is held by the Authority; or

       (b) disclose information requested

    to the extent that the information requested under FOIA is Exempt Information.

2.5 In relation to any request for Exempt Information made to the Authority under FOIA the Authority shall where applicable:

    (a) respond to any FOIA notice and in responding set out the relevant exemption(s) under FOIA applying to the Exempt Information and the basis upon which such exemptions apply (including where applicable the grounds for the Authority's assessment of the balance of the public interest) which is the subject of such FOIA notice; and/or

    (b) lodge an appeal against any decision of the Information Commissioner in relation to disclosure of Exempt Information where in the Supplier's reasonable opinion the information requested is exempt from disclosure under FOIA.

2.5 The Authority shall indemnify the Supplier for any and all costs (including legal fees) incurred by the Supplier:

    (a) in any successful application for an injunction to prevent disclosure by the Authority of Exempt Information; and

    (b) in any application for judicial review of a decision of the Authority to disclose information where disclosure by the Authority is held by such judicial review to have been unnecessary, unwarranted or unlawful.

Schedule [X]

Exempt Information

[List all information which the Supplier wishes to protect from disclosure]   **6–021**

Option 3

1. Definitions

"Potentially Exempt Information"	means the information (including but not limited to any document, report, contract or other material containing information) listed in [Schedule [X]], which information may be updated by the parties from time to time.
"FOIA"	means the Freedom of Information Act 2000 and all regulations made thereunder from time to time or any superseding or amending enactment and regulations.

6–022

2. Freedom of Information

6–023   2.1   The Supplier acknowledges that the Authority is subject to legal duties under FOIA which may require the Authority to disclose on request information relating to this Agreement or which otherwise relates to the Supplier.

2.2   The Authority acknowledges that certain information provided by the Supplier to the Authority under this Agreement constitutes information which is confidential to the Supplier or comprises personal information about the Supplier's personnel or third party personnel or which is information which would be prejudicial to the Supplier's commercial interests if disclosed to a third party.

2.3   The Supplier agrees that the Authority shall be entitled to disclose information in whatever form pursuant to a request made under FOIA save that in relation to any information which is Potentially Exempt Information the Authority shall use reasonable endeavours to notify the Supplier promptly of any request and before making any disclosure of Potentially Exempt Information the Authority shall take account of representations made within a reasonable time by the Supplier about the applicability to such Potentially Exempt Information of the FOIA Exemptions.

2.4   The Authority shall not:

(a) confirm or deny that information is held by the Authority; or

(b) disclose information requested

to the extent that in the Authority's opinion the information is eligible in the circumstances for a FOIA Exemption and therefore that the Authority may lawfully refrain from doing either of the things described in parts (a) and (b) of this Clause 2.4.

2.5   The Authority shall indemnify the Supplier for any and all costs (including legal fees) incurred by the Supplier:

(a) in any successful application for an injunction to prevent disclosure by the Authority of Exempt Information; and

(b) in any application for judicial review of a decision of the Authority to disclose information where disclosure by the Authority is held by such judicial review to have been unnecessary, unwarranted or unlawful.

Schedule [X]

Potentially Exempt Information

[The list below is for illustration only]   6–024

1. The bid documentation for [*name of project*] and all correspondence relating to it.

2. All documentation relating to [*name of Supplier*] pricing and financial modelling.

3. All documentation relating to technical solutions provided to the Authority.

4. All documentation relating to third party contractors of [*name of Supplier*].

5. All documentation relating to benchmarking exercises.

6. [*Other*]

7. The following clauses of this Agreement: [*insert list*].

APPENDIX 1

FREEDOM OF INFORMATION ACT—TABLE OF EXEMPTIONS

7–001

Section	Exemption Title	Status (absolute or qualifed)	Duration	Conclusive certificate?
21	Information accessible to the applicant by other means	Absolute (but does not apply to the duty to confirm or deny)	Unlimited*	
22	Information intended for future publication	Qualified	Unlimited*	
23	Information supplied by, or relating to, bodies dealing with security matters	Absolute[1]	Unlimited	Yes
24	National security	Qualified	Unlimited	Yes
26	Defence	Qualified	Unlimited	
27	International relations	Qualified	Unlimited	
28	Relations within the United Kingdom	Qualified	30 years	
29	The economy	Qualified	Unlimited	
30	Investigations and proceedings conducted by public authorities	Qualified	Unlimited (except for s.30(1) which lasts for 30 years)	
31	Law enforcement	Qualified	100 years	
32	Court records etc	Absolute	30 years	
33	Audit functions	Qualified	30 years	

* But note that the exemption falls away if information is 30 years old and has been transferred to the Public Records Office

[1] Section 23 continues to apply to historical records held at the Public Records Office, but only as a qualified exemption.

Section	Exemption Title	Status (absolute or qualifed)	Duration	Conclusive certificate?
34	Parliamentary privilege	Absolute	Unlimited	Yes
35	Formulation of government policy etc	Qualified	30 years	
36	Prejudice to the effective conduct of public affairs	Qualified (except in relation to information held by the House of Commons or the House of Lords, for which it is absolute)	30 years	Yes[2]
37	Communications with Her Majesty, etc and honours	Qualified	30 years (s.37(1)(a)) 60 years (s.37(1)(b))	
38	Health and safety	Qualified	Unlimited	
39	Environmental information	Qualified	Unlimited	
40	Personal information	Absolute (except where s.40(2) applies because disclosure would contravene a notice given under s.10 of the DPA)	Unlimited	
41	Information provided in confidence	Absolute	Unlimited	
42	Legal professional privilege	Qualified[3]	30 years	
43	Commercial interests	Qualified[4]	30 years	
44	Prohibitions on disclosure	Absolute	Unlimited	

[2] But only in relation to information held by either House of Parliament.
[3] But note the wording of s.42(2) in relation to the duty to confirm or deny.
[4] Note that there is no exemption to the duty to confirm or deny where the information is a trade secret.

APPENDIX 2

OFFICE OF GOVERNMENT COMMERCE FOI (CIVIL PROCUREMENT) POLICY AND GUIDANCE

This Appendix reproduces Annex A to the OGC Civil Procurement Policy **8–001** and Guidance paper. The document itself provides policy and guidance on how requests for civil-procurement related information under FOIA should be handled. It effectively sets out the government's initial view of the application of FOIA to public procurement information. In particular, the document contains:

(a) general guidance on freedom of information procurement issues;

(b) OGC policy on the application of key aspects of FOIA, to inform decision making; and

(c) a summary of OGC's disclosure "positions", based on a series of procurement-related "Working Assumptions". These Working Assumptions are the subject of this Appendix, set out in the attached table under headings 1–6.

The full document is available at
www.ogc.gov.uk/embedded_object.asp?docid=1002589.

Appendix 2

8–002 1. General procurement information

Item	Information type	Discussion	Working Assumption decision
1	Information on suppliers compiled from widely available sources (eg product catalogues, press stories)	Already in the public domain, so clear exemption applies. However, requesters could be directed to the original information sources to satisfy their information need.	Not to be released.
2	Information on suppliers aggregated from knowledge gained within the authority through their supplier dealings (eg performance over several contracts). Also includes derived information (eg opinions drawn from data).	If the aggregated information is critical of a supplier and released, it could (but may not) damage commercial interests. If it were known that only information relating to suppliers generally performing well would be disclosed, a refusal to disclose aggregated information on a particular supplier would effectively identify them as performing badly. Anonymised information may generally be disclosed.	Not to be released (except for anonymised information).
3	Information obtained from suppliers and not generally available (future product info, research plans, financial details).	This information will generally have been specifically requested by the authority and supplied with a reasonable expectation it would not be made public. Otherwise, companies may refuse to divulge the information, to the probable detriment of the public interest.	Not to be released.
4	Gateway review reports.	Refer to the Gateway review information Working Assumption.	Refer to the Working Assumption.

2. Initiation information (start of procurement planning up to readiness to issue bid documentation)

Item	Information type	Discussion	Working Assumption decision
1	All vision, strategy and planning documentation, including Business Cases.	The key document in this phase is the Business Case (strategic outline, outline or full). NHS guidelines for PFI/PPP contracts mandates the publication of Business Cases within a month of their final approval, but allows for the possible redacting of information. However, non-PFI work may operate in a different environment and direct correlation may not be appropriate. In some cases, information may be subject to release as a managed process for early supplier involvement. Only disclosure outside of this process is detrimental.	Not to be released in phase (unless part of a managed process for early release of information). Disclose when bid documentation issued.
2	Requirements information.	Early disclosure of requirements, unless part of the procurement strategy, could prejudice the tendering process and give unfair advantage to some suppliers. In some cases, information may be subject to release as a managed process for early supplier involvement. Only disclosure outside of this process is detrimental.	Not to be released in phase.

8–004 3. Tender information (release of tender documents up to selection of preferred bidder)

Item	Information type	Discussion	Working Assumption decision
1	All project management documentation, with the following exceptions.	This covers the typical documentation generated during management of selection when run as a project (*e.g.* Prince 2 products). Demonstrates procurement was properly managed, but release during tendering could damage process.	Not to be released in phase. Disclose when contract let.
2	Project Issue and Risk logs.	These may contain critical information about tenderers.	Not to be released in phase. Decide by case thereafter.
3	All information received from tenderers.	This covers tender documents, correspondence, negotiation notes, etc.	Not to be released in phase (thereafter, see table for following phase).
4	All evaluation information.	Covers evaluation reports.	Not to be released in phase (thereafter, see table for following phase).

4. Contract negotiation information (successful bidder notified up 8–005 to contract signature)

Item	Information type	Discussion	Working Assumption decision
1	Tender information received from unsuccessful bidders.	This covers tender documents, (inc prices). Non-UK case law indicates not in public interest to disclose, although note that exemption would not apply to any information not prejudicial to commercial interests.	Not to be released, except for non-sensitive information.
2	Tender evaluation information on unsuccessful bidders (including ranking).	Although commercially non-sensitive information could be disclosed, the public interest in favour of disclosure of sensitive information is generally weaker than that for winning bidders.	Generally disclose, except for sensitive information.
3	Identity of unsuccessful bidders.	Non-UK case law says no exemptions apply (unless security/H&S related).	Generally disclose (unless security/ H&S related).
4	Evaluation information for successful bidders.	Non-UK case law decided in favour of public interest disclosure.	Generally disclose.
5	Tender information received from successful bidder, with the exceptions below.	General tender information, including total tender price (but not supplier's costing information, see below). Note that if cost information could be deduced from price information (*e.g.* consultancy, where total price = days * day rate), then consultation may be needed before a decision on disclosure is reached.	Generally disclose (unless security/ H&S related).
6	Payment terms.	Non-UK case law is unclear what this covered in the particular case.	Generally disclose after contract signature.
7	Information on the supplier's approach to the work.	Non-UK case law here is unclear, but this is assumed to only apply where the supplier has a unique approach that could be considered a "trade secret".	Generally disclose except for information agreed as "trade secret".
8	Financial models.	For more complex work, detailed models of how the cash flow for both the authority and supplier would be managed over the life of the contract (eg recovering low initial capital charges through incentivised support work).	Not to be released.

Item	Information type	Discussion	Working Assumption decision
9	Price breakdown.	Price breakdowns, without knowledge of the underlying financial model, could be misleading and need proper presentation.	Not to be released (until no longer sensitive).
10	CVs and reference sites.	CV's are likely to come under the Data Protection Act. Reference site information was probably supplied to the bidder in confidence.	Not to be released.
11	Information on supplier's costing mechanisms.	This covers information relating to profit margins, day rates (where used to calculate a fixed price), overhead costs, etc. This may give advantage to a competitor.	Not to be released.
12	Information relating to contract negotiation.	Covers correspondence, meeting minutes, e-mails, contract change notices, etc. Decision will depend on sensitivity and content, and should not comprise suppliers negotiations with sub-contractors or the public authority's negotiations with any third parties.	Generally disclose except for information agreed as commercially sensitive, with time limits.

5. Contract delivery information (from start of work to completion)

Item	Information type	Discussion	Working Assumption decision
1	All project management documentation, with the following exceptions.	This covers the typical documentation generated during management of contract when run as a project (*e.g.* Prince 2 products). Demonstrates project was properly managed.	Generally disclose.
2	Project Risk logs.	The project should be able to explore issues freely and cooperatively between parties. Disclosure would damage this freedom, to the detriment of the project.	Not to be released in phase. Decide by case thereafter.
3	Exception reports.	These may contain critical information about suppliers. Disclosure could prejudice process (due to a reluctance to raise/accept). See discussion under item 2.	Not to be released in phase.
4	Lessons learnt report.	These may contain critical information about suppliers. Disclosure could prevent candour and hence restrict valuable information.	Not to be released.
5	Contract information (general).	Non-UK case law indicates that it is in the public interest to disclose **all** contract information, including total contract price and performance indicators, although commercially sensitive information may need to be removed in some cases.	Generally disclose (unless security/H&S related), but see below for exceptions.
6	Contract information requiring particular attention:		
7	Price breakdown.	See under tender information in previous table	Not to be released (until no longer sensitive).
8	Service level agreements.	Information provides key indicator that proper management is in place. Strong public interest element, probably low commercial impact.	Generally disclose.
9	Performance measurement procedures.	As above, with possibly even lower commercial impact.	Generally disclose.

Item	Information type	Discussion	Working Assumption decision
10	Incentive mechanisms.	Information provides key indicator that proper management is in place. Details of the mechanisms may be considered sensitive by suppliers, but there is a strong public interest element in disclosure. Summary information should be considered.	Generally disclose.
11	Criteria for recovering sums.	Stronger commercial argument, since it would indicate financial risk to which company is exposed. Subsequent knowledge of performance would mean financial impact could be deduced, possibly affecting company's financial position.	Generally disclose, but not full details.
12	Pricing mechanisms.	Covers milestone payments, price variation mechanisms (*e.g.* fee rate increases per year). Case law supports release of this information, based on public interest in disclosure.	Generally disclose.

6. Contract delivery information (from start of work to completion)—continued

Item	Information type	Discussion	Working Assumption decision
1	Dispute resolution procedures.	Information provides key indicator that proper management is in place. Strong public interest element, probably low commercial impact.	Generally disclose.
2	Invoicing arrangements.	Probably no commercial impact, so exemptions unlikely to apply. However, if they did, it is difficult to see any public interest in non-disclosure.	Generally disclose.
3	Contract management arrangements.	Information provides key indicator that proper management is in place. Strong public interest element, probably low commercial impact.	Generally disclose.
4	Exit strategies and break options.	Information provides key indicator that proper management is in place. Strong public interest element, probably low commercial impact.	Generally disclose.
5	Sub-contractor details.	Covers their identity, management arrangements, flow-down of contract conditions.	Not to be released (except for their identity).
6	Assessing or reporting on contract performance.	This covers information relating to performance against SLAs, KPIs, SPAs, benchmarks, etc. Mostly relevant to longer term service provision. Overall, likely to be in public interest to release, but financial sensitivity for supplier needs to expire.	Generally disclose once any financial sensitivity has expired.
7	Information on sums recovered.	Where contracts have liquidated damages clauses, the information possible is a) have damages been imposed, b) the amounts involved. The former could arguably be disclosed, but the liklihood is that the latter could then be deduced from other information. The latter is probably commercially/ financially damaging (but beware if covered under EIRs), but only for a definable period.	Not to be released until any financial sensitivity has expired.

Item	Information type	Discussion	Working Assumption decision
8	Information on project progress.	Covers progress review minutes, reports, correspondence. More relevant to start/end projects. Disclosure may be in public interest, but supplier reputation could suffer if major project known to be delayed (with fall in share price, loss of bids in progress, etc). Also, important that such information is put in context (*e.g.* delay may be due to new requirements or other valid reasons).	Generally disclose.
9	Product/service verification procedures.	Covers details of test documentation, eg strategy, procedures, acceptance plans. Also covers building acceptance/ commissioning plans. Possible "trade secret" and IPR issues, especially for service companies. Release of detailed procedures to competitors effectively enables re-use by them, possibly giving them competitive advantage.	Generally disclose except where "trade secrets" agreed.
10	Product/service verification results.	Covers results from above activities. Same comments as above, as procedures may be deduced from results.	Generally disclose except where "trade secrets" agreed.
11	Contract change information.	Same arguments as for contract. Disclosure of all information likely to be in the public interest.	As for contract.

APPENDIX 3

CODE OF PRACTICE
(FREEDOM OF INFORMATION ACT
2000, s.45)

**Guidance to public authorities as to the practice
which it would be desirable for them
to follow in connection with the discharge
of their functions under Part I of the
Freedom of Information Act 2000**

Having consulted the Information Commissioner, this Code of Practice is **9–001** issued by the Secretary of State for Constitutional Affairs under section 45 of the Freedom of Information Act 2000 (c.36) on 25 November 2004. The Code provides guidance to public authorities, as defined in the Act, as to the practice which it would, in the Secretary of State's opinion, be desirable for them to follow in connection with the discharge of their functions under Part I of the Act. Laid before Parliament on 25 November 2004 pursuant to section 45(5) of the Freedom of Information Act 2000.

I Introduction

1. This Code of Practice provides guidance to public authorities as **9–002** to the practice which it would, in the opinion of the Secretary of State for Constitutional Affairs, be desirable for them to follow in connection with the discharge of their functions under Part I (Access to information held by public authorities) of the Freedom of Information Act 2000 ("the Act").

2. Words and expressions used in this Code have the same meaning as the same words and expressions used in the Act.

II The provision of advice and assistance to persons making requests for information

3. The following paragraphs of this Code apply in relation to the provision of advice and assistance to persons who propose to make, or have made, requests for information to public authorities. They are intended to provide guidance to public authorities as to the practice which it would be desirable for them

445

to follow in the discharge of their duty under section 16 of the Act.

Advice and assistance to those proposing to make requests:

4. Public authorities should publish their procedures for dealing with requests for information. Consideration should be given to including in these procedures a statement of:

   • what the public authority's usual procedure will be where it does not hold the information requested (see also III— "Transferring requests for information"), and

   • when the public authority may need to consult other public authorities and/or third parties in order to reach a decision on whether the requested information can be released (see also IV —"Consultation with third parties").

5. The procedures should include an address or addresses (including an e-mail address where possible) to which applicants may direct requests for information or for assistance. A telephone number should also be provided, where possible that of a named individual who can provide assistance. These procedures should be referred to in the authority's publication scheme.

6. Staff working in public authorities in contact with the public should bear in mind that not everyone will be aware of the Act, or Regulations made under it, and they will need where appropriate to draw these to the attention of potential applicants who appear unaware of them.

7. Where a person is unable to frame his or her request in writing, the public authority should ensure that appropriate assistance is given to enable that person to make a request for information. Depending on the circumstances, consideration should be given to:

   • advising the person that another person or agency (such as a Citizens Advice Bureau) may be able to assist them with the application, or make the application on their behalf;

   • in exceptional circumstances, offering to take a note of the application over the telephone and then send the note to the applicant for confirmation (in which case the written note of the telephone request, once verified by the applicant and returned, would constitute a written request for information and the statutory time limit for reply would begin when the written confirmation was received).

This list is not exhaustive, and public authorities should be flexible in offering advice and assistance most appropriate to the circumstances of the applicant.

Clarifying the request: 9–003

8. A request for information must adequately specify and describe the information sought by the applicant. Public authorities are entitled to ask for more detail, if needed, to enable them to identify and locate the information sought. Authorities should, as far as reasonably practicable, provide assistance to the applicant to enable him or her to describe more clearly the information requested.

9. Authorities should be aware that the aim of providing assistance is to clarify the nature of the information sought, not to determine the aims or motivation of the applicant. Care should be taken not to give the applicant the impression that he or she is obliged to disclose the nature of his or her interest as a precondition to exercising the rights of access, or that he or she will be treated differently if he or she does (or does not). Public authorities should be prepared to explain to the applicant why they are asking for more information. It is important that the applicant is contacted as soon as possible, preferably by telephone, fax or e-mail, where more information is needed to clarify what is sought.

10. Appropriate assistance in this instance might include:

   • providing an outline of the different kinds of information which might meet the terms of the request;

   • providing access to detailed catalogues and indexes, where these are available, to help the applicant ascertain the nature and extent of the information held by the authority;

   • providing a general response to the request setting out options for further information which could be provided on request.

This list is not exhaustive, and public authorities should be flexible in offering advice and assistance most appropriate to the circumstances of the applicant.

11. In seeking to clarify what is sought, public authorities should bear in mind that applicants cannot reasonably be expected to possess identifiers such as a file reference number, or a description of a particular record, unless this information is made available by the authority for the use of applicants.

Limits to advice and assistance

9–004   12. If, following the provision of such assistance, the applicant still fails to describe the information requested in a way which would enable the authority to identify and locate it, the authority is not expected to seek further clarification. The authority should disclose any information relating to the application which has been successfully identified and found for which it does not propose to claim an exemption. It should also explain to the applicant why it cannot take the request any further and provide details of the authority's complaints procedure and the applicant's rights under section 50 of the Act (see "Complaints Procedure" in section VI).

Advice and assistance and fees

13. Where the applicant indicates that he or she is not prepared to pay the fee notified in any fees notice given to the applicant, the authority should consider whether there is any information that may be of interest to the applicant that is available free of charge.

14. Where an authority is not obliged to comply with a request for information because, under section 12(1) and regulations made under section 12, the cost of complying would exceed the "appropriate limit" (i.e. cost threshold) the authority should consider providing an indication of what, if any, information could be provided within the cost ceiling. The authority should also consider advising the applicant that by reforming or re-focussing their request, information may be able to be supplied for a lower, or no, fee.

15. An authority is not expected to provide assistance to applicants whose requests are vexatious within the meaning of section 14 of the Act. Guidance on what constitutes a vexatious request can be found in the DCA Handbook—"Guidance on Processing Requests". The Information Commissioner has also issued advice on dealing with vexatious and repetitious requests.

III Transferring requests for information

9–005   16. The following paragraphs apply in any case in which a public authority is not able to comply with a request (or to comply with it in full) because it does not hold the information requested, and proposes, in accordance with section 1(1)(a), to confirm that it does not hold that information.

17. If the authority has reason to believe that some or all of the information requested, but which it does not hold, is held by another public authority, the authority should consider what would be the most helpful way of assisting the applicant with his or her request.

18. In most cases this is likely to involve:

    - contacting the applicant and informing him or her that the information requested may be held by another public authority;

    - suggesting that the applicant re-applies to the authority which the original authority believes may hold the information; and

    - providing him or her with contact details for that authority.

19. However, in some cases the authority to which the original request is made may consider it to be more appropriate to transfer the request to another authority in respect of the information which it does not hold. In such cases, the authority should consult the other authority with a view to ascertaining whether it does in fact hold the information and, if so, whether it is obliged to confirm this under section 1(1) of the Act. If that is the case, the first authority should proceed to consider transferring the request. A request (or part of a request) should not be transferred without confirmation by the second authority that it holds the information, and will confirm as much to the applicant on receipt of a request.

20. Before transferring a request for information to another authority, the original authority should consider:

    - whether a transfer is appropriate; and if so

    - whether the applicant is likely to have any grounds to object to the transfer. If the authority reasonably concludes that the applicant is not likely to object, it may transfer the request without going back to the applicant, but should tell him or her it has done so.

21. Where there are reasonable grounds to believe an applicant is likely to object, the authority should only transfer the request to another authority with his or her consent. If the authority is in any doubt, it may prefer to advise the applicant to make a new request to the other authority, and to inform the applicant that the other authority has confirmed that it holds the information.

22. Where a request or part of a request is transferred from one public authority to another, the receiving authority should comply with its obligations under Part I of the Act in the same way as it would in the case of a request that is received direct from an applicant. The time for complying with such a request should be calculated by regarding the date of transfer as the date of receipt of the request.

23. All transfers of requests should take place as soon as is practicable, and the applicant must be informed as soon as possible once this has been done.

24. Where a public authority is unable either to advise the applicant which public authority holds, or may hold, the requested information or to facilitate the transfer of the request to another authority (or considers it inappropriate to do so) it should consider what advice, if any, it can provide to the applicant to enable him or her to pursue his or her request.

IV Consultation with Third Parties

9–006

25. There are many circumstances in which:

- requests for information may relate to persons other than the applicant and the authority; or

- disclosure of information is likely to affect the interests of persons other than the applicant or the authority.

26. It is highly recommended that public authorities take appropriate steps to ensure that such third parties, and those who supply public authorities with information, are aware of the public authority's duty to comply with the Freedom of Information Act, and that therefore information will have to be disclosed upon request unless an exemption applies.

27. In some cases is will be necessary to consult, directly and individually, with such persons in order to determine whether or not an exemption applies to the information requested, or in order to reach a view on whether the obligations in section 1 of the Act arise in relation to that information. But in a range of other circumstances it will be good practice to do so; for example where a public authority proposes to disclose information relating to third parties, or information which is likely to affect their interests, reasonable steps should, where appropriate, be taken to give them advance notice, or failing that, to draw it to their attention afterwards.

28. In some cases, it may also be appropriate to consult such third parties about such matters as whether any further explanatory material or advice should be given to the applicant together with the information in question. Such advice may, for example, refer to any restrictions (including copyright restrictions) which may exist as to the subsequent use which may be made of such information.

29. No decision to release information which has been supplied by one government department to another should be taken without

450

first notifying, and where appropriate consulting, the department from which the information originated.

30. Where information to be disclosed relates to a number of third parties, or the interests of a number of third parties may be affected by a disclosure, and those parties have a representative organisation which can express views on behalf of those parties, the authority may consider whether it would be sufficient to notify or consult with that representative organisation. If there is no representative organisation, the authority may consider that it would be sufficient to notify or consult with a representative sample of the third parties in question.

V Freedom of Information and confidentiality obligations

31. Public authorities should bear clearly in mind their obligations under the Freedom of Information Act when preparing to enter into contracts which may contain terms relating to the disclosure of information by them.　　**9–007**

32. When entering into contracts with non-public authority contractors, public authorities may be asked to accept confidentiality clauses, for example to the effect that information relating to the terms of the contract, its value and performance will not be disclosed. Public authorities should carefully consider the compatibility of such terms with their obligations under the Act. It is important that both the public authority and the contractor are aware of the limits placed by the Act on the enforceability of such confidentiality clauses.

33. The Act does, however, recognise that there will be circumstances and respects in which the preservation of confidentiality between public authority and contractor is appropriate, and must be maintained, in the public interest.

34. Where there is good reason, as recognised by the terms of the exemption provisions of the Act, to include non-disclosure provisions in a contract, public authorities should consider the desirability where possible of making express provision in the contract identifying the information which should not be disclosed and the reasons for confidentiality. Consideration may also be given to including provision in contracts as to when consultation with third parties will be necessary or appropriate before the information is disclosed.

35. Similar considerations will apply to the offering or acceptance of confidentiality obligations by public authorities in non-contractual circumstances. There will be circumstances in which such obligations will be an appropriate part of the acquisition of

information from third parties and will be protected by the terms of the exemption provisions of the Act. But again, it will be important that both the public authority and the third party are aware of the limits placed by the Act on the enforceability of expectations of confidentiality, and for authorities to ensure that such expectations are created only where to do so is consistent with their obligations under the Act.

VI Complaints procedure

9–008

36. Each public authority should have a procedure in place for dealing with complaints in relation to its handling of requests for information. The same procedure could also usefully handle complaints in relation to the authority's publication scheme. If the complaints cannot be dealt with swiftly and satisfactorily on an informal basis, the public authority should inform persons if approached by them of the details of its internal complaints procedure, and how to contact the Information Commissioner, if the complainant wishes to write to him about the matter.

37. When communicating any decision made to refuse a request, in reliance on an exemption provision, public authorities are obliged, under section 17(7) of the Act to notify the applicant of particulars of the procedure provided by the public authority for dealing with complaints (or to state that it does not have one). In doing so, they should provide full details of their own complaints procedure, including how to make a complaint and inform the applicant of the right to complain to the Commissioner under section 50 if he or she is still dissatisfied following the authority's review.

38. Any written reply from the applicant (including one transmitted by electronic means) expressing dissatisfaction with an authority's response to a request for information should be treated as a complaint, as should any written communication from a person who considers that the authority is not complying with its publication scheme. These communications should be handled in accordance with the authority's complaints procedure, even if, in the case of a request for information under the general rights of access, the applicant does not expressly state his or her desire for the authority to review its decision or its handling of the application.

39. The complaints procedure should provide a fair and thorough review of handling issues and of decisions taken pursuant to the Act, including decisions taken about where the public interest lies in respect of exempt information. It should enable a fresh decision to be taken on a reconsideration of all the factors relevant to the issue. Complaints procedures should be as clear and simple as possible. They should encourage a prompt determination of the complaint.

40. Where the complaint concerns a request for information under the general rights of access, the review should be undertaken by someone senior to the person who took the original decision, where this is reasonably practicable. The public authority should in any event undertake a full re-evaluation of the case, taking into account the matters raised by the investigation of the complaint.

41. In all cases, complaints should be acknowledged promptly and the complainant should be informed of the authority's target date for determining the complaint. Where it is apparent that determination of the complaint will take longer than the target time (for example because of the complexity of the particular case), the authority should inform the applicant and explain the reason for the delay. The complainant should always be informed of the outcome of his or her complaint.

42. Authorities should set their own target times for dealing with complaints; these should be reasonable, and subject to regular review. Each public authority should publish its target times for determining complaints and information as to how successful it is with meeting those targets.

43. Records should be kept of all complaints and of their outcome. Authorities should have procedures in place for monitoring complaints and for reviewing, and, if necessary, amending, procedures for dealing with requests for information where such action is indicated by more than occasional reversals of initial decisions.

44. Where the outcome of a complaint is a decision that information should be disclosed which was previously withheld, the information in question should be disclosed as soon as practicable and the applicant should be informed how soon this will be.

45. Where the outcome of a complaint is that the procedures within an authority have not been properly followed by the authority's staff, the authority should apologise to the applicant. The authority should also take appropriate steps to prevent similar errors occurring in future.

46. Where the outcome of a complaint is that an initial decision to withhold information is upheld, or is otherwise in the authority's favour, the applicant should be informed of his or her right to apply to the Commissioner, and be given details of how to make an application, for a decision on whether the request for information has been dealt with in accordance with the requirements of Part I of the Act.

APPENDIX 4

CODE OF PRACTICE
ON

(1) THE MANAGEMENT OF RECORDS
BY PUBLIC AUTHORITIES
AND

(2) THE TRANSFER AND REVIEW OF
PUBLIC RECORDS UNDER THE
FREEDOM OF INFORMATION ACT
2000

The Lord Chancellor, after consulting the Information Commissioner and the appropriate Northern Ireland Minister, issues the following Code of Practice pursuant to section 46 of the Freedom of Information Act.

Laid before Parliament on 20 November 2002 pursuant to section 46(6) of the Freedom of Information Act 2000.

Introduction

1. The aims of the Code are: 10–001

   1. **to set out practices which public authorities, and bodies subject to the Public Records Act 1958 and the Public Records Act (NI) 1923, should follow in relation to the creation, keeping, management and destruction of their records (Part I of the Code); and**

   2. **to describe the arrangements which public record bodies should follow in reviewing public records and transferring them to the Public Record Office or to**

places of deposit or to the Public Record Office of Northern Ireland (Part II of the Code).

2. This Code refers to records in all technical or physical formats.

3. Part One of the Code provides a framework for the management of records of public authorities and of bodies subject to the Public Records Act 1958 and the Public Records Act (NI) 1923, and Part Two deals with the review and transfer of public records. More detailed guidance on both themes may be obtained from published standards. Those which support the objectives of this Code most directly are listed at Annex A.

4. Words and expressions used in this Code have the same meaning as the same words and expressions used in the FOIA.

Part I: Records Management

5. Functional responsibility

10–002   5.1   The records management function should be recognised as a specific corporate programme within an authority and should receive the necessary levels of organisational support to ensure effectiveness. It should bring together responsibilities for records in all formats, including electronic records, throughout their life cycle, from planning and creation through to ultimate disposal. It should have clearly defined responsibilities and objectives, and the resources to achieve them. It is desirable that the person, or persons, responsible for the records management function should also have either direct responsibility or an organisational connection with the person or persons responsible for freedom of information, data protection and other information management issues.

6. Policy

10–003   6.1   An authority should have in place an overall policy statement, endorsed by top management and made readily available to staff at all levels of the organisation, on how it manages its records, including electronic records.

6.2   This policy statement should provide a mandate for the performance of all records and information management functions. In particular, it should set out an authority's commitment to create, keep and manage records which document its principal activities. The policy should also outline the role of records management and its relationship to the authority's overall strategy; define roles and responsibilities including the responsibility of individuals to document their actions and decisions in the authority's records, and to dispose of records; provide a framework for supporting standards, procedures and guidelines; and indicate the way in which compliance with the policy and its supporting standards, procedures and guidelines will be monitored.

6.3   The policy statement should be reviewed at regular intervals (at least once every three years) and, if appropriate, amended to maintain its relevance.

7.   Human Resources

7.1   A designated member of staff of appropriate seniority should **10–004** have lead responsibility for records management within the authority. This lead role should be formally acknowledged and made known throughout the authority.

7.2   Staff responsible for records management should have the appropriate skills and knowledge needed to achieve the aims of the records management programme. Responsibility for all aspects of record keeping should be specifically defined and incorporated in the role descriptions or similar documents.

7.3   Human resource policies and practices in organisations should address the need to recruit and retain good quality staff and should accordingly support the records management function in the following areas:

- the provision of appropriate resources to enable the records management function to be maintained across all of its activities;

- the establishment and maintenance of a scheme, such as a competency framework, to identify the knowledge, skills and corporate competencies required in records and information management;

- the regular review of selection criteria for posts with records management duties to ensure currency and compliance with best practice;

- the regular analysis of training needs;

- the establishment of a professional development programme for staff with records management duties;

- the inclusion in induction training programmes for all new staff of an awareness of records issues and practices.

8.   Active Records Management

Record Creation

10–005   8.1   Each operational/business unit of an authority should have in place an adequate system for documenting its activities. This system should take into account the legislative and regulatory environments in which the authority works.

8.2   Records of a business activity should be complete and accurate enough to allow employees and their successors to undertake appropriate actions in the context of their responsibilities, to:

- facilitate an audit or examination of the business by anyone so authorised,

- protect the legal and other rights of the authority, its clients and any other person affected by its actions, and

- provide authenticity of the records so that the evidence derived from them is shown to be credible and authoritative.

8.3   Records created by the authority should be arranged in a record keeping system that will enable the authority to obtain the maximum benefit from the quick and easy retrieval of information.

Record Keeping

10–006   8.4   Installing and maintaining an effective records management programme depends on knowledge of what records are held, in what form they are made accessible, and their relationship to organisational functions. An information survey or record audit will meet this requirement, help to promote control over the records, and provide valuable data for developing records appraisal and disposal procedures.

8.5   Paper and electronic record keeping systems should contain metadata (descriptive and technical documentation) to enable the system and the records to be understood and to be operated efficiently, and to provide an administrative context for effective management of the records.

8.6   The record-keeping system, whether paper or electronic, should include a set of rules for referencing, titling, indexing and, if appropriate, security marking of records. These should be easily understood and should enable the efficient retrieval of information.

Record Maintenance

8.7   The movement and location of records should be controlled to ensure that a record can be easily retrieved at any time, that any outstanding issues can be dealt with, and that there is an auditable trail of record transactions.

8.8   Storage accommodation for current records should be clean and tidy, and it should prevent damage to the records. Equipment used for current records should provide storage which is safe from unauthorised access and which meets fire regulations, but which allows maximum accessibility to the information commensurate with its frequency of use. When records are no longer required for the conduct of current business, their placement in a designated records centre rather than in offices may be a more economical and efficient way to store them. Procedures for handling records should take full account of the need to preserve important information.

8.9   A contingency or business recovery plan should be in place to provide protection for records which are vital to the continued functioning of the authority.

9.   Disposal Arrangements

9.1   It is particularly important under FOI that the disposal of records—which is here defined as the point in their lifecycle when they are either transferred to an archives or destroyed—is undertaken in accordance with clearly established policies which have been formally adopted by authorities and which are enforced by properly authorised staff.   **10–007**

Record Closure

9.2   Records should be closed as soon as they have ceased to be of active use other than for reference purposes. As a general rule, files should be closed after five years and, if action continues, a further file should be opened. An indication that a file of paper records or folder of electronic records has been closed should be shown on the record itself as well as noted in the index or database of the files/folders. Wherever possible, information on the intended disposal of electronic records should be included in the metadata when the record is created.   **10–008**

9.3   The storage of closed records awaiting disposal should follow accepted standards relating to environment, security and physical organisation.

Appraisal Planning and Documentation

9.4   In order to make their disposal policies work effectively and for those to which the FOIA applies to provide the information   **10–009** required under FOI legislation, authorities need to have in place systems for managing appraisal and for recording the disposal decisions made. An assessment of the volume and nature of records due for disposal, the time taken to appraise records, and the risks associated with destruction or delay in appraisal will provide information to support an authority's resource planning and workflow arrangements.

9.5 An appraisal documentation system will ensure consistency in records appraisal and disposal. It should show what records are designated for destruction, the authority under which they are to be destroyed and when they are to be destroyed. It should also provide background information on the records, such as legislative provisions, functional context and physical arrangement. This information will provide valuable data for placing records selected for preservation into context and will enable future records managers to provide evidence of the operation of their selection policies.

Record Selection

10–010 9.6 Each authority should maintain a selection policy which states in broad terms the functions from which records are likely to be selected for permanent preservation and the periods for which other records should be retained. The policy should be supported by or linked to disposal schedules which should cover all records created, including electronic records. Schedules should be arranged on the basis of series or collection and should indicate the appropriate disposal action for all records (*e.g.* review after x years; destroy after y years).

9.7 Records selected for permanent preservation and no longer in regular use by the authority should be transferred as soon as possible to an archival institution that has adequate storage and public access facilities (see Part Two of this Code for arrangements for bodies subject to the Public Records Acts).

9.8 Records not selected for permanent preservation and which have reached the end of their administrative life should be destroyed in as secure a manner as is necessary for the level of confidentiality or security markings they bear. A record of the destruction of records, showing their reference, description and date of destruction should be maintained and preserved by the records manager. Disposal schedules would constitute the basis of such a record.

9.9 If a record due for destruction is known to be the subject of a request for information, destruction should be delayed until disclosure has taken place or, if the authority has decided not to disclose the information, until the complaint and appeal provisions of the FOIA have been exhausted.

10. Management of Electronic Records

10.1 The principal issues for the management of electronic records **10–011** are the same as those for the management of any record. They include, for example the creation of authentic records, the tracking of records and disposal arrangements. However, the means by which these issues are addressed in the electronic environment will be different.

10.2 Effective electronic record keeping requires:

- a clear understanding of the nature of electronic records;

- the creation of records and metadata necessary to document business processes: this should be part of the systems which hold the records;

- the maintenance of a structure of folders to reflect logical groupings of records;

- the secure maintenance of the integrity of electronic records;

- the accessibility and use of electronic records for as long as required (which may include their migration across systems);

- the application of appropriate disposal procedures, including procedures for archiving; and

- the ability to cross reference electronic records to their paper counterparts in a mixed environment.

10.3 Generic requirements for electronic record management systems are set out in the 1999 Public Record Office statement Functional Requirements and Testing of Electronic Records Management Systems. Authorities are encouraged to use these, and any subsequent versions, as a model when developing their specifications for such systems.

10.4 Audit trails should be provided for all electronic information and documents. They should be kept securely and should be available for inspection by authorised personnel. The BSI document *Principles of Good Practice for Information Management* (PD0010) recommends audits at predetermined intervals for particular aspects of electronic records management.

10.5 Authorities should seek to conform to the provisions of BSI DISC PD0008—*A Code of Practice for Legal Admissibility and Evidential Weight of Information Stored Electronically (2nd edn)*—especially for those records likely to be required as evidence.

Part II: Review and Transfer of Public Records

10–012

11.1 This part of the Code relates to the arrangements which authorities should follow to ensure the timely and effective review and transfer of public records. Accordingly, it is relevant only to authorities which are subject to the Public Records Acts 1958 and 1967 or to the Public Records Act (NI) 1923. The general purpose of this part of the Code is to facilitate the performance by the Public Record Office, the Public Record Office of Northern Ireland and other public authorities of their functions under the Freedom of Information Act.

11.2 Under the Public Records Acts, records selected for preservation may be transferred either to the Public Record Office or to places of deposit appointed by the Lord Chancellor. This Code applies to all such transfers. For guidance on which records may be transferred to which institution, and on the disposition of UK public records relating to Northern Ireland, see the Public Record Office Acquisition Policy (1998) and the Public Record Office Disposition Policy (2000).

11.3 In reviewing records for public release, authorities should ensure that public records become available to the public at the earliest possible time in accordance with the FOIA.

11.4 Authorities which have created or are otherwise responsible for public records should ensure that they operate effective arrangements to determine:

a. which records should be selected for permanent preservation; and

b. which records should be released to the public.

These arrangements should be established and operated under the supervision of the Public Record Office or, in Northern Ireland, in conjunction with the Public Record Office of Northern Ireland. The objectives and arrangements for the review of records for release are described in greater detail below.

11.5 In carrying out their review of records for release to the public, authorities should observe the following points:

11.5.1 transfer to the Public Record Office must take place by the time the records are 30 years old, unless the Lord Chancellor gives authorisation for them to be retained for a longer period of time (see section 3(4) of the Public Records Act 1958). By agreement with the Public Record Office, transfer and release may take place before 30 years;

11.5.2 review—for selection and release—should therefore take place before the records in question are 30 years old.

11.5.3 in Northern Ireland transfer under the Public Records Act (NI) 1923 to the Public Record Office of Northern Ireland is normally at 20 years.

11.6 In the case of records to be transferred to the Public Record Office or to a place of deposit appointed under section 4 of the Public Records Act 1958, or to the Public Record Office of Northern Ireland, the purpose of the review of records for release to the public is to:

- consider which information must be available to the public on transfer because no exemptions under the FOIA apply;

- consider which information must be available to the public at 30 years because relevant exemptions in the FOIA have ceased to apply;

- consider whether the information must be released in the public interest, notwithstanding the application of an exemption under the FOIA; and

- consider which information merits continued protection in accordance with the provisions of the FOIA.

11.7 If the review results in the identification of specified information **10–014** which the authorities consider ought not to be released under the terms of the FOIA, the authorities should prepare a schedule identifying this information precisely, citing the relevant exemption(s), explaining why the information may not be released and identifying a date at which either release would be appropriate or a date at which the case for release should be reconsidered. Where the information is environmental information to which the exemption at Section 39 of the FOIA applies, the schedule should cite the appropriate exception in the Environmental Information Regulations. This schedule must be submitted to the Public Record Office or, in Northern Ireland, to the Public Record Office of Northern Ireland prior to transfer which must be before the records containing the information are 30 years old (in the case of the Public Record

Office) or 20 years old (in the case of the Public Record Office of Northern Ireland). Authorities should consider whether parts of records might be released if the sensitive information were blanked out.

11.8 In the first instance, the schedule described in 11.7 is to be submitted to the Public Record Office for review and advice. The case in favour of withholding the records for a period longer than 30 years is then considered by the Advisory Council. The Advisory Council may respond as follows:

a. by accepting that the information may be withheld for longer than 30 years and earmarking the records for release or re-review at the date identified by the authority;

b. by accepting that the information may be withheld for longer than 30 years but asking the authority to reconsider the later date designated for release or re-review;

c. by questioning the basis on which it is deemed that the information may be withheld for longer than 30 years and asking the authority to reconsider the case;

d. by advising the Lord Chancellor if it is not satisfied with the responses it receives from authorities on particular cases;

e. by taking such other action as it deems appropriate within its role as defined in the Public Records Act.

In Northern Ireland there are separate administrative arrangements requiring that schedules are submitted to a Sensitivity Review Group consisting of representatives of different departments. The Sensitivity Review Group has the role of advising public authorities as to the appropriateness or otherwise of releasing records.

10–015 11.9 For the avoidance of doubt, none of the actions described in this Code affects the statutory rights of access established under the FOIA. Requests for information in public records transferred to the Public Record Office or to a place of deposit appointed under section 4 of the Public Records Act 1958 or to the Public Record Office of Northern Ireland will be dealt with on a case by case basis in accordance with the provisions of the FOIA.

11.10 Where records are transferred to the Public Record Office or a place of deposit before they are 30 years old, they should be designated by the transferring department or agency for immediate release unless an exemption applies: there will be no formal review of these designations.

11.11 When an exemption has ceased to apply under section 63 of the FOIA the records will become automatically available to members of the public on the day specified in the finalised schedule (i.e. the schedule after it has been reviewed by the Advisory Council). In other cases, if the authority concerned wishes further to extend the period during which the information is to be withheld in accordance with the FOIA, it should submit a further schedule explaining the sensitivity of the information. This is to be done before the expiry of the period stated in the earlier schedule. The Public Record Office and Advisory Council will then review the schedule in accordance with the process described in paragraph 11.8 above. In Northern Ireland, Ministerial approval is required for any further extension of the stated period.

11.12 In reviewing records an authority may identify those which are appropriate for retention within the department, after they are 30 years old, under section 3(4) of the Public Records Act 1958. Applications must be submitted to the Public Record Office for review and advice. The case in favour of retention beyond the 30 year period will then be considered by the Advisory Council. The Advisory Council will consider the case for retaining individual records unless there is already in place a standing authorisation by the Lord Chancellor for the retention of a whole category of records. It will consider such applications on the basis of the guidance in chapter 9 of the White Paper *Open Government* (Cm 2290, 1993) or subsequent revisions of government policy on retention.

Annex A 10–016

Standards Accepted in Records Management

British Standards (BSI)

BS 4783	Storage, transportation and maintenance of media for use in data processing and information storage
BS 7799	Code of practice for information security management
BS ISO 15489-1	Information and Documentation—Records Management—Part 1: General
BSI DISC PD0008	Code of practice for legal admissibility and evidential weight of information stored on electronic document management systems
BSI DISC PD0010	Principles of good practice for information management

BSI DISC PD0012   Guide to the practical implications of the Data Protection Act 1998

Public Record Office standards for the management of public records

The Public Record Office publishes standards, guidance and toolkits on the management of public records, in whatever format, covering their entire life cycle.

APPENDIX 5

CODE OF PRACTICE ON THE DISCHARGE OF THE OBLIGATIONS OF PUBLIC AUTHORITIES UNDER THE ENVIRONMENTAL INFORMATION REGULATIONS 2004 (SI 2004 No. 3391)

The Secretary of State, after consulting the Information Commissioner, **11–001** issues the following Code of Practice pursuant to Regulation 16 of the Environmental Information Regulations 2004.

Laid before Parliament on 16 February 2005 pursuant to Regulation 16 of the Environmental Information Regulations.

I Training

1. All communications to a public authority, including those not in **11–002** writing and those transmitted by electronic means, potentially amount to a request for information within the meaning of the EIR, and if they do they must be dealt with in accordance with the provisions of the EIR. It is therefore essential that everyone working in a public authority who deals with correspondence, or who otherwise may be required to provide information, is familiar with the requirements of the EIR and this Code in addition to the FOIA and the other Codes of Practice issued under its provisions, and takes account of any relevant guidance on good practice issued by the Commissioner. Authorities should also ensure that proper training is provided.

2. Requests for environmental information may come in the form of verbal requests which has specific implications for training provision.

3. In planning and delivering training, authorities should be aware of other provisions affecting the disclosure of information such as the

467

FOIA, the Data Protection Act 1998, and anti-discrimination legislation (such as the Disability Discrimination Act).

II Proactive Dissemination of Information

11–003

4. Under Regulation 4, a public authority has a duty to progressively make information available to the public by electronic means which are easily accessible, and to take reasonable steps to organize information relevant to its functions with a view to active and systematic dissemination.

5. Consideration should be given to making web sites accessible to all and simple to use, so that information can be readily found, for example by enabling search functions and having an alphabetical directory as well as tree structures. Information should not be "buried" on a site.

6. Public authorities should consider how to publicise applicants' rights to information, for example as part of general information on services provided by the authority.

7. When public authorities are considering what information to disseminate proactively, they should not restrict themselves to the minimum requirements as listed in the Directive. For example, consideration should be given to disseminating frequently requested information, which will reduce individual requests for such information in the future.

III The Provision of advice and assistance to persons making requests for information

11–004

8. The provision of advice and assistance to persons making requests for environmental information differs from that provided to those making general requests for information under FOIA:

- requests for environmental information need not be in writing;

- EIR contains no equivalent to the "appropriate limit" exemption under section 12 of the FOIA; and

- the duty to provide advice and assistance under EIR requires the public authority to request that the applicant provide more particulars within 20 working days of the request where a request is formulated in too general a manner.

9. Every public authority should be ready to provide advice and assistance, including but not necessarily limited to the steps set out below. This advice and assistance should be available to those

who propose to make, or have made requests and help them to make good use of the Regulations. The duty on the public authority is to provide advice and assistance "so far as it would be reasonable to expect the authority to do so".

10. Appropriate assistance might include:

   – providing an outline of the different kinds of information that might meet the terms of the request;

   – providing access to detailed catalogues and indexes, where these are available, to help the applicant ascertain the nature and extent of the information held by the authority;

   – providing a general response to the request setting out options for further information that could be provided on request;

   – advising the person that another person or agency (such as a Citizens Advice Bureau) may be able to assist them with the application or make the application on their behalf.

11. This list is not exhaustive and public authorities should be flexible **11–005** in offering advice and assistance most appropriate to the circumstances of the applicant.

12. Public authorities should publish their procedures for dealing with requests for information. These procedures may include what the public authority's usual procedure will be where it does not hold the information requested. (See also VI—"Transferring requests for information"). It may also alert potential applicants to the fact that the public authority may want to consult other public authorities and/or third parties in order to reach a decision on whether the requested information can be released. Potential applicants may wish to be notified before any transfer of request or consultation is made. If this is the case, the published procedure should therefore alert them to say so in their applications. (See also VII—"Consultation with third parties".) The procedures should include an address or addresses (including an e-mail address where possible) to which applicants may direct requests for information or for assistance. A telephone number should also be provided and where possible the name of an individual who can provide assistance. These procedures should be referred to in the authority's publication scheme where it has one.

13. Public authorities may wish to consider publishing their procedures for reviewing refusals for requests. In addition, public authorities will also wish to consider providing information about other access regimes (where appropriate), provide guidance about frequently requested information, and provide information relating to previous disclosures.

14. Staff in public authorities in contact with the public should bear in mind that not everyone will be aware of the EIR or the FOIA and they should draw the legislation to the attention of potential applicants who appear unaware of them. Any question which cannot be dealt with on the spot hould be treated as a request for information.

15. A request for information under the EIR can be in any form and need not be in writing. However, for a response to be made by the public authority it will need contact details to either provide the information or refuse the request. A request in writing includes a request transmitted by electronic means. Where a person finds it difficult to specify very clearly the nature of their request, the public authority should ensure that appropriate assistance is given to enable that person to make a request for information. For example, if a request is formulated in too general a manner the public authority shall, as soon as possible and not later than 20 working days after receipt of the request, ask the applicant to provide more particulars and shall assist them in doing so. However, Public Authorities should be aware of the dangers of overbureaucratising procedures when responding to requests for routine information.

Clarifying the Request

11–006

16. Where the applicant does not describe the information sought in a way which would enable the public authority to identify or locate it, or the request is ambiguous, the authority should, as far as practicable, provide assistance to the applicant to enable him or her to describe more clearly the information requested. Authorities should be aware that the aim of providing assistance is to clarify the nature of the information sought, not to determine the aims or motivation of the applicant. Care should be taken not to give the applicant the impression that he or she is obliged to disclose the nature of his or her interest or that he or she will be treated differently if he or she does. It is important that the applicant is contacted as soon as possible, preferably by telephone, fax or e-mail, where more information is needed to clarify what is sought. Public authorities should also be prepared to explain why they are asking for additional information. The 20 day time limit stops running when a request for clarification is issued.

17. In seeking to clarify what is sought, public authorities should bear in mind that applicants cannot reasonably be expected to possess identifiers such as a file reference number, or a description of a particular record, unless this information is made available by the authority for the use of applicants.

18. If, following the provision of such assistance, the applicant is still unable to describe the information requested in a way that would

enable the authority to identify and locate it, the authority is not expected to seek further clarification. The authority should disclose any information relating to the application that has been successfully identified and found that it can disclose. It should also explain to the applicant why it cannot take the request any further and provide details of the authority's complaints procedure and where applicable the applicant's rights under section 50 of the FOIA (see "Complaints Procedure" in section XII below).

19. Where the applicant indicates that he or she is not prepared to pay any charge requested, the authority should consider whether there is any information that may be of interest to the applicant that is available free of charge.

20. There is no EIR equivalent to the "appropriate limit" under section 12 of the FOIA. A public authority is expected to deal with all requests for environmental information. However, cost may be relevant when considering whether to apply the exceptions relating to "manifestly unreasonable" or "too general". Where the applicant makes a request that is clear but which involves the provision of a very large volume of information, and specifies a cost ceiling, the authority should consider providing an indication of what information could be provided within the cost ceiling.

21. There are no special provisions for dealing with requests that appear to be part of an organised campaign. Such requests are to be expected and dealt with in the usual way. Repeatedly requested information may be best made available by means of a publication scheme. Being part of a campaign does not necessarily make a request "manifestly unreasonable".

Form and Format

22. Regulation 6 allows for the applicant to be given the information **11–007** available in a particular form or format unless there is another reasonable approach to supplying the information. A public authority should be flexible, as far as is reasonable, with respect to form and format, taking into account the fact, for example, that some IT users may not be able to read attachments in certain formats, and that some members of the public may prefer paper to electronic copies.

23. Although there is no specific reference in the Regulations to the provision of information in the form of a summary or digest, a request for environmental information may include a request for information to be provided in the form of a digest or summary. This should generally be provided so long as it is reasonably practical to do so, taking into account the cost. Many applicants will find a summary more useful than masses of data, and this

should be taken into account when considering proactive dissemination.

IV Timeliness in dealing with Requests for Information

11–008

24. Requests for information must be responded to within 20 working days. The 20 day time limit can be extended to 40 working days if the complexity and volume of the information requested means that the 20 working days deadline cannot be complied with. Unlike FOIA, there is no provision to further extend the time limit for cases where the public interest has to be balanced.

25. Public authorities are required to comply with all requests for information as soon as possible and they must not delay responding until the end of the 20 working day period under Regulation 5(2)(b) if the information could reasonably have been provided earlier.

26. Public authorities must aim to make all decisions as soon as possible and in any case within 20 working days, including in cases where a public authority needs to consider where the public interest lies. However, it is recognised there will be some instances where, because of the complexity and volume of the information requested it will not be possible to deal with an application within 20 working days. In such cases a public authority is expected to inform the applicant of this as soon as possible and within 20 working days, and should be as specific as possible in their response to the applicant indicating when they will receive the information and the reasons for the delay. The 20 days will halt at the point that the authority issues a request for payment of an advance charge, and commences again at the point payment is received. Authorities must in any case comply with or refuse the request within 40 working days. Authorities may find it helpful to formulate a policy about how to apply the provision on making a time extension.

27. It is of critical importance for the body receiving a request to identify the request for environmental information in the first instance, and then to meet the timetable. Monitoring the timeliness of responses is easiest where requests for information are in writing. Where requests for environmental information are made otherwise than in writing (e.g. by telephone or in person) public authorities will need a system for recording the request. This may, for example, involve making a written note of the request and asking the applicant to confirm its accuracy.

V Charges

11–009

28. The EIR does not require charges to be made but public authorities have discretion to make a reasonable charge for

environmental information. However, if they are providing access to a public register, or if the applicant examines the information at the offices of the public authority or in a drop in library or other place which the public authority makes available for that examination, access to the information shall be free of charge. When making a charge, whether for information that is proactively disseminated or provided on request, the charge must not exceed the cost of producing the information unless that public authority is one entitled to levy a market-based charge for the information, such as a trading fund.

29. Where a public authority proposes to make a charge, a schedule of charges should be made available (including, e.g. a price list for publications, or the charge per unit of work which will be incurred to meet the request). When an advance payment is required, the applicant should be notified and the public authority should invite the applicant to say whether they wish to proceed with the request, or part of it, or whether the request may be met in some other way (for example, by visiting the offices of the public authority to inspect the information or by making use of more easily identifiable data). Where a requirement for advance payment has been notified, the period between the notification and the receipt of payment will be disregarded in determining the response times for meeting requests (Regulation 8(5)). The request will remain active for up to 60 working days from the date of notification. If no payment is received during this time the request lapses but the applicant may make a new application at any time. When a fee payment is received the public authority should release the information promptly and within the appropriate time limit.

30. Public authorities should ensure that any charges they make are reasonable, and in accordance with the EIR and the guidance: *http://www.defra.gov.uk/environment/pubaccess/*

VI Transferring Requests for Information

31. A request whether in writing or received in any other form can **11–010** only be transferred where a public authority receives a request for environmental information that it does not itself hold and which is not held by any other person on its behalf. If a public authority in receipt of a request holds some of the information requested, a transfer can only be made in respect of the information it does not hold but is held by another public authority.

32. Public authorities should bear in mind that "holding" environmental information under the EIR includes holding a copy of a record produced or supplied by another person or body and, unlike FOIA, it extends to holding a record on behalf of another

person or body. Where information is held on behalf of another person or body it will be appropriate to consult on whether the environmental information requested should be supplied unless the outcome can be predicted with reasonable confidence. (See also VII—Consultation with Third Parties). (Special provisions apply to the National Archives and other public record holding bodies under Regulation 17 including the Public Records Office Northern Ireland).

33. The authority receiving the initial request must always deal with that request in accordance with the EIR. When the authority receiving the original request does not hold all the information requested it must still deal with the request for information it does hold. The authority must also advise the applicant that it does not hold part of the requested information, or all of it, whichever applies. However, before doing this, the authority must be certain as to the extent of information requested that it holds itself. If information is freely available via a third party's public register, an authority may point to that register as part of providing advice and assistance, but this does not alter the authority's responsibility to respond to the request, for example if the applicant requests the information in the format in which it is held by the authority.

34. If the authority to whom the initial request was made believes that some or all of the information requested is held by another public authority, the authority should consider what would be the most helpful and expeditious way of assisting the applicant with his or her request. In most cases this is likely to involve:

   – contacting the applicant and informing him or her that the information requested may be held by another public authority;

   – suggesting that the applicant re-applies to the authority that is believed to hold the information;

   – providing him or her with contact details for that authority;

   – if the public authority receiving the request and the authority holding the information are publicly perceived as indelibly linked, explaining to the applicant the difference between the two authorities.

11–011   35. However, in some cases the authority to whom the original request is made may consider it to be more appropriate to transfer the request for information that it does not itself hold to another authority. In such cases, the authority should always consult with the other authority with a view to ascertaining whether it does hold the information and, if so, whether it should transfer the request to it. A request (or part of a request) should not be transferred if there is any reason to doubt that the second authority holds the information. When consulting a second authority the identity of the person requesting the information should not be disclosed unless that person has consented.

36. Before transferring a request for information to another authority, the authority should firstly consider whether a transfer is appropriate. If a transfer is appropriate the authority should first obtain the consent of the applicant who may have valid reasons for not wishing their request to be transferred to a third party. If consent is given the applicant should always be provided with sufficient details concerning the date and destination of transfer.

37. Where a request or part of a request is transferred from one public authority to another, the receiving authority must comply with its obligations under the EIR in the same way as it would for a request that is received direct from an applicant. The time for complying with such a request will be measured from the day that the receiving authority receives the request.

38. All transfers of requests should take place as soon as is practicable, and the applicant should be notified as soon as possible once this has been done by issuing a refusal letter under Regulation 14.

39. Where a public authority is unable either to advise the applicant which public authority holds, or may hold, the requested information or to facilitate the transfer of the request to another authority (or considers it inappropriate to do so) it should consider what advice, if any, it can provide to the applicant to enable him or her to pursue his or her request. In this event the public authority should also issue a refusal letter in accordance with Regulation 14. The refusal letter should explain that the public authority does not hold the information.

VII Consultation with Third Parties

40. Public authorities must always remember that unless an exception   **11–012**
is provided for in the EIR in relation to any particular information, they will be obliged to disclose that information in response to a request. Authorities are not obliged by the EIR to consult in respect of information which may be wholly or jointly owned by third parties, but may make a commitment to do so.

41. All EIR exceptions are subject to the public interest test; unlike FOIA, the EIR contains no "absolute" exceptions. Moreover, lack of consent of a third party does not necessarily preclude disclosure, as in each case the public interest must be balanced. If the public interest in disclosing the information outweighs the

public interest in withholding it, the information must be disclosed. (Information on emissions must be disclosed in accordance with Regulation 12 and personal data must be considered in accordance with DPA requirements).

42. A public authority may consider that consultation is not appropriate where the cost of consulting with third parties would be disproportionate because, for example, many third parties are involved or there has been earlier consultation on the status and sensitivity of the information. It should be noted that in this context "third party" is specifically a person or body affected by the information that is the subject of the consultation. In such cases the authority should consider what is the most reasonable course of action for it to take in light of the requirements of the EIR, the potential effects of disclosure, and the public interest.

43. Where the consent of a number of third parties may be relevant and those parties have a representative organisation that can express views on behalf of those parties the authority may, if it considers consultation appropriate, consider that it would be sufficient to consult that representative organisation. If there is no representative organisation, the authority may consider that it would be sufficient to consult a representative sample of the third parties in question.

44. The fact that the third party has not responded to consultation does not relieve the authority of its duty to disclose information under the EIR, or its duty to reply within the time specified in the EIR.

45. In all cases, it is for the public authority that received the request, not the third party (or representative of the third party) to weigh the public interest and to determine whether or not information should be disclosed under the EIR. A refusal to consent to disclosure by a third party does not in itself mean information should be withheld, although it may indicate interests involved. Note that in the case of public records transferred to a public record office there is a requirement to consult (see Regulation 17).

VIII Environmental information Regulations and Public Sector Contracts

11–013 46. When entering into contracts public authorities should refuse to include contractual terms that purport to restrict the disclosure of environmental information held by the authority and relating to the contract beyond the restrictions permitted by the EIR. Public authorities cannot "contract out" of their obligations under the Regulations. This means that they cannot sign a contract that gives an undertaking to a private firm (or anyone else) that they will not comply with their obligations under the Regulations. Unless an exception provided for under the EIR is applicable in relation to any particular information and the balancing of public interest favours refusal, a public authority will be obliged to disclose that information in response to a request, regardless of the terms of any contract. Where personal data is concerned this will be done in accordance with the requirements of Regulation 13 and the Data Protection Act 1998.

47. When entering into contracts with non-public authority contractors, public authorities may be under pressure to accept confidentiality clauses so that information relating to the terms of the contract, its value and performance will be exempt from disclosure. Public authorities should reject such clauses wherever possible and explain the relevance of the public interest test. Where, exceptionally, it is necessary to include non-disclosure provisions in a contract, an option could be to agree with the contractor a schedule of the contract that clearly identifies information that should not be disclosed. But authorities will need to take care when drawing up any such schedule, and be aware that any restrictions on disclosure provided for could potentially be overridden by their obligations under the EIR, as described above.

48. In any event, public authorities should not agree to hold information "in confidence" which is not in fact confidential in nature. Authorities should be aware that certain exceptions including those for commercial confidentiality, and voluntarily supplied data, are not available when the information requested is about emissions into the environment.

49. Any acceptance of confidentiality provisions must be for good reasons and capable of being justified to the Commissioner.

50. It is for the public authority to disclose information pursuant to the EIR, and not the non-public authority contractor, unless that contractor received the request and is, itself, a body subject to the EIR. However, a public authority may have concerns regarding contractual matters and not wish the contractor to release information without consulting them. In these cases, contracts or other working arrangements should be made to ensure appropriate consultation about the handling of requests for information exchanged between the parties. Any such constraints should be drawn as narrowly as possible and according to the individual circumstances of the case. Apart from such cases, public authorities should not impose terms of secrecy on contractors.

51. With contracts in existence prior to EIR 2004 being enacted, if an authority receives a request for information whose release would

mean an actionable breach of confidence, the authority should refer to the guidance issued by the Information Commissioner: *http://www.informationcommissioner.gov.uk* Public authorities in this position should seek their own legal advice as appropriate.

52. Under the EIR, some contractors, including public utilities that have been privatised, are subject to the requirements of the EIR. *http://www.defra.gov.uk/environment/pubaccess/guidance/ index.htm*

IX Accepting Information in Confidence from Third Parties

11–014

53. A public authority should only accept information from third parties in confidence if it is essential to obtain that information in connection with the exercise of any of the authority's functions and it would not otherwise be provided. Even in these circumstances it will be necessary to explain the relevance of the public interest test and the fact that there could be circumstances in which the public interest in disclosure equals or outweighs the adverse effects of disclosure on a third party. In addition, public authorities should not agree to hold information received from third parties "in confidence" which is not confidential in nature (paragraph 47). Again, acceptance of any confidentiality provisions must be for good reasons, capable of being justified to the Commissioner. (Special provisions apply to archives (paragraph 32)).

X Consultation with Devolved Administrations

11–015

54. Public authorities should consult with the relevant devolved administration before disclosing information provided by or directly concerning that administration, except where:

- the views of the devolved administration can have no effect on the decision of the authority (for example where there is no applicable exception so the information must be disclosed under EIR); or

- where the outcome may be predicted with reasonable confidence and in the circumstances, consultation would be too costly or time consuming.

55. Similarly, the devolved administrations should consult with the relevant non-devolved public authority before disclosing information provided by or directly concerning that authority, except where the views of the public authority can have no effect on the decision whether to disclose, or where consultation would be disproportionate in the circumstances.

XI Refusal of Request

56. Where a request for information is refused or partially refused in accordance with an exception, the EIR requires that the authority notify the applicant which exception has been claimed and why that exception applies. Public authorities should not, unless the statement would involve the disclosure of information which would itself be withheld in accordance with the EIR, merely paraphrase the wording of the exception. They should state clearly in the decision letter the reason why they have decided to apply that exception in the case in question. The EIR also requires authorities, when withholding information, to state the reasons for claiming that the public interest in maintaining the exception outweighs the public interest in disclosure. Public authorities should specify the public interest factors (for and against disclosure) that they have taken into account before reaching the decision (again, unless the statement would involve the disclosure of information which would itself be withheld in accordance with the EIR). They should also include details of the complaints procedure. **11–016**

57. For monitoring purposes public authorities should keep **a record of all** applications where either all or part of the requested information is withheld, the basis on which it was withheld (including the exception or exceptions which were applied), and, where relevant, a full explanation of how the public interest test was applied and the factors which were considered. Public authorities should also keep copies of redacted information, together with a copy of the information that the applicant actually received in case of a subsequent complaint. Senior managers in each public authority will need this information to determine whether cases are being properly considered and whether the reasons for refusals are sound. The information will also be required if the applicant appeals against the refusal, or refers the case to the Information Commissioner. This could be done by requiring all staff that refuse a request for information to forward the details to a central point in the organisation for collation. Details of information on complaints about applications which have been refused (see XII—"Complaints procedure") could be collected at the same central point.

XII Review and Complaints Procedures

58. Each public authority must have a review procedure in place. This procedure may be used by any person who considers that their request has not been properly handled or who are otherwise dissatisfied with the outcome of the consideration of their request and where the issue is such that it cannot be resolved informally in discussion with the official dealing with the request. Information **11–017**

relating to the complaints procedure should be included in an authority's publication scheme if it has one, or made readily available elsewhere. Under Regulation 18, the enforcement and appeal provisions of the FOIA will apply in respect of a complaint made after 1st January 2005.

59. Any decision made in relation to a request under the EIR that contains a refusal must be in writing and public authorities are obliged under Regulations 14 (5) to notify the applicant of his or her right of complaint. They should provide details of their own complaints procedure, including how to make a complaint and inform the applicant of the right to complain to the Commissioner under section 50 of the FOIA if he or she is still dissatisfied following the authority's review. However, as a matter of good practice authorities should provide details of their complaints procedure when responding to all requests. It is for the applicant to decide whether they are content with the response they receive; they may have concerns that they wish to pursue in circumstances where the public authority claims to have fully complied with their request.

60. Any written reply from the applicant (including one transmitted electronically) expressing dissatisfaction with an authority's response to a valid request for information should be treated as a complaint, as should any written communication from a person who perceives the authority is not complying with its publication scheme where it has one. These communications should be handled in accordance with the authority's review procedure pursuant to Regulation 11, even if the applicant does not state his or her desire for the authority to review their decision or the handling of their application.

61. The complaints procedure should be a fair and impartial means of dealing with problems and reviewing decisions taken pursuant to the EIR, including decisions taken about where the public interest lies. It should be possible to reverse or otherwise amend decisions previously taken. Complaints procedures should be clear and not unnecessarily bureaucratic. They should be capable of producing a prompt determination of the complaint.

62. In all cases, complaints should be acknowledged and the complainant should be informed of the authority's target date for determining the complaint. Where it is apparent that determination of the complaint will take longer than the target time (for example because of the complexity of the particular case), the authority should inform the applicant and explain the reason for the delay. The complainant should always be informed of the outcome of his or her complaint.

63. Authorities must consider each complaint, decide whether they have complied with their requirements under EIR and respond to the complainant within 40 working days from the time when the complaint was received.

64. Records should be kept of all complaints and of their outcome. Authorities should have procedures in place for monitoring complaints and for reviewing, and if necessary amending procedures for dealing with requests for information where such action is indicated by more than occasional reversals of initial decisions.

65. Where the outcome of a complaint is that information should be disclosed which was previously withheld, the information in question should be disclosed with immediate effect.

66. Where the outcome of a complaint is that the procedures within an authority have not been properly followed by the authority's staff, the authority should apologise to the applicant. The authority should also take appropriate steps to prevent similar errors occurring in future.

67. Where the outcome of a complaint is that an initial decision to withhold information is upheld or is otherwise in the authority's favour, the applicant should be informed of his or her right to apply to the Commissioner and be given details of how to make an application for a decision on whether the request for information has been dealt with in accordance with the requirements of the EIR. As failure to deal with a complaint promptly may be grounds for complaint to the Information Commissioner, authorities should set out details of the timescale for dealing with complaints in their complaints procedure, which should be made readily available.

INDEX

[all references are to paragraph number]